A MESSIANIC D.

HONEY
Out of the Rock

KYLE SUTTON

A FONTLIFE Publication, LLC

A FONTLIFE Publication, LLC
Raleigh, NC 27603
Email: info@fontlifepublications.com
http://fontlifepublications.com/

International Standard Book Number: 978-1-62422-005-0
First Printing

Bulk Sales

The publisher offers excellent discounts on this book when ordered in quantity for bulk purchases, Bible studies or Sunday school classes. For more information, please contact the publisher at info@fontlifepublications.com.

Printed and bound in the United States of America by Lightning Source, Inc., La Vergne, TN USA 37086.

Reporting Errata

A FONTLIFE Publication, LLC strives to maintain the highest quality standards for its published works, hence they undergo constant review and refinement. Readers are encouraged to report any issues and view any existing errata. Errata that is submitted on http://fontlifepublications.com/ becomes visible on the site immediately after it is reviewed by the publisher or author, so it may be helpful to other readers or viewers who encounter the same problem. Confirmed errors are corrected in electronic versions and future printings of a book.

Disclaimer

This book does not necessarily express the views held by International Board of Jewish Missions (IBJM). This book is simply an independent source for insights into the Hebraic nature of the biblical faith once delivered to the saints.

All quoted Scripture is from the *King James Version* of the Bible. References are routinely made from the original, inspired languages, primarily Hebrew.

Front Cover Photo used with permission.
Courtesy of *Jim & Penny Caldwell*
Split Rock Research Foundation
Diamondhead, MS

The rock in this photograph is believed to be the rock in Horeb that Moses struck at God's command to supply water to the Israelites.

"And they thirsted not when he led them through the deserts: he caused the waters to flow out of the rock for them: he clave the rock also, and the waters gushed out." (Isaiah 48:21)

For more information visit: www.splitrockresearch.org

Cover Design by
Sarah Tesch
11-28 Media
Melbourne, Australia
http://11-28.net

Acknowledgements

Many thanks are in order. Of particular importance are the various Jewish believers who have come to faith in the last century and seek to enlighten Gentile Christians of the Hebraic nature of the Bible, including the New Testament: Gartenhaus, Eidershciem, Fruchtenbaum, Rambsel, Levitt, just to name a few. They have impressed Gentile believers to go back and approach the Bible with the mindset of its Hebrew authors. People like these give us keys and clues that we might open further doors of Bible discovery.

Dedication

This book is dedicated to my parents who raised me under the precepts of the Book; Dr. Ralph Sexton Jr., who took me on my first two trips through the Bible Land to discover it firsthand; Dr. William Day, who as founding dean of TBBC invited me to enroll in the church's Bible College; Homer Smith and Edward Sparks who together first drew my attention to the need of having a profound love for the Jewish people and taking the message of Messiah's love to them; and lastly, in chronology of influence in my life's direction into ministry, to Dr. Orman L. Norwood, who counted me faithful enough to become one of their many representatives.

Ancient Hebrew
The Early Paleo-Hebrew Alefbet[†]

Paleo	Modern	Name	Picture	Meaning	Sound
𐤀	א	Alef	Ox Head	strong, power, leader	ah, eh
𐤁	ב	Bet	Tent floor plan	family, house, inn	b, (v)
✓	ג	Gimel	Foot	gather, walk	g
𐤃	ד	Dalet	Door	move, hang, entrance	d
𐤄	ה	Hey	Man with arms raised	look, reveal, breath	h, ah
𐤅	ו	Waw	Tent peg	add, secure, hook	w, o, u
𐤆	ז	Zain	Mattock	food, cut, nourish	z
𐤇	ח	Hket	Wall	outside, divide, half	hh
⊗	ט	Tet	Basket	surround, contain, mud	t
𐤉	י	Yod	Arm and hand	work, worship, throw	y, ee
𐤊	כ	Kaph	Open palm	open, allow, tame	k
∠	ל	Lamed	Shepherd's staff	teach, yoke, to bind	l
ᴡ	מ	Mem	Water	chaos, mighty, blood	m
𐤍	נ	Nun	Seed	continue, heir, son	n
𐤎	ס	Samek	Thorn	grab, hate, protect	s
⊙	ע	Ayin	Eye	watch, know, shade	aghn
𐤐	פ	Pey	Mouth	blow, scatter, edge	p, f
𐤑	צ	Tsade	Man on his side	wait, snare, edge	ts
𐤒	ק	Quph	Sun on horizon	condense, circle, time	q
𐤓	ר	Resh	Head of a man	first, top, beginning	r
𐤔	ש	Shin	Two front teeth	sharp, press, eat, two	sh
+	ת	Taw	Crossed sticks	mark, sign, signal, monument	t

[†]For more understanding on this alphabet visit Jeff A. Benner's website: Ancient Hebrew Research Center at ancient-hebrew.org

"He made him ride on the high places of the earth,
that he might eat the increase of the fields;
*and he made him to suck **honey out of the rock,***
and oil out of the flinty rock; butter of kine, and milk of sheep,
with fat of lambs, and rams of the breed of Bashan, and goats,
with the fat of kidneys of wheat; and thou didst drink
the pure blood of the grape."

(Deuteronomy 32:13-14)

Preface

Daniel was one to whom hidden things were revealed—not just by way of dreams, but also by way of reading the Bible's clear text. Listen to what Daniel says about a critical discovery he made from a simple but careful reading of the scroll of Yirmeyahu:

> "...I Daniel understood by books the number of the years, whereof the word of the LORD came to Jeremiah the prophet, that he would accomplish seventy years in the desolations of Jerusalem" (Daniel 9:2).

Until Daniel read that specific portion of Yirmeyahu's scroll (Jeremiah 25:11), he had no idea if God would ever allow his people to return to the Holy Land. Daniel was doubly excited to discover that he and his people only had less than 20 years to wait until the end of their captivity.

Daniel acknowledges that God reveals "deep and secret things" to men (Daniel 2:22). He simply waits for prepared and ready vessels to whom He can reveal them and for those who are looking for the deep and secret things of His Word. Solomon understood this concept beforehand when he said, "It is the glory of God to conceal a thing: but the honor of kings is to search out a matter" (Proverbs 25:2).

Sometimes God conceals a thing in plain sight, and at other times, He makes you dig a while. This book comes about by digging mostly with Hebraic tools. When the soil of God's Word is lifted out, whether it is a word or a verse, it must be put through the fine sift of covenant imagery to define what it is truly. That is why the base of this daily devotional book is Hebraic thought. The word Hebraic is an adjective meaning "pertaining to, or characteristic of the Hebrews, their language or their culture." Yes, the wonderful layers of God's written Word are based upon the rich soil of Abraham's Semitic people.

Someone has said, "If you don't know covenant then you don't really know the Bible." God never operates outside of Covenant, and as you will find in this year's reading, there are more covenants that God operates in than just the Old and New. For example, there are *four levels of covenant* upon which man interacts with God. These run right through the Bible from Genesis to Revelation. They are the Servanthood, Friendship, Inheritance and Marriage Covenants. Moreover, not only are there four levels of covenant to consider, but there are also *four layers of Hebrew Hermeneutics* to put Scripture through. They are Pashat, D'rash, Remez and Sod. Both of these concepts are explained in a short series in this devotional.

If this sounds a bit strange, be reminded that the four gospels present four different perspectives of the same Redeemer. Matthew presents Yeshua as a Lion, Judah's King. Mark presents Him as an Ox—perfect Servant. Luke presents Him as a Person—perfect Man. And John presents Him as an eagle, perfect God. In one of Messiah's parables, He speaks of four types of soil upon which His Word falls (trampled upon ground, shallow ground, uncultivated ground and good ground). God placed four cardinal points on the compass (north, south, east and west), four seasons in a year (spring, summer, autumn and winter), four elements in our world (earth, water, wind and fire), and four time markers in our day (morning, evening, noon and midnight). God seems to love working with the number four. Is it any wonder, then, that various patterns of four would be given to us in which to view and understand Scripture? Did you know that there are even four different categories of prophecy—direct, typical, application and summary fulfillment? Michael Rydelnik of Moody Bible Institute covers these in his book, *The Messianic Hope*. We have just outlined four sets of Hebraic tools (with four types in each set) that may be used to dig out Scripture.

The inspiration for this devotional book came in the first week of January 2010, while doing a little research on Psalm 87:7, "All my springs are in thee." It was so thrilling to discover truths about Jerusalem's Temple and its various supplies of spring-fed water that I felt compelled to see what else could be drawn out of God's Word and, through this personal challenge, start a one-year book of discovery. Repeatedly, I was overjoyed at the things that were uncovered because of simply turning over "rocks." God has woven so much into His unfathomable Word that there is no end to what may be found in its rich soil.

When we are told to "study to show ourselves approved unto God," we can be assured that God stands ready to reward the student of His Word with a few rare gems. David's prayer was, "Open thou mine eyes, that I may behold wondrous things out of thy law" (Psalm 119:18). By this, David acknowledges that unless God chooses to reveal a certain thing to us we remain limited in our understanding. Paul confirms this by saying that Scripture is spiritually discerned (1 Corinthians 2:14). The Holy Spirit is the Author of the Book and He alone chooses when, where and how to disclose its sacred contents. After going through a dry spell, my prayer to the Lord was that He might let me find something amazing in His word. The next day, His response to that short, sincere prayer was staggering. He indeed is able to do exceeding abundantly above all that we ask or think (Ephesians 3:20).

What was uncovered confirms the old adage that the New Testament is in the Old Testament concealed, and the Old Testament is in the New Testament revealed. Would you believe that the risen Saviour's very first post-resurrection words and actions are not found in the New Testament gospels, but rather in plain view back in the Old Testament Torah? That's right! Moreover, this short passage in Deuteronomy reveals much, much more! It sets you directly in the middle of Gethsemane's Garden the night before the Saviour's death and highlights five events taking place there. What becomes so suddenly clear is that this Deuteronomy passage is much more than a proclamation; it is a prophecy—and a very important one.

There was a lot going on in Gethsemane's gauntlet that night, but in no way were those sorted events disjointed. The Deuteronomy passage confirms that the five Gethsemane events were, in reality, tokens of Yeshua's absolute, unquestionable divinity. Yeshua's divine supremacy is further revealed in this Torah treasure by a sixth and seventh token not to be missed. Tokens are touched upon often in this book, yet these seven tokens are the most riveting of all.

Scholars and students alike continue to wrestle over the incident of Peter's sword, but this find—in the author's estimation—not only settles the issue of why he was allowed to swing it, but does so on the premise that the Bible is one harmonious book. And because you've taken time to read this introduction, I will tell you where to find this eye-opening, heart-warming, faith-building discovery. It is a three-part devotional that must be read in successive order. It begins on August 18 with "Yeshua, the Great I Am," is followed by "The Great I Am in Gethsemane," and finishes with "Lord of the Sword." An expanded version of this study is available in a PowerPoint presentation at our website's homepage: *www.friendshipbc.com.au*

Yahweh told Israel, "at the mouth of two…or…three witnesses, shall the matter be established" (Deuteronomy 19:15). He was referring to civil judgments in the gates, but this rule also applies to doctrinal judgments concerning His Word. No truth in Scripture is supposed to stand alone. God regularly supplies another verse to confirm a truth—particularly a grand truth. This is why He says, "For precept must be upon precept, precept upon precept; line upon line, line upon line; here a little, and there a little" (Isaiah 28:10). Two scriptural witnesses to a biblical truth may both come from the Old Testament or one may come from the Old and the other from the New. For example, Paul tells us in the New Testament that Yeshua *was equal with God* the Father before coming to earth and also during His incarnation (Philippians 2:6). When we look to the Old Testament, particularly Zechariah 13:7, it confirms this fact and more. Yeshua, even in His flesh, was Yahweh's "fellow," His equal. These two passages confirm equality within the Godhead. The Bible is one cohesive Book and we see much of Messiah's majesty and glory in this light.

We know the Old Testament is incomplete without the New Testament, and the opposite is quite true. For this reason, there should be no blank page separating the two Covenants. The writers of the New Testament always had the Old Testament in view. The two were never divorced from each other in the apostles' thinking. We would do well to follow this pattern. Both Testaments remain open books in the single respect that they hold vast amounts of unfulfilled Scripture concerning Messiah's second coming. Consider also, that only once does the New Testament ever refer to the former Testament as being "old" (Hebrews 8:13). Alongside this is the fact that in the next verse the writer of Hebrews describes the former Covenant as being the "first" (v.14). So what do the Jewish people call this first Covenant? They call it the *Tanakh*, which is an acronym for *Torah* [the books of Moses], *Neviim* [the prophets] and *Ketuvim* [the historical writings].

The Old Covenant is indispensable to our understanding. In this respect, the Old and New Covenants are like two pillars or posts, which are necessary to form a doorway. At the threshold of the door stands Messiah, the omnipotent Son of God. Did He not say, "I am the door: by me if any man enter in, he shall be saved, and shall go in and out, and find pasture" (John 10:9)? The student of the Bible who wants to feed on Yeshua, the Bread of Life, will find ample, green pasture in both Covenants. The student who only studies Jesus from the New Testament only knows half of what he should know about Jesus. He testifies three times that all Scripture points to Him. Through the voice of the psalmist, He said, "Lo, I come: in the volume of the book [Old Testament] it is written of me" (Psalm 40:7). To the unbelieving Pharisees He said, "Search the scriptures [Old Testament]; for in them ye think ye have eternal life: and they are they which testify of me." (John 5:39). The day Yeshua arose He sought out two disparaging disciples on their way back to Emmaus. The narrative says, "And beginning at Moses and all the prophets, he expounded unto them in all the scriptures [Old Testament] the things concerning himself" (Luke 24:27). These two men needed a little refresher course on *Messiah in the Old Testament* and He gave it to them.

We must do away with preconceived biases when approaching God's Word or one might miss what is actually staring him in the face. Let me cite one example. Very few artistic renderings place a personality other than Moses at the burning bush. Because this singular image is etched into our minds, we can actually read right past this passage and miss the main Character. Yeshua [the Son of God] was right there in pre-incarnate form and became quite visible to Moses in the midst of the bush. The Exodus passage gives Him the title, Malak Yahweh—"the angel of the LORD." Elohim [God the Father] was also *represented* and spoke to Moses. Was the third Person of the Triune Godhead also present at that moment? If so, in what form? Could it have been the flaming fire that engulfed the bush that represents the Holy Spirit? Elsewhere, Scripture would confirm it. Moses later gave this testimony: "For the LORD thy God is a consuming *fire*, even a jealous God" (Deuteronomy 4:24). To summarize Moses' experience, the Father's voice was firmly heard, the Son's body was clearly seen, and the Spirit's zeal was warmly felt.

Yeshua, the Rock of Israel

"He is the Rock, his work is perfect: for all his ways are judgment: a God of truth and without iniquity, just and right is he." (Deuteronomy 32:4)

When it comes to ascribing proper deity to Yeshua, the Bible makes it plain and clear—He is the God of the Old Testament, not just the New. Just one example that illustrates this point is seen in the fact that Yeshua shares a familial title with His Father—the Rock of Israel. Ancient Hebrews thought in concrete terms and so they gave Yahweh this title as a token of what He meant to them.

A large enough rock is immovable, thus Israel could always count on Him to be there for them. A large rock is also impregnable, thus Israel could hide in Him in time of trouble. A large rock can also be immeasurable in its value as desert shelter and shade, thus Israel could receive this form of provision from Him as needed.

After this particular Rock is traced through the Bible, you discover that it is indeed the person of Yeshua. Paul makes it emphatic: "and that Rock was Christ...that followed them" (1 Corinthians 10:4). Deuteronomy 32:4 describes Yeshua as Israel's *perfect* Rock, yet in the wilderness He was also their *lightly esteemed* Rock (Deuteronomy 32:15). When Israel's Rock came in the flesh, they esteemed Him even less. At Calvary, before the whole nation's eyes, He became like the *smitten* Rock at Horeb (Exodus 17:6). This is the first mention of rock in the Bible, and it comes with great import. In addition, under direction of the Father, Yeshua was smitten "that the people may drink." This is why His followers remain satiated ever since.

In Moses' estimation, Yeshua was the *glorious* Rock (Exodus 33:21-23). In regards to Hannah, whose barrenness was reversed, Yeshua was her Rock *of rejoicing* and her Rock *of holiness*. He was her absolute *irreplaceable* Rock for she said, "neither is there any rock like our God" (1 Samuel 12:2). David, who spent many years running from Saul's hunters, experienced Yeshua as his Rock *of hiding* and described Him this way: "my fortress…my high tower…my refuge" (2 Samuel 22:2). He goes on to declare Yeshua as the *blessed* Rock, the *exalted* Rock, the Rock *of salvation* (v.47). On his deathbed, David proclaimed that Yeshua is the Rock *that speaks*. Read the last words of the Sweet Psalmist of Israel very carefully for he mentions each Member of the Trinity: "The <u>Spirit of the LORD</u> spake by me, and his word was in my tongue. The <u>God of Israel</u> said, the <u>Rock of Israel</u> spake to me, He that ruleth over men must be just, ruling in the fear of God" (2 Samuel 23:1-3).

In the Psalms, Yeshua is spoken of as a *strong* Rock that *leads* and *guides* you (31:2-3), a *bedrock* for your house to be built upon (40:2), a *high* Rock for you to take eternal shelter in (61:2-4), an *easily forgotten* Rock but One that stands ready to redeem you once you remember Him (78:35), a *praise-worthy* Rock that you can sing unto and make a joyful noise unto (95:1).

Isaiah describes Yeshua as a *great* Rock in a weary land (32:2). The prophet also describes Israel's Rock in a fearful way that is in keeping with Deuteronomy 32:4. He is a rock-solid *sanctuary* for the believing, but a Rock *of stumbling* for the unbelieving (8:14). Yeshua spoke in the context of Isaiah's prophecy warning that whosoever came unto Him broken over their sin would be saved. However, if they didn't come to him He would destroy them like a rock that grinds mill (Luke 20:17-18). Yeshua's claim of being Israel's perfect Rock, their perfect Judge, greatly agitated the Pharisees.

In the New Testament Yeshua made a clear reference to being Israel's majestic Rock *that begats little rocks* (Deuteronomy 32:18). Yeshua said to His chief disciple, "thou art Peter [*petros*—a piece of rock], and upon this rock [*petra*—a mass of rock] I will build my church" (Matthew 16:18). Yeshua's obvious claim was that He was Israel's Creator and now their New Covenant Founder for those who have saving faith. Now that we have shown from the whole of Scripture that Yeshua is the Rock of Israel, let's examine the Honey that flows out from this Rock.

Honey, out of the Rock

"Oh that my people had hearkened unto me, and Israel had walked in my ways! I should soon have…fed them also with the finest of the wheat:

and with honey out of the rock should I have satisfied thee." (Psalm 81:13, 16)

The first mention of honey in the Bible is found in Torah where God enfolds its flavor within the children of Israel's daily provision of manna (Exodus 16:31). The Good Shepherd referred to that honey-sweetened manna as spiritual food when He described how His Father, "gave them bread from heaven to eat" (John 6:31). One key verse in Torah directly links manna typologically to God's pure Word: "And he humbled thee, and suffered thee to hunger, and fed thee with manna, which thou knewest not, neither did thy fathers know; that he might make thee know that man doth not live by bread only, but by every word that proceedeth out of the mouth of the LORD doth man live" (Deuteronomy 8:3).

A link has now been made between honey-sweetened manna and the Word of God, yet a psalmist links honey itself directly to the Word. He says, "How sweet are thy words unto my taste! yea, sweeter than honey to my mouth!" (Psalm 119:103). So there you go. God's words, His sayings, are literally compared to honey. What is even more interesting is how the honey "bee" and the "word" are linked on the Hebrew level. In Hebrew, "bee" is *deborah* and "word" is *debar*. These two words share the same root, *dabar*, which means to *arrange*. The bee arranges its honey in a very orderly fashion and God arranges His written Word in ways that we might draw on them for ages to come.

Honeybees place their hives in a variety of locations, even in the crevasses of rocks. In the text verse above, Yeshua promises to feed you with the hidden honey of His Word if you will only walk in His ways. He has "hidden manna" waiting for you also (Revelation 2:17). And seeing that Yeshua is your *sacred* Rock, may your heart and soul be richly blessed each day of the year as you journey through *HONEY Out of the Rock*.

All My Springs Are in Thee
Part 1

"The LORD loveth the gates of Zion more than all the dwellings of Jacob....all my springs are in thee." (Psalm 87:2, 7)

Yahweh has placed His sacred springs in the holy mountains of Jerusalem—within the gates of Zion (v.1-2). God's springs are there because it is "the city of God" (v.3). And if He has chosen to dwell there, then fountains of life must certainly be found in its midst. So special is this city that the "LORD shall count, when he writeth up the people, that this man was born there" (v.6). The word *born* appears twice in this chapter and thus draws the reader's attention to the need for spiritual rebirth (v.5). The text verse brings comfort to every believer in times of drought and despair reminding you that your daily source of satisfaction is not to be sought for out in the world; rather, it is to be sought *within*. The Son of God made this reality clear when He stated with such plainness, "If any man thirst, let him come unto me, and drink. He that believeth on me, as the scripture hath said, out of his belly shall flow rivers of living water" (John 7:37-38).

Yeshua made this reference to the dark *inner recess* of a believer's belly knowing that it was a common Oriental belief that the spirit of a deity could dwell in a dark chamber called an *adytum*. The Temple of Yahweh was dedicated on the festival of Tabernacles. He filled it with His presence and clouds of glory, which caused Solomon to say, "The LORD said that he would dwell in the thick darkness" (1 Kings 8:12). [See also Exodus 20:21, 2 Samuel 22:12.] From His thick, cloudlike abode atop Mount Sinai to His heavily-veiled Tabernacle to His inner-most Sanctum within the windowless, stone Temple at Jerusalem, the God of Abraham set forth one important requirement for His earthly existence among men—a pavilion of darkness. Yahweh's radiance is much too glorious, holy, and powerful for finite man to behold. One glorious day this will dramatically change "for we shall see Him as he is" (1 John 3:2).

As you pray this morning, thank the Father for making His voluntary choice to inhabit you with His Holy Spirit. As you meditate on His indwelling presence, praise Him from the quietness of your heart.

All My Springs Are in Thee
Part 2

According to W. Robertson Smith, "The adytum, or dark inner chamber, found in many temples both among the Semites and in Greece, was almost certainly in its origin a cave; indeed in Greece it was often wholly or partially subterranean."

A wonderful parallel is found in the fact that the incarnate Son of God was conceived within the secret chamber of a virgin's womb. Moreover, this unique Deity was very likely birthed inside the darkened setting of a shallow hillside cave where animals were sheltered. The Bethlehem countryside had no shortage of small caves, and the common practice of peasants was to build their houses up against them. They would sleep in the front part and their animals would be brought in at night and sheltered in the rear where the low-ceiling cave was. The little oil lamps shining in baby Messiah's windowless chamber were minimal for dispersing the darkness. Those oil lamps were somewhat figurative of the Menorah's seven lamps that barely lit Yahweh's outer sanctuary.

Later, Messiah's preaching ministry was predominately to those dwelling in spiritual darkness—Gentiles of Galilee (Matthew 4:15). Matthew writes, "The people which sat in darkness saw great light; and to them which sat in the region and shadow of death light is sprung up" (v.16). Matthew speaks of Messiah's light springing up like the dawn. Indeed, Messiah grew up in the area, was schooled in the area, and one day began proclaiming eternal life to all dwelling in that area. For three and half years, the Galilee area sprang up with the illuminating words of Yeshua. From Him, Jerusalem also experienced brief bursts from this. He would have placed His well of salvation in their midst permanently if they had only desired it and asked.

As you pray today, rejoice that Yeshua entered your world of darkness with the light of His Word. Thank Him for convicting you of your sins, cleansing you from your sins, and then settling down within your innermost chamber.

All My Springs Are in Thee
Part 3

Not only did the Son of God spring forth to life from within a little cave of Bethlehem, 33 years later, He sprang from atoning death to life-everlasting within the darkened chamber of a pristine tomb. The rich man's brand new burial chamber was hewn out of rocky earth along Golgatha's hillside, and much like the inaccessible Holy of Holies, this adytum of the sleeping Deity was sealed off accordingly. Though Messiah was truly dead, the spring of life remained embedded deep in His soul. At an irreversible moment in history, He sprang yet again as light and life, joy and peace, love and hope eternal.

One of the strangest things the Spirit of God has ever chosen to do of His own free will is to abide permanently within the hearts of mankind. However, this can only happen so long as the cleansing blood of the Son has first purified a man's heart. The first occurrence of the Spirit's indwelling took place exactly 50 days after the Day of First Fruits, the day when Yeshua rose again and walked out of His dark tomb. Fifty is the biblical number of the Holy Spirit, and that fiftieth day from First Fruits was a high Feast day called Shavuot. Where did this historical Spirit-giving event take place? It took place in the heart of Jerusalem within the Temple courtyards. At 9 a.m. on that high feast day, the disciples were no longer in the Upper Room. Instead, they were right where one would expect to see faithful Jews—at Yahweh's Temple. This new spring in Jerusalem sprang unexpectedly, but the faithful were not caught unaware.

Two thousand years later, God continues to take up residence within blood-washed tabernacles of men everywhere. When the darkness of this fallen world seems to swallow you up, just remember that this present darkness is just the entrance leading you to seek Him further in the Most Holy Place, the inward secret chamber of your heart. Today, be reminded that God's glory within you shines brighter even though the present time seems darker.

All My Springs Are in Thee

Part 4

In his work, *The Temples That Jerusalem Forgot,* Ernest L. Martin states, "temples required a spring." Archaeological evidence yields one such example—the temple at Panias. Today its foundation is all that visibly remains. Panias draws its name from the false god it was built to honor, Pan—the god of fear. Herod Phillip built this pagan temple in 20 BC (at the base of Mt. Hermon in Northern Galilee) to enclose the site of its adytum, a rather large cave. From somewhere within that secret chamber a significant spring flowed and continues to flow to this present day. The spring waters exit the cave's mouth helping to form the headwaters of the Jordan River.

For a prototype concept of temples and springs, we should look back to the time when Yahweh was dwelling in His cloud-covered sanctum upon Mt. Sinai's peak 8,000 ft. above the Arabian sands. From a close-by source, the LORD suddenly caused pure water to spring forth from a very large rock splitting it wide-open and supplying Israel with abundant life over the next two years.

Ezekiel envisioned Messiah's millennial Temple as having a life-giving stream issuing forth from its very threshold (Ezekiel 47:1). The prophet describes how the water gets deeper and deeper as it moves outward beyond the courts of the Temple reaching the point where it is deep enough to swim in (v.5). Ezekiel even mentions the healing properties of the sanctified river (v.9-10). Zechariah adds that the magnitude of fresh water will be so great that its path will have to be split in two, half of it emptying into the Mediterranean Sea and the other half going down to heal the Dead Sea (Zechariah 14:8).

The world is like a desert; it can be a very thirsty place. Before venturing out into the dry landscape of this sin-swept world today, be refreshed in prayer by the God of Abraham. Take time also to wade out into the deeper, life-giving waters of His holy Word.

All My Springs Are in Thee
Part 5

Beyond the collection of winter rain in cisterns, the only flowing source of water for the ancient City of David was the Gihon Spring. In the days of Hezekiah—due to a coming invasion—this spring was conducted into the city via a cleverly designed tunnel. Unfortunately, the Gihon Spring possessed insufficient head pressure to meet the needs of Solomon's Temple, which was situated some 80 feet higher. A more significant volume of water was required to wash away the blood of the daily sacrifices.

According to rabbinical records, water was conveyed to the Temple, *Beit HaMikdash,* by skillfully designed pipes. Exposed remains of the underground aqueducts Solomon built can be seen today at various points along their route. The Temple's supply of fresh water was drawn altogether from four different springs. The furthermost spring, Ein Arrub, was in Hebron 20 miles south, and the nearest spring, Ein Etam, was in Bethlehem where they were collected into three enormous reservoirs known as Solomon's Pools. These were mainly used to wash the sheep before bringing them up to the Temple.

Israel's loving God permitted a sufficient supply of living water to enter Jerusalem—via Solomon's creative genius—allowing Him to say, "All my springs are in thee." The Gihon Spring represents the steadfast supply of God's inwardly abiding Holy Spirit. Jerusalem's other four conduits of spring water remind us of other helps God provides such as the Water of Life [Yeshua Himself], the water of His Word, the still waters of meditation, and the refreshing waters of that are found in fellowship with the saints.

In your quiet time today, reflect on God's goodness and how He supplies all your daily needs from sources of His choosing. The Father doesn't want you to dry up on the vine. He wants you tender, green, and flourishing.

January 6

All My Springs Are in Thee
Part 6

God's joyful declaration to Jerusalem, "All my springs are in thee," reveals to us that there are indeed multiple sources of contentment that come to us from His secret and untraceable chambers. In Messiah's conversation with the Samaritan woman the word *water* was used seven times, the number of perfection. The conversation began with the subject of whose spring was more satisfying, Yeshua's or Yacob's. Then it shifted to the issue of how to obtain the perfectly satisfying water Messiah was offering. With that matter solved, Yeshua quickly gave out His generous invitation: "whosoever drinketh of the water that I shall give him shall never thirst; but the water that I shall give him shall be in him a well of water springing up into everlasting life" (John 4:14).

New Covenant believers should consider the wonders of God's eternal springs. One spring gives forth vital baptismal waters to the new man, another spring provides waters of renewal, and another grants healing waters for the weak and heavy-laden. The Fountain of Living Waters Himself has graciously placed within us *all His springs* that we might have "sufficiency in all things" (2 Corinthians 9:8). He even graciously provides waters for consecration and sanctification. Of all the springs that flow into the believer's life, Messiah's red-flowing stream is the most precious and most wondrous of them all. The prophet makes mention of this most gracious spring saying, "In that day there shall be a fountain opened to the house of David and to the inhabitants of Jerusalem for sin and for uncleanness" (Zechariah 13:1).

No matter what your need is today, your internal springs of God's Holy Spirit shall wonderfully provide for you. Take time today to point some other thirsty soul to this heavenly Source.

All My Springs Are in Thee
Part 7

The Hebrew word for water is only given to us in plural form, *mayim*. This speaks of the abundance of God's life-giving supply. Yeshua's proclamation, "If any man thirst let him come unto me and drink" is in complete synch with Yahweh's earlier claim in Psalm 87, "all *my* springs are in thee." Yeshua was rightfully claiming to be the sacred *Owner* of Israel's celestial springs; that is, the Source of their spiritual contentment. Most hand-dug wells are named after their owners. Isaiah reveals the name of the most satisfying Fountain of Life God ever provided to Israel. He declares, "With joy shall ye draw water out of the wells of salvation" (Isaiah 12:3). The Hebrew noun for salvation is *yeshuah*. How telling! Yeshua presented Temple gatherers with a necessary challenge that day: They must first seek after the *Owner* of the well.

It is from Yeshua's own resurrected temple that Israel's living springs now flow. This highlights another fact: Yeshua must have His *own* particular plans for their divine use. These eternal springs represent a continual "supply of the Spirit" and are not for our satisfaction only. Springs are provided also for the purifying of our flesh (Philippians 1:19). Notice the Spirit's cleansing power in these words of the LORD: "I...entered into a covenant with thee...and thou becamest mine. Then washed I thee with water" (Ezekiel 16:8-9). The Redeemer's heavenly springs not only wash away the believer's daily defilement; they also remove the guilt and shame caused by defilement. Paul sums up the fact that this purifying effect is made possible "by the washing of regeneration, and renewing of the Holy Ghost; Which he shed on us abundantly through Jesus Christ our Saviour" (Titus 3:5-6).

As you go through this year, may you be found each and every day at Yeshua's springs of life. The Saviour provides them for you and expects to see you using them regularly. Thank Him today for His heavenly provision.

From Year to Year

"And Samuel judged Israel all the days of his life. And he went from year to year in circuit to Bethel...Gilgal, and Mizpeh, and judged Israel in all those places." (1 Samuel 17:15-16)

Samuel was one of the most revered prophets under whom the nation ever served. Some prophets were met with biases, apathy, resistance, rejection and sometimes—ill treatment such as starvation and death.

When it was noised abroad that the venerated judge was coming to town, many were fraught with tension. Others were filled with hope as they knew he would hear their case in all fairness and deliver unto them due justice. For Samuel it was the same thing over and over again, year after year—the same old cities and the same old faces. Perhaps there was a new face here or there or a new case different from all the others thus making him feel like he was breaking new ground. But for the most part, it was business as usual for the aging prophet. The upside for Samuel was that this was God's will. Samuel had once enjoyed the wonder years of growing up in the Tabernacle under the protective wings of Yahweh—feeling His divine presence and hearing His calming voice. Year after year in the tent of Yahweh was refreshing, but year after year refereeing arguments was far different. Samuel's job was to continue, simply being faithful in what he was instructed to do no matter how old he was.

As this new year dawns upon you, you may feel like everything is the same as it has always been: the same old town, the same old faces, the same old places, the same old work place, and perhaps even the same "old" church! But you know something? It doesn't have to be like that. It's you that needs the "facelift," a new freshness from God. This year you may not be able to persuade one saint to change for the better or persuade one soul to bow the knee to Yeshua, but you can and must stay on the firing line. Don't slack-up, back up or give up.

Today, determine in prayer to keep making your circuit, and as you go, God will give you staying power and bring victory after victory even in the darkest hour.

Hold Fast All Year

"Hold fast till I come. And he that overcometh, and keepeth my works unto the end, to him will I give power over the nations." (Revelation 2:25-26)

Marathon runners routinely agonize their way through a grueling 26-kilometer course. Although their bodies are overcome with pain, their determination remains the same. Quitting is never an option or they will never see the finish line. The most interesting thing about marathon runners is that they persevere to the end even if they are in last place. Our calling is to be endurance runners and to run the gospel race with patience (Hebrews 12:1).

First, God has challenged you to *keep His commandments* unto the end. These are the running shoes. He has also told you to *remember Him* unto the end. Moses said, "remember the LORD thy God: for it is he that giveth thee power" (Deuteronomy 8:18). *Trust Him* unto the end and don't worry because you have your Trainer/Coach with you every step of the way. He promises, "I am with you alway, even unto the end of the world" (Matthew 28:20). Also, *learn from Him* unto the end for He has already run the race before you as no one has ever run it or will run it! *Wait on Him* unto the end. This does not mean to stop the race. He says, "For I know the thoughts that I think toward you, saith the LORD, thoughts of peace...to give you an expected end [*tikvah,* hope]" (Jeremiah 29:11).

Keep your vision of the finish line, and if necessary, recite daily, "LORD, make me to know mine end, and the measure of my days" (Psalm 39:4). First place is not the goal; finishing the race is! Occasionally He will let you catch a glimpse of the finish line to encourage you. This will also help you to *rejoice in Him* unto the end.

Finally, *love Him* unto the end. John says of Messiah, "Having loved his own which were in the world, he loved them unto the end" (John 13:1). This means that you can also *cast all your care upon Him* unto the end because He truly cares about you (1 Peter 5:7). Ask the Lord today to help you make it to the end with honor.

Ⓦinning the Ⓓaily Ⓑattle

"…and God divided the light from the darkness." (Genesis 1:4)

Not a single day shall pass by this year in which you will not meet with decisions between light and dark, right and wrong, good and evil. You will face *daily* challenges, sometimes feeling the turmoil of unseen spiritual warfare.

In the original language of this verse, we discover something etymologically interesting. The Hebrew word for divide is *badal*. This is where the word *battle* comes from. Although the Hebrew pronunciation is slightly different, the only real thing that has changed for *battle* is its spelling. *Badal* means "to divide: to separate, distinguish, differ, sever." Each of these distinctive descriptions took place after God first created the evening and the morning. What is more, these concepts also take place in a literal battle. First, a *separation* of opposing ideologies comes about which may then *divide* the citizenry, eventually leading to a civil, internal war. The need quickly arises for citizens to *distinguish* on which side they are going to be. This is further accomplished by making a clear *difference* in the visual appearance of their uniforms as they ultimately go into the *divisive,* bloodletting battle.

When you wake up and put on your shoes each morning as a believer, the previous day's spiritual battle resumes. Yes, it's on again! The uniform you choose to put on determines whether you experience defeat or victory at the end of the daylong battle. As a good soldier in the LORD's army, will you *distinguish* between the light of His Word and the dark counsel of the ungodly? (Psalm 1:1) Will you carefully discern the *difference* between the light of God's Spirit and the false light of seducing spirits? (1 Timothy 4:1) Will you rightfully *divide* between what belongs to God—your spirit, soul and body—and what belongs to the dark prince, like the things that are in the world? (1 Thessalonians 5:23; 1 John 2:15)

Winning the daily battle is not very hard, but deciding which uniform to put on sometimes is! Today after putting on the right battle uniform ask the Lord for help so that you wear it for His glory all day long.

Five Monumental Mountains

"For they were departed from Rephidim, and were come to the desert of Sinai...and there Israel camped before the mount." (Exodus 19:2)

Each of the following mountains speaks of a different aspect of our Saviour. From these we can more readily discern what our respective places are before Him and what our attitudes should reflect.

MT. SINAI is the first mountain, and here we behold Yeshua as our *Judge*. The key to the Judge's heart is found in your <u>diligence</u> towards His holy laws: "But take diligent heed to...love the LORD your God, and to walk in all his ways, and to keep his commandments, and to cleave unto him, and to serve him with all your heart and...soul" (Joshua 22:5).

MT. ZION is the mountain reserved for Yeshua to rule from as our *King*. "Beautiful for situation...is mount Zion...the city of the great King" (Psalm 48:2). The King's servant must possess a strong sense of <u>duty</u>. "So...when ye shall have done all those things...say, We are [not for profit] servants: we have done that which was our duty to do" (Luke 17:9).

MT. OLIVET is the mountain that speaks of Yeshua as our *Teacher*. "And as he sat upon the mount of Olives, the disciples came unto him privately, saying, Tell us, when shall these things be?" (Matthew 24:3). This Teacher is so serious about <u>discipleship</u> that He lays out three basic requirements to follow. If you ignore these, you cannot be His disciple (Luke 14:26, 27, 33).

MT. of TRANSFIGURATION was the place of unveiling of our *High Priest*. "Jesus...was transfigured before them: and his face did shine as the sun, and his raiment was white as the light" (Matthew 17:1-2). Peter's desire to camp out a while was good, but at that time, not in Yeshua's perfects will. Yeshua welcomes our godly <u>desire,</u> yet "what things soever ye desire" must meet His approval before He grants them (Mark 11:24).

MT. CALVARY, near Moriah's peak, presents Yeshua as our *Redeemer*. "And when they were come to...Calvary, there they crucified him" (Luke 23:33). His demonstration of supreme love should bring about our own manifest <u>devotion</u>. If you love Him, then show it openly today.

ℒively 𝒮tones

"Who is there among you of all his people? his God be with him, and let him go up to Jerusalem, which is in Judah, and build the house of the LORD God of Israel." (Ezra 1:3)

The Spirit of God moved upon Cyrus, king of Persia, to allow Judean exiles to return and build their God a stone temple in the appointed place. So it is today. God's Spirit is still stirring up the hearts of those that belong to Him that they may build Him a house, albeit using a different type of stone.

The first stone laid in Yahweh's New Covenant house (the church) was the cornerstone, Yeshua the Messiah. He was selected because of His perfection. All other stones are laid plumb and level in accordance to His standard of perfection. Referring to Psalm 118:22, Peter says that Yeshua is the "living stone, disallowed indeed of men, but chosen of God, and precious...also it is contained in the scripture, Behold, I lay in Zion a chief corner stone...and he that believeth on him shall not be confounded" (1 Peter 2:4, 6). Peter also described the believers that make up the rest of God's house. He said that we are "lively stones" and that we "are built up a spiritual house...acceptable to God by Jesus Christ" (1 Peter 2:5).

Maybe you're a stone that makes up the bottom row of foundation stones. If so, then you are an *elder*—steadfast and dependable. Maybe you are a stone that frames the door of the house. If so, then you're an *usher* who welcomes other worshippers. Maybe you are a stone that frames a window. If so, then you're a *teacher* or *youth worker* who joyfully brings the light of the Word into God's house. Maybe you are a stone that makes up the roof. If so, then you provide *prayer* cover for those who attend. Maybe you are a circular stone in a tall stack that completes one of the many columns. If so, you're vital *support* for a host of activities that take place in and around God's house. Maybe you are a stone laid in the floor to give people a sure place to plant their feet. If so, then you're a *helper* who can be counted on for anything. Today, thank the Lord for how He has placed you in His holy Temple.

Yeshua, What a Friend

"I will never leave thee, nor forsake thee." (Hebrews 13:5)

Friends may occasionally disappoint you due to their "me-first" attitude. Because this nature is engrafted at birth, we tend to settle for such flawed relationships having little or no recourse. By nature, earthly friends have countless human limitations, but the Son of God has none whatsoever. Yeshua is the most spectacular Friend one could ever want for several reasons.

First, He promises what no other friend can ever promise: "I will never leave thee, nor forsake thee." Paul takes this quote directly from Joshua 1:5 thus making Yeshua to be supreme Deity. True friends are indispensable because of their warmth and strength in times of hardship. A real friend may be hindered by his own circumstances, but Yeshua is the One Who is always there when you need Him. He will never tell you that He has other pressing engagements or obligations. When you call out to Him in your time of need, His response comes back so confidently: "Fear not. I'm right here."

Next, Yeshua delivers what no other friend can. He has the ability to meet your deepest and most desperate needs. Your earthly friend may amaze you with his acts of kindness or ability to steady-up a situation, but the Son of God is a supernatural Friend Who can totally transform any situation if He so desires. Even if He doesn't transform the *crisis*, He will certainly transform *you*. You may not find the storm dissolving around you, but you will soon find your fears dissolving.

Finally, the Saviour loves you more than any friend could ever love you. The average friend can only love you from his short supply of emotions; however, Yeshua loves you from the eternal supply of His cross and promises you saying, "Yea, I have loved thee with an everlasting love" (Jeremiah 31:3).

Today, praise *Yeshua HaBen*, Jesus the Son, for all His supreme and loving attributes. He certainly is a Friend like no other.

A Marvelous Journey

"In my Father's house are many mansions: if it were not so, I would have told you. I go to prepare a place for you. And if I go and prepare a place for you, I will...receive you unto myself; that where I am, there ye may be also. And...the way ye know." (John 14:1-4)

Come on a marvelous journey to Emanuel's Land.
> He's waiting and patiently holding out His pierced hand.
His land shall ever be robed with a soft sunrise.
> There in that land you'll never have to dry your eyes.
It has bright blue skies where rainless bows do appear,
> Yet before your eyes shall never, ever disappear.
Breaking waves whisper songs upon the sandy tides,
> N'er flowing out to rob the inlets of their salty prize;
A place where birds sing songs that mortals never dreamed,
> And foals run far from their mothers being fully weaned.
The perfect dream home has been prepared just for you,
> By the One who died a selfless and sinless Jew.
Receive Him and His gift today as your very own.
> His offer to you is not in any way a loan.
He gave you life, not once but actually twice.
> You owe Him a debt; but strangely, He paid the price.
Aimless, hopeless one, come toward the Son of God!
> You'll find Him walking upon the tall, silver sod.
When you see Him, thank Him—but only on your knees.
> He has given you a set of bright and golden keys!
Keys that shall split the glorious pearl gates apart,
> Leading to the quiet inner chambers of His heart.

Disappointments, heartaches and bereavements will come this year, and some of the old ones may still follow you from last year. In either case, look forward to your bright future beginning today. Take your sorrows to Yeshua this morning and then leave them with Him.

Chosen from the Crowd

"Blessed is the man whom thou choosest, and causest to approach unto thee, that he may dwell in thy courts:" (Psalm 65:4)

This psalm came from the golden-hearted king of Israel who knew what it felt like to hold out his scepter to allow or disallow someone into his presence. Due to logistics, a king could only choose a few from the crowd to gather in his courts for the day. Their petitions were often weighty and only added to his many other woes. What he really desired was someone to lighten his own load and lift his heart from the cares of his kingdom. Whoever was chosen stood among the privileged few. They were then able to speak freely and just enjoy the aura of the king's royal presence.

The first word in our text is "blessed." The word in Hebrew is *asher*, meaning happy. And who wouldn't be happy to be among the chosen on a given day? The next word, "choose," comes from the root word *bakhar* and means to select. If you go to a tree to select fruit you only look for ripened ones. These are called *bakhurim*. Ripened fruit is also ready to fall to the ground if not selected quickly; therefore, the king looked closely and considered who was not going to cling to the tree of life much longer under their heavy burden. He would hold out the golden scepter to that drooping soul who would then "approach" or *karawb*, that is, to draw near.

Paul was chosen to enter King Messiah's heavenly court. He encourages all that are heavy-hearted saying, "Let us draw near with a true heart in full assurance of faith, having our hearts sprinkled from an evil conscience, and our bodies washed with pure water" (Hebrews 10:22). James adds, "Draw nigh to God, and he will draw nigh to you…Cleanse your hands…purify your hearts…Humble yourselves in the sight of the Lord, and he shall lift you up" (James 4:8, 10).

Today, with the help of the Spirit, seek someone out of the crowd and encourage them with the gospel.

Dissolving Your Doubts

"Forasmuch as an excellent spirit, and knowledge, and understanding, interpreting of dreams, and showing of hard sentences, and dissolving of doubts, were found in the same Daniel..." (Daniel 5:12)

Our doubts can lead to worries, and worries may lead to fear. When fear comes, it ties us in knots and renders us incapable of having full faith in the Lord. Yeshua was constantly chastising His followers and listeners for their spirit of doubt and unbelief. The amount of baggage one carries determines the distances he can go with real strength. While Peter was walking on water towards the Master of the Sea, his doubts quickly turned to worry and worry turned to fear causing him to cry out, "Lord, save me!" Immediately the Master stretched forth His hand, and caught Peter. He also caught Peter with a question: "O thou of little faith, wherefore didst thou doubt?" (Matthew 14:31).

If your stomach is all tied up in knots, there is no way you can experience the joy of the Lord or serve God with gratitude! Yeshua said, "I am come that they might have life, and that they might have it more abundantly" (John 10:10). Sometimes we believe but not with true joy. The resurrected Messiah entered the Upper Room in living color: "and while they yet believed not for joy, and wondered [doubted], he said unto them, Have ye here any meat?" The abundant life is not meant to depend upon the abundance of pleasant circumstances, but rather, the abundance of God's grace. The devil preys upon your weaknesses, your human limitations. He loves to get your faith all tangled in knots causing you to doubt your salvation and your Saviour.

What are you doubting and worrying about today—or yesterday? Doubt looks at the *past* and *present*, but faith looks to the *future* in great anticipation and wonder toward God's bright tomorrow. Dissolve your doubts and begin focusing on the God of the impossible.

Adopted & Adored

"God sent forth his Son...that we might receive the adoption of sons." (Galatians 4:4-5)

God knew of my cold and *adamant* heart; nevertheless, He mercifully healed me from the *adder's* bite. He then pointed out an *addendum*—walk in the light. My new Father lovingly began teaching me to *adapt* a different way of life and to become *addicted* to the ministry. Being a permanent *addition* to Yahweh's royal family, He continues to *address* all my needs. The LORD is so *adept* and so *adequate*. Being God's prized possession, He *adheres* to me like *adhesive* with His Spirit. He never has to say *adieu, ad infinitum*. His home is not *adjacent* to me; it is in me. Being His pet, He *adjudicates* for me. When necessary, He *adjures* me not to remain *adrift*, but to *adjust*, having graciously *admeasured* to me the miraculous seeds of faith. He watchfully *administrates* my life. He is my *Admiral* (Hebrews 2:10) and I hold Him in great *admiration*. My good qualities He *admits* so long as they are not an *admixture* to His saving grace. He *admonishes* me because He doesn't want me to stay an *adolescent*. My *Adonai* has wonderfully *adopted* me. He *adores* and *adorns* me giving me an *adrenal* rush!

He wants me to daily *absorb* His Word and become a spiritual *adult* lest I become a spiritual *adulterer* and thereby *adumbrate* or overshadow His laws. He also expects me not to be *adust* (melancholy), but instead, to *advance* His kingdom without gaining an *advantage* for myself. He asks me to wait patiently for the Second *Advent*, yet also to run the race *adventurously*. To help me complete these sublime goals, He fights off the *adversary* who is so *adverse* to me. Further still, my Father carries me through *adversity* while I laboriously *advertise* His gracious banquet invitation to humanity. What is more, He continually *advises* me, *advocates* for me, and from His *adytum* carefully fashions me into the image of His Son. He does this with His holy *adze*—a sharp wood dressing axe.

Today, thank the heavenly Father for adopting you and continually adoring you.

Rising to the Call

"Gideon threshed wheat by the winepress, to hide it from the Midianites. And the angel of the LORD appeared unto him, and said...The LORD is with thee, thou mighty man of valour." (Judges 6:11-12)

Gideon first appears as one of the most unlikely heroes in the Bible. He didn't look very valiant while working secretly in a time of oppression. Why then did the angel call Gideon a *man of valour* when he was a fearful man? Because that was what Gideon would become after rising to meet God's challenge. Similarly, the LORD called Abraham the *father of many nations* at a time when he was only the father of one, and Messiah called Peter a *rock* at a time when he was anything but stable. The LORD doesn't call people according to their abilities; He calls them according to their purpose in life.

Gideon got off to a rather slow start, but he did get started. He wasn't so full of valour at the beginning, but he became valiant. Did you know that Gideon's calling and purpose initially began at birth when God inspired his parents to name him *Ghid-yon*? This word comes from *gadah'*, which means, "to *fell* a tree; cut, hew down." Thus, Gideon's name means *feller* or *warrior*, one who cuts down. This is exactly what Gideon's first mission was: to "throw down the altar of Baal...and cut down the grove...by it" (v.25). Later, with God's help, Gideon cut down the Midianites as if they were merely wheat!

The secret to victory is in the rising. The calling that God gives you will always be greater than your ability; otherwise, you wouldn't have to rise. Receive the calling God gives you even if it doesn't feel comfortable or if it feels way too big for you. And as you rise, don't do so because of who *you are,* but because of Who *God is.*

Rise to your calling today. Take the mantle that has been laid upon you, go in it, and *grow* in it!

The Gospel According to You

"According to the glorious gospel of the blessed God, which was committed to my trust." (1 Timothy 1:11)

When the Master said to His faithful followers, "Go ye into all the world, and preach the gospel to every creature," He was entrusting them with the good news (Mark 16:15). Later He entrusted Paul with it and eventually young Timothy (2 Timothy 1:14). In this current generation, Messiah has entrusted you with this life-saving gospel message; but the lost may sit back and *watch* your gospel before they will ever *want* your gospel.

First, they will watch your LIBERATION, the signs of broken prison chains from your former, sinful lifestyle. It is your job to help the lost understand that "if any man be in Christ, he is a new creature" (2 Corinthians 5:17). When fully received, the gospel message transforms lives. Sometimes the transformation is dramatic like Zacchaeus, the greedy tax collector who sought to restore his stolen fortune; or John, one of the "sons of thunder" who learned to balance truth with love; or Saul who once tried to stamp out the church, then turned to nurture it.

The lost will also observe your LABOR to see just how much you care about their physical wellbeing, and then they will know that you care for their souls. The apostle Paul spent long hours with multitudes and individuals so that none were left with any doubt that He really cared for their everyday needs. He left His legacy saying; "I have showed you all things, how that so laboring ye ought to support the weak" (Acts 20:35).

The unredeemed will also be looking for your LAMENT over their never-dying souls. Jeremiah prayed for more tears. If you have no tears for the lost, then you would do well to pray for the fountain of your heart to be slowly opened.

Lastly, they will behold your LAUGHTER to see if your encounter with God has brought you greater joy than that which the world has brought them. With these things in mind, may the Lord refresh you today with tears and joy as you go carrying His blessed gospel.

ᘒearch ᘒt ᘒgain

"They answered and said unto him, Art thou also of Galilee? Search, and look: for out of Galilee ariseth no prophet." (John 7:52)

The Pharisees put this rhetorical question to Nicodemus to silence him. They didn't really care what the Scriptures foretold of the promised Messiah. If they had cared, they would have searched again themselves. They had a strong bias against Northern Israel and its former Baal-worshipping tribes. After the Northern tribes were carried away by Assyria, various nationalities were brought in; thus, any future Israelites from this region may have had questionable bloodlines. If the tribe of Judah was to witness its Messiah, they *assumed* He would only arise out of their immediate area.

Israel's spiritual guides knew that the Messiah was to be born in Bethlehem according to Micah 5:2, but had they searched the prophetic writings once again they would have been able to pinpoint the area of Messiah's public ministry—the rolling hills of Galilee. Isaiah foretold many details concerning the supernatural Man upon whose shoulders Israel's government of peace would come to rest (Isaiah 9:6-7). The very opening lines of this poetic vision reveal Messiah's headquarters, "the land of Zebulun and the land of Naphtali...by the way of the sea, beyond Jordan, in Galilee of the nations [*goyim,* gentiles]" (Isaiah 9:1). Isaiah also described the future illuminating effects of the Man Who would call Himself the Light of the World: "The people that walked in darkness have seen a great light: they that dwell in the land of the shadow of death, upon them hath the light shined" (Isaiah 9:2). If an *Israelite* lives in Yeshua's illuminating Word long enough, this soul will truly become an *Israelight.*

Why not commit to reading your Bible all the way through this year? Maybe you've never done this before. It's an incredibly exciting journey to search through it page-by-page, line-by-line. You'll discover things you missed from your last reading, and you'll see more brightly Him Who is the fairest of ten thousands. Today, as you read the Bible, search it out for hidden treasures that will encourage your heart.

Your Kinsman Redeemer

"Enter not into the fields of the fatherless: For their Redeemer is mighty; he shall plead their cause with thee." (Proverbs 23:10-11)

In biblical days, if a married woman became widowed her means of income was suddenly and severely reduced. If any debts were owed and could not be quickly repaid, a creditor might take ownership of the family's property. If the family did not agree to sell their property, the creditor could make the woman and her children indentured servants. The law permitted one to sell himself until the debt was paid in full (Leviticus 25:47). Though a child remained fatherless, the land was to be returned on *yovel,* the Jubilee year. But that could be a very long wait! These unfortunate circumstances could be suddenly reversed if "his uncle, or his uncle's son, or any that was nigh of kin unto him" came to his rescue (Leviticus 25:48). In Hebrew, such a person was known as a *goel,* meaning redeemer. However, besides having the necessary, natural love he also needed to have the financial means.

From the courts of glory, God could not redeem the fallen, fatherless sons of men because He was not a blood relative, a human. Out of necessity, God decided to make a way and provide you with the perfect Kinsman Redeemer. This appointed One descended from heaven and came through the earthly bloodline of Adam's helpless race in the form of a man-child. Yeshua was the Father in *humble* manifestation, and He demonstrated His divine *love* just by coming to dwell among us (John 14:9). Moreover, your heavenly Father possesses the *divine* means to redeem trusting souls; "the church of God, which he hath purchased with his own blood" (Acts 20:28).

Do you feel like you're orphaned, lonely and abandoned, maybe even taken advantage of by those who have subversive agendas? Let Yeshua, your loving Kinsman Redeemer plead your hapless cause, for he "is able also to save them...that come unto...him" (Hebrews 7:25). Spend time in the Redeemer's presence today. Tell Him how grateful you are for so great a salvation.

Calling on the Sacred Name

"And God spake unto Moses, and said unto him, I am the LORD [YHWH]: And I appeared unto Abraham unto Isaac, and unto Jacob, by the name of God Almighty [El Shaddai], but by my name Jehovah [YHWH] was I not known to them." (Exodus 6:2-3)

God's covenant name was not first revealed to Moses at the burning bush. Adam knew it. Eve made mention of Yahweh's covenant name (Genesis 4:1). Whenever you see LORD in all capital letters—, which appears nearly 6,800 times—it means Yahweh. Seth had a son and named him Enos; "then began men to call upon the name of the LORD" (Genesis 4:26). The Hebrew root for Enos is *anash* meaning to be "frail, feeble, or incurable; mortal." Because Seth called on the sacred name for help, his son was spared an infant death and lived to be 950 years old. Abraham invoked the covenant name upon entering the unfamiliar land of Canaan (Genesis 12:8). After experiencing a war within her womb, Rebekah inquired of Yahweh and received an answer that settled her fears (Genesis 25:22).

After Israel's 430-year exile in Egypt Yahweh asked Moses the rhetorical question: "by my name Jehovah was I not known to them?" This *question mark* is recorded in the margin of a special Masoretic text that was written to aid in the proper singing of the Torah. Nine hundred years after Moses, God used His personal-relationship name prolifically with Jeremiah and reprimanded Israel's false prophets by saying that their "fathers have forgotten my name" (Jeremiah 23:27). They had replaced it with a mere title—Baal, which means Lord.

The heavenly Father knows you by name and longs for all His covenant children to know Him by name and call upon it in time of need. In Psalm 91:14-15 Yahweh pledges six things when you call upon His sacred name: He will deliver you, set you on high, answer you, be with you, honor you, satisfy you, and show you His "salvation"—which in Hebrew is *yeshuah*. Today, use God's *personal* name Yahweh as you talk to Him, and do so in the name of His Son, Yeshua.

You Are Not Forgotten

"Behold, I have graven thee upon the palms of my hands" (Isaiah 49:16)

God penned His Ten Commandments with His index finger before the eyes of Moses (Exodus 31:18). Nine hundred years later in Belshazzar's fearful presence, the fingers of a man's hand were seen mysteriously writing upon the plaster wall of the king's palace (Daniel 5:5). Six hundred years after that, the Son of God stooped down and with His finger wrote on the ground (John 8:6).

There is no reason why our text verse can't be taken literally. It's quite common for a young person in love to take an ink pen or marker and begin writing the name of their loved one directly onto his or her hand. The Son of God was raised from the grave with a body of normal human proportions. His hands are the same size as ours, but His eyes are much, much sharper. Naturally, believers' names would have to be written so small that only He could see them. Technology since 1985 has allowed mankind to write on such a small scale that the entire contents of an encyclopedia can be made to fit on the head of a pin. What man struggles to do, our LORD does with the greatest of ease. Perhaps our names are even inscribed in a spiraling fashion around the nail prints of His pierced hands.

Whatever the case may be, not a day shall pass this year that Yahweh Yeshua cannot glance down at His pierced palm to behold your precious name. You are so dear to Him. He *died* for you and ever *lives* for you. He has not forgotten you. You may think He has at times, but He hasn't. He thinks of you, waits patiently for you, and watches over you so that nothing can bypass His perfect will for your life.

Little lamb, take rest today! You're *on* His mind, *near* His heart and *in* the palm of His hand.

Your Constant Companion

"That which we have seen and heard declare we unto you, that ye also may have fellowship with us: and truly our fellowship is with the Father, and with his Son Jesus Christ." (1 John 1:3)

The beloved disciple begins his letter using his own eyewitness account and cites his source of eternal joy: close fellowship with the incarnate God. John speaks of the grand privilege of having seen Yeshua on a daily basis and hearing His invigorating words which he and a select few were afforded. As a result of having been daily infused with Messiah's divine speech, He now calls Yeshua the Word of Life (v.1).

John's desire was that every blood-bought believer would be able to experience his or her own unique fellowship with the Lord. He says, "And these things write we unto you, that your joy may be full" (v.4). The Christian life is filled with ups and downs, but to John that mattered little compared to the continual fellowship and subsequent joy found in the Father and Son. The word *fellow* means "a person of equal rank; a peer." This equality is made possible only by God's condescension. The Father could not stoop down, but the Son could and did—being fashioned "in the likeness of sinful flesh" (Romans 8:3).

Now, as you know, long distance relationships seldom last. This is why you are encouraged to keep near Him at all times. When God commanded you to come out of darkness, you were also simultaneously "called unto the fellowship of his Son" (1 Corinthians 1:9). This is the heavenly ordained place in which you are to dwell continually.

John's revelation clearly says that the living Saviour longs to have fellowship with you. You are a member of His body, so He is incomplete without you. This is why He patiently stands at your heart's door waiting daily to continue joy-filled communion with you. Once you have discovered the glory of uninterrupted fellowship with Him, your life and joy will never be fuller.

As you go about your day, be mindful of the One Who has chosen to share it with you. Acknowledge His presence through meaningful dialogue.

The Joy & Pain of Forgiveness

"So shall ye say unto Joseph, Forgive, I pray thee now, the trespass of thy brethren, and their sin; for they did unto thee evil:" (Genesis 50:17)

In the original language there are two words predominantly used which mean to *forgive*. The first of these is used in our text. It is the word *nasa,* which means to *lift.* When you forgive someone, you are lifting a weight of negative emotions from that person. You are lifting their spirit and making them to know joy again. You experience that joy as well. The word *nasa* in its Paleo-Hebraic form reveals more. It is spelled *nun, samekh, hey* and carries the meaning of one who *continues* to *protect* and *look* after another. Unforgiveness says, "I don't care about you anymore," but forgiveness says, "I will always care about you." Unforgiveness says, "We are like poured-out water," but forgiveness says, "We are now like gathered waters."

The other word for forgive is *salakh,* as in "the LORD shall forgive her" (Numbers 30:12). This word means to *pardon.* When you forgive someone that has caused you pain, you choose to keep that pain to yourself and not place it back on the other person. This is exactly what the ancient Hebrew picture language reveals about the word *salakh,* spelled *samekh-lamed-kaph.* The letter *samekh* is depicted by a thorn—a true depiction of pain—and means to *protect* or *grab.* The letter *lamed* is depicted by a shepherd's staff—a beneficial tool—and means to *bind.* The letter *kaph* is depicted by an open palm—a symbol of peace—and means to *allow* or *tame.* When someone wrongs you, it is because he or she is in pain. You *pardon* that person by *grabbing* their pain [protecting them from it] and *binding* it to yourself, thus *allowing* him or her to be free of pain.

Now consider what the Good Shepherd has done for you. "And you...in your sins [thorns and pain]...hath he...forgiven you all trespasses [pardoned]; Blotting out the handwriting of ordinances that was against us [protecting]...and took [grabbed] it out of the way, nailing [binding] it to his cross" (Colossians 2:13-15). Today, seek to lift and remove someone's emotional pain. Give them a heart-felt pardon in Jesus' name!

Keeping the Marshall Cool

"He that is slow to anger is better than the mighty; and he that ruleth his spirit than he that taketh a city." (Proverbs 16:32)

In some countries, a marshal is a military official of the highest rank. Ordinarily a marshal is one who carries out court orders. He does not need to get angry in order to accomplish his set objective for he has power over others. He can remain calm in his work. The Hebrew word used here for "ruleth" is *mashal*. Sound familiar? It is a primitive root meaning, "to have rule, dominion, power as a governor."

If a marshal gets upset, out of control, and starts shooting at anything that moves, everyone starts running for cover. They run and hide in fear lest they get struck by one of his many stray bullets. This leads us to our next point—keeping the marshal cool.

Believe it or not, the word *cool* also comes from the Hebrew. Joseph used this Semitic word with his brothers when he promised to "nourish" them (Genesis 45:11). *Kul* is a primitive root meaning, "to *keep in*; figuratively, to *maintain, forbear.*" Joseph was promising his brothers that he would keep them in; that is, provide shelter and food for them. Herein lies the secret of keeping the marshal's emotions calm, cool and collected. We must learn to *keep in* our emotions and not let them become so outwardly visible. We must always work to *maintain* a high degree of self-control. It is important to remain unruffled by the actions and words of others and choose to *forbear,* or wait.

May the Holy Spirit help you today to rule your emotions quietly like Yeshua ruled His.

A Bittersweet Life

"And she said unto them, Call me not Naomi, call me Mara: for the Almighty hath dealt very bitterly with me." (Ruth 1:20)

Naomi [Heb. *my pleasantness*] had left Bethlehem under drought conditions with a husband and two sons. Years later, she returned with only one relative, Ruth, her daughter-in-law. Her lament to the citizens of Bethlehem was, "I went out full, and the LORD hath brought me home again empty" (v.21). She invoked the people's pity desiring to be called by a different name from that time forward—Mara, which means *bitter*. In her bitterness, she forgot to be continually thankful before the LORD.

Though nothing can ever fully replace blood kin, Naomi was overlooking the one *pleasant* thing she had returned with—Ruth. Naomi had not yet learned to appreciate the *pleasant* Moabitess who was faithfully clinging to her. At the moment of Naomi's confession, Ruth must have felt very insignificant and unappreciated. After all, her mother-in-law had just strongly urged her to go back home to her own people. Ruth had her own right to cry out with bitterness, but instead seemed to remain hopeful and thankful that she had at least someone to whom to cling. When Ruth said, "your God will be my God," she was clinging to Naomi in a covenant way.

How many times in life do you cry before God and others that your lot in life is not what you dreamed it would be? Do you expect to get to your perfect mountaintop without first passing through a valley or two? Would you ever fully appreciate the sweetness of God's red mountaintop vineyards if you had never compared that taste with the bitter pools that sometimes collect in the gray valley below?

Beloved, embrace the cold of night as well as you do the warmth of the noonday for God has made them both. Ask the Saviour today to help you trust Him and receive from His hand both the bad and the good (Matthew 22:10). In this way, you shall enjoy the warmth of His tears *and* the healing glow of His smile.

A Song with Wings

"Awake, awake, Deborah: awake, awake, utter a song: arise, Barak, and lead thy captivity captive." (Judges 5:12)

Every morning at the break of dawn for the past three months or more I have been awakened out of my sound sleep by a bird who roosts in a neighbor's nearby tree. This Australian bird makes the most distinct call that goes forth in two parts. The early-riser lifts its loud but lofty voice while his friend a block away hears the sound and repeats it. It sounds like an echo because of the perfect repetition. As the sound returns, the noisy, winged-creature sends out its other musical call that is also repeated by the distant bird. This cycle goes on for approximately ten minutes before the two-line chorus is finally over and the bird takes its morning flight through the lower heavens. Having a different sort of biological clock, I gladly go back to sleep.

The only other creature that God ordained for heavenly *flight* is man, and he too has been given a song. Mankind sings all manner of songs that lift his spirit, but once he receives eternal life he notices the difference and begins to sing of his Redeemer, "he hath put a new song in my mouth, even praise unto our God" (Psalm 40:3). Unfortunately, the inevitable happens: The reborn soul loses his song of redemption for one reason or another. But God is always worthy of the believer's praise. This was made so clear to me just this morning.

When the bird wakes me up at 5:30 a.m. I abruptly go to the window and close it, but this morning the bird's joyful song was accompanied with pouring rain. I listened a few minutes as the feathered-one's song ascended upwards through the dimly lit sky like incense rising in the holiest of temples. Its message to the world—"God is worthy to be praised, even when the sky is falling!"

Let God know all the things that you're thankful for today, even if your life is raining down problems.

Our Infinite God

"And one cried unto another, and said, Holy, holy, holy, [kadosh, kadosh, kadosh] is the LORD of hosts: the whole earth is full of his glory." (Isaiah 6:3)

Isaiah described seeing seraphim, angels of fire, but he also saw what very few have seen—the Lord (v.1). Consider four things about Yahweh. First, His *glory appears* at every turn. He has designed this world so that only those who refuse to see could ever miss His holy thumbprint upon His finished work of creation.

Further still, His *greatness amazes* those who are small in their own eyes. Man's pride in his own accomplishments often clouds his vision of the One Who alone is great. In the construction of Solomon's Temple God commanded that not so much as a hammer be heard on site. Yahweh wanted Israelites to be amazed with Him, not the House. This is why Yeshua declared, "That in this place is one greater than the Temple" (Matthew 12:6). Isaiah saw Yeshua "sitting upon a throne, high and lifted up, and his train filling the temple" (v.1).

There is none like the God of Jacob whose *goodness abounds*. Isaiah recognized his own uncleanness in the sight of the Holy One, but the Lord had a remedy prepared. A seraph flew over with a live coal in his hand, which he had taken with the tongs from the altar. He laid it upon Isaiah's mouth and said, "Lo, this hath touched thy lips; and thine iniquity is taken away, and thy sin purged" (v.7). God will abound unto you also and keep you cleansed from sin.

Finally, observe the manner in which His *grace abides*. The Lord said, "Whom shall I send, and who will go for us?" (v.8). He said this because He was ready to extend grace once again to a wayward people who seemed to care little for Him. His grace abides even when we don't.

Today, be on the lookout for God's glory to appear, His goodness to abound, His greatness to amaze, and His grace to abide!

Destined for Greatness

"Among those that are born of women there is not a greater prophet than John the Baptist: but he that is least in the kingdom of God is greater than he." (Luke 7:28)

He that would have everything must possess nothing. He that would have servants must be a servant. He that would be first must be last. And he that would be the greatest must be the least. What a challenge this is for men robed with sinful flesh.

Unfortunately, it is not within our fallen natures to be *little*, let alone *least*. Are you content while hidden in a corner, unnoticed and insignificant in the world's eyes? If you want to be greater than John, then get ready to have no certain dwelling, get ready to eat only what the Lord provides, and begin caring more about God's opinion of you than what your friends think of you. Embracing ridicule, scorn and discouragement, along with returning good for evil will become the order of the day. Performing the will of God without a whim will quickly have to become your second nature. Helping the homeless rather than renovating your own home will also be a very necessary requirement. Your brother's plight will have to mean more to you than your bank account does, and the list goes on. This is a very tall order indeed, but not impossible to achieve.

The Saviour described the greatest saint in God's kingdom with one simple word—*least*. This word in its Greek form is instantly recognizable. It is the word *micro* meaning small. Herein lies the secret of spiritual greatness. John already had this strategy figured out. Referring to the Son of God he exclaimed, "He must increase, but I must decrease" (John 3:30).

In order to be counted as *extraordinary* in the kingdom you must count as your *ordinary* service doing the will of God without being lifted up in the eyes of men. Today, ask God to help you adapt to being the least.

Monumental Faith

"And these all, having obtained a good report through faith."
(Hebrews 11:39)

The Scriptures clearly reveal that monumental faith *pleases the Lord.* Just prior to the above verse, Paul states that it is impossible to please God outside a life of faith (Hebrews 11:6). Our use of faith pleases Him so much that He shows His contentment by rewarding us. Paul confirms this saying that "he is a rewarder of them that diligently seek him" (Hebrews 11:6). When we operate in the realm of faith, it's like building a monument to the Lord showing how much we trust Him. In the end Messiah will exclaim, "Well done, good and faithful servant" (Matthew 25:23).

Monumental faith also *produces great results.* Through faith Peter did what the other disciples thought only their mighty Messiah could do—walk on water! Students were naturally expected to imitate their rabbis, but Yeshua encouraged them to do even greater things than He did (John 14:12).

Having monumental faith in the Lord's return *purifies our hearts.* "So Christ was once offered to bear the sins of many; and unto them that look for him shall he appear the second time without sin unto salvation" (Hebrews 9:28). With expectant faith, the believer looks for Lord Yeshua's return and prepares his heart by removing impurities and needless things.

It is only a monumental faith that *persuades the lost.* Paul's unswerving faith in the Saviour struck a nerve in Agrippa, great-grandson of Herod the Great. He said, "Almost thou persuadest me to be a Christian" (Acts 26:28). Paul may not have persuaded Agrippa, the last of the Herods, but he persuaded countless thousands with his vibrant faith.

People are looking for believers with real faith. May the Lord help you today to convince the world that our God reigns both now and in the world to come.

Deep Waters Yield Great Harvests!

"Now when he had left speaking, he said unto Simon, Launch out into the deep, and let down your nets for a draught." (Luke 5:4)

Fishermen seem to have a different color of blood than most people—theirs is more like deep blue! What Yeshua inspired Simon Peter to go after was a draught, a *load* of fish. The word draught (pronounced *drahft*) is a Middle English word meaning a measured portion or amount drawn from a given load. This word is still used every day all over the world though it's spelled differently.

Before the Master could prod Simon to launch out into the deep, He first had to motivate the tired and discouraged fisherman to "thrust out a little from the land" (v.3). Peter thought he was only making his great Teacher a little speaking platform on water so He could break free from the smothering crowds. But Peter got more than he bargained for. Had Yeshua told Simon to drag his heavy fishing vessel off the sandy bottoms of the lakeshore to go deep-sea fishing, he would have likely never pulled up the anchor. But Peter's subsequent obedience yielded him a mother-load of fish. He *drew* them out from the depths of the sea with awe and wonder. In time, his zeal was redirected to throw out a glorious gospel net in which he caught 3000 human souls in a single day! Funny enough, after he caught them that Pentecost day, he ordered them all to be washed and cleaned in baptismal *waters*.

The Captain of your salvation will never place you in deep waters without first helping you get your feet wet. The Saviour will lead you gently along, set your gospel compass, build your confidence, and strengthen the fabric of your faith until at last you're ready to launch out into the fearless deep. He will also help you to stay as long as necessary in order to bring home the gospel prize. Today, get direction from the Master of the Sea on exactly where to *let down* your gospel net for waiting souls.

Growing in Covenant Relationship
Part 1

"In love...grow up into him in all things, which is the head, even Christ." (Ephesians 4:15)

Four meaningful, progressive covenants in the Old Testament have their fulfillments in the New. The *Blood Covenant* is the first of these. The purchased slave begins in lowly *servanthood* with his new Owner. He only knows God as someone Who has bought him out of difficult circumstances and simply serves Him as Master.

The *Salt Covenant* is the next level. You grow closer to your Lord and obtain favor through steadfast obedience. This allows you to become His *trusted friend*. Abraham proved his unquestioning friendship by giving Yahweh his only son. Abraham moved along rapidly with the LORD and achieved the amazing status of God's friend (2 Chronicles 20:7). The Son of God ate salt with His faithful servants and proclaimed them all to be His friends (John 15:15).

The *Sandal Covenant* is performed when the servant/friend acquires an *inheritance*. God promised Abraham and his descendants that the land of Canaan would be theirs to inherit (Genesis 15:7). This promise was fulfilled when Yahweh said to Joshua, "Every place that the sole of your foot [i.e. sandals off] shall tread, that have I given unto you" (Joshua 1:3). Paul spoke of our full inheritance when he wrote, "He that spared not his own Son, but delivered him up for us all, how shall he not with him also freely give us all things?" (Romans 8:32).

The *Marriage Covenant* is the closet of all unions and comes to pass when the servant/friend/heir becomes the Owner's *bride*. Messiah spoke of believers as children of the bridal chamber (Mark 2:19-20). We as His servants are still fully owned, but now also fully loved. The story of Ruth wonderfully exemplifies the perfect cycle of this four-covenant concept.

Today, seek to please your Master with good stewardship, good friendship, and a united heart.

The Blood Covenant

Part 2

"Present your bodies a living sacrifice, holy, acceptable unto God, which is your reasonable service." (Romans 12:1)

The blood covenant is the first of God's four progressive covenants, and He initiates each level. Here God invites the believer to enter into a relationship as *servant*. The key to good servanthood is sacrificing your own reputation. That is what God's Son did when He came to earth. He "made himself of no reputation, and took upon him the form of a servant" (Philippians 2:7).

In biblical times, a servant who desired no reputation of his own and for love's sake refused to leave his master, could undergo a ritual that involved the letting of his blood. After the servant's clear profession before the judges, his master would take him to a doorpost and bore his ear through with an awl. This was the token signifying that he wanted to serve him forever (Exodus 21:6). Messiah was the Chief of servants, and He set the benchmark for all who would say they truly love the Father. His declaration was telling: "I do always those things that please him" (John 8:29). Paul sought to live a sacrificial life, one that would please God and not himself. Turning away from his own reputation he said, "I die daily" (1 Corinthians 15:31). Messiah pledged blessings to those servants whom He found busy carrying out their daily service at His return (Luke 12:37).

When a person places faith in the risen Messiah, the first step of obedience is to undergo believer's baptism. This signals death to the old, self-serving life. If you are a man, you are now called a *servant* of the LORD, and if you're a woman, you are now the LORD's *handmaiden*. The voluntary servant is now eligible to participate in a highly symbolic blood ritual—drinking "the blood of grapes," or as Messiah referred to it, "the fruit of the vine" (Genesis 49:11; Luke 22:18). Drinking from the Master's cup (communion) should be observed often. He placed no restrictions on the frequency of this act (1 Corinthians 11:26). By drinking the "blood of grapes," you are *renewing* the blood covenant, that is, obedience to the Son. Today, renew your commitment to *serve* the living God in quiet prayer.

The Salt Covenant

Part 3

"Ought you not to know that the LORD God of Israel gave the kingdom over Israel to David for ever, even to him and to his sons by a covenant of salt?" (2 Chronicles 13:5)

The sign of salt identifies the Salt Covenant. When God invited Israel into a close fellowship with Him through the sacrificial system, no covenant sacrifice was to be offered without being salted (Leviticus 2:13). Those that kept fidelity with Yahweh, therefore, viewed salt as divine. Salt has other qualities than just seasoning. It is also known for its wonderful abilities to purify, preserve and even heal.

Salt conveys the idea behind *hospitality* as no meal is normally eaten without it. In the Near East, when someone passes you the salt you return by saying, "You do me honor." Because of its permanent nature, salt also represents *loyalty*. DaVinci's *Last Supper* appears to depict Judas inadvertently knocking over the salt canister signifying his disregard for loyalty. When two people had eaten together, they would say with great import, "There is salt between us." These traits of fidelity, hospitality and loyalty were the hallmarks of *friendship* and were sealed up in the concept of salt.

In Bible times, when two people wanted to enter into a covenant of friendship they would recite the terms of their covenant, open up their salt bags with which they travelled, exchange salt from one pouch to the other, and then shake the pouches. The symbolism demonstrated that the only way their pact could be broken was for each person to retrieve their own granules of salt from the other person's pouch, which was impossible to do. Once their covenant of friendship was spoken and made, it was binding. Messiah shared salt-seasoned meals with His disciples and declared His fidelity to them by calling them *friends* (John 15:15). You enter this same friendship covenant with Him when you eat communion bread, which symbolizes His body that was once covered with His own salt-ladened sweat in the Garden of Gethsemane (Luke 22:44).

In prayer today, ask the Lord to help you stay *true to salt*.

35

The Sandal Covenant

Part 4

"And Abram said to the king of Sodom...I will not take from a thread even to a shoelatchet...lest thou shouldest say, I have made Abram rich." (Genesis 14:22-23)

Abraham knew that all he would ever *inherit* would come from God's hand, not men. This first usage of the word shoe in the Bible has to do with one person giving another his sandal as tangible evidence of the transfer of property. "Now this was the custom in former times in Israel concerning redeeming and concerning changing, for to confirm all things; a man plucked off his shoe, and gave it to his neighbor: and this was a testimony in Israel" (Ruth 4:7).

Both Moses and Joshua were told by Yahweh to divest themselves of their sandals on the inaugural eve of receiving their inheritance. Leaving behind a flock of sheep, Moses inherited a nation at the burning bush. Joshua who spied out the Promised Land inherited a standing army to go and conquer it. When these two plucked off their sandals, it signified total surrender of their personal ambitions. Only with this mindset could God them to lead His people. This covenant demanded that the whole nation occasionally stop and remove their sandals before Him. He told them, "Every place whereon the *soles* of your feet shall tread shall be yours" (Deuteronomy 11:24). There is some evidence to suggest that they actually did just this—even the children. At Har Karkom in the Sinai desert outlines of paired-sandals have been found etched into granite. Could these strange tokens be the title deed to the Promised Land? According to Split Rock Research Foundations, thousands of these same sandal-glyphs exist in Saudi Arabia along the perimeter of the country's border. Later, 70 New Testament gospel heralds were given authority to tread under foot serpents and scorpions as they walked in sandal-covenant possession within the borders of Israel (Luke 10:19).

Before going into prayer this morning, put off your shoes. Afterwards, put on the Saviour's humble, yet hallowed sandals and go possess the kingdom.

The Marriage Covenant
Part 5

"Turn, O backsliding children, saith the LORD; for I am married unto you:" (Jeremiah 3:14)

Marriage remains the highest form of covenant on earth. From God's dealings with mankind, we see that it is also the oldest form of covenanting. Marriage still comes with a very special token—a ring. Its circular shape symbolizes the unbreakable nature of the covenant. One of the most important unions in history is that of Yahweh to His covenant people Israel. Before going into somber silence for 400 years, God reminded the men of Judah of their unfaithfulness in marrying outsiders. His accusation was that the tribe had "married the daughter of a strange god" (Malachi 2:11). Ezra had to deal with this particular problem. So that Yahweh might continue to "seek a godly seed," He sternly told the men of Judah to "take heed to your spirit, and let none deal treacherously against the wife of his youth" (v.15).

In the fullness of time Israel's covenant Head came down and personally set the record straight. The Pharisees pressed Yeshua to give His opinion on the issue of divorce. He pointed back to the union of Adam and Eve saying, "What...God hath joined together, let not man put asunder" (Mark 10:9). This can be illustrated by the following Hebrew wedding custom. Under the *huppah* [wedding canopy] a newly joined couple drinks wine from a single glass and then crushes it under their feet symbolizing their exclusive union. No one else can drink from that cup. Moving to New Covenant marital status, Paul says, "For we are members of his body, of his flesh, and of his bones...This is a great mystery: but I speak concerning Christ and the church" (Ephesians 5:30, 32). The grandest wedding of all time is drawing nearer by the day, but God continues gathering His bride.

Today, ask the Lord to help you prepare accordingly using Revelation 19:7 as a praise chorus: "Let us be glad and rejoice, and give honor to him: for the marriage of the Lamb is come, and his wife hath made herself ready."

ℋarassing 𝐸vil

"See, I have this day set thee over the nations and over the kingdoms, to root out, and to pull down, and to destroy, and to throw down, to build, and to plant." (Jeremiah 1:10)

At a very young age, Jeremiah was given a task to guide Judah's obstinate rulers and minister to the impoverished remnant left in Judea. However, before he could build and plant, he first had to pull down and destroy the heady ideas of Judah's kings and then throw down all possibilities of resisting Babylon. He did all this with the Word of the LORD.

There is a little helpful Hebrew secret behind the words "throw down." It is the word *hâras.* We use the word harass all the time. It means to disturb persistently. If a person is persistently disturbed long enough, he will become cast down and break apart mentally or emotionally. The believer's job is not to spiritually harass people, but rather, harass evil. In the New Covenant, we are also advised to cast down evil things that encroach upon us. Paul writes that we are to be like warriors; that is, "Casting down imaginations, and every high thing that exalts itself against the knowledge of God" (2 Corinthians 10:5).

The word *hâras* comes from *hâr* meaning a mountain or hill. As a believer, you seek to dwell on the mountaintop, but the evil one isn't going to help you in that pursuit. He will instead hinder you. He will war against your mind and set up his battlements. Your job is to break down the enemy's dark walls that surround and crowd out your spiritual life. In finality, you should *throw them down* the mountain. You are more than a conqueror through Yeshua (Romans 8:37). If you don't throw evil influences far down under your feet, those things can and will build back up in your life again. If you want to be a biblical builder, you must first learn to throw down the sinful things that surround you. Then you'll be able to shout *hurrah* and be free from evil's grip (James 4:7).

Lean upon the Spirit for help today. Seek His divine assistance in prayer to help you accomplish your set task.

Supposing About God

"And Jesus himself began to be about thirty years of age, being (as was supposed) the son of Joseph, which was the son of Heli." (Luke 3:23)

The general populace of Israel only supposed or assumed that Yeshua was of human origin. Had they taken time to investigate and ask His mother, she would have gladly told them of her son's miraculous conception. Well, believers can fall into the same kind of trap as the people in Messiah's day. Believers *suppose* something is so when they should really know for a fact. They guess about theological concepts when they should really be studying and building a strong foundation for their belief system. Paul said, "Study to show thyself approved unto God, a workman that needeth not to be ashamed, rightly dividing the word of truth" (2 Timothy 2:15).

A believer finds himself at a great disadvantage when he begins supposing various things about the person of God. We are not to *suppose* that things will just pan out, or *suppose* that God will intervene in a certain way. Paul described Yeshua as the God Who goes beyond our expectations. He said, "Now unto him that is able to do exceeding abundantly above all that we ask or think, according to the power that worketh in us" (Ephesians 3:20). The Holy Spirit Who works in us does not *suppose* that He can do great things—He knows He can. The trouble He has is getting us to believe that He can.

The worst supposing of all is when believers *suppose* that the Son of God is way up in heaven and can't be bothered to walk among His people anymore. We need to see the mighty Saviour superimposed upon the doorway of our congregation as well as the pulpit, the choir, the baptistery and the altar. This brand of faith will charge the very atmosphere of our weekly meetings. At church it is okay if everything goes as it was supposed to so long as it went the way the Spirit wanted it to.

As you go into prayer and out the door today, *believe* that God can and will do all His good pleasure (Philippians 2:13).

Gospel Crumbs

"And she answered and said unto him, Yes, Lord: yet the dogs under the table eat of the children's crumbs." (Mark 7:28)

Messiah had the poor in mind when He gave the Torah to Moses. He forbade Israel to harvest the corners of their fields completely. It was also forbidden for a landowner to glean his fields or vineyard. Concerning the leftovers, He said, "thou shalt leave them unto the poor, and to the stranger: I am the LORD your God" (Leviticus 23:22). Apparently, this custom carried over into the home where bread that fell from a table was considered gleanings appointed to the poor. What is more, the family table was viewed as a consecrated altar by ancient peoples. Bread was holy and the salt that accompanied it. If any morsels fell to the floor, they were not to be reclaimed.

With His great love for the poor, Yeshua spoke of this well-known custom in His parable of the poor paralytic who desired "to be fed with the crumbs which fell from the rich man's table" (Luke 16:20-21). Some rich people, like the one in Yeshua's parable, may have been sure to let some bread fall on purpose. Messiah was the Champion of the poor and His very first message started like this: "The Spirit of the Lord is upon me, because he hath anointed me to preach the gospel to the poor" (Luke 4:18). The word poor in every culture is synonymous with hunger, desire and lack. By contrast, the poor are usually the ones who eagerly respond to what the gospel has to offer.

The Syro-Phoenician woman needed a miracle. Messiah's response was, "it is not proper to take the children's bread, and to cast it unto the dogs" (v.27). The Jewish nation viewed dogs as unclean or impure as house pets, but gentiles likely held no such prohibition. Thus, she spoke in recognition of her own custom that crumbs from the table might be shared by whoever hungered. This won Messiah's heart, and the spiritually poor woman received not a crumb, but a whole loaf!

Today, don't forget the gospel-poor, those who have never *tasted* the Bread of Life.

Adorning the Doctrine of God

"...showing all good fidelity; that they may adorn the doctrine of God our Saviour in all things." (Titus 2:10)

The word *doctrine* comes to us from a Greek word meaning teaching or instruction. The heavenly Father doesn't want us to walk mechanically in His teachings; He wants us to walk in a way that shows how much we love His word. By definition *adorn* means "lend beauty to, or to enhance the glory of." The translators gave us the word "adorn" from the Greek word *kosmeos* meaning, "to put in proper order, to decorate." Kosmeos is where we get our modern word cosmetics.

Believers can adorn the doctrine of God by simply being *orderly*. We must do the things that God has given us to do in the right order, in the right way and in the right spirit. We also adorn God's instructions by being *lowly*. This was the central theme of Paul's address to the Christians at Philippi. We can also adorn His word by being *obedient*. When we act according to the gospel, in a sense we are wearing the gospel. We make it visible and beautiful to others who may be watching. Solomon said, "My son, hear the instruction of thy father, and forsake not the law of thy mother: For they shall be an ornament of grace unto thy head, and chains about thy neck" (Proverbs 1:8-9).

Acts 2:42 tells us that the first-century believers obeyed the apostles' doctrine faithfully. They wanted to adorn the Saviour's high commands with which He had instructed them. Isaiah drew upon this concept when he prophesied of Israel's complete obedience in the golden Messianic age: "Thou shalt also be a crown of glory in the hand of the LORD, and a royal diadem in the hand of thy God" (Isaiah 62:3).

How well do you adorn God's holy doctrines? Do you make them look like beautiful ornaments in which others would desire to be wrapped? Do you *glow* with the gospel or do you *groan* because of it? Today, ask God to help you adorn His word by keeping it happily.

The Healing Touch

"And when Jesus was come into Peter's house, he saw his wife's mother laid, and sick of a fever. And he touched her hand, and the fever left her: and she arose, and ministered unto them." (Matthew 8:14-15)

Like any good shepherd, Yeshua was always looking for sheep in need of help. Physical healing also brings about restoration of mental and spiritual wellbeing. Messiah's normal custom was to speak words of life simply to the ones in need. But oh, how His love was demonstrated when He laid His holy hands directly upon them.

One of Israel's greatest prophets, Elijah, was once in need of emotional repair. "And as he lay and slept under a juniper tree, behold, then an angel touched him, and said unto him, Arise and eat" (1 Kings 19:5). The root word for touch is *nagah* meaning, "to *lay the hand upon;* by implication to *reach.*" The angel reached out to Elijah waking him up twice until he finished eating his soul-restoring meal. The weary prophet was so strengthened by the angel's outreach of love that he "went in the strength of that meat forty days and forty nights" (v.8). After Yeshua brought back Peter's mother-in-law from the brink, she immediately began the arduous process of cooking for company.

There is a practical lesson in this story. Although the gracious Lord looks on you with pity and often helps you out of your predicaments, He helps you so that you can get back to helping others. He touches you so that you can touch the lives of others. God does to you what He wants you to do to others; namely, have compassion. And you don't have to go to a nursing home to find people in great need. Everyone has a great need in his or her life. And physical discomfort is not always with which someone needs help. Not a soul walks this earth who is without some heavy burden, some load of care.

As the LORD has reached *you*, go reach *others* for Him today.

Look, Worship, Breathe!

"And God said unto Moses, I AM THAT I AM: and he said, Thus shalt thou say unto the children of Israel, I AM hath sent me unto you." (Exodus 3:14)

The Hebrew name God presents Himself with is *Hayah Asher Hayah.* The verb *hayah* means to exist or be. Asher is commonly translated as *who*, so God's name also means, "I AM WHO I AM." He shortens it to say *Hayah*, "I AM." Moshe just had his typical day turned into a most extraordinary one after he saw a bramble engulfed by fire and remain intact. One named *Malakh Yehovah,* the Angel of the LORD, appeared standing in the midst of it. But as Moshe drew closer, *Elohim,* God, began speaking out of the midst of the bush (v.2, 4). These two divine Beings at the scene form the basis of a profound truth.

The heavenly Father is bound hand in hand with His Son. The three ancient Paleo-Hebrew letters for *Hayah* draw this exact picture. The letter *hey* depicts a man with both his hands raised. God has said that He raises His hands to the seed of the house of Jacob and to the Gentiles (Ezekiel 20:5; Isaiah 49:22). The word *Hayah* has two *hey's,* so this word represents two divine Persons linked by the letter *yod* which depicts a *hand*. This hand refers to a third personality, the Holy Spirit. The Holy Spirit manifested Himself to Moses at the bush as fire (Deuteronomy 4:24). The *yod—an arm with a hand—*means work or worship. The *arm* of the LORD is synonymous with His saving power: "The LORD hath made bare his holy arm...and all the ends of the earth shall see the salvation of our God" (Isaiah 52:10).

In summary, the letter *hey* means, "look, reveal, or breathe." *Yod* here refers to worship. Thus, the pictorial form of I AM, *Hayah,* invites man to *look* at the *revealed* God, *worship* Him and *breathe*; that is, live. "Look unto me, and be ye saved, all the ends of the earth: for I am God" (Isaiah 45:22).

Today, humbly ask the LORD to reach out and reveal His saving grace to one of your lost relatives or friends.

By the Shepherd's Side

"The LORD is my shepherd; I shall not want." (Psalm 23:1)

Salvation or safety exists wherever the Shepherd is. This song of salvation from the trusting sheep finds its real inspiration in the Shepherd and Bishop of souls (1 Peter 2:25). "I shall not want" means that you are complete in Him and shall never lack any good thing (Colossians 2:10). Your insatiable desires are sure to diminish once you enter Yeshua's divinely prepared sheepfold. There He causes His own to "lie down in green pastures" making it a haven of perfect rest. Because the lamb states, "he leadeth me beside the still waters," you are assured that you can drink at your leisure and slow your pulse to the rhythm of the calm brook He has led you to.

The great Shepherd also knows how to mend shattered dreams and broken hearts. This seems to be His specialty, whereby the sheep regain their confidence saying, "He restoreth my soul." The shepherd also specializes in bringing out His own virtues in you. This we know for the lamb says, "he leadeth me in the paths of righteousness for his name's sake." In the Shepherd's presence, strength and conviction grow on the lamb as fast as its wool does causing him to say, "I will fear no evil: for thou art with me." Under the Shepherd's watch-care, you have a refuge from all unfriendlies. The sheep exclaims from his own personal experience, "thy rod and thy staff they comfort me." You can be comforted in this, too.

If the sheep is attacked or lost, he knows that the Shepherd already possesses the safety kit to perform the rescue. If the sheep sustains any flesh wounds, he also knows that the Shepherd will surely anoint him on the "head with oil." The abundance of the Shepherd's storehouse causes the lamb to burst out, "my cup runneth over" and the abundance of the Shepherd's loving-kindness makes the lamb to shout, "surely goodness and mercy shall follow me all the days of my life." Moreover, he foresees everlasting joy "in the house of the" Shepherd.

Today, thank the Shepherd for all He means to you.

Treasure in Your Attic!

"And the child Samuel ministered unto the LORD before Eli. And the word of the LORD was precious in those days; there was no open vision." (1 Samuel 3:1)

Israel had only been living in the land for about 250 years, and most of that time was spent fighting the Canaanites under Joshua and succeeding judges. Israel had not yet entered into a time of peace and prosperity because of their casual attitude toward the things of God. Instead of having time to hear the Word of God, they only heard the clamoring sound of rams' horns calling them to charge or retreat. The days of Samuel heralded a new era in the economy of God. He began to speak to Israel once again and give great spiritual leadership through His devoted prophet. Growing up in the Tabernacle, Samuel had spent much time in the secret place of the Most High, but the time came to bring the treasured Word of the LORD out into the open.

If you are a believer then you know that the greatest treasure in the entire world is the Word of God. Millions of souls have died over this very treasure. They died while trying to live it, read it, translate it, copy it, hide it, share it, transport it, preach it and teach it, or just trying to breathe one word of it. Only a handful of copies of the first English Bibles printed on the famous Guttenberg press still exist today. These copies can sell for between four and ten million dollars. The contents of it don't read much differently than the copy you possess right now. The truth is your personal copy of the Bible is of inestimable value. If you read it and live by it, then this treasure is hidden in the secret chambers of your heart, and you can say like David, "Thy word have I hid in mine heart, that I might not sin against thee" (Psalm 119:11).

As the end of days and the coming of Messiah Yeshua draws near, it is time to bring the treasure out of the attic of our hearts and into the broad streets where others can see and judge its worth. Because the Word of God has the power to awaken and save souls, pray about sharing it with someone today.

Five Precious Things

"That the trial of your faith, being much more precious than of gold that perisheth, though it be tried with fire, might be found unto praise and honour and glory at the appearing of Jesus Christ." (1 Peter 1:7)

In his two letters, Peter uses the word *precious* seven times. Because precious means, "something highly esteemed or cherished," the apostle wants us to estimate properly what has been given us. The first thing of worth he mentions is the *precious testing* the believer goes through. Trials may seem like a tragedy to the believer, but God sees the end of the test in triumphant shades of glory. He sees your faith being refined to purer strains.

Peter then goes on to point out that "ye were not redeemed with corruptible things, as silver and gold...but with the *precious blood* of Christ" (1:18-19). From that priceless, redeeming blood, the believer gets a much clearer estimation of his own value. God could not say I love you in any greater way than He did 2000 years ago.

Next, Peter speaks of Yeshua as the *precious cornerstone* saying, "he that believeth on him shall not be confounded" (2:6). If the Cornerstone faced rejection, so shall many other stones belonging to God's house. Peter also speaks "to them that have obtained like *precious faith*...through the righteousness of God and...Jesus Christ" (2 Peter 1:1). Peter is talking about the common bond shared by those who have also entered into the covenant of life.

Finally, Peter says that God has "given unto us exceeding great and *precious promises*: that by these ye might be partakers of the divine nature" (2 Peter 1:4). Among the many promises of God we hold dear, the two most prized are the promise of His indwelling Spirit and the promise of a new incorruptible body on resurrection day.

Count these five *precious* things on your right hand in your prayer time, and then raise it to Him in loving gratitude.

When Family & Friends Fail You

"My kinsfolk have failed, and my familiar friends have forgotten me." (Job 19:14)

In her ignorance, Job's wife could not stand beside him; instead, she delivered her guilty verdict and told him to curse God and die (2:9). The Bible is not short of tragic stories that tell of the rejection of family and friends. Ever since creation's fall, life continues to be like a chain of weak, rusty links. When the pressure becomes too great, the chain breaks.

Family and friends do not have to turn completely on you to make life unbearable; they only have to turn their backs and give you the cold shoulder. The Hebrew word for forget is *shakeakh*, a primitive root meaning "to *mislay*; that is, to *be oblivious* of, from lack of memory or attention." By this, it is easy to describe what one feels like in such a condition—mislaid, cast aside, shelved, deserted. You pass these people every day in the streets. They may even desire you to smile at them in hopes that you will notice and value them as a person.

There is, however, good news. You can pray for your family and friends and await the results. The chain can be mended for God is able. "And the LORD turned the captivity of Job, when he prayed for his friends: also the LORD gave Job twice as much as he had before" (42:10).

The best family relationship you can ever enjoy is with the family of God, and the best Friend you'll ever have is the Son of God. Paul advised individual believers not to forsake regular assembly with the saints (Hebrews 10:25). This *strong* fellowship with the saints helps to offset your *sour* relationships that tend to occur through time. When you feel friendless, that's when you need the saints all the more. When you get around them, you'll flourish like a desert palm tree.

After praying and seeking the Lord's leading, ring a brother or sister in the Lord and encourage them.

The Dawn Sacrifice

"Jesus went unto the mount of Olives. And early in the morning he came again into the temple, and all the people came unto him; and he sat down, and taught them." (John 8:1-2)

Looking at the setting of this event, we are provided with some clarity through the original language. The Greek word for "early in the morning" is *orthros* meaning the *rising* of light; dawn. This is when the Temple doors were opened each day. Because the Hebrew mind thought in concrete terms, Messiah seldom taught without using tangible illustrations to make His points clear. This morning would be no exception as "the scribes and Pharisees brought unto him a woman taken in adultery" (v.3). She was caught in the act and, under the Law, was worthy of the death penalty. The Pharisees were ready to sacrifice her then and there so that others would fear both God's holy law and their appointed authority.

While the Pharisees' were preparing their dawn sacrifice for an imminent bloodletting by stoning, the priesthood was beginning their preparations for the ordained daily sacrifice—a lamb. The mid-morning Levitical sacrifice was to invoke the *mercies of God* and was to take place under a well-lit sky. By contrast, the Pharisees' dawn sacrifice was brought forth to invoke the *wrath of God* and was presented too close to the darkness to ever be acknowledged by the Father of Lights.

This situation provided the perfect illustration of God's mercy. Under the law, Messiah had to uphold the law's justice and condemn the woman's disregard for it; however, He cleverly designed a way to abrogate the law legally by getting rid of the witnesses to her crime. After the witnesses all left one by one, the merciful Judge of Israel said to her, "Woman, where are those thine accusers? ...go, and sin no more" (v.10-11). To a different group of pre-dawn Pharisees He then turned and said, "I am the light of the world: he that followeth me shall not walk in darkness, but shall have the light of life" (v.12).

After praying this morning, be ready to extend mercy towards another when and where it becomes most needed.

Have You Had a Bath Today?

"And on the seventh day he shall purify himself, and wash his clothes, and bathe himself in water, and shall be clean at even." (Numbers 19:19)

The primary goal of biblical bathing was generally equated with the removal of physical impurities, and within Israel's holy camp there were "diverse washings" (Hebrews 9:10). Archaeologists have unearthed hundreds of ritual baths in and around Jerusalem. Besides the ritual bath to *remove defilement* from sin, there were three main types of baptism. The first of these is the baptism for *repentance*. This type of immersion was compulsory for entrance into the Messianic kingdom and was accompanied by public confession of sin. In typology, going completely under water represents death, and emerging from it represents the new man being spiritually reborn. This baptism's meaning is greatly amplified after Yeshua's resurrection and is still required today.

Water immersion was also necessary for personal *dedication*. Scribes would bathe before writing the sacred name of God, and devoted worshippers would take ritual baths on the eve of the Sabbath to show their solemn dedication to Yahweh. This practice is still carried out today. Those who were about to enter ministry, such as Levites entering the priesthood, or prophets graduating from school, or kings ascending the throne underwent the ritual bath, *mikveh*. Yeshua's baptism could not have been for repentance of sin; rather, it was for His inaugural dedication into public ministry as Prophet, Priest and King!

The third reason for baptism involved the rite of *marriage*. In the early morning hours of the wedding day, a bride would be led by her bridal maids to a ceremonial bath where she would bathe in running water.

Follower of the Lamb, have you literally been through the waters of *repentance*? Have you *dedicated* yourself to live completely for God? Has the Lord given you some *ministry* to which you should be tending? Are you a well-washed bride purified, prepared and waiting for a heavenly *marriage*? Today, purify your heart to serve the living God.

February 19

The Medicine God

"Jesus...withdrew himself...and great multitudes followed him, and he healed them all." (Matthew 12:15)

The golden seal or token of Yeshua's ministry rested upon Malachi's prophecy. Messiah would arise with healing powers "in His wings [Mosaic fringes]" (Malachi 4:2). The power to heal was the theme of His very first sermon. He began by reading from Isaiah: "The Spirit of the Lord is upon me...he hath sent me to heal" (Luke 4:18). He followed this message up with His very first prophecy declaring that in His final moments before death His rejecters would mockingly put Him to the test saying, "Physician, heal thyself" (Luke 4:23). If He could do that, He would be considered more than a medicine man. Yahweh alone was the One Who could forgive *all* sins and heal *all* sicknesses (Psalm 103:3).

Israel's Medicine God was so powerful that the very saliva from His mouth held curative powers (Mark 7:33, 8:23). Once He made a mixture of spit and clay for a blind man's eyes (John 9:11). Pure words from the tip of His tongue could also restore life to the depressed, diseased, demoniac, and even the dead, leaving the crowds astonished. Many pried their way through congested crowds to be healed by a touch from His hand. Moreover, those who touched the Mosaic hem of His garment were also instantly and completely made whole (Deuteronomy 22:12). Some travelled from far countries to get to the Medicine God, and not one ever went back home with his head hanging down. *All* were healed and healed completely.

On that dark day when the beloved Physician's own head was hanging down in despair, scoffers shouted, "Save [fig. *heal*] thyself, and come down from the cross" (Mark 15:30). Yeshua could have healed Himself that very moment but decided it was more important to heal our sins with His crimson stripes (Isaiah 53:5). He didn't come down from the tree, but chose instead to do something even more impossible—to come out of His grave! He forever proved to be Israel's mighty Medicine God when He *healed Himself* three days later saving Himself from death and decay (John 10:18).

Today, praise the great Physician for healing you from all your sin and its inward shame.

Shiloh

"The sceptre shall not depart from Judah, nor a lawgiver from between his feet, until Shiloh come; and unto him shall the gathering of the people be." (Genesis 49:10)

Nearing death in Egypt, Jacob prophesied over his twelve sons. He foretold that Judah's tribe would produce the kingly line and that it would not cease until bringing forth its Messianic King. Jacob was moved of the Spirit to use the word *Shiloh,* an epithet of Messiah meaning "to be *tranquil;* that is, *secure* or *successful."* These three words accurately describe Yeshua's heavenly character and earthly ministry.

Yeshua is the *tranquil* Governor. This was predicted by Isaiah: "the government shall be upon his shoulder: and his name shall be called…the Prince of Peace. Of the increase of his government and peace there shall be no end" (Isaiah 9:6-7). Apart from nature, the world has little tranquility to offer. It is often short-lived because the world is always calling you back to its hurried pace. But never fear! Shiloh is near and able to go with you into the workplace and whirlwinds of life. Thus, He can give you constant calm.

Yeshua is also Israel's *secure* Governor. The heavenly Father said to Israel, "I will commit thy government into his hand…And the key of the house of David will I lay upon his shoulder; so he shall open, and none shall shut; and he shall shut, and none shall open. And I will fasten him as a nail in a sure place" (Isaiah 22:21-23). There is great security in His everlasting arms.

Yeshua is a most *successful* Governor. Isaiah pictured this saying, "and he shall be for a glorious throne to his father's house" (Isaiah 22:23). Beloved, your success will only be achieved by identifying with Shiloh's success. The reason the multitudes gathered around Shiloh the first time He came was because He alone made them feel tranquil and secure (Matthew 13:2).

Do you need peace, tranquility and security today? Then gather around Yeshua's tranquil throne in prayer.

There's Hope in the Red Rope

"And it shall be, when the LORD hath given us the land, that we will deal kindly and truly with thee. Then she let them down by a cord through the window: for her house was upon the town wall." (Joshua 2:14-15)

Having abandoned all hope in Jericho, Rahab switched sides and joined faith with the hope-filled people of Israel. As in all good covenant making, Rahab made the two spies swear that their army would save her family (v.12). The men's response was customary in oath making. They spoke of the pain of death if they broke their vow pledging, "Our life for yours" (v.15). She quickly made her league with the two spies, and then let them down the wall by a cord [Heb. *khebel,* a rope]. As the spies were going down, they remembered that Rahab had asked for a true token—symbolic proof. Thus, one of them whispered back up the wall in good fidelity, "Behold, when we come into the land, thou shalt bind this line of scarlet thread in the window which thou didst let us down by" (v.18). Covenanting is a reciprocal process, so the scarlet cord that saved the two men became the perfect token of Rahab's future salvation.

Notice in verse 18 how the word "cord" changes to "line," *tikvah,* meaning *hope,* or *expectancy.* Israel's national anthem is entitled HaTikvah, "The Hope." Sadly, Israel places her hope in her mighty army instead of her mighty God. Israel's flag only has blue stripes, but may they be reminded that there's only hope in the rope if there's red in the thread!

Hope in a believer's life can easily be misplaced if it's not firmly secured in the tightly twisted scarlet threads of blood that once flowed down the Saviour's sacrificial body. It is only through this eternal covenant token alone that the God of Heaven promises to show His kindness. Good works for salvation are only a *false* hope (Leviticus 17:11).

As you go into the Saviour's presence today, thank Him for providing you with His royal red blood that gives you perfect hope.

Granted One Wish

"And Jesus answered and said unto him, What wilt thou that I should do unto thee?" (Mark 10:51)

The blind man was quick to bring forth his request saying, "Lord, that I might receive my sight" (v.51). Yeshua granted the blind man the request of a lifetime and said, "Go thy way; thy faith hath made thee whole" (v.52). Immediately the blind man received his sight. After this desperate man gained his sight back, he was sure not to lose it so easily again for he "followed Jesus in the way" (v.52). Yeshua tested the man's new outlook on life by directing him to go his own way, but the man had gained heavenly sight in the process. His eyes were fastened squarely on the Saviour, and what a sight he beheld as he followed Him in the way! If the man actually followed Yeshua *all* the way to Jerusalem, then within a week's time he would have beheld the great Passover Lamb in all of His glory—a sight he would never forget.

What if the Lord of all the Earth graced you with His presence and granted you one request. What would your request be? Would your single request have only yourself in mind, or would it include your friends, family and neighbors? Would your request be "Lord, that I might liberate every drug addict in this city with the power of your word?" How about, "Lord, that I might encourage every local orphan boy and girl with your gift of love?" How about, "Lord, that I might win many of my work mates through telling them of your saving grace?" Or how about, "Lord, that I might proclaim the gospel of peace to a people sitting in dark places around the world?"

The Holy One is ready and waiting to grant this type of request if you will only call out to Him. Maybe you could show your gratitude to the One Who pulled you out of the bottomless pit by saying unto Him—like Saul of Tarsus did—"Lord, what wilt thou have me to do [for You]?" (Acts 9:6). It won't take the Son of God long to answer such a request. He has been waiting for this moment for a long, long time. Today, pray that God's Spirit will direct you to make the perfect request.

You're Bound to Remember

"Remember them that are in bonds, as bound with them; and them which suffer adversity, as being yourselves also in the body." (Hebrews 13:3)

The Jerusalem church was not born very long before experiencing chains and imprisonment. After about 11 years, this first assembly of believers began to be met with opposition, resentment, deprivation and full-on assault—better known as persecution.

Paul knew what persecution was like because he used to be the chief persecutor of New Testament saints. Later on after he got saved, he experienced the weight and burden of chains first-hand. Besides his many internments, he spent two full years in a cold, damp cell in Caesarea waiting for his long journey to Rome. He spent these remaining days of ministry in chains. In his letters, he appeals to us not to forget the persecuted ones. If you're bound next to someone, you're bound to remember his or her needs. Sadly, the western, prosperous church has failed miserably in following this command. In vain, some churches attempt to remember the persecuted church once a year on a national day of prayer and remembrance. What a tragedy—just one day a year! The worst feeling in the world is not just physical pain, but the emotional pain of being forgotten. We should never lift up any prayer to God without mentioning our brothers and sisters living in bondage, confinement, lack, loneliness and uncertainty of life.

The church can carry out Paul's apostolic command, "remember them that are in bonds," in a wide variety of ways. There are a number of organizations that work exclusively on behalf of the suffering church. Voice of the Martyrs, founded by Jewish believer Richard Wurmbrand, is an excellent organization. These groups minister to the various needs of suffering saints, and churches like yours can get more involved by financially supporting them. You can write to imprisoned saints all over the world through these organizations. If your church is in neglect of this scriptural command, then bring it to the leadership's attention. You can also make the first donation!

Today, seek the Lord about how you can make a difference.

The Sanctuary Sentinel

"Behold, bless ye the LORD, all ye servants of the LORD, which by night stand in the house of the LORD." (Psalm 134:1)

After the evening sacrifice was offered up, the crowds began to return home. By sunset the doors of the Sanctuary were shut for the night; however, it was Yahweh's desire that some of the Levite singers remain in the Temple chambers to be "employed in that work day and night" (1 Chronicles 9:33). They were free from their formal service, but were to be like the redeemed ones above who "are before the throne of God, and serve him day and night in his temple" (Revelation 7:15). The singers did not watch upon the walls; they kept watch upon their hearts and kept songs upon their lips for the glory of God. Those who lived close to the Temple could also hear these faint melodies while they bedded down for the night.

It is difficult to fall asleep while standing. Perhaps that is why the dictionary defines a *sentinel* as "one that watches or stands as if watching." It has been a custom for Jewish worshippers to pray standing (Luke 18:13). Even so, there is a Hebrew prayer called the *Amidah*, which means to stand. Yeshua, Who spent whole nights in prayer, also advised believers to watch and pray through the night watches and to avoid the embarrassment of falling asleep (Mark 13:35-36). The pattern has been firmly established that wherever saints are, they should never let-up in their sacrificial praise to the Most High God. The apostle to the gentiles was quite familiar with the temple practices and so "at midnight Paul and Silas prayed, and sang praises unto God: and the prisoners heard them" (Acts 16:25).

David was a sentinel. He said, "At midnight I will rise to give thanks unto thee" (Psalm 119:62). Sentinels are still needed around the clock today. If you can't sleep at night, and find the restlessness difficult to contend with, maybe it is of the Lord. Maybe He wants you to praise Him in thankful prayer or to lift up a song of adoration. It is not easy to be a midnight sentinel, but remember that He loves to hear the praises of His people. Let Him hear from you some night soon!

Cure for the Blues

"And if thou draw out thy soul to the hungry, and satisfy the afflicted soul; then...the LORD shall guide thee continually, and satisfy thy soul in drought, and make fat thy bones: and thou shalt be like a watered garden, and like a spring of water, whose waters fail not." (Isaiah 58:10-11)

The self-centered Christian life can lead to a miserable existence. You were not born anew just to become focused on your own wellbeing. That's what you did so consistently before you were touched by God's grace. Messiah has now filled you with the warmth of His sunshine. He says to us, "Look not every man on his own things, but every man also on the things of others" (Philippians 2:4). The simple cure for *your* blues is to look upon *other people's* blues. You will often find that they are bluer than you are. Once you grasp this reality, you face two options. You can join that person and tell them of your blues—which will only make them bluer—or you can chase their blues away by shining God's love upon them.

A believer-friend of mine had chronic depression and stayed mostly to himself. When I lived in his city, I saw him at least once or twice a week to encourage him but never seemed to have much visible success. However, my friend was temporarily put in the position of having to chauffer a visiting foreigner (whom he had never met) back and forth to his son's murder trial and had to translate for him. This went on for three weeks. During this time of "drawing out" his life for someone else, my friend had little time to sing the blues and became a totally different person. He was being well watered from on high.

In Hebrew, *draw out* also means "cause to extend." Sometimes it is not easy to *draw out* heart and soul or *extend* your hand to another, but it is a commandment. Moreover, it is your own cure for the blues! Be cured of your blues today by being the cure for someone else's.

Today, seek the Lord's guidance for whom you should extend a helping hand to next.

Supported by God

"Josiah was eight years old when he began to reign...And he did that which was right in the sight of the LORD, and walked in all the way of David his father, and turned not aside to the right hand or to the left." (2 Kings 22:1-2)

Josiah was one of the few good kings that Judah was privileged to have. Although he began to reign at a tender young age, his success was due to the fact that his heart stayed tender towards God. Josiah's Hebrew name is *Yosiyah,* which means, "founded of Yah." It seems that Josiah had quite a godly heritage and never had the desire to walk away from his inheritance. Maybe this is because Josiah recognized early on the joy and stability that comes from having God for a foundation.

Having Yahweh's knowledge and helpful Spirit as his undergirding support, Josiah began to shore up Jerusalem's poor and ailing foundations. The people were far from God because of a succession of bad kings. After Josiah initiated a repair project for the House of the LORD, one high priest found a copy of the Torah. After hearing this scroll read, Josiah rent his garments and had great fear for what was to become of his Judean countrymen. He assembled all the people to the Temple and personally read "all the words of the book of the covenant which was found in the house of the LORD" (23:2). The citizenry was not simply sent home after the public reading but were made to enter into a covenant that they would keep the words of the Book "with all their heart and all their soul" (23:3). Josiah leaned upon one of the two giant pillars in front of the Temple doorway and used it as a witness to their oath. From that point, the young king set out to destroy all the idols in the land.

You may not have had God as your sure foundation at an early age, but now that you do have Him, humbly seek Him in the Spirit of prayer and see what He might have you do on some broader scale that your whole community might be drawn closer to Him. He delights in using just one devoted person at a time to change the lives of many.

Putting Spectacles on God's Word

"Thy words were found, and I did eat them; and thy word was unto me the joy and rejoicing of mine heart:" (Jeremiah 15:16)

One night in Bible College, an instructor told us that the Puritans greatly revered God's Word and used an interesting little formula when reading it. We will get to their formula in a minute, but let's first find out how to prepare our hearts before reading God's word.

Begin with getting still. Don't sit down to break the Bread of Life in a hurry; you won't receive more than a crumb of nourishment in that fashion. We do live in a fast-paced world, but we don't serve a fast-paced God. He sits back on His throne. God said that being still is a pre-requisite to knowing Him (Psalm 46:10). Still your mind from the busy nature of the day's upcoming schedule and still your heart from any cares of the world. God will take care of today if you will take care of His Word and saturate yourself in it. After getting still, pray over God's Spirit-revealed Word. You want more out of God's Word than a simple reading, so you might want to pray what David prayed: "Open thou mine eyes, that I may behold wondrous things out of thy law" (Psalm 119:18).

The Puritans made a helpful acronym out of the word *spectacles* spelled like this—SPECS. After choosing a passage and reading it through, they began by looking at the *sense* or meaning of the passage. Reading back through the passage, they ask a series of questions: Are there any *promises* to claim or *principles* to live by? Are there any good *examples* for me to follow, or *errors* to avoid? Are there any *commands* I must obey? Are there any *sins* I must forsake?

If God's Word is the joy and rejoicing of your heart like it was for Jeremiah, then you are sure to love this little outline. Today, don't just give God's Word a glancing over. Give it the *spectacles* of love and sincerity. Put your SPECS on a passage and then prayerfully pour over it.

Joy in the Journey!

"And they took their journey from Succoth, and encamped in Etham, in the edge of the wilderness. And the LORD went before them by day in a pillar of a cloud, to lead them the way;" (Exodus 13:20-21)

Along the edge of the wilderness, the children of Israel rested but still faced a daunting journey ahead. They were not headed for scenic coastal waters, but a harsh landscape of peril and uncertainty. No one in their right mind wanted to spend very long in such wanting conditions, yet the Great Shepherd eagerly desired to lead His sheep into this no-man's land.

Their overshadowing cloud was not an ordinary one. The first time they ever laid eyes on God's majestic cloud it appeared as a tornado of fire standing between them and a fierce, approaching army. From day to day, it stood upright as a majestic king and gently swirled upwards into a pavilion of comforting shade. It glowed nightly with a warm golden hue that children of men had never before seen. Perhaps it occasionally moved about as a child prances around with delight. At times, it rested firm in place like a mighty pillar upon a foundation, and other times it gave out firm audible directives. In that barren, dry and thirsty land, the glory cloud was everything they needed it to be.

Following God is anything but dull. Wherever His presence dwells there is fullness of joy (Psalm 16:11). Even from behind desolate and locked-tight prison bars, persecuted Christians experience God's goodness and His glory with a joy that surpasses understanding. Strange surroundings do not have to rob you of joy and contentment because El Shaddai still surrounds you.

Today, your confidence and quiet assurance rests in the fact that God will go before you to lead you in the way. Going to a dreary workplace? Going to a hospital for a check-up or test? Going to a funeral? Going to the dentist? Never fear! Your Shepherd-Saviour goes before you. Recognize His presence, take comfort and joy and venture on.

Purim & House Moving

"Then the king Ahasuerus said unto Esther the queen and to Mordecai the Jew, Behold, I have given Esther the house of Haman, and him they have hanged upon the gallows, because he laid his hand upon the Jews" (Esther 8:7)

The author of evil loves the game of chess because he has no shortage of kings, bishops, knights, rooks or pawns. He will always find these at his disposal to do his bidding in any generation. The devil's rooks and pawns seldom know that he is using them. On the other hand, knights, bishops and kings know full well the level of evil in which they choose to get involved. Their lust for control and power blinds their vision of the Almighty One's end game. He *always* wins. If Haman knew he would inevitably lose his soul, his sons and his sanctuary, he would have chosen to play a less risky game.

Each year during Israel's worldwide Purim celebrations children play a game called Lots. They are mimicking how Haman cast lots to decide which day to do away with the Jews of Persia. Well, Satan is still plotting. Just in the 20th century alone, Satan's kings were Hitler, Stalin, Nasser, Hussein and Arafat. In 1973, Satan chose a new day to do away with the Jews—October 6th, the day of Yom Kippur. Satan didn't succeed. Praise the LORD! In the dawn of the 21st century, he is trying to succeed with his chess piece, Ahmadinejad. This Persian seems to have the exact same spirit as his ancient predecessor, Haman, but he will not succeed either.

The king of darkness not only hates the whole house of Abraham, but also hates the house of Messiah. However, we have a more sure Word of prophecy. Yahweh is about to checkmate Satan. God's apostolic bishop said so: "the God of peace shall bruise Satan under your feet shortly...Amen" (Romans 16:20).

Today, spend time praying for the nation of Israel and persecuted believers worldwide that God would come to their rescue quickly.

Go Through the Gates

"Go through, go through, the Gates; prepare ye the way of the people...and thou shalt be called, Sought out, A city not forsaken." (Isaiah 62:10, 12)

The gates of Jerusalem have been given a variety of names over the centuries. Let's walk through them as Nehemiah chapter three presents them. Each one speaks of a different aspect of the believer's life and the experiences he needs during his earthly sojourn.

The first gate is the *Sheep Gate*. This speaks of coming to the Lamb of God Who takes away your sins. The *Fish Gate* shows us the need to become fishers of men. The *Old Gate* reminds you that the framework for your actions lies not in the philosophies of men, but within the old paths of God's written Word. The *Valley Gate* leads the devoted one through difficult places like suffering, trials and testing, each one producing humility and fruit. The *Dung Gate* was where the refuse was carried out of the city to be burned. For the believer to grow in grace he must rid himself of all that is unholy and impure. The *Fountain Gate* led the way down to the Gihon Spring, Jerusalem's only original source of spring water. This life force represents the Holy Spirit, which refreshes, renews, replenishes and empowers the believer after having removed the refuse from his life.

The *Water Gate* refers to God's Word that sanctifies as you read it and heed it. The *Horse Gate* that once led to Solomon's stables emphasizes that a spiritual war is continually being waged. The *East Gate,* which faces the Mount of Olives, is where Yeshua, the King of Kings, will present Himself upon His glorious return. The *Inspection Gate* speaks of the future judgment seat of Christ and His assessment of how well we performed our duties as His servants.

As you talk to God today, ask Him to help you have a continual readiness in your spirit to be led through each of these gates at the appropriate time.

The Sheep Gate

"Then Eliashib the high priest rose up with his brethren the priests, and they builded the sheep gate." (Nehemiah 3:1)

The Hebrew word for sheep is *tsehone* meaning to *migrate*. The psalmist drew from this analogy when he said, "For he is our God; and we are the people of his pasture, and the sheep of his hand" (Psalm 95:7). Not only was the faithful remnant within Israel considered a flock belonging to Yahweh, there were others drawn out of the nations. Yeshua said, "other sheep I have, which are not of this fold: them also I must bring, and they shall hear my voice; and there shall be one fold, and one shepherd" (John 10:16).

Located along the north wall, the Sheep Gate speaks of salvation, the beginning of a believer's journey. After being ritually washed of all impurities at Solomon's pools in Bethlehem, sheep soon entered this gate with trusting subjection to their shepherds. Having no will of their own, they were passively led to be sacrificed. Newborn believers, having been washed of all sin, are also to surrender their own will in loving devotion to God and become accustomed to the surrounds of a new "sheepfold" (John 10:1). As devotion is fully given to the Great Shepherd, a keen sense of hearing His voice rapidly develops. He said, "My sheep hear my voice, and I know them, and they follow me" (John 10:27). As a newly washed lamb, you begin to appreciate Who is standing at the door of the sheepfold. You learn that by using His door alone you will "be saved [safe], and shall go in and out, and find pasture" (John 10:9). The Shepherd of the sheep exits the gate at the ordained time, then calls "his own sheep by name, and leads them out" (John 1:3).

Little lamb, have you committed your will and way to fully and unerringly trust and follow the strong, loving Shepherd? He will do you no harm, nor will He sacrifice you to the wolves. He asks for your unfaltering trust from the very beginning. It is wise not to shrink back from this, and much safer to simply wait when He says wait and to go when He says go. Today, regain perfect sight and sound of the Shepherd.

The Fish Gate

"But the fish gate did the sons of Hassenaah build." (Nehemiah 3:3)

The Fish Gate was the closest entrance to the city's fish market. Fishmongers coming with their prized white meat from one of Israel's two seas would have been familiar with this gate. Some of the fish caught by Peter, James and John would have eventually made their way through this gate; perhaps they even accompanied them at times. This gate, just after the sheep gate, takes the believer on to his next progression in the New Covenant journey—*catching souls.*

The prophet's analogy that God "makes men as the fishes of the sea" continues its theme where God draws men out of sin's deep, dark waters by way of evangelism (Habakkuk 1:14). In accordance with this theme, Messiah called fishermen to be His very first apprentices saying, "Come ye after me, and I will make you to become fishers of men" (Mark 1:18). The Master of the Sea produced a miracle catch of fishes for His disciples even though they had toiled all night and caught nothing. He did this to show them they would not be able to catch *the souls of men* apart from His guidance.

Peter fervently trained for three years how to properly fish for men, but he got discouraged after his Master was not daily by his side, so he went back to fishing for fish (John 21:3). Why was he not out zealously telling everyone that he had seen Israel's Messiah in His glorious resurrected form? This shows how easily we can get sidetracked from what we really need to be doing; namely, sharing the good news of salvation. Peter never got sidetracked again after Yeshua performed the second miraculous catch of fish from the seashore (v.6). The chief apostle became so suddenly enthusiastic that he drew the net to land and counted the fish as if they were the souls of men (v.11). The shofar call of evangelism sounded loudly in Peter's heart once again.

Today, ask Yeshua to give you "fishing fever" for the souls of men—a fever that will never go away.

The Old Gate

"Moreover the old gate repaired Jehoiada the son of Paseah."
(Nehemiah 3:6)

Our journey of Jerusalem takes us through the Old Gate. Leading from it are old paths that are not very susceptible to change. Oh, the surrounding scenery may change over time, but the *path of obedience* to and from the King's house does not. The King describes Himself as being "the same yesterday, and today, and for ever" (Hebrews 13:8). Since no improvements can be made on His statutes, we see a host of them restated in the New Testament.

One of Yahweh's faithful prophets said, "Stand ye in the ways, and see, and ask for the old paths, where is the good way, and walk therein, and ye shall find rest for your souls" (Jeremiah 6:16). Weariness of heart and soul is certain to occur if you venture off this ancient *path of rest.* A tried and proven path has wonderfully upheld many pilgrims.

Messiah Yeshua encourages sojourners not to deviate when they begin to experience discomfort along the *narrow path* (Matthew 7:14). This old road must be trodden by each generation alike. If it remains well worn and easily identifiable, the next generation shall find their way over it quite happily. The Hebrew word for "path" is *orakh* meaning well travelled. Unfortunately, one generation may not be so faithful in keeping the path beaten down as the previous generation was. This makes the path hard to find for the next generation who seeks it. The solution is not to make *new* paths. God's remedy is for each of us to be a "restorer of paths to dwell in" (Isaiah 58:12).

The Paleo-Hebraic letters that make up the word *orakh* tell us a great deal. The *alef* means strong, the *reish* means beginning and the *khet* means outside. Put these together and they speak of a *strong beginning outside* the city. A strong beginning does not guarantee a strong finish, but it certainly helps. During your quiet time today, pray that the Holy Spirit will help you stay on the path and finish the journey strong.

The Valley Gate

"The valley gate repaired Hanun, and the inhabitants of Zanoah; they built it." (Nehemiah 3:13)

The Valley Gate was situated along the southwestern corner of the city and led to the valley of Hinnom, the deepest of three valleys surrounding Jerusalem. The Bible usually portrays a valley as the believer's place of trial and sorrow. Yeshua alluded to the pilgrim's valley when He said, "In the world ye shall have tribulation: but be of good cheer; I have overcome the world" (John 16:33).

The pilgrim is not to fret throughout his valley walk, for God's *protection* is continually available. Israel had no shortage of valley experiences; neither did they have a shortage of God's protection and watch-care. When it was reported that the Syrians were boasting, "Yahweh is God of the hills but not God of the valleys," Yahweh proved otherwise by slaying 100,000 of their footmen (1 Kings 20:28-29).

Not only is Yahweh's protection available in the valley, so is His *provision*. The psalmist says, "He sendeth the springs into the valleys, which run among the hills" (Psalm 104:100). The continual "supply of the Spirit" shall never leave the pilgrim in drought or despair (Philippians 1:19). He cares for you and has promises to "satiate the weary soul" (Jeremiah 31:25). Confidently and quietly He sends you assurance saying, "I will satiate the soul of the priests...and my people shall be satisfied with my goodness, saith the LORD" (Jeremiah 31:14).

The valley experience can be a lonely walk, but the Redeemer's protection and provision are also accompanied by His constant *presence*. You will not see Him, but you will see His handiwork. At intermittent seasons, the valley floor and hills become carpeted with bright rose-red lilies called *shoshanim*. These are His visible tokens to you that He once ventured outside the gate bearing your reproach all the while leaving behind a blood-sprinkled trail. No wonder Yeshua is called the *Rose of Sharon* and the *Lily of the Valley* (Song of Solomon 2:1). Today, may your valley experience be brightened with tokens of His protection, provision and presence.

The Dung Gate

"*But the dung gate repaired Malchiah the son of Rechab.*" (Nehemiah 3:13)

This gate takes its name from the many *ash pots* that were carried through it. The Dung Gate bears a very belittling, yet meaningful title. The city's waste was carried out through this southeastern gate and down to the valley of Hinnom where it was summarily burned. An ancient sewer also lies just beneath. Before the Jordanians enlarged this gate in 1952, it was only big enough for a man and a donkey to pass through.

It is important for a believer to take constant assessment of what needs to be done away with in his life. The removal of refuse is essential to keeping the believer's temple clean. The Holy Spirit's desire and duty is "to present you holy and unblameable and unreproveable in his sight" (Colossians 1:22). This is why He speaks to your heart when something needs to be removed from your life. Since no one is perfect, there are always times when areas of sin must be carefully managed. "*If* we say that we have no sin, we deceive ourselves" (1 John 1:8). As you prayerfully follow the Spirit's leading and obey His Word, the defilement is taken away and your temple is properly cleansed. John says, "*If* we confess our sins, he is faithful and just to forgive us our sins, and to cleanse us from all unrighteousness" (1 John 1:9). These are two very big *ifs* in Scripture.

The rubbish must be removed from our lives and our temple cleansed so that we can experience the wonders and fullness of God's divine presence. This daily removing and cleansing process is also necessary to refine the pilgrim so that he can effectually go through the next gate. The Son of God "gave himself for us, that he might redeem us from all iniquity, and purify unto himself a peculiar people, zealous of good works" (Titus 2:14).

May your prayer time this morning allow the Holy Spirit ample space to sweep all the corners of your house.

The Fountain Gate

"But the gate of the fountain repaired Shallun the son of Colhozeh...and the wall of the pool of Siloah by the king's garden." (Nehemiah 3:15)

The Fountain Gate was located nearest the city's vital water supply—the pool of Siloam [*Shiloakh*]. The upper and lower pools were fed from the fresh flowing Gihon spring situated uphill a short distance away on the slopes of the hill Ophel. Yeshua once sent a blind man from the Temple Mount down to this pool to be healed after anointing his eyes with clay (John 9:6). It is only after the believer has passed through the dung gate to dispose of the ill contents of his house that he can go through the Fountain Gate that grants access to the pools of life.

During Judah's exile in Babylon, Yahweh explained their former error saying, "they have forsaken me the fountain of living waters, and hewed them out cisterns, broken cisterns, that can hold no water" (Jeremiah 2:13). Only the Spirit of God can supply a believer from moment to moment with the true waters of life. His Spirit looks for cleansed and expectant vessels to fill and does so that the inner-pool of His children's hearts may never run dry. Not surprisingly, a worshiper does not get clean before coming to the fountain; rather, he sheds his filthy garments back at the Dung Gate and then approaches the Fountain Gate in order to be more fully cleansed.

Three prophets foresaw the time when a fountain would break forth at Messiah's millennial Temple. Y'hezkel spoke of it issuing from the Temple's threshold and flowing to the Dead Sea to heal the sea from bareness (Ezekiel 47:1). Yoel saw it watering and refreshing a wilderness valley (Joel 3:18). Zecharyah understood the fountain's spiritual value, to remove worshippers' sin and uncleanness (Zechariah 13:1).

Prayer and confession is the current remedy for cleansing from unrighteousness (1 John 1:9). May the Fountain Gate swing wide for you today as you make your journey onwards and upwards to the Holy City.

The Water Gate

"Moreover the Nethinims [Temple servants] dwelt in Ophel, unto the place over against the water gate toward the east, and the tower that lieth out." (Nehemiah 3:26)

The Water Gate, which faced the Mount of Olives, took its name from an underlying water system. In 1967, Israel regained control of the Old City and soon began digging along the eastern wall in the area of Ophel where the city of David formerly existed. Archaeologists found the remains of Solomon's Water Gate. Two interesting discoveries made at the dig were large water cisterns and 40 clay storage jars with rope handles used for drawing water.

In biblical typology, water represents the *Word of God* because of its cleansing effect. The psalmist puts forth a riddle and tells the answer: "wherewithal shall a young man cleanse his way? by taking heed thereto according to thy word" (Psalm 119:9). The Word of God has an amazing way of washing away the dark and defiled corners of man's mind. After the tribe of Judah returned from worldly Babylon and rebuilt the city walls, they had one thing left remaining—to wash their minds of Babylon. And how did they do that? By the Word of God. Now, notice where this took place: "And all the people gathered themselves together as one man into the street that was before the water gate; and they spake unto Ezra the scribe to bring the book of the law of Moses...And Ezra the priest brought the law before the congregation...And he read therein before the street that was before the water gate from the morning until midday" (Nehemiah 8:1-3).

Five hundred years later Yeshua said to His followers, "Now ye are clean through the word which I have spoken unto you" (John 15:3). The disciples needed their minds completely cleansed before serving Him in His kingdom, and so do we.

After prayerfully reading a portion of Messiah's Word today, ask Him to anoint your mind and "cleanse it with the washing of water by the word" (Ephesians 5:25-26).

The Horse Gate

"From above the horse gate repaired the priests, every one over against his house." (Nehemiah 3:28)

This six-chambered gate lay along the steep slopes of Ophel and was an entrance to the stronghold of Zion. It also led to Solomon's stables. Horses were never used to transport goods because other animals were better suited for that. Horses were known for their speed, and Israel was specifically warned not to multiply them (Deuteronomy 17:16). Instead, Yahweh desired to be Israel's true strength and their enemy's dread whenever they went into battle. Nonetheless, a certain amount of horses was necessary for the quick dispatch of messengers and the swift movement of officers.

The Horse Gate speaks of *spiritual warfare*. From the day a believer is drawn out of darkness, he becomes a soldier of Light. Along with this enlistment he has a target placed on his back (Ephesians 6:12). The Lord doesn't expect His infantrymen to stay in the infirmary ward, but to be engaged in the spiritual conflict. Because this great battle between opposing kingdoms is not against flesh and blood, the soldier of Light is given a very special sword to fight with—the King's very own. It is called "the sword of the Spirit." Its two edges are the *written* word and the *spoken* word (Ephesians 6:17). The evil one fears the written Word of God for it has proclaimed his own defeat. The spoken Word, quoting God's Word, will also have an impact (2 Kings 7:1). With this double-edged sword and prayerful readiness "to endure hardness as a good soldier of Jesus Christ," the soldier of Light is always on the cutting edge of battle preparedness (2 Timothy 2:3-4).

The Horse Gate also speaks prophetically of the King of King's return from glory. When the Son of God comes, He will be mounted on a battle horse—not the foal of a donkey—and in righteousness will "judge and make war" (Revelation 19:11).

If your level of priestly warfare needs a little repair, ask the Spirit of Yahweh to assist you today. The battle is certain to grow more and more intense in these last days.

69

The East Gate

"After him repaired also Shemaiah the son of Shechaniah, the keeper of the east gate." (Nehemiah 3:29)

Along with the previous gate, the East Gate represents the Second Coming of Christ. Ezekiel explained his vision saying, "Then he brought me back the way of the gate of the outward sanctuary which looketh toward the east; and it was shut. Then said the LORD unto me; *This gate shall be shut*, it shall not be opened, and no man shall enter in by it; because the LORD, the God of Israel, hath entered in by it, therefore it shall be shut. It is for the prince; the prince, he shall sit in it to eat bread before the LORD" (Ezekiel 44:1-3).

According to one account, the first part of this prophecy was fulfilled in 1517 when the Turks conquered Jerusalem. Suleiman the Magnificent commanded that the city's ancient walls be rebuilt, and during the course of rebuilding, he ordered the Eastern Gate to be sealed. He became aware that Israel's returning Prince would one day come through this very gate. A Muslim cemetery was started at the gate's entry assuming that Mosaic Law would prohibit Israel's priestly King from coming in contact with the remains of the dead. It has been also reported that Jordan's King Hussein made plans to open up the Eastern Gate in June of 1967 but was prevented from doing so by Israel's sudden recapture of the Old City of Jerusalem. What is without dispute is that this large gate remains sealed today in expectation of Jerusalem's Davidic King.

The Eastern Gate faces the sun's rising and wonderfully awaits the coming Messiah Who shines far, far brighter (2 Peter 1:19). Yeshua predicted the suddenness of His coming: "For as the lightning cometh out of the east, and shineth even unto the west; so shall also the coming of the Son of man be" (Matthew 24:27).

With these words in mind, are you ready if the King arrived today? Are you prayed up? Are you busy serving in His kingdom and looking for His imminent return? Today, cooperate with the Spirit's inner work as He makes "ready a people prepared for the Lord" (Luke 1:17).

The Inspection Gate

"After him repaired Malchiah the goldsmith's son unto the place of the Nethinims, and of the merchants, over against the gate Miphkad." (Nehemiah 3:31)

Very little is known about this last gate in our survey as it is only mentioned once in Scripture. *Miphkad* means "assignment." Since this gate was adjacent to the Sheep Gate, one could speculate this was the place assigned where sacrificial animals were inspected for blemishes. After inspection, they would be assigned to Yahweh's altar for sacrifice or be sent away as unacceptable. Important decisions were always made at the gates of a city. This gate's name is drawn from the root word *pawkad*, which means "appointment."

All the nations of the world have an appointment with destiny. Not long after Lord Yeshua triumphantly returns, He will commence His holy inspection and righteous judgment of nations (Matthew 25:31-46). One criterion the nations will be judged by is their treatment of Israel, the King's covenant people through Abraham (Genesis 12:3).

The apostle Paul advised New Covenant believers that they also have their own *appointment* with destiny. He said, "For we must all appear before the judgment seat of Christ; that every one may receive the things done in his body, according to that he hath done, whether it be good or bad" (2 Corinthians 5:10). Redeemed ones cannot lose their salvation, but they can certainly lose their rewards (1 Corinthians 3:15). Concerning the receiving of rewards, Yeshua spoke of *assigning* good stewards ruler-ship over cities in His millennial kingdom (Luke 19:17). The apostles were told that if they were faithful they would be *assigned* to thrones where they would sit and judge the twelve tribes of Israel (Luke 22:30).

The King has given every believer an assigned place in this current spiritual kingdom, and we are to take our assignments with weight. Let us encourage one another to do our very best and to not lose heart or fall by the wayside. Pray that the Spirit aids you with your assignment today whether it is at home, school, work, church or elsewhere.

ℋℯ 𝒦nows 𝒴our 𝒩ame

"And the LORD said unto Moses, I will do this thing also that thou hast spoken: for thou hast found grace in my sight, and I know thee by name. And...I will make all my goodness pass before thee, and I will proclaim the name of the LORD before thee." (Exodus 33:19)

Moses wanted to get a first-hand glimpse of the One with Whom he had been talking to and dwelling. God granted the nomadic shepherd his request based on two criteria. The first reason is that Yahweh favored Moses. The Hebrew word for grace is *khane* and comes from the root *khanan* meaning to *bend* or *stoop* in kindness. Then Yahweh stated that He would grant the request because He knew Moses' name. God first called out Moses' name from the burning bush. He obviously knew everything about him. Now it was God's turn to reveal more of Himself to Moses. He did so by focusing upon His covenant name, Yahweh.

In Near East culture you cannot separate a person's identity from their name; they are one and the same. After cutting two more stone tablets Moses ascended the mountain the next morning: "And the LORD descended in the cloud, and stood with him there, and proclaimed the name of the LORD. And the LORD passed by before him, and proclaimed, The LORD, The LORD God, merciful and gracious, longsuffering, and abundant in goodness and truth" (Exodus 34:5-6). Moses' one-of-a-kind mountaintop experience must have been more than for which he could have hoped.

The LORD also knows your name. If your trust resides within the covenant bounds of His Son's substitute sacrifice, then you can rest assured that His covenant mercy, covenant grace, covenant longsuffering and covenant goodness will come to visit you from time to time. All you have to do is ask. That is what covenant partners are for so long as you are also prepared to do what He asks you to do when He calls your name.

How Peculiar Are You?

"Thou hast commanded us to keep thy precepts diligently." (Psalm 119:4)

The psalmist reflects upon a strange set of laws that Israel is expected to safeguard. In Hebrew, the word "precept" is *piqqud*, a mandate. God's *piqqud* is very *peculiar*; that is to say, "distinctive in nature or character from others." I was once handing out gospel tracts on an Australian street corner when a pedestrian called me weird. I took that as a compliment. Across the globe man's inborn ways all seem to have the familiar quality, "Do as you please," but it is not so with the God of Heaven. His peculiar call to holiness mandated that the whole nation wear four distinctive blue-intertwined fringes on their garments to remind them of His commandments (Numbers 15:38). Israel is to be a *peculiar* people because God Himself is peculiar by virtue of His holiness. Yahweh's distinctive precepts are referred to 21 times in this Psalm making it quite *peculiar* from all other Psalms.

The psalmist's desire to become *peculiar* for God causes him to say, "Make me to understand the way of thy precepts [piqqudek]" (v.27). The psalmist asks this because he understands something else beforehand. *Piqqud's* root is *pawkad* and it means, "to *visit* (with friendly or hostile intent)." The psalmist stands, even trembles with the knowledge that God shall come in due season to visit His people, perhaps at any moment—and unannounced. The psalmist longs for a *friendly* visit from the Holy One being mindful of Yahweh's former frightening words: "Whosoever hath sinned against me, him will I blot out of my book...in the day when I visit I will visit their sin upon them" (Exodus 32:33-34).

Although we carry God's abiding grace as our proud banner, we shouldn't continue in sin's magnetic and pathetic path. Quite the contrary! We are called to honor and obey God's holy precepts. Call on God's help today if you are not as peculiar as you ought to be. In doing so, He will desire to meet with you as a friend.

The Countdown

"Teach us to number our days, that we may apply our hearts unto wisdom." (Psalm 90:12)

The Hebrew word for number is *manah*, which means, "to *weigh* out; by implication to *allot*; to *enumerate*." There are at least three reasons we should number our days and consider the weight of each one.

The first reason is *because our time on earth is limited.* James said, "Whereas ye know not what shall be on the morrow. For what is your life? It is even a vapour, that appeareth for a little time, and then vanisheth away" (James 4:14). Each individual is born into this world with a set number of days. The psalmist realized this saying, "My times are in thy hand" (Psalm 31:15). In our youth, we tend to live like there is no tomorrow and later on, we are inclined to gauge our remaining days based on our health; but this is a false assumption. As the decades roll by, we become more aware of the countdown, but we should not wait until we are too old to measure our time on earth. Each day is all that we have, and we should use it to the fullest for Him.

We should also number our days *because it is a wise thing to do.* The psalmist's desire was "that we may apply our hearts unto wisdom." The writer of Proverbs speaks much of wisdom using the word 120 times. He advises against numbering your days in a prideful manner saying, "Boast not thyself of to morrow; for thou knowest not what a day may bring forth" (Proverbs 27:1). God teaches us to live in light of eternity. Albert Schweitzer said, "The tragedy of life is what dies inside a man while he lives."

Lastly, weigh out your days wisely *because Yeshua could come at any moment!* His very last words were, "behold, I come quickly" (Revelation 22:12). We might very possibly see Him before we see the grave. He elaborated on His sudden coming saying, "my reward is with me, to give every man according as his work shall be."

As you apply your heart unto wisdom in prayer, may you then go out and make the most of today.

The Shomer & the Shayeet

"In that day the LORD with his sore and great and strong sword shall punish leviathan the piercing serpent, even leviathan that crooked serpent; and he shall slay the dragon that is in the sea." (Isaiah 27:1)

Yeshua is Israel's great *Shomer*, her Guard. In this verse, He promises to defeat Israel's worst enemy, Leviathan, which is Satan. A guard can be a watchman over many things: city walls, sleeping soldiers, defenseless sheep or new vineyards. Scripture normally presents Yeshua as a Guard watching over His sheep, but here in verse 2 as a Guard watching over His tender vineyard. He says with great compassion, "I the LORD do keep it; I will water it every moment: lest any hurt it, I will keep it night and day" (v.3). The word here for keep is *natsar* which also means, "to *guard, protect,* or *keep.*"

A shomer protects his sheep by constructing a four-sided hedge of thorns. When the sheep come inside, they are sheltered from devouring predators that come in the night. A shomer uses thorny plants like the *shah-yeet* to build his hedge because predators would think twice before breaking through. Israel's great Shomer now boasts of His absolute might by calling all challengers. He shouts, "who would set the briers and thorns against me in battle? I would go through them, I would burn them together" (v.4). This passage is highly prophetic. Yeshua was once placed in the unavoidable situation where He was forced into protecting His sheep with fiery covenant love.

While the vulnerable Israelite sheep were gathered within the protective walls of Zion's fold one Passover eve, Leviathan descended upon the Great Shepherd and set briers against Him in battle. The serpent pierced Yeshua heels, hands and side; he also set thorns about the Shepherd's holy head (Matthew 27:29). However, Leviathan was horribly humiliated and defeated three days later when the Shepherd broke through unharmed.

Oh, trembling lamb, have you fully comprehended the Shepherd's keeping power? Meditate on it prayerfully and this will keep you from being fearful today.

The Raised Hand

"I have lift up mine hand unto the LORD, the most high God, the possessor of heaven and earth." (Genesis 14:22)

The raised hand has various meanings and is still found within many cultures. The Hebrews used the right hand *when making vows and oaths*. So prolific was the use of their raised hand that its very depiction showed up as a letter in their ancient Paleo alphabet—the letter *kaph*. Abraham spoke this verse, but mortals are not the only ones who raise their hand as a sign of the covenant. John recorded: "the angel which I saw stand upon the sea and upon the earth lifted up his hand to heaven, And sware by him that liveth for ever and ever" (Revelation 10:5, 6). Ezekiel also documents nine occasions where Yahweh uplifts His own right hand towards Israel swearing before them for either good or bad.

Another reason for the outstretched right hand was *to place a blessing on someone*. Jacob "stretched out his right hand, and laid it upon Ephraim's head" (Genesis 48:14). The priestly blessing over Israel required the use of outstretched hands. "Aaron lifted up his hand toward the people, and blessed them" (Leviticus 9:22). The Scriptures record the last thing Messiah did on earth: "he led them out as far as to Bethany, and he lifted up his hands, and blessed them" (Luke 24:50). All praise belongs to our Great High Priest by Whose pierced hands we remain blessed. Many believers worldwide still follow the psalmist's command to "Lift up your hands in the sanctuary, and bless the LORD" (Psalm 134:2).

A third and very significant reason for extending our hands upward to God is that He might *readily receive our petitions*. David said, "Hear the voice of my supplications…when I lift up my hands toward thy holy oracle" (Psalm 28:2). Jeremiah's command was, "Let us search and try our ways…Let us lift up our heart with our hands unto God in the heavens" (Lamentations 3:40-41).

Today, consider Paul's 1Timothy 2:8 plea "that men pray every where, lifting up holy hands."

The Lamp of God

"Bring thee pure oil olive beaten for the light [meorah], *to cause the lamp* [nayr] *to burn always* [tamiyd]. *In the tabernacle of the congregation without the veil, which is before the testimony."* (Exodus 27:20-21)

Just as the fire was never to go out upon the brazen altar, it was never to be extinguished before the Most Holy Place. Light is representative of the glory of God (Revelation 21:23). Yahweh instructed Israel to keep a light burning brightly before Him as a token of His veiled presence. In our text, the word for light is *meorah* meaning a *luminous* body. From this word came menorah referring to the golden lamp stand. *Orah* is the feminine form of *Or* meaning light and is the origin of the word aura, "an invisible breath or emanation; a distinctive air or quality that characterizes a person or thing."

Shortly after Israel entered the Promised Land, they set up the Tabernacle at Shiloh. About three centuries later Eli the high priest became complacent. He even reached the point of negligence. "And ere the lamp of God went out in the temple of the LORD, where the ark of God was" (1 Samuel 3:3). But there's more. While Samuel lay down to sleep, "the LORD called Samuel: and he answered, Here am I" (v.4). Eli's monumental failure brought about his removal from his Aaronic post and caused Yahweh to select a young boy immediately who was fully dedicated to making the One True God preeminent among His people.

Since the destruction of the Second Temple, the rabbis thought to replace the seven-branched lamp stand with a single-light to go inside a synagogue. This eternal flame, *ner tamid,* is suspended over the veiled cabinet that houses the synagogue's Torah scroll. The *ner tamid* is most often an electric light bulb—only a pale reminder of God's pure light and His formerly abiding presence.

Is your inner lamp burning as brightly as it ought to be? Ask the Spirit to illuminate the aura of Yeshua's holiness through you today.

When Will They Know?

"And I will sanctify my great name...which ye have profaned in the midst of them; and the heathen shall know that I am the LORD, saith the Lord GOD, when I shall be sanctified in you before their eyes." (Ezekiel 36:23)

At least 46 times Ezekiel penned the words, "and they shall know." Yehezkel prophesies that the spiritually unplowed nations who surround Israel will one day know of Yahweh's fame. The nations are lost because they are uninformed of God's holy ways. Moreover, they are lost partly because Israel herself is lost. Israel's present unsanctified condition makes them unable to lead the way in righteousness. In the past Israel acted like the heathen nations around them and struggled to be a light unto the gentiles. Yahweh, therefore, dealt with them accordingly.

What exactly will the uninformed nations know? That Yahweh alone is God and, therefore, worthy of all worship. The heathen will also know, along with Israel, that Yahweh is the One Who sanctifies vessels for His own use.

When will the lost sea of nations ever learn of Yahweh's truth and holiness? First, when He punishes Israel for their idolatrous ways. Second, when He punishes the nations for their idol worshipping and mistreatment of Israel. And third, as our text verse suggests, when Israel as a nation gets right with God and becomes sanctified. However, they will not become sanctified until they learn that they can't do this on their own! "Thus saith the Lord GOD; I will yet for this be inquired of by the house of Israel, to do it for them" (36:37). In the words of Jonah, "Salvation is of the LORD" (Jonah 2:9).

Today, the born-again saints are supposed to visibly attract Israel to do the right thing, to live subserviently for King Yeshua (Romans 11:11). After the gentiles achieve fullness, Israel will ultimately surrender to God's plan of the ages and find "fullness" in Yeshua (v.12). Pray today that the Holy One will help you become more fully sanctified and that Israel will clearly see their need for a heart-felt change.

Affinities & Afflictions

"They have forgotten the LORD their God. Return, ye backsliding children, and I will heal your backslidings." (Jeremiah 3:21-22)

How easy it is to lose awareness of the One Who once breathed new life in you and continually supplies you with breath! May the following play on words serve as an illustration of the dreadful process of turning one's back on God.

The backslidden life begins by making a decision to follow the Shepherd only from *afar*. Faithfulness towards the crucified One is then soon replaced with misguided and unholy *affairs*. Sadly, the saint loses most of his *affect* upon the lost. Hardening the heart, the prodigal son cuts off all godly *affiliations* with the House of God and makes even more *affinities* with the world. Strangely, the backslider still *affirms* his faith in Messiah, but oddly *affixes* his heart to Vanity Fair. The kingdom of darkness now heavily *afflicts* him, and having lost all *affluence* upon a lost world, the runaway servant becomes, to both God and man, an *affront*!

The remedy to turning back to God begins with a heavenly call. Only through the Father's refusal to give up on His prodigal child can such a one be afforded the opportunity to return home (Luke 15:20). The call of Messiah's Spirit bursts upon the scene, at which time, the wayward one's ears quickly perk up. His heart becomes smitten of the LORD. This causes him to assess his impoverished condition and his embarrassing lack of covenant faithfulness. The backslider senses mercy at the door and takes a monumental moment to consider his only option—*turn back* to God or *turn into* a pillar of salt; that is to say, become a monument to his own disobedience (2 Corinthians 13:7). Hopefully he recognizes that God's mercy wonderfully outweighs the consequences of his foolish actions.

If you or someone you know needs to turn back to his or her former standing with God, pray today that the Comforter will assist the runaway to return home quickly and become strengthened and stable.

You are a Biblical Character

"And Paul dwelt two whole years in his own hired house, and received all that came in unto him, Preaching the kingdom of God, and teaching those things which concern the Lord Jesus Christ, with all confidence, no man forbidding him." (Acts 28:30-31)

There are characters mentioned in the Bible, both good and bad, who lived their lives not knowing their life summary was going to be recorded for all generations to see. What if God decided to write a sequel to the Bible? Would you be glad for Him to write a paragraph or chapter on your life or would you blush at the thought of how little you had done for Him?

Although the Word of God is absolutely complete, one book in the New Covenant remains completely open—the Book of Acts. This book is the only one in the New Testament (with the exception of James) that has no ending, no salutation and no sign off. Acts is not a book of *doctrine*; rather, it's a book of *doing*, a history of the beginning of gospel ventures. There is no *Amen* at the end of Acts because there are more gospel acts that God's people must carry out. If God did decide to make a written record of the events that take place from first-century AD all the way through to the final 1000th year of Messiah's reign on earth, then there would be a complete record of all that transpired during the 7000-year history of man.

One thing is for sure; God is taking an account of the deeds done in His name. When Messiah Yeshua came along, some gave of their substance to Him; others brought sick folk to Him to be healed; some gave Him lodging; some praised Him; others thanked Him. Later, one helped Him carry His cross. Some wept for Him. A small group anointed His body and buried Him. After His resurrection and ascension, thousands began to carry the good news of His glory and saving power to people everywhere. For now, the question is this: "What will you be known for when the Book of Acts finally closes?"

Today, begin seeking the will of God for gospel projects He has purposely planned for you.

The Light

"Blessed be…God…for wisdom and might are his…He revealeth the deep and secret things: he knoweth what is in the darkness, and the light dwelleth with him." (Daniel 2:20, 22)

Daniel describes God's constant companion in mystery form—*the Light*. The Aramaic word is *neheerah*. It means "illumination, (figuratively) wisdom." This is one of Messiah's glorious titles. The creation of the heavens and earth did not come until Yeshua, as pure *Light* and creative *Wisdom*, first appeared upon the scene (Genesis 1:3). Yeshua's claim to be the Light of the World was a full claim to deity. He was also drawing metaphorically from Psalm 18:28 when He promised His listeners that those who faithfully follow Him "shall not walk in darkness, but shall have the light of life" (John 8:12).

A brief look at the psalmists' frequent use of light reveals much about our amazing Messiah. The psalmist equates *Messiah's light* with: the countenance of the LORD's face (4:6); salvation and rest (27:1); seeing eternity (36:9); earthly hope (38:10); truth (43:3); the glory cloud (78:14); our sins revealed (90:8); righteousness (97:11); God's very clothing (104:2); and the understanding of God's Word (119:130). But the most unusual *coupling of light* in the Psalm is found in this verse: "God is the LORD, which hath showed us light: bind the sacrifice with cords, even unto the horns of the altar" (118:27). God showed Israel His Messianic light when He offered them His Son upon the cross. And the horns that protruded from that holy altar were in the form of Roman spikes. If you have received Yeshua as your sacrificial Offering, then you have truly seen the Light and can praise God for illuminating your darkness.

Solomon says, "But the path of the just is as the shining light, that shineth more and more unto the perfect day" (Proverbs 4:18). Take this verse into your prayer time. Adore the Son and ask Him to fill you with His light and wisdom so that you might leave all darkness behind and make the most of the opportunities that are before you today.

The Lamp of God's City

"Blessed be the name of God...He revealeth the deep and secret things: he knoweth what is in the darkness, and the light [neheerah] dwelleth with him." (Daniel 2:20, 22)

Rabbinical sources attribute the mystery of God's abiding companion, "the light," to be a figure of the Messiah. They understood the Aramaic word *nehorah,* "light," to be one of Messiah's secretive titles. They also affirm that creation's first light that appeared upon the formless earth was also the illumination of God's anointed One. The question is asked, "Whose is this light which falls upon the congregation of the Lord?" and the response is given: "It is the light of the Messiah" (Pesikta Rabbati 62.1). Another rabbinic passage confirms this to be so in view of the psalmist's revelation—"In thy light, shall we see light" (Yalkut Shimeoni). Yeshua's claim to be the Light of the World was no small elucidation to His full status as God.

Daniel speaks figuratively of *neheerah,* "illumination," as wisdom, but the root of this word, *nehorah,* literally means daylight. Because of the natural association of these two concepts, Jewish law forbade holding trials or counsels at night lest they forsake the light of God's wisdom.

It was at Earth's darkest hour that Messiah sprang upon the horizon as both Light and Wisdom to commence creation. The counterpart to the Book of Daniel is the Book of Revelation, and here we find the prophecy of Messiah's eternal light in the New Jerusalem—after the earth is recreated. "And the city had no need of the sun, neither of the moon, to shine in it: for the glory of God did lighten it, and the Lamb is the light thereof. And the nations of them which are saved shall walk in the light of it" (Revelation 21:23-24).

This morning, prayerfully ask Yeshua to fill you with His holy light and wisdom that you may go out of your house today glowing with His humble countenance and heavenly mindset.

Separated & Filled

"But...it pleased God, who separated me from my mother's womb, and called me by his grace, To reveal his Son in me, that I might preach him among the heathen." (Galatians 1:15)

Before God could equip Paul as the herald of His grace, He first had to separate him for that one particular use. Paul's phrase, "from my mother's womb," acknowledges that the Lord's plan had always been to save and sanctify him. In due time He separated Saul from his ignorant ways. This happened on the Damascus Road. It was also right then and there that Yeshua filled Saul with His Spirit and redirected his life.

From the beginning, God's pattern has always been to first separate, then to fill. Just look at the creation story, and we see Him separating or dividing. On day one, He *separated* the light from the darkness (Genesis 1:4). On day two, He *divided* the waters that were under the firmament from the waters that were above the firmament (1:7). On day three, He *separated* the waters under the heaven and let the dry land appear (1:9). Then after making these distinctions, He began to fill the earth with abundant life. On day three, He *filled* the dry land with grass, herbs and fruit trees (1:11). On day four, He *filled* the day with the sun and *filled* the night with the moon and stars (1:16). On day five, He *filled* the deep waters with moving creatures and the barren sky with birds (1:20). On day six He *filled* the earth with animals and man (1:27). After God ended His work, He took the last remaining day, sanctified and *separated* it from the other days and then filled it with rest (2:2-3).

At the moment God saves you, He separates you from the world for a divine purpose. To help you accomplish this, He instantly fills you with His Spirit (Acts 2:4). He also fills you with His goodness and knowledge (Romans 15:14), His comfort (2 Corinthians 7:4), His fullness (Ephesians 3:19), His joy (2 Timothy 1:4), fruits of His righteousness (Philippians 1:11) and knowledge of His will (Colossians 1:9). This day will you allow the Holy One to completely separate you from the world and your own purposes, and then allow Him to fill you with all these wonderful things?

Weaned & Loaned

"I will not go up until the child be weaned, and then I will bring him, that he may appear before the LORD, and there abide for ever." (1 Samuel 1:22)

Many treasures are found within this heart-warming story. Not only did Hannah desire a child to take away her reproach, she desired a "man child" that she might give him back to Yahweh as a servant (v.11). In this chapter, the three-letter root word *sha'al* appears six times, once in its two-letter form. It is translated various ways: to *inquire, request, demand, ask,* also to *lend.* When presenting little Samuel to Eli, Hannah said, "The LORD hath given me [*sh'elah-ti*] my petition [*sha-alti*] which I asked of him. Therefore, I have lent him [*heeshil-teehu*] to the LORD; as long as he liveth he shall be lent [*shaul*] to the LORD" (v.27-28).

In Hebrew, you don't say something is "mine," you say it is "to me." Everything you have comes from God, so whenever you give to Him you are really just giving back what once belonged to Him. He *loans* things to you, then sometimes *asks* you to *loan* them back to Him for a season. Hannah not only understood this principle, but also met God in prayer on this very basis. God loves to answer these prayers.

Hannah "weaned" little Samuel like any proper child. The Hebrew word is *gamal,* which also means, *"benefit, reward, ripen."* Her intent was to give Yahweh the best gift possible, but first she wanted to give the child the *benefit* of bonding with a mother's daily smile, *reward* him with mother's daily prayers and *ripen* him with mother's daily milk. Then the child would be fit for the Master's use.

If you have been properly weaned on the Word of God, then place yourself permanently on loan to Him. Yahweh will surely use you. And if you have a child, then loan him or her to the LORD. Start by ripening that future servant on the "sincere milk of the word" and the nourishment of daily prayer (1 Peter 2:2).

God's Word & Yours

"And the LORD appeared again in Shiloh: for the LORD revealed himself to Samuel in Shiloh by the word of the LORD. And the word of Samuel came to all Israel." (1 Samuel 3:21; 4:1)

These two verses run back to back. There is no break between them, only a breath or pause. The narrative tells us that the LORD appeared to Samuel as *the Word*. This implies Yeshua, for He *is* the Word of God (John 1:1). Yeshua always spoke in a calm, audible voice to His young servant, as he grew up in the Tabernacle complex. Whether the little prophet was playing with other little Levite children or helping Eli carry out his duties as high priest, he never missed hearing a single word from the mouth of the LORD. As a fully-grown man Samuel was very careful not only to hear Yeshua's words, but also to let "none of his words fall to the ground" (1 Samuel 3:19). This was Samuel's way. For this reason, the LORD made him a wonderfully respected ruler over His people who readily recognized that the word of Samuel was in fact the word of the LORD.

Letting Yahweh's words fall to the ground is to show carelessness. On the other hand, to hide them in your heart is to show your utmost reverence for them. Yeshua said, "He that hath *my commandments*, and keepeth them, he it is that loveth me: and he that loveth me shall be loved of my Father, and I will love him, and will manifest myself to him" (John 14:21). As we daily take in Yeshua's words, reading them verse-by-verse and letting them sink into our heart, they become our words to both live by and die by.

When Yeshua's words become our words, we can lovingly take them to those around us to guide them, steady them, strengthen them and nourish them. We can also warn them with God's word should they seek to walk outside the will of God as the people did in Samuel's later years (1 Samuel 8:9-10).

Today, take extra care with God's words as you read. As you live by the power of them, you will become able to benefit others with them.

From Egypt to Israel

"So Joseph died, being an hundred and ten years old: and they embalmed him, and he was put in a coffin in Egypt." (Genesis 50:26)

The very last words from each of the five books of Moses tell a story. The fascinating story of redemption began in *Egypt* (Genesis 50:26). Israelites were there for four centuries and in bondage through the latter part. As each brief generation passed, they were buried in Egypt. In unexpected power and glory, God miraculously showed up and redeemed Israel, releasing them from captivity. They then set out on their *journeys* (Exodus 40:38). The newly born nation didn't immediately journey into the Promised Land; rather, they stopped and set up camp for two years at the base of a mountain in the *Sinai* (Leviticus 27:34). There they received instructions regarding their new relationship with the One True God. Some 38 years later Israel finally came to the end of their sojourn. At that point, they stared across the Jordon River at the well-watered land of *Jericho* (Numbers 36:13). After the priests crossed the river with the ark, the people followed at a prescribed distance until all were completely over and safely in Canaan which they renamed *Israel* (Deuteronomy 34:12).

A present-day comparison could be made from this story. When God's redemptive agent, Yeshua, delivers you from the bondage of sin, He immediately writes His law upon your heart. From that point, He takes you on a series of journeys that are designed to keep you humble and continually leaning upon Him. Yeshua is a faithful Shepherd and expects you to trust Him and walk with Him through the desert valleys. He doesn't expect you to walk it alone. His satisfying nature as the Water of Life and Manna from Heaven make Him your staying power. The Great Shepherd will surely see you all the way home until it is time for you to cross over Jordon.

Take time today to thank your heavenly Shepherd for all He has done for you in the past and for what He is doing in your life just now.

A Standing Servant

"And Elijah the Tishbite...said...As the LORD God of Israel liveth, before whom I stand, there shall not be dew nor rain these years, but according to my word." (1 Kings 17:1)

Elijah used the divine oath "before whom I stand" on many occasions. He knew that faithful servants of Yahweh stand and wait upon Him, and praise Him, even through the night (Psalm 134:1). We also are expected to be standing and serving our Lord. Paul was another good servant whom we can emulate.

If we want to be a standing servant like Paul, we should first be on *standby* to discover more about Who the living God really is. Paul asked, "Who art thou Lord?" (Acts 9:5). The believer should never get to the point where he feels there is little left to discover about his Master. When you meditate over the Word, you should be on *standby* for the Lord to reveal more of Himself to you.

Paul asked another question, "What wilt thou have me to do?" (v.6). He instantly placed himself on standby to do the Lord's bidding. There is plenty to do for the sake of the kingdom. The Lord said to Paul, "Arise, and go into the city, and it shall be told thee what thou must do" (v.6). There comes a time when a servant must also *stand up*. Servants were rarely afforded the luxury of sitting down anyway; they stood on their feet constantly. Even when they ate, they had to remain standing. The priests had to stand up to perform their holy work. Not even the great high priest was given a seat.

Paul also *stood out* from the crowd as Yeshua's choice servant. Yeshua said, "he is a chosen vessel unto me, to bear my name before the Gentiles, and kings, and the children of Israel" (v.15). God has specifically chosen each of us for a particular task that only we can do for Him. This means we each stand out in a special way.

Since you stand out so much, be sure to "walk worthy of the vocation wherewith ye are called" (Ephesians 4:1). May the Lord strengthen you today to stand and serve Him faithfully.

Messiah & Mayim

Part 1

"...he that sent me to baptize with water, the same said unto me, Upon whom thou shalt see the Spirit descending, and remaining on him, the same is he which baptizeth with the Holy Ghost." (John 1:33)

Water or *mayim* greatly represents life, for without it we cannot exist. The fourth gospel writer recorded much of Messiah's ministry in its relationship to water.

The mystery begins in chapter one with *water to be buried in!* The people came to the baptismal waters to confess their sins publically and to turn from them. It was a sobering experience and represented death to the old man. Today, all those who claim Messiah's saving name and shed blood are supernaturally buried with Him and raised to new life. Your duty is to make sure the old man stays buried!

In chapter two, the setting is Cana. Here we find *water in which to be overjoyed!* John writes that they wanted wine (v.3). What they really wanted was joy, and Messiah became the dispenser of it through the waters He so sweetly and abundantly blessed. Yeshua can turn your joyless day into a spectacular one as long as you, "do whatsoever He saith unto you" (v.5).

In chapter three, John records a conversation about *water to be birthed in!* Messiah directed one interested Sanhedrin member to something extremely needful saying, "Except a man be born of water and of the Spirit, he cannot enter into the kingdom of God" (v.4-5). All souls enter this world via natural amniotic waters, but each must go through supernatural waters in order to enter into the next world.

In chapter four where water is mentioned nine times, the beloved disciple describes *water to be drawn in!* At Jacob's well the Samaritan woman came to draw water. She also had a great spiritual thirst because she said to Messiah, "Sir, give me this water, that I thirst not, neither come hither to draw" (v.15). Today, draw from the blessed waters of Messiah's eternal Word.

Messiah & Mayim

Part 2

"Now there is at Jerusalem by the sheep market a pool...In these lay a great multitude of impotent folk, of blind, halt, withered, waiting for the moving of the water...whosoever then first after the troubling of the water stepped in was made whole of whatsoever disease he had" (John 5:2-4).

Here John reveals *water in which to be healed!* Yeshua healed an unlikely candidate and thereby showed Who had the actual power behind the highly revered waters. If you're looking for holy water for your infirmity, there is only One Who has it and can administer it. Many call Him the Great Physician, and His timing should remain unquestioned.

In chapter seven, John speaks of *water in which to be satisfied!* "Jesus stood and cried, saying, "If any man thirst, let him come unto me, and drink" (v.37). Only the Saviour's steadfast love and mercy can satisfy a longing soul. David described his thirst for God as a deer who pants in a parched desert. Take your desperate thirst to Yeshua today.

In chapter thirteen Messiah displayed *water in which to be washed!* He poured water into a basin and began to wash the disciples' feet "and to wipe them with the towel wherewith he was girded" (v.5). Only Messiah Yeshua can wash away your daily defilement. Have you been to Him today with a confessing spirit? He's waiting for you with basin and towel.

John's final stop along his tour of Messiah's miracle water pools is chapter nineteen where he points to *water to believe in!* At the Cross a Roman soldier pierced Messiah's side and immediately there came out blood and water (v.34). John saw this happen and recorded it "that ye might believe" (v.35). Messiah's shed blood allows Him to forgive you of all sin. His shed water then washes you from sin's guilt and shame, thus giving you a brand new start in life.

John was a fisherman and therefore understood the power of water, but what amazed him most was the power of Messiah's mighty waters. Do you believe today?

How Great is Your Gratitude?

"There was a certain creditor which had two debtors: the one owed five hundred pence, and the other fifty. And when they had nothing to pay, he frankly forgave them both. Tell me therefore, which of them will love him most?" (Luke 7:41-42)

This brief parable becomes a play within a play that is intended to reveal an overlooked truth. The main play has as its main characters Yeshua, the merciful Judge of Israel; an unnamed woman of scorn who is rejoicing in her newly acquired debt-free status; and a self-righteous Pharisee named Simon who seems completely unaware that he needs any forgiveness from God.

Messiah's riveting riddle takes center stage in a banquet that is supposed to be held in His honor. Although Yeshua is addressed by the title Master, the great Torah Scholar of Israel is shown no real honor by His host. Simon omits the normal formalities of kissing a venerable rabbi's hand, or at the very least as among equals, kissing Yeshua's cheek. He also omits giving his honored Guest any water to wash His feet, which was more than customary for a banquet. Lastly, Simon does not greet the Master with a bit of olive oil upon His forehead.

By contrast, the changed woman kisses the Master's feet not once, but repeatedly and pours out her tears upon His feet. Having nothing with which to dry them, she decides to let down her hair as a sacred towel, regardless of the shame it quickly brings. What she had originally come prepared to do was to anoint the Master with a small vial of perfumed oil that she normally wore upon a long necklace. It was all she had, but it was expensive and lavish.

Do you realize the size of the shameful debt from which you have been freed? Does your gratitude towards the blood of Yeshua show the proper amount of honor for such great forgiveness? Then spare no expense today and disregard any possible shame your act of devotion may bring.

The Dawn Breaker

"And in the morning, rising up a great while before day, he went out, and departed into a solitary place, and there prayed." (Mark 1:35)

The foul spirits hovering over Israel's camp created darkness greater than a thousand midnights, but during the time of her Messiah, she could rest calmly while His great Light pierced that unholy veil. The dawn never arose so early over the land of Israel as it did in the days of Israel's anointed Intercessor. Yeshua ruled over disease, depression, destitute hearts, death and demons. He ruled supremely over every form of darkness. He ruled in prayer.

The Son of Man preceded the dawn not only for Israel's benefit, but also for His own. Those early hours were the only moments He could commune with His Father without rush or interruption. Oh, how many times do we rush into the Father's presence and say goodbye before we've really said good morning! Yeshua knew His Father well and took delight in drawing near in prayer. If He had waited until after dawn to rise and pray, the crowing cock would have pierced the silence that the Saviour loved so well.

There is yet another reason why the Dawn Breaker lit up the last watch of the night. It was for you. Yeshua knew that there are many like Eyobe who struggle through the night. His cry was, "When shall I arise, and the night be gone? ...I am full of tossings to and fro unto the dawning of the day" (Job 7:4). When it's dark around your dwelling, the Son of God still intercedes for you so that His prayerful words might be as "a light that shineth in a dark place, until the day dawn, and the *day star arise in your hearts*" (2 Peter 1:19).

The Hebrew word for dawning is *neshef*, which comes from a root meaning *breeze*. The prayerful breeze coming off your lips today will also give light to a dark world and make for a wonderfully fresh and hope-filled day.

ᵂhen ℬlood & ᵂater ℳix

"And I took your sin, the calf which ye had made, and burnt it with fire, and stamped it, and ground it very small, even until it was as small as dust: and I cast the dust thereof into the brook that descended out of the mount." (Deuteronomy 9:21)

Up on the mountaintop Yahweh informed Moses that He was about to destroy Israel, but He couldn't do it unless Moses stopped his intercessory work. This is why the LORD said, "Let me alone" (v.14). When Moses went down the mount, he *cast* the commandments out of his hands and then attempted to pacify God's wrath by slaying unrepentant souls. But Moses did something else before ordering this slaughter. He ordered the golden calf to be immersed in fire, beaten flat and ground to powder. Then he personally *cast* the purified gold dust into the flowing brook. According to his book, *The Chemistry of the Blood*, Dr. M.R. DeHaun states that the gold dust instantly and completely dissolved creating a solution known as colloidal gold. This ancient remedy has been used to cure a variety of mental and emotional instabilities. It has a rose-red hue or even blood-red hue depending on the ratio of the mixture. Moses, the great intercessor, made the children of Israel drink it—but why? (Exodus 32:20). This author believes that the red drink stood as a symbolic substitute for the blood of the Old Covenant in the same way the "blood of the grape" did (Deuteronomy 32:14). The next day Moses went *back up* into the presence of Yahweh, fasted another 40 days, and continued interceding. The LORD hearkened unto Moses at that time (Deuteronomy 9:19).

Moses' intercessory actions are very typological. Yeshua took red juice, symbolic of the New Covenant, and forced it upon His disciples saying, "Drink ye all of it" (Matthew 26:27). And while on the cross, Yeshua interceded for the world's great sin. He begged the Father to forgive both Jew and Gentile (Luke 23:34). Later a soldier pierced His side and out flowed one holy mixture of "blood and water" (John 19:34). Reminiscent of Moses, Yeshua went *back up* into heaven 40 days after His resurrection to the Mount of God where He continues His intercession for our daily sins.

This morning thank the Son of God for His present intercessory work and previous outpouring on your behalf.

Removing the Scourge

"And there came a leper to him, beseeching him, and kneeling down to him, and saying unto him, If thou wilt, thou canst make me clean." (Mark 1:40)

Leprosy was a dreadful disease and greatly feared. Careful attention was given to its detection, and if necessary, subsequent treatment or containment was administered under Levitical law. The Hebrew word for leper is *tsarah,* a primitive root meaning "to *scourge,* figuratively, to be *stricken* with leprosy." The Hebrew name for this disease draws a picture of divine chastisement; that is, a person being scourged or whipped for some manner of sin—most likely an unforgivable sin. A person who contracted leprosy suffered the worst *scourge* of humanity being so unsightly and deplorable. Accompanying this personal calamity was a horrendous famine of friends and family. A stricken one could never draw near to their family again unless they became miraculously healed.

Having heard that an instant cure was available, one poor leper boldly came up to Messiah and anxiously begged for healing. Yeshua was moved with compassion and "put forth his hand, and touched him, and saith unto him, I will; be thou clean" (v.41). The Son of God did not have to touch the leper physically to administer healing, but in doing so, He foreshadowed His own future disfigurement. Yeshua cared so much about removing our sinful scourge that He allowed Himself to be literally scourged in our place. Isaiah described the marring of Messiah's face and body (Isaiah 52:14). He also described the nation's response: "we hid as it were our faces from him" (53:3). Isaiah's reasoning was that they "did esteem him stricken, smitten of God, and afflicted" (53:4). Ancient rabbis referred to this man depicted in Isaiah as *the Leper Scholar.* Isaiah explained the reality of the situation saying, "But the chastisement [scourging] of our peace was upon him; and with his [leprous] stripes we are healed" (53:5).

Oh, spot-free lamb, now that you have been cleansed, avoid contamination today by staying close to *the Cure*—Yeshua!

The Second Coming of Moses

"And the LORD said unto Moses, When thou goest to return into Egypt, see that thou do all those wonders before Pharaoh, which I have put in thine hand." (Exodus 4:21)

At the age of 40, the mighty prince of Egypt stepped out for the first time to deliver his Hebrew brethren from their heavy burdens. He was not met with overwhelming acceptance; rather, the response was, "Who made thee a prince and a judge over us?" (2:14). Although the Hebrews were under harsh slave conditions, they were perfectly content for Moses to go back to his royal palace and stay out of their lives. Their wish was granted. The next day he vanished into a far country—Midian. They would be on their own without any advocacy until God saw fit to send Moses back.

What a surprise it must have been for the oppressed Hebrews to behold this very same man returning to them one generation later. He came, not with the scepter of a man, but with the rod of God—duly authorized and thoroughly empowered. "And Moses…gathered together all the elders of the children of Israel: And…spake all the words which the LORD had spoken unto Moses, and did the signs in the sight of the people. And the people believed…then they bowed their heads and worshipped" (4:29-31). Their attitude towards him had changed, and as a result, their complete deliverance began straightway. Moses accomplished on the second occasion what he intended to do on the first. The difference is the second time his kinsmen submitted to his authority.

Maybe you have been trying to win someone to the Lord for a very long time or trying to succeed in some spiritual endeavor. Maybe you have seen little success. Perhaps you've only seen failure. Today, give your endeavor to the Almighty and He will do the unusual. Lay your burden, your heart's desire before Him and ask Him to show you the way to accomplish the burden that He has laid upon your heart. Success is sure to come in Yeshua's name!

The Second Coming of Messiah

"So Christ was once offered to bear the sins of many; and unto them that look for him shall he appear the second time without sin unto salvation." (Hebrews 9:27)

Moses' two appearances typified the two advents of Israel's promised Messiah. Yeshua's first coming was not as they had supposed, but was in a very humble manner. When Messiah came the first time, He was also rejected as their rightful Prince and Judge. Yeshua spoke a parable concerning this matter: "But his citizens…sent a message after him, saying, We will not have this man to reign over us" (Luke 19:14). Like Israel under Egypt, their concession was to remain under the dominance of Rome. Because of Israel's stubborn refusal, the royal Prince from the House of David vanished into a far country—Heaven. These were His stern and prophetic words: "I will go and return to my place, till they acknowledge their offence, and seek my face: in their affliction they will seek me early" (Hosea 5:15).

As it was with Moses, Israel will also be surprised when Messiah comes back the second time. His appearance will not be lowly with just a shepherd's staff as in His first coming, but will be mighty and have a drawn sword and a scepter of iron (Revelation 19:15). At His second coming, the Chief Shepherd will gather Hebrews from the ends of the earth. His inspirational news has been foretold: "I will pour upon the house of David, and upon the inhabitants of Jerusalem, the spirit of grace and of supplications: and they shall look upon me whom they have pierced" (Zechariah 12:10). As it was with Moses, their attitude toward Messiah will also change, for the prophet says, "they shall mourn for him as one mourneth for his only son" (v.10). As it was with Moses, every member of Jacob's clan will also humbly bow his or her head and worship (v.12). Because of their unified submission to their returning Redeemer, Israel will immediately experience victory over their oppressors (v.8).

Today, ask the Saviour to help ready you for His second coming. It is not very far away.

Bread of the Kingdom

"And Boaz said unto her, At mealtime come thou hither, and eat of the bread, and dip thy morsel in the vinegar. And she sat beside the reapers...and she did eat, and was sufficed." (Ruth 2:14)

The word vinegar comes from the Latin word *vinum* meaning wine, and *acer*, which refers to sharp or sour. In time, the two words were combined and became *vinegre*. The vinegar of biblical days was wine that had gone flat; it was then fortified with eggs or figs and diluted with water. It was commonly used as a sauce at mealtimes. Ruth used it to savor and soften her bread; Abraham summarized the unique nature of bread saying, "I will fetch a morsel of bread, and comfort ye your hearts; after that ye shall pass on" (Genesis 18:5); and Solomon expounded a key creed of the kingdom: "eat thy bread with joy" (Ecclesiastes 9:7).

In the days of the Romans, vinegar was the drink of slaves or servants. When Messiah, the Bread of Life, cried out "I thirst," He expected a drink of water from some sympathetic soul, but instead only received the taste of a little vinegar (John 19:30). The very next thing He did was say, "It is finished," and then "he bowed his head, and gave up the ghost" (v.30).

Boaz and Ruth prefigure the Messiah and His grafted-in Gentile bride. Ruth ate simple bread and humble wine in the presence of her new lord. This greatly typifies New Covenant communion with our Lord. Yeshua memorialized His atoning death by offering His disciples two tokens; small portions of tasteless bread and sips from His bitter cup. We also understand that in receiving these tokens they were expected to share in His suffering. Just as Ruth was *sufficed* with what was set before her, we as Messiah's bride need to accept our lot in life which is to lean on our Master, to labor in His fields and glean such souls as we can find, and to regularly sit among the other reapers—the saints—and participate in communion.

Today, be satisfied with the simple things the Master provides you, and then go out and glean in the fields.

Poor Man's Bread

"Seven days shalt thou eat unleavened bread therewith, even the bread of affliction: that thou mayest remember the day when thou camest forth out of the land of Egypt all the days of thy life." (Deuteronomy 16:3)

This was not likely the first time the poor Hebrew slaves had ever tasted *lechem oni,* the *bread of poverty,* nor would it be their last. God didn't want Israel to forget their low status when salvation first came their way. Pride has a way of deceiving us all. We should not think that because we are washed and cleansed of sin that we are suddenly worthy of God's blessings. Only the Lamb is worthy.

Not only does this poor man's bread remind Israel of her formerly low estate, but it also reminds New Covenant saints of Messiah's low estate on the eve of His last Passover. "And he took bread, and gave thanks, and brake it, and gave unto them, saying, This is my body which is given for you: this do in remembrance of me" (Luke 22:19). *Lechem oni,* also known as the *bread of affliction,* points more clearly to the type of person it was suited for—a condemned prisoner (1 Kings 22:27). After eating the bread of affliction with His talmidim, Yeshua voluntarily submitted Himself to be afflicted for us.

Paul speaks of Messiah's extreme poverty very poetically: "For ye know the grace of our Lord Jesus Christ that, though he was rich, yet for your sakes he became poor, that ye through his poverty might be rich" (2 Corinthians 8:8). The Saviour invites all His followers to share equally in His poverty, and if necessary, even His affliction (John 15:20). We are also left with a challenge to embrace Messiah's poverty with James' declaration: "Hearken, my beloved brethren, Hath not God chosen the poor of this world rich in faith, and heirs of the kingdom which he hath promised to them that love him?" (James 2:5).

Unto this day, the persecuted church eats the bread of poverty and suffers literal affliction. May you reverently remember to pray for them and their many needs today.

Triumph at the Trial

"And having spoiled principalities and powers, he made a show of them openly, triumphing over them in it." (Colossians 2:15)

The Son of Man enjoyed a triple triumph over the prince of darkness. This began at His trial, which was a mockery of real justice. It was held under the cover of darkness, was so poorly planned, and caused such embarrassment that the lords of the mock trial finally had to settle for unconvincing false witnesses (Matthew 26:60). Thinking Rome would give them the verdict they desired, Yeshua was sent to Pilate. Three times the governor declared, "I find no fault in Him." After a very disturbing daytime dream, Pilate's wife broke protocol and sent an urgent message to her husband in the judgment hall. She became the second faithful witness testifying that the Man from Nazeret was a just man to be feared (Matthew 27:19).

Judas was trembling with anguish, the priests were trembling with anger, Pilate was trembling with perplexity, his wife was trembling in her sleep, but Messiah was calmly triumphing through each of His six hearings. Because no guilty verdict could be legally given, He was tried repeatedly. The priests broke 22 laws, yet Yeshua broke none. The prophet's statement, "He was taken from prison and from judgment" (Isaiah 53:8) accurately foretells how Messiah would encounter a senseless repetition of judicial proceedings before being falsely and fatally sentenced. The unbiased, yet unregenerate judge delivered the outcome of the trial: "Not guilty, innocent of all charges!" Nevertheless, Pilate sentenced Him to death. But before doing so, he gave a Mosaic token; he washed his hands of any implication in this innocent Man's death (Deuteronomy 21:6).

From Messiah's followers' narrow viewpoint, it looked as if He suffered total defeat, but later they understood the prophecy: "the chastisement of our peace was upon him; and with his stripes we are healed" (Isaiah 53:5). The tragic ending of Messiah's trial was in reality an absolute triumph! Show your gratitude to Him today by receiving wrong if it comes and by doing something kind for others.

Triumph at the Tree

"And having spoiled principalities and powers, he made a show of them openly, triumphing over them in it." (Colossians 2:15)

Pilate was determined to let the humble Galilean Rabbi go free, but God had preordained just the opposite. Not only did the Just One triumph at His trial, He triumphed upon His tree. The leadership gathered and "consulted that they might take Jesus by subtlety, and kill him. But they said, *Not on the feast day,* lest there be an uproar among the people" (Matthew 26:4-5). Messianic fever was never any higher than at the season of Passover, and Rome's occupation created a desperate need for another deliverer like Moses. Israel's former days under judges and kings proved that they were uncomfortable in going against their enemies without God's appointed man at the forefront. The Judean assembly's earthly scheme to wait until after the Feast was overturned from above; the Lamb of God was offered up as planned on the very day of Passover.

As the perfect *Paschal Lamb,* Yeshua also triumphed in bringing full atonement in dying by loss of blood alone and not from suffocation, which is what would have happened if the Roman soldiers had broken His legs while He was still alive (Exodus 12:46, Psalm 34:20). As the *Light of the World* hung between heaven and earth He triumphed by blocking out the sun's natural light for three long hours. As the *Rock of Israel,* He triumphed by rending the rocks with one violent earthquake in Jerusalem the moment His Spirit left Him. Although the veil of His flesh was horribly torn, the new *Priest of Israel* triumphed when He tore the veil of the old Temple from top to bottom just after His Spirit left Him (Matthew 27:51).

Israel's wayward leaders regarded Yeshua only as someone who was being afflicted by God for trying to lead the nation astray, but in reality He "was wounded for our transgressions and [was] bruised for our iniquities" (Isaiah 53:5). He entered the dark domain of death to keep us from it for all eternity. May you give Him a proper praise offering today for His valiant and triumphant fight to the death.

Triumph at the Tomb

"See now that I, even I, am he...For I lift up my hand to heaven, and say, I live for ever." (Deuteronomy 32:39-40)

The third stage of Yeshua's triple triumph took place in His tomb. How He came to rest there was in itself a miracle. Nicodemus came to Pilate and begged for Messiah's body lest it receive a burial as Rome's other condemned subjects—the ash heaps. The lifeless *King of the Jews* triumphed by receiving a burial worthy of any great king. The funeral was conducted by two of Israel's highest officials, Joseph of Arimathaea and Nicodemus. Together the two Sanhedrin members took His body with 100 pounds of myrrh and aloes, wrapped it in linen and laid it in a sepulcher where no man had ever been laid before (John 19:39-41).

Even though the *King of the Jews* lay low in the house of the dead, fears of a staged resurrection—or even a real one— caused the chief heads in Jerusalem to beg Pilate for a group of soldiers to guard His tomb. Pilate not only consented, but was also moved of God's Spirit saying, "make it as sure as ye can" (Matthew 27:65). The tomb was quickly sealed with the authority of Rome. Two iron pins were driven and cemented with molten lead where the great stone came to rest. The guards then placed their backs to the wall, but death's silence was inevitably broken when a rumbling came from the netherworld on the first day of the week. The Father's prophetic promise came to pass, "I will prolong His days" (Isaiah 53:10)! The *Son of God* sat up in newness of life and walked straight through the sealed tomb. Clothed in glory, He raised His right hand to the sky and shouted, "I live for ever!" fulfilling Scripture as *the Great I Am.* Soon afterwards, a seismic shaking rocked Jerusalem's sleepy residences as an angel rolled away the stone. This act sheared off the iron pins [which remains visible today], exposed the empty grave, and nearly scared the battle-hardened soldiers to death! Actually, they passed out in fear (Matthew 28:4).

Take time today to praise Yeshua for His resurrection power and for the way in which He overcame death for you.

Don't Drop the Ball!

"Take heed to the ministry which thou hast received in the Lord, that thou fulfil it." (Colossians 4:17)

Samson did not do too good of a job fulfilling his ministry. He kept getting sidetracked. Had he tended to ministry properly, he would have kept his status as Israel's deliverer, as well as his eyes, his freedom and his life. Solomon *slacked away* from his ministerial duties and got preoccupied with living in excess luxury. Two of Aaron's sons fulfilled their ministry but in the *wrong way*. Also, an unnamed man of God was told to deliver a message and not to turn aside until he had left that country's borders (1 Kings 13). He didn't fulfill his ministry because he was *tricked* into believing that God had changed His mind.

Many saints did fulfill their God-given roles. One who stands out is Paul. In the end, he could say with confidence, "I have fought a good fight, I have finished my course, I have kept the faith" (2 Timothy 4:7). Will you be able to say that upon your deathbed? Over time, vast numbers of Bible College graduates and preachers have simply walked away from their ministerial callings for one reason or another, but Paul says, "Let every man abide in the same calling wherein he was called" (1 Corinthians 7:20). Paul counted it an incredible privilege to be given a special assignment from on high. He was thankful in three ways saying, "I thank Christ Jesus our Lord, who hath *enabled me*, for that he *counted me* faithful, *putting me* into the ministry" (1 Timothy 1:12).

This apostle not only tells ministers to take heed to the calling, to live in that calling and to be thankful for the calling, but also to carry it to its fullest degree! He says, "make full proof of thy ministry" (2 Timothy 4:5). If God has called you to home school your children, don't think of stopping. Has He called you to a tract distribution ministry? Stick with it and expand on it! We are not to stop on a whim, but to press on until the King comes. Ask Him for His divine assistance today to help you complete your assignment.

April 12

The Cup of Sanctification

"The cup of blessing which we bless, is it not the communion of the blood of Messiah?" (1 Corinthians 10:16)

Throughout the Messianic world, the Passover Seder begins with a standard blessing over the first cup: "Behold this cup of sanctification. Let it be a symbol of our joy tonight as we celebrate the festival of Pesach!" Sanctification, *kiddush,* means, "to set apart" and comes from the root word *kadosh* meaning "holy." God's purpose was to set Israel completely apart from all other nations. In turn, Israel was supposed to set apart Yahweh, the One True God, from all other gods. Even so, because Israel's God is holy, Israel is to reflect His character by being holy. One great way of illustrating this principle is found in God's instruction for Israel to cleanse their houses of all leaven, to take that week and completely set it apart from all other weeks of the year.

In the days just before Yeshua's final Passover He thoroughly sanctified the House of God cleansing it of all leaven. He turned over tables of corruption and prohibited Temple-goers from carrying any unclean vessels, which caused quite a stir. He had earlier warned casual worshippers of only cleaning "the outside of the cup" (Luke 11:39). Paul continued this theme advising a group of careless believers with the warning, "Christ our Passover is sacrificed for us: Therefore let us keep the feast, not with old leaven, neither with the leaven of malice and wickedness; but with the unleavened bread of sincerity and truth...Ye cannot drink the cup of the Lord, and the cup of devils: ye cannot be partakers of the Lord's [Passover] table, and of the table of devils. Do we provoke the Lord to jealousy?...All things are lawful for me, but all things edify not" (1 Corinthians 5:7-8, 10:21-23). Paul also said, "Jesus also, that he might sanctify the people with his own blood, suffered without the gate" (Hebrews 13:12).

May Lord Yeshua give you a holy determination to keep your spiritual house cleansed all year so that you may enjoy beautiful and unbroken fellowship with Him.

The Cup of Remembrance

"This cup is the new testament in my blood: this do ye, as oft as ye Drink it, in remembrance of me." (1 Corinthians 11:25)

The main reason for the annual observance of Passover is to bring to *remembrance* what great things the LORD has done for Israel. He delivered His people from Egyptian captivity and bondage; therefore, this Cup of Remembrance is also known as the *Cup of Deliverance*. Because of all the strange things that took place on the original night of Passover, an overriding question was most likely asked by many children: "Father, why is this night so different from all other nights?" It was only through a succession of plagues culminating with the death of the firstborn that Pharaoh finally agreed to let Israel go out from Egypt. Because of this, the Cup of Remembrance is also known as the *Cup of Plagues*.

Due to Messiah's shocking Passover announcement that one of His disciples would betray Him, the overriding question became "Lord, is it I?" Just like the original night of Passover, the disciples were feeling very uneasy and restless.

Focus for a moment upon the last two *plagues*. They literally happened once again on the day of Pesach, 30AD. Like the three-day *plague* of darkness that fell over Egypt just before the firstborn sons died, Matthew records a three-hour *plague* of darkness that fell upon the land of Israel in the hours just before the death of God's only begotten Son. "Now from the sixth hour there was darkness over all the land unto the ninth hour" (Matthew 27:45). John's gospel highlights the only Person on that Passover Who actually drank [as it were] from a *cup of plagues* (John 19:30). Man filled it with vinegar, but God filled it with His wrath! At the end of the day the Father declared to His Son, "Behold, I have taken out of thine hand the cup of trembling, even the dregs of the cup of my fury; thou shalt no more drink it again" (Isaiah 51:22).

Take time today to remember the events surrounding your personal salvation from sin and shame, and then thank Him for working His wonders to bring you out from your lifestyle of bondage and slavery.

The Cup of Redemption

"I will take the cup of salvation [Heb. *yeshuah*], *and call upon the name of the LORD."* (Psalm 116:13)

This Cup of Redemption reminds us of God's promise to His people when He faithfully declared, "I will redeem you with a stretched out arm" (Exodus 6:6). Redeem means to buy back something that once belonged to you. Israel had become the possession of Pharaoh and the house of Egypt, so it became necessary for God to send Moses to buy Israel back for Himself. What was the purchase price? One slain lamb per household with its blood smeared on the doorpost as a token, a sign.

A parallel to this can be seen in the ancient betrothal ceremony where a father would take his son to the potential bride's house. The ceremony involved filling and drinking from four different cups; however, this was more like a time of bargaining than anything else. A price would have to be agreed upon between the two fathers to buy the bride out of her father's house. This price was called a *mohar* or dowry. There were many other factors to be discussed during the visit, but the one determining factor was whether the bride agreed to marry him or not. In some cases, the bride had never seen the groom before. After the meal, the cup was filled for the third time. This one was known as the Cup of Redemption. If she consented to be bought out from her father's house, she would simply pick up the cup and drink from it.

This is the very cup from which the psalmist agrees to drink. He calls it the *Cup of Salvation*, or in Hebrew, the Cup of Yeshuah. Yeshuah is a noun, and *Yeshua* is a proper noun—Messiah's covenant name. He is the lover of your soul Who sets His cup before you and waits for you to drink! This New Covenant Groom took "the cup after supper, saying, This cup is the new covenant in my blood, which is shed for you" (Luke 22:20). That very night He began to pay the ultimate price to buy you out from your house of bondage. His *stretched out arm* upon the cross says it all.

Today, go and walk worthy of the great redemption price that has been paid for you.

The Cup of Praise

"Thou art my God, and I will praise thee: thou art my God, I will exalt thee." (Psalm 118:28)

It has been a long-standing tradition to sing Psalm 113-118 during the first night of Passover. In gratitude for redemption and freedom, Israelites began the nighttime *Seder* singing, "Praise ye the LORD. Praise, O ye servants of the LORD, praise the name of the LORD" (113:1).

One gospel narrative wonderfully informs us of Yeshua's Last Seder saying, "when they had sung an *hymn*, they went out into the mount of Olives" (Matthew 26:30). They didn't sing a hymn as we do today; they sang a *hallel*, a psalm. Psalm 118 was the *hallel* sung towards the end of the evening and would have been fresh in Yeshua's mind when He walked out into the night towards the Garden of Gethsemane. This particular *hallel* is packed with prophecy concerning Messiah's final hours. Have a look: "The LORD is my strength and song, and is become my salvation...I shall not die, but live, and declare the works of the LORD. The LORD hath chastened me sore: but he hath not given me over unto death. Open to me the gates of righteousness: I will go into them, and I will praise the LORD...the stone which the builders refused is become the head stone of the corner. This is the day that the LORD hath made; we will rejoice and be glad in it...Blessed be he that cometh in the name of the LORD: we have blessed you out of the house of the LORD...God is the LORD, which hath showed us light: bind the sacrifice with cords, even unto the horns of the altar" (v.14-27).

Now that you know Messiah Yeshua has brought you redemption and eternal refuge, it is only fitting to praise Him today for His acts of loving-kindness on your behalf. This is the day that the LORD has made; rejoice and be glad in it! Let your holy Saviour know how grateful you are by praising His exalted name all throughout the day.

The Kidron Curse

Part 1

"For it shall be, that on the day thou go out, and pass over the brook Kidron...that thou shalt surely die: thy blood shall be upon thine own head." (1 Kings 2:37)

Nothing good is ever mentioned concerning this brook that is situated along the seismically active valley floor between Mt. Moriah and Mt. Olivet. The Kidron is mentioned 11 times in the Tanakh [the number of judgment and disorder]. In Hebrew Kidron means a *dusky* place. This name is drawn from the word *kadar* meaning "to be *ashy*, that is, *dark* colored; by implication, to *mourn*." All three of these words are true of the Kidron. It was a deep, *dark* valley where the residents of Jerusalem dumped their daily refuse to be burned resulting in continual fires and mounds of *ashes*. Because of the various pagan altars found there, it was also cursed. This made the Kidron Valley a place of gross spiritual *darkness*. Many tombs were located in this region and so the eerie sounds of *mourners* were often heard there.

Shimei's name means *famous* or *my fame*. Shimei comes from the root *shema* meaning "something *heard*, i.e. a *sound, rumor, announcement*: abstractly *audience*—fame, loud, report, speech, tidings." Shimei fulfilled his prophetic name. He acquired *fame* among the ten northern tribes as the man who drew an *audience* by *loudly* cursing David and violently casting stones at him as he fled Jerusalem. In contrast, a thousand men of Benjamin followed Shimei when he went to deliver his humble, apologetic *speech* and welcome David back to his rightful Judean throne. At that time, Shimei took up residence in Jerusalem. After David died, Solomon would not let him leave. "And it came to pass at the end of three years, that two of the servants of Shimei ran away...And they told Shimei, saying, Behold, thy servants be in Gath. And Shimei arose, and saddled his donkey" and went after them (1 Kings 2:39-40). Shimei crossed the Kidron, the token of Solomon's curse, and brought upon himself a death sentence. A soldier thrust him through upon his return.

Today, live within the boundaries of the Bible and be greatly blessed.

The Kidron Curse

Part 2

"Jesus...went forth with his disciples over the brook Kidron, where was a garden, into the which he entered" (John 18:1).

Yeshua willfully crossed the Kidron knowing that the *curse of the world's sins* awaited Him on the Olivet slopes and knowing, like Shimei, that He would surely die as a result. This only reference to the Kidron in the entire New Testament is immediately followed by the mentioning of the most *cursed man* in the Bible: "Judas...which betrayed him, knew the place" (v.2).

Messiah humbled Himself in the garden that He might suffer the curse for Israel's breach of Mosaic Law. Paul explains: "Messiah hath redeemed us from the curse of the law, being made a curse for us: for it is written, Cursed is every one that hangeth on a tree" (Galatians 3:13). Like Shimei, Yeshua was only going over the Kidron to reclaim His wayward servants—us. Messiah also rode a donkey, [albeit in a separate but related event], which is quite profound (Genesis 49:11 & Zechariah 9:9).

Yeshua's act of heroism makes Him the most *famous* Person ever to walk the earth. Remembering more assorted meanings of Shimei's name, consider the following things while Messiah was on the cross. The dying Saviour's *speech* was marked for all ages to ponder! A *rumor* spread that He could be calling Elijah to come rescue Him. The many scoffers could hear Yeshua's loud voice. The *sound* of His death cry, "It is finished," rent the veil of the Temple and shook the foundations of Jerusalem. That final *announcement* also reinstated the sunlight whereby His *audience* could once again lay their sinful eyes on Him. Like Shimei, a soldier also thrust Yeshua through. A true *report* was sent to Pilate that the Nazarene was dead, but glad *tidings* surfaced three days later that He had risen from the dead—our curse lifted forever!

You are no longer under the dominion of any curses, bondages or strongholds, so go forth today walking in full freedom as the reclaimed servant of King Yeshua.

Sign Language of the Torah

"Cursed be he that confirmeth not all the words of this law to do them. And all the people shall say, Amen." (Deuteronomy 27:26)

Yahweh pronounced a curse upon those who didn't "confirm" [Heb. *stand up*] His entire law [Heb. *torah*]. Every covenant came with a visible token as a reminder. The token for the Covenant of Law was the Sabbath (Exodus 31:13). On the Sabbath God could see Israel's token of obedience and they could see His token supply of double-manna which fell the day before. Tragically, Israel broke the terms of the covenant, but God kept them intact for 1500 years until such a time that He could renew His covenant under a new Mediator (Ezekiel 36:27; Hebrews 12:27). This Person was Yeshua, and He was prefigured right in the word *Torah*.

In the days of Moses Israel's alphabet consisted of pictographs. The "t" [*tav*] was depicted by a pair of crossed sticks, and it represented a *sign*. The "o" [*vav*] looked like a tent peg *and* meant *secure* or *hook*. The "r" [*reish*] featured the head of a man and represented the idea of *top* or *first*. The final letter "h" [*hey*] pictured a man with his hands raised, and it implied *look* or *reveal*. Here's how the reader could have conceptualized the *word* Torah: "SIGN of the covenant—a CHIEF MAN securely FASTENED with RAISED ARMS for all to LOOK upon."

This pattern was established with Moses, Israel's chieftain, who prevailed for them in battle against Amalek. But this only happened when Aaron and Hur personally secured Moses' hands in a raised position (Exodus 17:11-12). Israel's very next leader, Joshua, brought victory for them by stretching out his arm with a spear and keeping it stretched out until the battle was won (Joshua 8:26). This word-picture of Torah wonderfully points to Yeshua, Israel's foremost *Chieftain*, Whose *raised arms* were *securely hooked* to a cross, the *sign* of the New Covenant.

Find strength, determination and victory today, by looking back at Yeshua's outstretched arms.

Shelam, Shalam, Shalom

"Jesus...said, It is finished: and he bowed his head, and gave up the ghost." (John 19:30)

Yeshua was not a Greek philosopher; rather, He was a Torah scholar Who immersed Himself in the ancient Hebrew language. His everyday speech was couched in Aramaic, a Semitic cousin language. When the Judean captives returned from Babylon five centuries earlier they brought back this Chaldean tongue. On top of this, two centuries prior to Yeshua the nation had the Greek culture forced upon them. Israelites who spoke Greek were known as Hellenists (Acts 6:1). Though Yeshua's first language was Hebrew, the gospel accounts give us occasional glimpses of His Aramaic tongue. To a dead damsel He said, "Talitha cumi" (Mark 5:41). From the cross He exclaimed, "Eloi, Eloi, lama sabachthani?" (Mark 15:34). In keeping with these Semitic sayings, His final Aramaic cry from the cross would have been *"Shelam!"*

Shel-ahm' means "to complete, restore: deliver." This word sounds a lot like *shalom* because it comes from the same primitive Hebrew root, *sha-lahm* meaning "to be safe; figuratively to be completed, at peace; [in various applications] make an end, finish, make good, perfect, prosper, restore, make restitution, repay." All these words speak of the Son's enduring work at Golgotha.

We are *"complete* in Him" (Colossians 2:10) having been *restored* from eternal ruin. Yeshua made us *safe* for all eternity! He *made good* on the promise to Abraham *repaying* man's sinful debt that we might be at *peace* with the Father Whose wrath is now forever satisfied. By Messiah's selfless sacrifice He "hath *perfected* forever them that are sanctified" (Hebrews 10:14). What is more, we shall also spiritually *"prosper* in his hand" (Isaiah 53:10). Full *restitution* with the Father has been made and nothing left unfinished. Hallelujah!

Show your deep gratitude to Yeshua today! Help finish the unfinished work of the gospel. Let the Spirit lead you today as you go from place to place.

In His Deaths

Part 1

"And he made his grave with...the rich in his death." (Isaiah 53:9)

In Hebrew, this word death is in the plural form, *mo-tah-yot* meaning *deaths*. The plurality denotes grandeur and intrigue; but let's examine the various aspects of His death for a moment.

Death's Estate. He poured out His soul "unto death" (v.12). The word for death is *mote* meaning "the state or place of death." Messiah's temporary dwelling place and inheritance was the grave. Oh, what a debt we owe Him and can never, ever repay!

Death's Esteem. Isaiah identified with his unbelieving people when he said, "we esteemed him not" (v.3). Mote was the Canaanite god of death. Although the word *mote* may seem very foreign, its Hebrew root *moot* means "to die, causatively to kill" and is part of our every day vocabulary. The expression "That is a *moot* point" means something that is doubtful or of little or no practical value or meaning. After "he was cut off out of the land of the living" Yeshua's own followers never dreamed He would rise from the dead and saw no practical value or meaning in His death (v.8).

Death's Estuary. Yeshua became *moot* and lay lifelessly in a "moat" just outside the Pharisees' religiously fortified walls of Jerusalem. Moat is an Old French word meaning "mound, clod" and could date back to the Hebrew root *mote* meaning death. Moats were trenches often filled with water and surrounded by steep mounds made from the dirt extracted from the 30-foot-deep trench. If the enemy were hit with an arrow and badly disabled, they could fall down the steep mound into the estuary and quickly drown. Compare a moat to a freshly dug grave which has a mound of dirt piled beside it. Perhaps this is the original idea of moat—the *moot* [the dead] were placed in the *moat*. Messiah's estuary was not below ground, but Messiah spoke prophetically through the psalmist saying, "Thou hast laid me in the lowest pit, in darkness, in the deeps" (Psalm 88:6).

Today, meditate on the humbling fact that God the Son died for you and was buried with your sins.

In His Deaths

Part 2

"He was oppressed, and he was afflicted, yet he opened not his mouth...as a sheep before her shearers is dumb, so he openeth not his mouth." (Isaiah 53:7)

Death's Estrangement. Another related word to *moot* is *mute* which means "silent; refraining from speech or utterance; incapable of speech." This describes our once lowly Saviour Who refrained from speaking at His trial and was later made incapable of speech through death. Isaiah 52:15 says that when Messiah's horrific yet atoning salvation story is told throughout the world "kings shall shut their mouths at him [i.e. *become mutes*]: for that which...they had not heard shall they consider." The prophet begs each generation of believers not to be mute concerning the gospel. He says, "who shall declare his generation?" Will you declare His wonderful words?

Death's Estimation. Messiah's death was of utmost importance for all people. Without His shed blood, the world would still lie in sin. Another related word that comes from *moot* is *mutilate,* which means to disfigure or mar. In His punishment for our sins Messiah was "marred more than any man" (52:14). In gross error, the Sanhedrin esteemed Yeshua "smitten of God" and likened Him only to a false prophet (53:4). But Isaiah clearly gave us the Father's dramatic estimation of the suffering Servant's worth: "So shall he sprinkle many nations" (52:15).

Death's Esthetics. Unlike Saul, David or Solomon, there was no natural beauty about Messiah that would make the people desire that He become their king. Isaiah notes Messiah's absence of physique or majesty saying, "there is no beauty that we should desire him" (53:2). The visionary prophet opens to us Yeshua's true spiritual beauty saying, "He was wounded for our transgressions...the chastisement of our peace was upon him; and with his stripes we are healed" (v.5).

How do you behold Him? Is He not the fairest of ten thousand to your soul? Worship Him today and praise Him for unselfishly suffering and dying for your soul.

A Perfect Picture of Yeshua's Name

"The name of the LORD is a strong tower: the righteous runneth into it, and is safe." (Proverbs 18:10)

In the Near East, a person's name was equivalent to their physical person. At Yeshua's conception, an exalted name was placed upon Him. Yeshua, the contracted form of Yehoshua, means, "Yehovah is Saviour." There is more to discover from the glorious depths found within Yeshua's sacred name by looking at the Paleo-Hebraic letters that form it. They draw a picture of His safe, tower-like cross.

The first letter in Yeshua's name is *yod,* and is depicted by an arm with a closed or open hand representing two concepts—*work* and *worship.* Upon the cross, Yeshua's hand did all the work that will ever be necessary for salvation and for His name is to be worshiped. The next letter is the *sheen,* which is depicted by two front teeth meaning *two* and *sharp.* Two is the biblical number for *union* and *division.* The name Yeshua gloriously unites those who have believing faith and sharply divides those who don't. Yeshua said, "Suppose ye that I am come to give peace on earth? I tell you, Nay; but rather division" (Luke 12:51). The third letter is *vav* and is depicted by a wooden tent peg; hence a nail. Its meaning is "to *add, secure, hook.*" Yeshua's body was hooked to the cross by sharp nails. Those who believe He bore their sins in this manner are added into His eternal Book of Life.

Now focus on the final letter, the *ayin,* which is depicted by an eye and means *shade.* Yeshua's towering cross stands as His token of protective shade which shields all who come to Him from the life-threatening elements of this fallen world. To those who are still fleeing from the fiery pains of their sin, Yeshua says, "him that cometh to me I will in no wise cast out" (John 6:37). This reassuring fact makes His refuge a place of true safety. All that He requires for entrance into His eternal refuge is a simple but sincere call of His saving name (Joel 2:32).

Spend some time today worshipping Yeshua's name and praising Him for the eternal safety and refuge He is providing you.

Taking Refuge in Yeshua

"Let us therefore come boldly unto the throne of grace, that we may obtain mercy, and find grace to help in time of need." (Hebrews 4:16)

Yesterday we saw that refuge or safety could be taken in the strong tower of Yeshua's name. The believer is encouraged to run to Him any time there is need of His safety or help. We are told to come boldly, for His home is also *our home*. The plaque beside the entrance says, "The eternal God is thy refuge, and underneath are the everlasting arms" (Deuteronomy 33:27). This wonderful description of the Saviour is known as *anthropomorphism* —"attributing human attributes to a deity." But wait! God the Son literally grew a body with arms at His incarnation, and being raised again with an everlasting body, He now possesses the strongest arms of any man in the whole universe. Now, think about that a while!

A beautiful picture of refuge was laid out for Israel in God's provision of six cities of refuge (Joshua 20:2). There were three on this side of Jordan and three on the other side. When an innocent person fled from an avenger of blood, he was safe once he reached one of the cities. His case was heard, and he was then given a place to dwell among them (v.4). The word for refuge is *meh-o-nah*. This word *meonah* also means habitation or dwelling place and has the letter *ayin* at its center. As we saw yesterday, the *ayin* in Paleo-Hebrew represents shade, and thus protection. The innocent slayer was only safe as long as he remained inside that city's ordained place of protection (v.5). After the high priest died, the slayer could return to his own city (v.6).

The wonderful thing about taking refuge in Yeshua is that this High Priest is eternal and never dies. In fact, He ever lives to make intercession for you (Hebrews 7:25). The psalmist makes his boast: "Trust in him at all times; ye people, pour out your heart before him: God is a refuge for us" (Psalm 62:8). If you have any kind of need today, flee to Yeshua's exalted throne. Stay there and plead your case before Him. He will assuredly grant you shelter until your worries are over.

Why Messiah Got Up from the Grave

"Behold, he that keepeth Israel shall neither slumber nor sleep."
(Psalm 121:4)

Israel's Shepherd was not like the shepherds of other nations; He was on constant watch. Yahweh says, "Thy shepherds slumber, O king of Assyria...thy people is scattered upon the mountains, and no man gathereth them" (Nahum 3:18). The word for sleep in our text is *yaw-shane,* a primitive root meaning, "to *be slack;* by implication to *sleep;* figuratively to *die."*

Messiah boldly proclaimed before His vulnerable flock, "I am the Good Shepherd" (John 10:11). He encouraged them by saying that He would fight to the death to protect them from "the wolf," meaning Satan. Sometime later, the Good Shepherd was fatally wounded in His encounter with the wolf. Afterwards, He was laid to rest but couldn't stay in that state lest the sheep be scattered and devoured. His love was stronger than the grave, so by His own power He caused Himself to rise up and put on strength (John 10:18). In doing so the Good Shepherd became the Great Shepherd and set out to re-gather His flock (Hebrews 13:20).

Returning to our text verse, the Great Shepherd of Israel can now be found standing and interceding upon Zion's highest hill—heaven. It is from there that the sheep's Helper now intently watches us (v.1). The Shepherd's name is merciful and mighty and one with the Father (v.2). He promises to keep your feet from slipping so you won't fall over a cliff (v.3), and He promises always to have His eye on you (v.4). Not only is He your Keeper, but also your divine Shelter (v.5). With this available protection, the sun's burning heat or the night's bitter chill will no longer worry you (v.6). Yahweh says He will preserve your soul forever (v.7). His preservation extends even to your daily routine of going out and coming in (v.8).

Messiah got up from the grave so that He could continue doing what He does best—watching over you night and day. So have a fearless day today and a peaceful night's rest.

Catching the Afterglow

"And after six days Jesus taketh with him Peter, and James, and John, and leadeth them up into an high mountain apart by themselves: and he was transfigured before them. And his raiment became shining, exceeding white as snow; so as no fuller on earth can white them." (Mark 9:2-3)

These three comprised Messiah's inner circle and were only separated from Him on rare occasions. They were constantly at His side and on various occasions held special privileges like seeing the mighty revealing of His full deity, power and glory. The *exceeding high* mountain was probably Mt. Hermon, Israel's highest by far, which has three distinct summits at 9,232 feet. It can be trekked in less than eight hours.

When they beheld Yeshua's glory, Peter wanted to immediately set up a camp and stay awhile. The Son of God definitely wanted them to experience His mountaintop glow, but there was something even more special He wanted them to catch—His *afterglow*. This was to take place on another mountain called Calvary! "And as they came down from the mountain, he charged them that they should tell no man what things they had seen, till the Son of man were risen from the dead" (v.9). The three were stunned at His glory but bewildered at His strange command; therefore, "they kept that saying with themselves, questioning one with another what the rising from the dead should mean" (v.10).

In due season the disciples learned exactly what Messiah's rising from the dead meant. Once they caught the *afterglow* of His amazing resurrection, they were never the same. His afterglow was truly more glorious than they could have ever imagined.

Yeshua's resurrection *afterglow* is also freely available for you to catch if you have eyes of faith. Dear saint, can you see Him now in all of His resurrection power? Today, if you will draw close to Him in quiet communion and stay long enough in His presence, you will begin to glow with all of His redeeming, radiant, royal love.

The Forsaking of Shiloh
Part 1

"But go ye now unto my place which was in Shiloh, where I set my name at the first, and see what I did to it for the wickedness of my people Israel." (Jeremiah 7:12)

Shiloh (meaning *tranquil*) was a beautiful city in the Samarian hill country. After the conquest of Canaan, "the whole congregation of the children of Israel assembled together at Shiloh, and set up the Tabernacle of the congregation there" (Joshua 18:1). This *Tent of Meeting* rested in Shiloh for a total of 369 years. Tractate Zevahim 14 informs us that the *Mishkan,* or Tabernacle, was restructured with "a building of stone below, and cloth above." Many of the large tent-stake holes for securing the ropes to the animal-skin roof were bored in bedrock and are still visible today.

The calamitous time came when Israel met the Philistines at Aphek. They suffered utter defeat and the loss of the ark. Eli, the high priest, along with his two sons, Hophni and Phinehas, and 30,000 foot soldiers all died in one unforgettable day (1 Samuel 4). Not only did the Philistine army parade their new showpiece, the Ark, back to the temple of Dagon in Ashdod, evidently one contingent of troops advanced upon Shiloh to destroy the Hebrews' religious capital (1 Samuel 5:2). Fearing the loss of all the Tabernacle treasures, the priests hurriedly whisked them away into a secret place. The ark was recovered seven months later, and within a few decades, it was brought up to Jerusalem by David to rest in a public place.

What set this dismal chain of events into motion was *not* the unsanctioned removal of the ark, but Israel's love of "graven images" (Psalm 78:58). Phinehas' distraught wife, who suddenly went into labor upon hearing the tragic news, could only repeat over and over again before dying, "The glory is departed from Israel" (1 Samuel 4:22).

As you linger in prayer this morning, thank the LORD for His promise to never leave you nor forsake you. But also ask Him if there's something unsanctioned you have done that is grieving Him.

The Forsaking of Shiloh
Part 2

"When God heard this…he forsook the tabernacle of Shiloh, the tent which he placed among men." (Psalm 78:59-60)

The Hebrew word translated forsook comes from the root *natash* meaning, "to *pound*, that is, *smite*," however, it also means, "to *leave* or *let alone*." Once Yahweh decided to withdraw His protective presence and *leave* the center of Israelite worship, the advancing Philistine armies began to *smite* and *pound* the encampment at Shiloh. The psalmist describes how God in His wrath, "delivered his strength [*Israel*] into captivity, and his glory [*the ark*] into the enemy's hand" (v.61).

It is often helpful to use the principle of first-mention to allow the Bible to define the original sense of a word clearly. In doing so now, we discover that the word "Shiloh" is a prophetic reference to Israel's Messiah. Jacob attached this epithet to Judah's future King saying, "The scepter shall not depart from Judah, nor a lawgiver from between his feet, until Shiloh come; unto him shall the *gathering of the people* be" (Genesis 49:10). When Shiloh, the tranquil "Prince of Peace" arrived, the impoverished *multitudes gathered* around Him to hear His words of comfort. Shiloh didn't care much for the crowded city life but preferred the tranquil Galilean hill country. This didn't deter thousands of desperate souls from tracing His divine footsteps to obtain a permanent cure for all their physical woes. The most prominent reason Shiloh came was to cure sinful hearts.

Like the citizens who were forced to leave the capital city of Shiloh, the time came in cyclical fashion when Yeshua's disciples "all forsook him, and fled" (Mark 14:50). Moreover, God the Father "forsook the [*human*] tabernacle of Shiloh [*Yeshua*], the [*holy*] tent which he placed among men." At the cross Yeshua expressed his feeling of being utterly forsaken by the Father (Mark 15:34). If the Father had an answer, it would be this—"for the wickedness of my people Israel" (Jeremiah 7:12). Meditate on this today and praise Shiloh for making peace between you and God.

117

The Forsaking of Shiloh
Part 3

"My God, my God, Why hast thou forsaken me?" (Psalm 22:1)

After Shiloh uttered these pitiful words from Golgotha's tree, some bystanders thought He was calling for Elijah's help. One adversary mockingly brought Shiloh a little vinegar to moisten His mouth that He might cry out all the more. In great fulfillment of the forsaking typology, this mocker then exclaimed, "Let alone [*step back, leave, forsake*]; let us see whether Elijah will come" (Mark 15:36). According to Scripture, no one came: "Lover and friend hast thou put far from me, and mine acquaintances into darkness" (Psalm 88:18).

Messiah was left for dead and forsaken by heaven and earth alike. Only a few Galilean followers standing nearby in the supernatural noonday dark could mournfully lament how the Glory had departed from Israel. Reflecting on Psalm 78:60, Yahweh delivered His Glory (Yeshua, the anti-type of the ark) into the enemy's hand and His strength (Israel) into Roman captivity. Israel has seen more than its fair share of sorrowful sunsets; but because the sun also rises, Shiloh will return at the end of days and gather all Israel unto Himself and "cut off the names of the idols out of the land, and they shall no more be remembered" (Zechariah 13:2).

Do you ever feel abandoned? Have friends and family left you alone to swim or sink? Do your feelings of isolation seem to overwhelm you? Well, first, realize that these are opportunities for you to come to know your Redeemer in a deeper way through "the fellowship of his sufferings" (Philippians 3:10). This will also give you a better appreciation for "the power of his resurrection." Second, be reminded that Shiloh has not forsaken you, nor will He, nor can He because of His promise (Hebrews 13:5). He may withhold His blessings if you have grieved Him in some way, but His glory shall never depart from you. If necessary, let any and all idols go from your grasp today. In place thereof, hold on to His promise with one hand and hold out praise to Him with the other.

The Bread of Death

"In the sweat of thy face shalt thou eat bread, till thou return unto the ground; for out of it wast thou taken: for dust thou art, and unto dust shalt thou return." (Genesis 3:19)

In the Book of Beginnings, there are many references to bread. These present pictures of the Lord's *death*, our *communion* with Him, and the *comfort* His Spirit brings. Let us look at just the first picture of bread—death. The very first mention of bread (above) casts a prominent shadow upon the subject of death. God uses bread to illustrate Adam's curse. Since bread is made from ground wheat, every time Adam began grinding wheat to dust he was reminded of his ultimate future. It was his constant prelude to death. Abraham likened death to dust saying, "I...am but dust and ashes" (Genesis 18:27).

Like Adam and all his descendants who sweated as a sign of their mortality, the man Messiah Yeshua one day willingly crossed the bridge of immortality and became covered in sweat, "great drops...falling to the ground" (Luke 22:44). It was not hot sweat, but cold sweat as death's door began to swing open for Him. Soon, like His sweat, Yeshua Himself would go into the earth. This all began in Gethsemane, a garden like the place where Adam first experienced his sweaty prelude to death. Just a few short hours before the Son of God began His descent into the earth, He drew the analogy between bread and His death saying, "Take, eat: this is my body, which is broken for you...For as often as ye eat this bread...ye do show the Lord's death till he come" (1 Corinthians 11:24, 26). Even earlier Messiah made another prominent reference to His body and food saying, "I am that bread of life" and "my flesh is meat indeed" (John 6:48, 55).

When you partake of the communion bread, you are partaking in the Saviour's death. But you must also be dead to sin to appreciate its worth fully. In your quiet time today, consider the immensity of the Bread of Life and the Bread of Death.

Why the Resurrection?

"For thou wilt not leave my soul in hell; neither wilt thou suffer thine Holy One to see corruption." (Psalm 16:10)

With seven being the number of perfection and completion, let us count the seven reasons why God raised Messiah from the dead. First, *there was a promise given,* and therefore, the promise must be kept. We see this clearly in our text verse. Second, *it proved that Yeshua was Who He said He was*—God's unique Son (Romans 1:4). Yeshua's incredible claim to deity was at last vindicated. Third, *it gave Messiah victory over His enemies.* Messiah prophesied through the psalmist saying, "I will extol thee, O LORD; for thou hast lifted me up, and hast not made my foes to rejoice over me. O LORD, thou hast brought up my soul from the grave" (Psalm 30:1, 2). The fourth reason He was raised from the dead was *to bring praise to the Father.* "Wilt thou show wonders to the dead? Shall the dead arise and praise thee?" (Psalm 88:10). When Yeshua arose, this question became a fulfilled prophecy.

Fifth, Yeshua's rising again *gives us complete and lasting atonement.* Once again, Messiah speaks from the grave saying, "What profit is there in my blood, when I go down to the pit?" (Psalm 30:9). Indeed, there could be no atonement without an eternal High Priest to officiate over the sacrificial blood. The apostle wrote that Yeshua "was delivered for our offences, and was raised again for our justification" (Romans 4:25). Sixth, the resurrection *gives believers a new way of walking.* "Therefore we are buried with him by baptism into death: that like as Christ was raised up from the dead…even so we also should walk in newness of life" (Romans 6:4). Seventh, the resurrection of Messiah *gives us an unfailing token* of our own future bodily resurrection. "Knowing that he which raised up the Lord Jesus shall raise up us also by Jesus" (2 Corinthians 4:14).

Why the resurrection? The simplest way of answering this question is this: It changes everything! May these thoughts on the resurrection change your day and your outlook as you meditate on them in prayer this morning.

ℳiracle 𝒫ower

"Who are kept by the power of God through faith unto salvation ready to be revealed in the last time." (1 Peter 1:5)

The shepherd of the Jerusalem flock encourages us by saying we "are kept by the power of God." This is exciting news for those times when we tend to forget Whom the great Keeper of Israel is (Psalm 121:4). The Hebrew word for keeper is *shomer* meaning guard or watchman. God successfully guarded the souls of Abraham, Isaac and Jacob during times of drought. He also kept Israel safe and guarded them with a pillar of fire when the Egyptian army came after them. One morning the citizens of Jerusalem awoke to find 185,000 Assyrian soldiers lying dead outside their city walls. His power was so manifest at those times that the most faint-hearted of believers must have been supernaturally revived.

If God has no problem keeping our bodies safe, then He will do no less of a miracle with our souls. Knowing this, you can rest in your "faith unto salvation." You can also go on to do great things for your Saviour without fear of death; otherwise, fear inhibits your gospel progress. Fresh soldiers on a battlefield sometimes get so struck with fear that they become immobilized. They can't move their feet. Someone has to get them off the battlefield quickly or into a place of safety. God doesn't want His gospel soldiers to be like this, so He may let us experience a little battle-readiness from time to time—conditioning for our Great Commissioning.

With these assurances in place, your salvation is "ready to be revealed in the last [set] time." David, Daniel and Paul also talked about the last days when our bodies would go through a miraculous change—from mortality to immortality. Because the early church was aware of this fact, they went out and did great things for God. Peter's confidence in full salvation caused him to burst into doxology exclaiming, "Blessed be the God and Father of our Lord Jesus Christ, which according to his abundant mercy hath begotten us again unto a lively hope by the resurrection of Jesus Christ from the dead" (v.3-4).

Today, let praise, not fear, regulate your heartbeat.

Cradled in the Glory of God

"And the name of Amram's wife was Jochebed...and she bare unto Amram Aaron and Moses, and Miriam their sister." (Numbers 26:59)

Yochebed's name means "Yah is glorious," and this name was highly prophetic. Moses' mother cradled him close in those first months being so fearful that her baby would be taken and killed. After he was too big to hide, Yochebed took a basket, waterproofed it, and set it sailing down the river. By faith, she left the outcome in Yahweh's hands. Moses' time in the dark basket and out of his mother's arms was short-lived. Yochebed was quickly summoned into the presence of royalty where she experienced God's predestined plan. She could return home and continue cradling her baby until he was fully weaned. Knowing that Moses was destined for the inside of Egypt's palace walls, Yochebed must have felt God cradling them both.

Forty years later Moses was praying on top of the Mountain of God. There he asked a reasonable, yet very assuming question to Yahweh: "Show me thy glory" (Exodus 33:18). Moses saw his opportunity to be cradled in the divine Light. His request was fulfilled with only one precondition. Yahweh responded saying, "it shall come to pass, while my glory passes by, that I will put thee in a cleft of the rock, and will cover thee with my hand" (Exodus 33:22).

Blood-washed saint, rest assured that Yahweh cradles you as well as the rest of His covenant children, albeit in different ways. These precious moments are sometimes fleeting, but nonetheless wonderful and powerful in their restorative affect—moments that can hardly be forgotten. Moses spoke of every believer's opportunity to be cradled in God's glory. He declared, "The eternal God is thy refuge, and underneath are the everlasting arms" (Deuteronomy 33:27).

Once you are nestled in the Saviour's glorious bosom you will discover that His strong arms bear the covenant marks of His eternal love for you. Spend time cradled in Yeshua's arms today.

Here, Drink This

"But Jesus said unto them, Ye know not what ye ask: can ye drink of the cup that I drink of?" (Mark 10:38)

Every devoted subject within a kingdom deeply desires the honor and privilege of sitting next to the king and drinking from his cup. James and John were two such people and urgently placed their requests before their Davidic Lord (v.37). When they did, their question was met with an even more incredible question: "Can ye drink of the cup that I drink of and be baptized with the baptism that I am baptized with?" Presumptuously and with lit-up faces the two disciples replied, "We can!" The lead disciples, James and John (v.35) wanted to share the Messiah's Victory Cup, but they knew not that He was referring to a different cup (v.39). The Father chose a strange baptism for His only begotten Son, but there was a big benefit in it. The Father has also chosen baptisms of suffering that equally benefit His adopted sons and daughters.

Only a little more than a decade after Messiah's baptism of death, James received his when Herod beheaded him with the sword (Acts 12:2). Tradition holds that John received his baptism when Emperor Domitian ordered him thrown into a cauldron of boiling oil. When the apostle remained unharmed, the emperor had him banished to the island of Patmos. Tertullian, a third-century Christian historian, seems responsible for reporting this event as a historical fact. Throughout the ages, King Messiah has regularly handed His cup of suffering to countless numbers of devoted followers. Each in turn drank the dregs of an untimely and unimaginable death. Some were tied to stakes to await high tide—baptismal waters that would turbulently flow over their heads.

There are many organizations that help the persecuted saints, and every non-persecuted church or saint should be intricately involved. As you seek Lord Yeshua's will today, ask Him how you can help those who are daily facing such fiery trials of faith.

Necessary Gardening

"They made me the keeper of the vineyards; but mine own vineyard have I not kept." (Song of Solomon 1:6)

How easy it is for a believer to get caught up in life's many requirements to the neglect of his own essential, spiritual well-being! He labors hard to produce a physical harvest for his earthly master, but upon returning home finds little or no motivation to produce a good harvest for himself.

Perhaps the lack of motivation is found in the fact that you have never tasted the unique sweetness that hangs from that overly familiar vine in your own backyard. You let the birds pick from its low-yielding clusters while thinking, "I'll just let them enjoy its goodness. I haven't the time to collect what little is there." Yet the birds fly away from your abandoned treasury filled with joy and singing the merriest of songs. No, they cannot *tend* to your vineyard, but they have sense enough to *taste* it.

Perhaps your disregard for your own vineyard is due to the regular allotment of grapes your earthly master allows you to bring home from his vast vineyards. How can you be sufficed with the pale and bitter grapes this world's barren soil brings forth when the soil in your own vineyard has been fertilized with the King's royal blood nourishing it and producing the richest, reddest grapes on earth?

To be blessed, happy, and thriving you will need to find time to tend your own spiritual vine regularly. Meditate daily on the Word of God for your vital enrichment and pray over which branches you should trim from your cluttered vine. Also, be sure to protect your vineyard from *winter's* frostbite and *spring's* "little foxes, which spoil the vine" (2:15). Finally, fear not when *summer's* long, hot, dry days seem to never end. Your vineyard will endure that coming drought and yield you a perfect, fruitful harvest at autumn's onset.

Moses the Baptizer

"Moreover, brethren, I would not that ye should be ignorant, how that all our fathers were under the cloud, and all passed through the sea; And were all baptized unto Moses in the cloud and in the sea." (1 Corinthians 10:1-2)

Within Judaism, ritual immersions must take place under rabbinical supervision. As Israel exited Egypt's dark world of slavery and bondage, the nation's first immersion took place under Moses' authoritative name. That baptism pictured a future baptism in the regenerating waters of the Holy Spirit under the name of the Son of God (Titus 3:5). As the Messianic age began to dawn, a Levite came first with the authority to baptize repentant Israelites. His name was Yohanan ben Zecharyah—John, the son of Zacharias. His purpose was to prepare people to hear and receive the Messiah.

Once the faithful remnant understood Yeshua's role and authority, they came to Him to be baptized, not John (John 3:26). Yeshua's baptism speaks of many things; one of which is spiritual enlightenment. That is why the gospel writer records Yeshua's sermon on light and then ties it to His authoritative baptism (v.22). When the Jewish remnant came to Messiah, they were coming to His holy light (v.19-21). A short time later Gentiles also desired Messiah's spiritual illumination and underwent His baptism. Paul speaks of the believers' collective immersion saying, "For by one Spirit are we all baptized into one body [Messiah's], whether we be Jews or Gentiles...and have been all made to drink into one Spirit" (1 Corinthians 12:13). If you have received Christ, then you have definitely received His Spirit baptism. You are safe and sure to reach the other side of eternity!

Have you been illuminated by the Holy Spirit to see that Yeshua is fully God and that He fully died for *all* your sins—past, present and future? If so, have you submitted to His literal water baptism since coming to full faith? Though this baptism is only symbolic, it is necessary so that you can fulfill all righteousness (Matthew 3:15). This morning as you come to Messiah's glorious light in prayer, allow Him to manifest His plan and purposes for you concerning this day.

The Choice Vine

"Binding his foal unto the vine, and his ass's colt unto the choice vine; he washed his garments in wine, and his clothes in the blood of grapes: His eyes shall be red with wine, and his teeth white with milk." (Genesis 49:11-12)

This poetic prophecy refers to Messiah whom Jacob affectionately titles *Shiloh* in verse 10. The donkey and her foal are Messiah's transport to the choice vine; that is to say, the cross. And the blood of grapes, an acceptable substitute for real blood when making a covenant, speaks of Messiah's bloody death. This prophecy was cryptic at the time, but further prophecy and its fulfillment brings light upon it.

The Hebrew word for choice vine is *soreq*, which denotes the sense of *redness*—the richest variety of grapes. A related prophecy is given that adds detail more than a thousand years later. In Zechariah 9:9, a young donkey remains the central token of Jacob's prophecy. Now, we see that this donkey has never been ridden, nor does it refuse its new Master. Zechariah informs us that Shiloh is perfectly righteous, humble, and is Jerusalem's long-awaited Messiah. Shiloh arrives 500 years later, and only days after His triumphal entry on the back of the untamed beast, the Romans begin to draw blood. After scourging Him they "put his own clothes on him, and led him out to crucify him" (Mark 15:20). The *redness* of flowing blood quickly stained the fabric of Shiloh's garments fulfilling the ancient prophecy.

The *redness* of Shiloh's eyes was mainly due to the constant flow of blood coming from the wounds inflicted by His crown of thorns. This reality created a situation where He could see sinful mankind through the blood-red film that remained over His eyes. An experiment worth trying is to view the red letters in your Bible through transparent red film. The red letters will appear as white as the background! No other two matching colors will duplicate this process. Jacob's reference to Shiloh's white teeth speak of the pure truth that proceeds from His mouth. Though your sins be red like crimson, they shall be whiter than snow when the Holy Spirit places the Son's royal-red blood upon your heart's door (Isaiah 1:18). Today, praise Yeshua for providing so great a salvation for you.

The Faithful Servant

"And I will raise me up a faithful priest, that shall do according to that which is in mine heart and in my mind: and I will build him a sure house; and he shall walk before mine anointed for ever." (1 Samuel 2:35)

An unnamed man of God came and brought these words to Eli as he neared 100 years of age. Yahweh had grown weary with His high priest's lack of steadfastness. What He wanted was a faithful priest. Here the word for faithful is *naaman* from the root *aman* meaning to *believe* or *trust*. God uses the word *naaman* again when He speaks of building Eli's replacement a "sure" house—a *firm* house. In the next chapter, *naaman* appears yet again where it is translated "established" meaning something *attested* to. "And all Israel from Dan even to Beersheba knew that Samuel was established to be a prophet of the LORD" (3:20). Eli's problems were not *being faithful* in the maintenance of the menorah, not *being firm* with his wayward sons, and not *attesting* to the truth that the ark should remain in the Tabernacle.

God is looking for the quality of faithfulness and trustworthiness in His saints. This quality is measured by how well our lives attest to His commandments. We live in a generation of quitters who cannot endure hardness and testing. They fold under the slightest of pressure and struggle to shine through the present darkness. Messiah challenged His followers saying, "Who then is that faithful and wise steward, whom his lord shall make ruler over his household, to give them their portion of meat in due season?" (Luke 12:42). The everyday diet of the Near East was vegetarian; therefore, Yeshua was actually referring to making a grand celebration—killing the fatted calf—for those servants who remained steadfast in their duties. Paul also emphasized the key to good servanthood saying, "it is required in stewards, that a man be found faithful" (1 Corinthians 4:2).

This morning, ask the Lord to help you in an area where you might need more steadfastness like Bible reading, prayer, giving, worship, showing loving kindness, or sharing the Good News with others.

A Mother's Day Plea

"Now there cried a certain woman of the wives of the sons of the prophets unto Elisha, saying...my husband is dead; and thou knowest that thy servant did fear the LORD: and the creditor is come to take unto him my two sons to be bondmen." (2 Kings 4:1)

The recently widowed woman had never demanded anything from the miracle-working prophet, but the time finally came. Her troubles were about to be doubled, so she cried out to Israel's great intercessor and was heard. Elisha's initial response brought her no comfort: "Tell me, what hast thou in the house?" (v.2). If the widow had anything in her house to pay her husband's debt, she would have already done so. A pot of oil was the only thing she had of any immediate value, but it was worth so little. However, the widow's *lack* was God's *luster*. God loves to shine when our world is at its darkest. The prophet told the bereaved and distraught widow to borrow all the vessels in the village she could muster and get to pouring. By day's end, she was the biggest wholesaler of olive oil in the area. After selling her precious commodity at the market there was not only enough money to rid her of heartless creditors, but also to rid her of other cares for the next little while (v.7).

Whether you are down to your last two pennies or last two sons, God stands ready to save. After all, His name is Saviour. When you are no longer in control that is when the Saviour is ready to step in and show *His* control. He is strongest when you are at your weakest. This is why He allows you time to lose sight of your own strength before He allows you to see all of His. When you cry for His help He may give you a special assignment in return—a test of trust—but don't be discouraged! His aid is on the way. High-ranking officials on earth have their aids, and God is certainly not without His. Sometimes we call them angels; other times we call them neighbors or friends.

Take your need to the Lord today. He has the perfect supply. He will meet your need of the hour and not a minute too late.

Lift Off!

"For if ye forgive men their trespasses, your heavenly Father will also forgive you: But if ye forgive not men their trespasses, neither will your Father forgive your trespasses." (Matthew 6:14-15)

Time and again, aeronautical engineers at NASA have combined their talents to launch various kinds of rockets and spaceships into outer space. Spacecraft weigh a lot, and so the ability to successfully overcome earth's gravity and put a rocket into weightless orbit above earth's atmosphere is a great challenge. The final stage of their effort begins with the exciting words, "We have lift off!" When this takes place, hearts are made glad and jubilation fills the air.

There is a little secret behind the name NASA. The four letters are an acronym for National Aeronautical Space Administration, but these four letters are also an ancient Hebrew word. *Nasa*, pronounced nah-sah, means, "to *lift.*" God uses the word when He asks us to *forgive* someone. What God desires from us is simply to *lift* someone's burden off of them. It really doesn't matter how they obtained the heavy burden; what is important is that we *lift* that burden off of them. When someone says to you, "Do you forgive me?" what he or she is asking for is your assistance in removing an unwanted load from his or her soul. They are depending on you because only you can lift it from them.

The word forgive is conceptually the most important word in the entire Bible. Unforgiveness is its ugly twin and carries an incalculable weight. When you forgive someone, you help them experience the "weightlessness" and freedom from the heavy pull of their transgression, their error.

God permanently *lifted* your heavy burden of sin, shame and sorrow. So why not go and do likewise? Today, think of someone who might need your forgiveness. Break their bonds with your healing words and a prayer of forgiveness and reconciliation.

Mother's Finest

"For I was my father's son, tender and only beloved in the sight of my mother." (Proverbs 4:3)

Mothers' finest boys in the Bible were *not* usually the firstborn sons who held the birthright position. Although firstborn sons were the rightful heirs, the favored ones were often the next born. Second-born sons are sometimes listed first in a grouping like *"Abram,* Nahor, and Haran" and *"Shem,* Ham, and Japheth." Abraham and Shem are only listed first because of their prominence in the Messianic line.

Earth's very first mother, Eve, had two sons. Her finest son was Abel, the second born who brought God the acceptable offering. Noah's wife had three sons. Her finest was not Japheth the elder, but rather Shem, in whose tents God said He would dwell (Genesis 10:21; 9:27). Terra's wife had three sons. Her finest was Abraham, a second born who became the father of the Hebrew people and people of faith. Sarah had two sons. Her finest was not Ishmael, but Isaac the second born. He obediently submitted to his father's every request. Rebekah had two sons. Her finest was not Esau the first born, but Jacob who wrestled with the angel and became a prince with God. Leah had six sons. Her finest was Levi, a second born who became the progenitor of the priestly tribe. The wife of Jesse had eight sons. Her finest was not the eldest but the youngest, David. He became the fearless giant killer and Judah's venerated king.

There was one first born named Joseph (belonging to Rachel) who was highly favored and went on to save his entire clan from starvation. Miriam of the New Testament, also known as Mary, had five sons altogether (Matthew 13:55). Her finest was also a firstborn, Yeshua, Who conquered death, hell, and the grave and now rules the universe and sits upon His Father's throne.

Today, whether you are a first-born or second-born child, be sure to make your firm identification with "the first born among many brethren," and that is Yeshua (Romans 8:29). Also, this Mother's Day give your mother a special thank you for all she's done for you over the years.

You Are So Blessed!

"And he led them out as far as to Bethany, and he lifted up his hands, and blessed them." (Luke 24:50)

Luke ended his gospel account of Yeshua's glorious life and ministry with this beautiful story. He recorded Messiah's final act as He stood on the backside of the Mount of Olives with His devoted ones. "And it came to pass while he blessed them, he was parted from them, and carried up into heaven" (v.51). Luke didn't reveal the exact words Lord Yeshua spoke over His disciples upon the Mount of Ascension; nevertheless, what the Eternal High Priest most likely said—especially with His hands outstretched—was the priestly blessing known as the *Birkat Kohanim*.

This prayerful benediction was always done publically and goes like this: "The LORD bless thee, and keep thee: The LORD make his face shine upon thee, and be gracious unto thee: The LORD lift up his countenance upon thee, and give thee peace" (Numbers 6:24-26). Yahweh instructed the priests saying, "And they shall put my name upon the children of Israel; and I will bless them" (v.27). This blessing was also known as *Nesiat Kapayim*, the lifting of the hands, and the high priest always recited it from a raised rostrum in keeping with Leviticus 9:22. In wonderful fulfillment of this little detail of the raised platform, the new Melchizedek Priest began slowly and supernaturally ascending to heaven as He neared the end of His recitation over them. No other high priest had done this before, nor ever shall.

You are so blessed this day because your Great High Priest Yeshua has put His name upon you and ever lives to bless you and make intercession for you. Don't go out the front door today dreading what might go wrong or what went wrong yesterday. Instead of leaving home with doubt and discomfort, head out in Yeshua's name shining in His strength, love and blessing! Be led forth with peace for the High Priest of our profession has placed His divine blessing upon you that includes His protection, His favor and His shalom. Do what the disciples did after Yeshua blessed them—continually praise and bless God (Luke 24:53).

$\mathcal{N}eed \; \mathcal{A} \; \mathcal{F}acelift?$

"And they came to Jericho: and as he went out of Jericho with his disciples and a great number of people, blind Bartimaeus, the son of Timaeus, sat by the highway side begging." (Mark 10:46)

The key to this story is in the meaning of Bartimaeus' name. Mark clearly draws our attention to it. Timaeus comes from the Hebrew word *tah-may'* meaning "foul, defiled, polluted, unclean," and *bar* is Aramaic for "son." Thus, this blind beggar was not known by his *own* name, but by his father's degrading name. All blind Bartimaeus' days were gray and clouded. Not one day passed by that his head wasn't hung down in despair or disgrace. His lot in life was to sit on the dusty sidelines and cry, "Woe is me." But one day he heard that Messiah was exiting the city, and so "he began to cry out...Jesus, thou son of David, have mercy on me" (v.47).

The Greek word for cry is *krad-zo* meaning to *shriek,* or *scream.* This was his one chance. There would never be another! "And many charged him that he should hold his peace: but he cried the more a great deal" (v.48). Yeshua heard him, hailed him and then healed him. From that day forward, it was all sunshine and roses because the *son of the defiled* had come face to face with the Son of David and was elevated from a pauper to a prince.

Some say Yeshua never claimed to be God; but in fact, one scripture He fulfilled speaks very dramatically of God. "The LORD maketh poor, and maketh rich: he bringeth low, and lifteth up. He raiseth up the poor out of the dust, and lifteth up the beggar from the dunghill, to set them among princes, and to make them inherit the throne of glory" (1 Samuel 2:7-8).

If you have always felt belittled, maybe this has happened so that your desire would be always towards God, that He might have pity on you. Maybe your finances, health or happiness has changed recently causing your face to hang down low. Well, don't be dismayed! "Be of good comfort, rise; he calleth thee" (Mark 10:49). Today, do as Bartimaeus did. Cast away your garments of gloom and come to the Saviour. Receive a facelift, for in His presence is the fullness of joy.

The Sign of the New Covenant

"In whom also ye are circumcised with the circumcision made without hands, in putting off the body of the sins of the flesh by the circumcision of Christ: Buried with him in baptism," (Colossians 2:11-12)

Greeks thought in abstract ways, but Hebrews thought in concrete terms. Promises by individuals, therefore, were seldom taken seriously unless they were also accompanied with a visible token of the promise. It could be almost anything, but it had to be something one could see, touch or keep. The token of the Mosaic Covenant was something visible that both God and man could see—a scar.

The Mosaic circumcision involved the removal of part of man's unneeded flesh, but God's ultimate aim was to remove the unwanted stony layer around man's adamant heart. "And the LORD thy God will circumcise thine heart...to love the LORD thy God with all thine heart, and with all thy soul, that thou mayest live" (Deuteronomy 30:6). This type of circumcision happens the moment one receives Yeshua as LORD and Saviour. Only God can see this circumcision, so He gives the born-again believer a *visible token* of His inner work that both you and He can see— water baptism. The outward sign of a circumcised heart is also a *changed life*. Other people can see this, too.

Receiving the new birth without receiving water baptism is like receiving a marriage partner without receiving a ring, the token of the other person's lasting commitment. With reciprocal love, the Son of God received from mankind his strange token—a baptism of death, a literal grave! Now it's your turn to receive His baptism by simply going under water and dying to the self-life (Romans 6:3)! Let me highlight this. When new converts living in deeply persecuted lands profess faith in the Saviour and undergo water baptism, they also commit themselves to the possibility of a different kind of baptism—literal death.

Are you this committed to the cold waters of baptism? Has your heart truly been changed? Be fully committed to the Lord before going out today.

The Backspace Key

"Neither let him which is in the field return back to take his clothes." (Mark 24:18)

Recently while typing I couldn't help but notice the most well worn key on my keyboard—the *backspace*. We are prone to hit this button more than any other. It is one thing to hit the backspace on a keyboard, but another thing altogether to *back up* on our kingdom walk. Our King also declared, "No man, having put his hand to the plow, and *looking back*, is fit for the kingdom of God" (Luke 9:62). Despite His urgent warning, "many of his disciples *went back*, and walked no more with him" (John 6:66). How sad! Even though they had beheld His miracles and tasted of His manna, they weren't unlike their forefathers who *turned back* again to Egypt "in their hearts" (Acts 7:39). How often we, too, turn back in our hearts while allowing others to believe we're still moving forward.

Even the best of followers can struggle to stay in perfect step with the divine Son. Remember Yeshua's orthodox parents who took Him to the Temple for a festival? They had to go "*back again* to Jerusalem, seeking him" (Luke 2:45). Sometimes we're too quick to leave our assemblies, our prayer closets and our Bibles when instead we should linger a while longer to just dwell in His presence.

Sometimes we're like Hananiah and Sapphira who "*kept back* part of the price" (Acts 5:1-2). We hit the backspace key when it comes to giving saying, "Oh, I need this fifty. I'll just give the five." Because of our tendency to backslide, the writer to the Hebrews brings us encouragement saying, "For yet a little while, and he that shall come will come, and will not tarry. Now the just shall live by faith: but if any man *draw back*, my soul shall have no pleasure in him. But we are not of them who draw back unto perdition; but of them that believe to the saving of the soul" (Hebrews 10:37-39).

Today, ask the Lord to help you avoid hitting that "backspace key," and pray that He will help you to use the "control key" of His Spirit all through the day.

Beth Aven & the Avon Company

"And Joshua sent men from Jericho to Ai, which is beside Bethaven, on the east side of Bethel." (Joshua 7:2)

In Canaan, two cities were just opposite each other—Beit El, the *House* of *God,* and Beit Aven, the *House* of *Vanity.* These two cities symbolized the two ways of life. A person has the option of either living for God or living for the vain and empty things often found in life. The House of Vanity drew its name from the emptiness, uselessness and wickedness of relying upon idols. The classical Hebrew word *aven* also bears a relationship to *avon,* translated as "iniquity or perversity," which implies some form of "moral *evil* or *mischief.*" Although *avon* is pronounced *ah-vone,* its spelling is immediately recognized as the name of one of the leading sellers of beauty supplies in the world.

An Irishman who sold books door-to-door for a publishing house in the 1880s originally began the Avon Company. His sales were down, so he formulated some perfumes and gave away small samples to entice women to buy his books. Because they were more interested in his perfumes than his books, he began a perfume company, and the rest is history.

In this modern Church age, we have often let vanities grow around us like weeds. In the process, we have ignored God's desire to grow in us. Old Bibles are being replaced with Bibles that are more modern and contemporary songs are replacing old hymns. Electric guitar strings are drowning out piano strings, and more frequently, the cross is being taken down and replaced by a world globe or some other artistic centerpiece. The true gospel is being supplanted with feel-good messages and repentance is a word that no longer seems to fit. The House of Vanity disdains the thought of godly repentance and replaces it with a new mantra—"Realize your potential." Yeshua, to Whom the House of God belongs, said, "without me ye can do nothing" (John 15:5).

Today, ask the Lord to show you something in your life that you have been relying upon that is empty and meaningless; then get rid of it or turn from it.

Are You Set?

"All these...were chosen to be porters in the gates...whom David and Samuel the seer did ordain in their set office." (1 Chronicles 9:22)

Porters were of the Levitical tribe. Their job was to watch at every gate from the inner court all the way to the outer court. Their watch included the Temple doors. They were to be on guard for unclean persons who might be coming in. Some who felt they were inwardly unclean or unworthy willingly stood afar off (Luke 18:13). The porters warmly greeted incoming worshippers, but sometimes they had to refuse someone who was ceremonially unfit. A porter's job was not an easy one; extreme vigilance was necessary (Mark 13:34). The porter's job was not always thankworthy because rejected worshippers could become offended or even indignant. Nonetheless, if the House of Yahweh was to be a holy place, it would have to be kept free of any and all defilement.

Just shortly before the time of Christ, Samaritans came in and defiled the Temple compound by scattering dead men's bones in various places. At that time, the porters must have been a bit careless in their set duties. The root of the Hebrew word for "set office" is *emunah*. Emunah is the word commonly translated as faith meaning *"firmness; (figuratively) security; moral fidelity."* As the duly appointed Temple security, porters had to be spiritually and physically upright, and when necessary, very firm with those who were not. They had to be extremely *set* in their *office* or the house of God would become just a "house of cards" ready to tumble at any moment.

Are you set in your holy office, as a porter would be? Are you "showing all good fidelity" to the LORD (Titus 2:10)? If you aren't, you are jeopardizing the sanctity of your assembly. If need be, take a time out today and get reconciled to God, sanctified in your heart, and refreshed in your spirit because it is to the sanctified soul "that the porter openeth" (John 10:3). And once you enter His house you can truly set your heart to praise Adonai Yeshua.

Raptured!

"The voice of my beloved! behold, he cometh leaping upon the mountains, skipping upon the hills." (Song of Solomon 2:8)

The long winter waiting period of the bride and groom suddenly culminates with sight and sound. Gray skies are replaced with blue. Barren brown earth quickly becomes overspread with green carpets decked with colorful wild flowers. Birds now shower the air with glad songs, and trees that had seemed dead now show forth their blossoms (v.11-13).

The bride was listening daily to the familiar voices of family, friends and her many fair maidens; but now all those wonderful voices are replaced, even drowned out by the single voice of the groom who is "altogether lovely" (5:16). This speaks of our heavenly Groom, the Son of God. He is coming in grandeur never before seen. He is so much larger than life that He makes His ever-bounding path to our hearts by running and jumping from one mountain peak to another. He will stride the rough hills as though they're mere stones in a riverbed until He's within our reach. Our Beloved is appearing so suddenly, however, that we have only a short time to wake from our slumber. He beckons us, His bride, saying, "Rise up, my love, my fair one, and come away" (2:10). After we join Him hand in hand, nothing will ever separate us again.

This ancient story from Solomon's poetic writings pictures the imminent rapture of the saints. Whether our *bodies* are walking the earth or lying in the ground when the Beloved Saviour descends from heaven with His shout, our slothful demeanor will instantly turn to alertness. Paul says that the saints who lie in the ground shall rise first, followed immediately by living believers. Both these groups will meet the Lord in the air "and so shall we ever be with the Lord" (1 Thessalonians 4:16-17). Paul also says "that now it is high time to awake out of sleep: for now is our salvation nearer than when we believed" (Romans 13:11).

Today could be the day, so be on watch.

May 18

Did You or Didn't You?

"Thus did Noah; according to all that God commanded him, so did he." (Genesis 6:22)

The same can be said for Moses, Israel's wilderness tour guide: "Thus did Moses: according to all that the LORD commanded him, so did he" (Exodus 40:16). Others in the Bible did as the Lord directed them. "And Aaron did so;" and "so did Joshua;" and Gideon, "he did so;" and Josiah, "so did he." You get the idea. Each of these saints simply found the courage to be doers of God's Word. We need to be like them and do as they did.

"And Moses and Aaron went in unto Pharaoh, and they did so as the LORD had commanded: and Aaron cast down his rod before Pharaoh, and before his servants, and it became a serpent" (Exodus 7:10). It is only when we *do so* biblically that we shall see the hand of God moving on our behalf or on behalf of others in need of His love, mercy and salvation. Had it not been for the simple obedience of Yeshua's followers one particular day, there would have been chaos after He multiplied the loaves in front of the starving. "And he said to his disciples, Make them sit down by fifties in a company. And they *did so*" (Mark 9:14).

Peace and tranquility can only come into the lives of those who are careful to do all that has been required of them. To put it another way, God will only do so once we have done so. When you stand before Lord Yeshua's judgment seat, the main question will be a very simple one: "Did you or didn't you keep all my commandments?" (John 14:15).

Today, ask God to give you uprightness, strength and courage like Josiah, who at age eight *"did that* which was right in the sight of the LORD...and declined neither to the right hand, nor to the left" (2 Chronicles 34:2). Once you have done this today, you'll be glad you did.

The Silver Bullet

"...and the blood of Jesus Christ his Son cleanseth us from all sin." (1 John 1:7)

The term "silver bullet" has been used as a general metaphor referring to any straightforward solution perceived to have incredible effectiveness or that will easily cure a prevailing problem. Sin can be a prevailing problem for believers. If sin is left unchecked in our lives, it may bring on symptoms. We need to be inwardly honest. "If we say that we have no sin, we deceive ourselves, and the truth is not in us" (v.8).

Is there a silver bullet for sin and uncleanness in the believer's life? Yes! The blood of God's own Son dramatically cleanses us from all sin. Good works only *mask over* the symptoms. In the Bible silver is representative of the redemptive power of God. Sin sells us away to the world as some cheap commodity, but the blood of Messiah buys us back revealing to us that we are of inestimable value and not for resale at any price! Yohanan encourages every believer to seek the regular use of God's straightforward solution. "And if any man sin, we have an advocate with the Father, Jesus Christ...the propitiation [atonement] for our sins" (1 John 2:1-2). The blood of Yeshua is the "silver bullet," but it must have gunpowder to propel it forward. Prayerful, heart-felt confession is the "gunpowder" that sends the sinless blood of Messiah streaming into action. The beloved apostle informs us, "If we confess our sins, he is faithful and just to forgive us our sins, and to cleanse us from all unrighteousness" (1 John 1:9).

Not a day shall go by that you won't need heaven's remedy for your earthly sin—a bad thought, a bad word, a bad deed, a wrong reaction. Whatever the sin may be, the Just One stands ready to cleanse you and restore you to full fellowship, so readily make confession to Yeshua part of your day.

Thirty-Eight Long Years

"And the space in which we came from we came from Kadeshbarnea, until we were come over the brook Zered, was thirty and eight years; until all the generation of the men of war were wasted out from among the host, as the LORD sware unto them." (Deuteronomy 2:14)

Israel didn't wander the desert for 40 years because the first two were spent at Sinai. The number 38 is mentioned only four times in the Bible, and each time the number appears slavery is pictured. The Israelites were enslaved in the wilderness because of their own sin and unbelief. They were also enslaved to their fears rather than trusting God by faith.

The second occasion says, "in the thirty and eighth year of Asa king of Judah began Ahab the son of Omri to reign over Israel" (1 Kings 16:29). This time, the ten northern tribes became enslaved by their own king, the most evil one under whom they ever lived. The third occasion states that in "the thirty and eighth year of Azariah king of Judah did Zachariah the son of Jeroboam reign over Israel in Samaria...And he did that which was evil in the sight of the LORD, as his fathers had done...who made Israel to sin" (2 Kings 15:8).

Fourthly, in the New Testament we find a man enslaved by disease—a byproduct of original sin—the exact same length of time Israel wandered in the desert. "And a certain man was there, which had an infirmity thirty and eight years" (John 5:5). He could never reach the pool on his own; outside help was needed. Only Messiah had the power to free him from his slavery of body and soul. (Adapted from *Biblical Mathematics* by Edward F. Vallowe.)

After 38 long years, God delivered Israel from *sin* and *unbelief* and brought them into the Promised Land. But if you are striving against sin and walking in full belief, you won't have to wait that long for the Saviour to deliver you (Hebrews 12:4). Regardless of how much you need His help, the secret is not to give up on Him. Today, pray, seek His face and call out to Him. Read His life-changing Word. Praise Him and then wait patiently. He will come to you in due season.

The Sabbath Table

"And...he went through the corn fields on the Sabbath day; and his disciples began, as they went, to pluck the ears of corn." (Mark 2:23)

Uncooked oatmeal for breakfast is not all that appetizing, but when your home is the great outdoors and kindling a fire to boil water is forbidden, you do the best you can. Messiah and His followers were prophetic heralds of the unfolding kingdom and knew how to rough it without complaining. Though the Lord's Sabbath table was humble that day, the disciples were grateful for it. Eating with family is the essence of the Sabbath day.

Shabbat means *intermission,* and its root means to *cease* or *rest.* In Paleo-Hebrew, Shabbat's three letters really tell the story! The letter *sheen* represents two teeth, and one of its meanings is to eat. The letter *bet* pictures a tent or house and represents a family. The letter *tav* is illustrated by two crossed sticks and represents a sign. In Exodus 31:13, Yahweh confirms His Sabbath covenant to Israel saying, "it is a sign between me and you throughout your generations." Another meaning of the letter *tav* is a monument, and the seventh day is the monumental day of the week to which the children of Abraham happily look. The Sabbath includes at least three festive meals, but because this work-free day is such a delight, no one wants it to end at sunset. So families and their friends gather around the table and share a late meal and godly conversation well into the night. In Acts 20:7 Luke shows us this very idea. He writes, "And upon the first day of the week [at sunset], when the disciples came together to break bread, Paul preached unto them, ready to depart on the morrow; and continued his speech until midnight."

Today, gather around a table with family or godly friends and feed on the freshest bread you can find in Messiah's kingdom—the Word of God. After all, it is His table. Rest from your worries and enjoy fellowship with the Lord of the Sabbath.

Are You an Eyewitness?

"And ye also shall bear witness, because ye have been with me from the beginning" (John 15:27)

From the very beginning of Messiah Yeshua's public ministry, He chose a small company of men to live with Him day in and day out. They must have absolutely been breathless being so close to the epicenter of a many, mighty miracles.

Peter was never lacking for sermon material when he bore *witness* of the Saviour. He just told it as he saw it; and consequently, his first Spirit-empowered *witness* yielded 3000 genuine converts. Not too many days later, one of his heaven-blessed *sermons* produced 5000 more born-again souls. That sermon landed him in jail. At his hearing, his *testimony* was this: "For we cannot but speak the things which we have seen and heard" (Acts 4:20). Peter and his gospel companions were brought before courts on numerous occasions, which provided further opportunity to *speak* of things that they had experienced firsthand; the greatest of these things was Yeshua's rising from the dead. Before those magistrates, they stood and "with great power gave the apostles *witness* of the resurrection of the Lord Jesus" (Acts 4:33). Their main line of defense was simplistic and effective: "we are his witnesses of these things" (Acts 5:32). Years down the road Peter reminds the next generation of followers saying, "For we have not followed cunningly devised fables, when we made known unto you the power and coming of our Lord Jesus Christ, but were *eyewitnesses* of his majesty" (2 Peter 1:16).

Today, go forth telling the lost what great things the Lord has done for you. Start from the very beginning and give some person an eyewitness account of the miraculous changes that have come to pass in your life. Each believer has a story to tell and each one is different in its own right, but all point toward the lovely Son of God. Tell your story of transformation with compassion, courtesy and courage; then leave the convicting results up to God.

The Bread of Presence

"And it came to pass, as he sat at meat with them, he took bread, and blessed it, and brake, and gave to them. And their eyes were opened, and they knew him; and he vanished out of their sight." (Luke 24:30-31)

Each Sabbath the priests placed twelve fresh loaves of bread on the golden table adjacent to the veiled presence of Yahweh. The LORD wanted warm fellowship with His priestly servants. Fellowship is naturally enhanced by shared food. Yahweh said, "thou shalt set upon the table shewbread before me alway" (Exodus 25:30). In Hebrew, *showbread* is plural, *lehkem panaim.* Panaim literally means, "faces" and is normally translated as presence. The *bread of presence* was set before the presence of God. Though Yahweh was veiled, this special bread was His faithful token that He was ready to commune with His covenant people. Once the new bread was exchanged for the week-old bread, the priests all shared the bread by taking a very tiny piece. This was a foreshadowing of New Covenant communion.

Raised from the dead less than 24 hours earlier, Yeshua was already missing fellowship with His kinsmen. So the incarnate God concealed His identity and drew near to a pair of disciples who were walking to Emmaus. When the two men arrived at their destination, they extended their hospitality to the *veiled Deity.* Though Yeshua was only a guest in the house, He acted as host. What is more, He conducted the very first post-resurrection communion service. Holding up the bread *before His face,* He recited the ancient Hebrew prayer, "Blessed are you, O Lord our God, King of the Universe, Who brings forth bread from the earth." Why this prayer? Because He is the *Bread of Life* brought forth fresh from the earth! In the text verse above, by mentioning the exact same *four things* Yeshua did with the bread at the Last Supper, Luke is hinting [*remez*] to what actually happened in Emmaus. The very first post-resurrection communion was taking place, and the Lord was there! At the Last Supper Yeshua "took bread, and gave thanks, and brake it, and gave unto them, saying, This is my body which is given for you: this do in remembrance of me" (Luke 22:19). When He said this in Emmaus, it opened their eyes! He then suddenly removed His *visible* presence, but left them with the symbolic token of His *abiding* presence—the communion bread.

Who Will Go?

"Also I heard the voice of the Lord, saying, Whom shall I send, and who will go for us?" (Isaiah 6:8)

Isaiah's calling began with a mighty visitation. While in the Sanctuary, he saw Yeshua sitting upon His throne with heavenly creatures surrounding Him and exalting His name. "And the posts of the door moved at the voice of him that cried, and the house was filled with smoke" (v.4). This was no vision; it was reality. The humble priest didn't expect to live, having seen God in person. From the depths of his sin-awareness, he exclaimed, "Woe is me!" (v.5) This is in keeping with Manoah who explained to his wife, "We shall surely die, because we have seen God." Perhaps this type of thinking developed among the saints after Enoch vanished once he had met the LORD (Genesis 5:24).

Isaiah didn't depart for heaven because God had other plans for him. The LORD sent a Seraph to cleanse Isaiah's lips so that he might speak the pure words of the LORD from that day forward. Isaiah recalls the next thing that happened: "I heard the voice of the Lord." The high calling came to be a prophet, and he responded in the affirmative saying, "Here am I; send me" (v.8). Yahweh sealed Isaiah's calling with a one-time life assignment, "Go, and tell" (v.9).

Isaiah identifies Israel's Sovereign as *Yehovah Tsevaot*, "the LORD of hosts" (v.5). The word *"hosts"* refers to a mass of people, especially an army. Some 700 years later LORD Yeshua announced this same campaign strategy to His specially trained New Covenant commanders and all who would follow them—"Go ye...and teach all nations" (Matthew 28:19). If you surrender and go out with the gospel, you will be among the ranks of the elite. Take the council of Peter with you: "If any man speak, let him speak as the oracles of God" (1 Peter 4:11).

Today there will be plenty of souls crossing your path who know nothing of God's goodness, mercy or love; so be prayed up and prepared to proclaim the good news.

"Lord, We Went"

"Go ye into all the world, and preach the gospel to every creature."
(Mark 16:15)

It was not too long after the gospel message first went out to the world—perhaps a century—that pilgrims began making their way to the Holy Land, particularly Jerusalem and Bethlehem. In a Hendersonville, NC *Time-News* article dating December 19, 1979, details are given of Magen Broshi's discovery deep below a 4th-century AD church in Jerusalem.

This archaeologist from the Israel Museum found a nearly yard-long plaque of polished stone set into a rough wall. It contains a drawing of a Roman merchant ship with main sail, rigging and oars. Its hull is made of black granite. Broshi believes the mysterious broken mast the pilgrims depicted in the drawing represents their very own ship, which encountered a storm during the journey. The plaque also includes a Latin inscription *Domine Ivimus* meaning, "Lord, we went." Magen believes that the pilgrims came from the western end of the empire motivated by Psalm 122:1, and wanted a record of their accomplishment.

The resurrected Lord's final instruction to His devoted followers was, "Go ye into all the world, and preach the gospel to every creature." Maybe you have not been personally called to go into another country, but you have certainly been called to go into the entire neighborhood, or into the entire city where you live. After all, the Lord has already placed you there by design. When you get to heaven and look the Saviour in the eye, will you be able to say, "Lord, I went?"

You have your sailing orders. So why not take the gospel challenge of a lifetime? Here's how to get started! Pray, and then find a small map of your neighborhood or some other suburb in the city. Next, secure the help of a fellow saint and a fresh supply of quality gospel tracts as cargo from your pastor. Get others to pray for you and then venture out with the wonderful, life-changing Word of God.

The LORD's Release

"At the end of every seven years thou shalt make a release. And this is the manner of the release: Every creditor that lendeth ought unto his neighbour shall release it; he shall not exact it of his neighbour, or of his brother; because it is called the LORD'S release." (Deuteronomy 15:1-2)

Yahweh's Old Testament command instills into our New Testament theology two important salvation principles. First, God chooses a set time to release us from our unrepayable sin-debt. He works in our lives through the gospel to bring us to a state of repentance, at which time we place all our trust in the Son and the redemption price of His sinless blood. Whenever God sends forth the message of free salvation through the preached Word, He is announcing to hearers their day of release. As Yeshua said to Zacchaeus, "This day is salvation come to this house" (Luke 19:9). Yeshua had it all planned. He released the chief publican of his great sin-debt on the day of *His* choosing. And when He did, He acted in grace. The biblical number for grace is five, and the word *release* is used exactly five times in the cluster of these first three verses on the LORD's release. Here is the fifth usage: "Of a foreigner thou may exact it again: but that which is thine with thy brother thine hand shall release" (v.3). The Son of God came down to join the brotherhood of mankind so that He could release from debtors' prison all men who look to Him for mercy.

Second, when the LORD releases us from our sin-debt He doesn't send us out empty; He sends us out filled with His Spirit! "And when thou sendest him out free from thee, thou shalt not let him go away empty: Thou shalt furnish him liberally out of thy flock, and out of thy floor, and out of thy winepress: of that wherewith the LORD thy God hath blessed thee thou shalt give unto him" (v.13-14). On the very same day that God releases you from your house of spiritual bondage He gives you something vital: "the supply of the Spirit of Jesus Christ" (Philippians 1:19). Make no mistake about it; when God saves you He also immediately supplies you with the nine-fold fruits of His Holy Spirit (Galatians 5:22). All in all, this is the greatest day of your life!

Today, praise the LORD for His sovereign grace and unconditionally abundant provision.

Ready, Set, Go!

"And thus shall ye eat it; with your loins girded, your shoes on your feet, and your staff in your hand; and ye shall eat it in haste: it is the LORD'S passover." (Exodus 12:11)

When Yahweh instituted Passover He told His people that Nissan would become the beginning of months. Israel's Mosaic redemption began with the command to apply a lamb's blood to the entrance of their dwellings. The blood saved them because it sanctified [separated] them from the Egyptians, a type of the world. This was followed by another injunction—"Be ready to go." When Israel did go out of Egypt, they were baptized in the Red Sea and remained on the move for the next two generations. This also foreshadows the requirements for New Covenant believers.

As the Lamb of God, Messiah Yeshua provided His atoning blood for all nations. We should not refuse the Spirit's sanctifying application of this in our daily life. Salvation is followed by a host of injunctions. You may be like the believing crowd on the day of Pentecost who said to Peter, "What shall we do?" (Acts 2:37). He gave them a very clear answer: "be baptized" (v.38). Years later Paul came to believe in Messiah as Lord. After receiving God's grace he asked, "Lord, what will you have me to do?" (Acts 9:6). The response came quickly: "Arise, and *go* into the city."

The Lord has much for His people to do once they come to Him for salvation. Lord Yeshua gave His newly saved followers a direct assignment—"go and sin no more." Matthew records the Lord saying to others: go preach (10:7), go and show (11:4), go get in a ship (14:22), go and tell (18:15), go and sell (19:21), go into the village (21:2), go into the highways (22:9), and go into the city (26:18). The last time the Lord ever directed His people in an action-oriented way He said, "Go ye...and teach all nations, baptizing them in the name of the Father, and of the Son, and of the Holy Ghost" (28:19).

Are you *ready* to serve today or are you so relaxed that you've become a little dull of hearing? Today, get *set*, and as the Lord sees your obedient prayerful posture, He will direct your paths and show you the way to *go*.

Hang on to the True Vine

"I am the true vine...Abide in me...As the branch cannot bear fruit of itself...He that abideth in me, and I in him, the same bringeth forth much fruit: for without me ye can do nothing." (John 15:1-5)

In the eighth century BC Yahweh said, "I found Israel like grapes in the wilderness" (Hosea 9:10). As a likely result of this fond term, the *grapevine* became a prominent symbol for the nation. This symbol of blessing has been found stamped on coins from the Maccabean period (167-63 BC). The adornment of the Second Temple included an elaborate golden grapevine with clusters hanging upon a golden trellis. This ornate decoration was affixed over the entrance of the Holy Place and wealthy worshipers could donate a cluster to the vine if they desired. The less affluent could sponsor a single grape or leaf if they wished. Messiah used this very well-known and ongoing project to illustrate a spiritual truth. If the people really loved the Father they would have to attach themselves to His Son—Israel's source of abiding life.

The "near-sighted" worshippers of Yahweh were only interested in *adding* to the glory of the Temple's ornate vine, but the Master emphasized a point they knew all too well. In order to *add* clusters to a living vine, one must regularly *cut away* unneeded branches. Each year after the autumn harvest, 90 percent of that year's new growth has to be pruned. A vine bears two types of branches, ones that produce fruit and ones that don't. The latter cannot be allowed to produce only foliage and take away strength from the rest of the plant.

Oh, little green branch; don't become weary this year during the Father's winter pruning season. Life circumstances may become unpleasant, but see that you continue to abide in the rich sap of Yeshua's Word. Don't shrink back when the Father's pruning devices swoop in to take away those needless distractions from your hurried life. Then you'll be glad when summer arrives and the Spirit bears precious fruit in your life. "Thus saith the LORD, As the new wine is found in the cluster...Destroy it not; for a blessing is in it" (Isaiah 65:8).

The Well of Salvation

"They went to Beer: that is the well whereof the LORD spake unto Moses, Gather the people together, and I will give them water." (Numbers 21:17)

Israel's sojourn through the rugged, parched and arid landscape left them in constant drought mode clinging to life. Their salvation was only as close as water could be found. The lesson that took them more than once to learn was that as long as their mighty wonder-working God was near, so was water. He alone was their salvation and He alone could provide for them.

The first thing we discover about the well of salvation is that it is a *specific* well—"the well whereof the LORD spake unto Moses." People around the world go blindly searching for springs of youth and happiness but forget to simply listen to the LORD and rely upon His hand-drawn map, the Bible, to point them in the right direction. Once finding this well, and drinking, one realizes that it is a *satisfying* well. The LORD said to Moses, "Gather the people together, and I will give them water." The Great Shepherd knows how to satisfy His thirsty lambs best. His well produces sweet, soul-reviving water.

It is also a *surprising* well. "Then Israel sang this song, Spring up, O well; sing ye unto it…The princes digged the well…with their staves" (v.18). Israel was earlier surprised when Moses' rod struck a rock and water came forth. Now they were equally surprised when water began bubbling up after merely scratching around the sand with sticks and singing a song of thanksgiving.

Finally, it is a *sovereign* well, for they dug "by the direction of the lawgiver" (v.18). A sovereign is a person of royalty or someone who is above all others in character, importance and excellence. This describes with perfection the Son of God Who owns the well of salvation. Isaiah writes, "Therefore with joy shall ye draw water out of the wells of *salvation* [Heb. *yeshuah*]" (Isaiah 12:3).

This morning prayerfully gather around Yeshua's unfailing Word. It's a true wellspring of hope and will satisfy you all day long.

Wearing Messiah's Mantle

Part 1

"So he...found Elisha...who was plowing with twelve yoke of oxen...and Elijah passed by him, and cast his mantle upon him." (1 Kings 19:19)

The word mantle appears 14 times in the KJV, and its simplest definition is an *outer garment*. In Bible numerology, the number 14 represents salvation, which is interesting because the outer garment was a person's *year-round salvation* from the desert's frigid night air. Messiah's Spirit-mantle is the token of our eternal salvation.

Elijah didn't ask Elisha if he wanted to wear his mantle; he just threw it over him and walked on. Messiah Yeshua transferred His mantle of authority to us when He walked by us in mercy and grace on our day of salvation. To understand the nature of Messiah's mantle, look at its Hebrew meaning. The word for mantle is *adderet* which means "something *ample*; a garment, mantle, robe." This word is derived from *addiyr* meaning "wide, large (figuratively) powerful."

When Elijah called Elisha to follow him, the young man left his plowshare but first went back and said farewell to his family. Messiah's demands, however, come with greater expectations. Yeshua referred to Elisha's sentimental nature when speaking to His would-be follower. He said, "No man, having put his hand to the plow, and looking back, is fit for the kingdom of God" (Luke 9:62). Wearing Messiah's mantle is a high calling and comes with a high price. On Elijah's translation day, he permanently cast his mantle upon his faithful follower just as Messiah Who cast His Spirit-mantle down on us after going up to heaven.

Adderet also means, "glory, goodly." Messiah's mantle is, therefore, not only an ample token, but also a *glorious* token. He said, "Tarry ye in the city...until ye be endued [*enduo*, clothed] with power from on high" (Luke 24:49). Today, treat your divine empowerment as clothing *invested* upon you by your glorious Master, Lord Yeshua. Sink into it, use it, grow in it and seek to fill it up (Ephesians 4:13).

Wearing Messiah's Mantle
Part 2

"I will greatly rejoice in the LORD, my soul shall be joyful in my God; for he hath clothed me with the garments of salvation," (Isaiah 61:10)

Salvation is not given to the self-righteous. Messiah's mantle is a *life-saving garment* given to those who have faith enough to simply reach out and take hold of it (1 Timothy 6:12). It is a free gift and can never be earned (Romans 6:23). Messiah's mantle is also a *joy-filled garment*. The prophet Isaiah rejoices knowing that what has been given him can never be taken away. The Hebrew word Isaiah uses for joyful is *guul*, which means, "to *spin* around or go in *circles*." Children do this often because they are truly and naturally joyful.

A comforting feature of Messiah's mantle is that it is a *sufficient garment*. Paul had a great need in his life, but Messiah said to him, "My grace is sufficient for thee: for my strength is made perfect in weakness" (2 Corinthians 12:9). Paul received this admonition saying, "Most gladly therefore will I rather glory in my infirmities, that the power of Christ [His Spirit-mantle] may rest upon me." In a similar way, Messiah's mantle is a *humble garment*. It takes humility to wear the hairy garment of a prophet. The disciples' Messiah-like nature did not go unnoticed by the self-righteous Pharisees for they all "marveled; and...took knowledge of them, that they had been with Jesus" (Acts 4:13).

Messiah's mantle is also a *holy garment*. You are told to "put off...the old man [your own mantle], which is corrupt...and...put on the new man [Messiah's mantle], which after God is created in righteousness and true holiness" (Ephesians 4:22-24). Messiah's mantle is also a *demanding garment* for you are told to "Put on...bowels of mercies, kindness, humbleness of mind, meekness, longsuffering; Forbearing one another, and forgiving one another, if any man have a quarrel against any: even as Christ forgave you, so also do ye. And above all these things put on charity" (Colossians 3:12-14). This morning ask Messiah Yeshua to help you wear His mantle in a way that fully honors Him.

Heavenly Interests

"But he turned, and said unto Peter...Thou art an offence unto me:
for thou savourest not the things that be of God, but those that be of men."
(Matthew 16:23)

In verse 21 Yeshua said that He must go to Jerusalem and be killed, yet He would rise again in three days. That seemed too much for impulsive Peter to handle. Therefore he rebuked his own Master saying, "Be it far from thee, Lord: this shall not be unto thee" (v.22). The chief disciple entertained only thoughts of a kingdom victory that suited his zeal—one with swords drawn. That was his way, but not his Master's. Peter was ready to get to the mountaintop experience of the kingdom and sit by his Master's throne, not his Master's grave. He simply had no interest in anything that got in the way of his preconceived plans.

The Prince of Peace had some very harsh words of correction for His near-sighted student. What is more, Messiah wanted all His followers to put away their dreams of kicking the Romans out by force and simply focus on their Redeemer. If that weren't enough for them, they would have to adjust, not Him! He had a message for all of them, but none of them seemed to catch it. He wanted them to become *clothed in humility*, thus taking the kingdom of darkness by stealth. He warned them saying that they were the salt of the earth, and that if they lost their savor, their testimony would be irreversible. He added that they would then be undesirables, and consequently, "trodden under foot of men" (Matthew 5:13). If they were to be in line with Him, they would have to become like Him—*cloaked in meekness*! That was the essence and the extent of His kingdom. The Son of Man reminded them not to follow the world's method of getting what it wants when He said, "And from the days of John the Baptist until now the kingdom of heaven suffereth violence, and the violent take it by force" (Matthew 11:12).

What is it that you savor or think about from day to day? How do your ministry interests and pursuits line up with the Master's? Today, pray for more humility, meekness and kingdom-mindedness.

Godly Pursuits

"Know ye not that they which run in a race run all, but one receiveth the prize? So run, that ye may obtain." (1 Corinthians 9:24)

Like Paul who ran to win the prize, many believers today also run to win. Some saints, on the other hand, are poorly motivated to run at all. They are running many other races that count for nothing in the end. Every believer has a special place in the race. The reason it is a race is because time is limited. What we must do, we must do quickly. The Master has said, "work...while it is day: the night cometh, when no man can work" (John 9:4).

Jacob was also a saint in pursuit. He ran to win the blessings of God. Ruth was a wonderful pursuer of God. When she looked her mother-in-law in the face and proclaimed, "Thy people shall be my people, and thy God my God," she was showing her preparedness to run in a covenant way. The Moabitess became highly focused on her new, godly heritage. David was a champion runner. He ran to finish what General Joshua left undone—to dispossess the land of its enemies. When Yeshua was only twelve years old, He was already in full pursuit for the kingdom's sake. And what exactly was that godly pursuit? Tending to His Father's business of winning the Jews (Luke 2:49). From that day forward, He was always contending for the faith. Many other New Testament saints pursued godly goals. Phillip the evangelist pursued lost souls, and Phoebe pursued good servanthood in her church. The list goes on (Romans 16:1).

In what godly pursuit are you currently involved? Do you want to make a real difference? It doesn't matter if you think you have nothing to contribute. God will give you what you are lacking so that you can run the race and run well. What you need, quite simply, is just a steadfast supply of *want to*! He will take care of the rest. Ask the Lord today to help you with your *want to* and then get ready to receive His *how to*. Then run for His glory alone. Amen?

The Grandest Wedding of All

Part 1

"And the third day there was a marriage in Cana of Galilee; and...Jesus was there." (John 2:1)

The fact that Yeshua chose to perform His very first miracle at a wedding wonderfully foreshadows the grandest wedding that will ever take place—the union of the Saviour and His New Covenant bride! When Yeshua turned water into wine, He saved the best till last (v.10). This fits right into the theme of the grandest wedding of all time.

This future union will be the *most joyous* wedding ever. What the people at Cana really wanted was joy, so Yeshua gave them a token of what His capabilities were (v.3). However, if you want real and lasting joy you must do whatever He bids you to do (v.5). This wedding will also be the *most royal* of all because Messiah is "the Prince of the kings of the earth" (Revelation 1:5). The cost of the dowry alone with which Messiah bought you makes this the *most expensive* wedding ever conceived. Peter says that we "were not redeemed with corruptible things, as silver and gold...but with the precious blood of Christ" (1 Peter 1:18-19). This future wedding will be the *most prepared* one in history. When Yeshua said, "I go to prepare a place for you," He must also have had in mind the many wedding preparations (John 14:2).

For 2000 years now, the collective bride has been eagerly waiting and listening for the midnight call: "Behold, the bridegroom cometh; go ye out to meet him" (Matthew 25:6). This length of time makes this the *most highly anticipated* wedding of all time. To date, this heavenly event remains the *most highly publicized* and *most inclusive* wedding of all time. The invitation from heaven's royal court has been formally sent out to all nations: "The Spirit and the bride say, Come. And let him that heareth say, Come. And let him that is athirst come. And whosoever will, let him take the water of life freely" (Revelation 22:17). This is not an invitation to be a guest at the wedding, but to be a part of the bride! Today, ask the Spirit to help you prepare for this soon-coming union.

ᏔᏋ Grandest Wedding of All

Part 2

"For the Lord himself shall descend from heaven with a shout, with the voice of the archangel, and with the trump of God." (1 Thessalonians 4:16)

These heavenly heralds will make this wedding day the *most highly announced* marriage in history. What else would one expect to happen since this will be *the largest* wedding ever imagined. The list of marriage participants is drawn out of every kindred, tongue, people and nation. In their excitement and gratitude they will arrive with a melody on their lips singing "a new song, saying, Thou art worthy to take the book, and to open the seals thereof: for thou wast slain, and hast redeemed us to God by thy blood" (Revelation 5:9).

We know that this shall be the *most-sacred* joining of souls ever because "Christ...loved the church, and gave himself for it; That he might sanctify and cleanse it...[and] present it to himself...not having spot, or wrinkle, or any such thing" (Ephesians 5:23-27). This royal wedding will be the *most triumphant* of all ages. "And I heard as it were the voice of...mighty thunderings, saying, Alleluia: for the Lord God omnipotent reigneth. Let us be glad and rejoice, and give honour to him: for the marriage of the Lamb is come, and his wife hath made herself ready...Blessed are they which are called unto the marriage supper of the Lamb" (Revelation 19:6-9).

Do you have the proper wedding garment in order to be received into this wedding of the ages (Matthew 22:12)? If so, is your garment clean, free from spots? Are there any wrinkles that need smoothing out? Have you formally thanked the Bridegroom's Father for paying your purchase price and have you fully accepted that price as sufficient? Have you stopped preparing your temporary place here below to have more time to tell others how to get in on this grand occasion? Are you anticipating, watching, waiting and listening for the Bridegroom's sacred voice and the trumpet's upward call? The time is drawing near! Today, prayerfully ask the Holy Spirit to help you get rapture-ready.

✤igns & ᶃonders

"Then said Jesus unto him, Except ye see signs and wonders, ye will not believe." (John 4:48)

Almost every reference to signs and wonders in the Tenach points to that period in Egypt when Israel stood in disbelief and hardness of heart. For Israel's sake, He continued the miracles for 40 years. This did not change their heart one bit. The two Old Testament prophets who performed the most miracles, Elijah and Elisha, did so because Israel had once again fallen into such a horrible state of unbelief. As expected, it was for this exact same reason that Yeshua, the Prophet of Galilee, had to produce so many signs and wonders for Israel. He didn't enjoy having to produce physical evidence of His Messiahship. He ridiculed the nation often for their lack of saving faith.

The phrase "signs and wonders" appears 29 times between both Covenants. According to Edward Vallowe, the number 29 is associated with "departure or going away." He cites that the 29th time the name Noah, Abram/Abraham, Isaac, Jacob, Laban or Samson appears a *departure* of some sort takes place. Signs and wonders were never meant to be God's modus operandi. During forty years in the wilderness, Yahweh performed signs and wonders daily for the unbelieving Israelites, but these particular miracles *departed* the day after Israel crossed over Jordan. Faith alone was then unapologetically required from the nation. When the Messiah and His apostles came along 1500 years later, they were also forced to give Israel irrefutable tokens over a forty-year period because of their lack of faith. At the end of that generation the signs quickly dried up just as they had done in the past (1 Corinthians 13:8-10; 2Timothy 4:20). Israel and the Jews were forced once again to believe by biblical faith alone (Luke 16:31).

Yeshua sternly warned the last-days generation in Israel of a different sort of event that would precede His return—false prophets showing false signs and wonders (Matthew 24:24). He told them to *depart* to the mountains (v.16).

Take time today to seek direction and guidance from God's infallible, unchanging Word and *don't depart* from it.

Feeling Strange?

"I am a stranger in the earth: hide not thy commandments from me."
(Psalm 119:19)

David may have enjoyed a few short carefree years growing up in Bethlehem, but it wasn't long before he was feeling isolation coming from every side. It all began when he was handed the job of caring for the family's sheep. Like any normal boy, little David would have preferred being closer to home than scouring the lonely Judean landscape looking for pasture and fending off predators. The alienated feelings only intensified when Samuel separated him from among his seven brothers to be king. His brothers never treated him the same again (1 Samuel 17:28).

Not long after this the young fellow was requisitioned and brought to Gibeon to play soothing songs in Saul's melancholy house (1 Samuel 16:22). Then when the teenager began to taunt the Philistines over and over, the women back home began to sing his praises. This did not sit well with Saul, and the subsequent attempts on David's life left him rejected, running, and with little refuge. David's many years as a fugitive—perhaps spanning two decades—left him feeling homeless, hungry and hallow. He was routinely refused aid and comfort by various villages. Dens and caves became his princely palace and *misery* and *martyrdom* were often his mantra. Even as a reigning king, he once had to flee to the wilderness when one of his own sons turned on him. At the end of the day, no one knew the terrain of Judea and Samaria like David.

Maybe you receive little thanks for the good service you do in the Lord's work; or worse, you only suffer retribution. Well, then, you must do as David did in the text verse: keep close to the greatest of all travelling companions, the Bible. Also, find fellow believers who will be considerate of your plight. Yeshua, foremost, is one of these. He suffered constant rejection and felt like a stranger (Psalm 69:8). After consorting with Yeshua and His word today, you will settle down in your spirit and go on to victory.

The Fold and the Flock

"I will surely gather the remnant of Israel; I will put them together as the sheep of Bozrah, as the flock in the midst of their fold: they shall make great noise by reason of the multitude of men." (Micah 2:12)

The word for sheep is *tseh-one* meaning to *migrate*. This accurately describes the Hebrew flock that has migrated more than any other people on earth have. The Shepherd of Israel once had a large flock, but it became scattered, torn and reduced to a mere remnant. On the bright side, He pledges to gather them one day from lonely horizons. Shortly after the Shepherd gathers His sheep back to their end-time place of rest, they will need to expand the borders of the ancient fold (Ezekiel 45:1).

When the scattered sheep of Israel return, their spiritual resting place will be Zion. "For out of Jerusalem shall go forth a remnant...out of mount Zion: the zeal of the LORD of hosts shall do this" (Isaiah 37:32). The word for Zion is *tsee-yone*; its root means *conspicuous*. This accurately describes Jerusalem, a heavily fortified city that sits on a hill. Since a permanent sheepfold has rock walls, it is only natural that the heavenly Shepherd would look down from above and view Jerusalem as the protective enclosure for His beloved little sheep. Yes, the Shepherd of Israel built the walls of *Tsee-yone* for His *tseh-one*.

There are other enclosures that He provided His sheep with like Zair, Zeba and Zoar, but He "loveth the gates of Zion more than all the dwellings of Jacob" (Psalm 87:2). Zion's many gates make it easier for His sheep going in and out to pasture. When Israel's Shepherd appeared in flesh and blood, He said, "I am the door of the sheep...by me if any man enter in, he shall be saved, and shall go in and out, and find pasture" (John 10:7, 9).

Little lamb, are you seeking the spiritual safety of the Saviour's enclosure every day and night? He wants you to come in and take comfort within the fold's safety. He says, "I will cause you to pass under the rod, and I will bring you into the bond of the covenant" (Ezekiel 20:37). Nightfall is quickly approaching. He's watching and waiting for you at the door of the fold ready to count you after you pass under His authoritative rod.

His Workmanship

"For we are his workmanship, created in Christ Jesus unto good works, which God hath before ordained that we should walk in them." (Ephesians 2:10)

The first time we find the word *workmanship* in the Bible it is seen as the gifting of metallurgy and stone cutting endowed to Bezaleel (Exodus 31:3). The Hebrew word is *melakah* meaning "deputyship, ministry, employment." Melakah is derived from *malak* meaning, "to *dispatch* as a deputy or messenger."

God equipped Bezaleel and then dispatched him to his employment or holy duties. Sometimes God dispatches us and equips us as we go, but He doesn't always do His work up front. We are a work in progress. The Son of God dispatched His messengers with one central message and one simple command: "as ye go, preach saying, The kingdom of heaven is at hand" (Matthew 10:7). A messenger delivers a message, but it is sometimes hard work because the message is often laid upon hard hearts. This is why Messiah also dispatches His workmen with "unction," that is to say, the Spirit's *anointing* (1 John 2:20). He is also responsible for the messenger's other essentials like food. This is why Yeshua told His full-time disciples not to take their own provisions informing them, "the workman is worthy of his meat" (Matthew 10:10).

The Master Craftsman is also working on *all* his workmen to develop their understanding of Him and His holy ways. Although this is mainly Yahweh's responsibility, He extends a portion of this responsibility to His workmen saying, "Study to show thyself approved unto God, a workman that needeth not to be ashamed, rightly dividing the word of truth" (2 Timothy 2:15). The LORD wants to do a work in you and through you that both you and the world may be blessed by it. If you're a child of the King, then you're never without employment and equally without excuse. Be engaged in the work the Saviour has called you to lest He say unto you, "Why stand ye here all the day idle?" (Matthew 20:6). Seek the Lord's enablement in prayer today before going about your duties.

What's in the Name Yahweh?

"According to thy name, O God, so is thy praise unto the ends of the earth:" (Psalm 48:10)

In verse 1, the psalmist praises God by His covenant name: "Great is the LORD"—*Yahweh*. Four verses later he says, "For this God is our God for ever and ever" (v.14). The psalmist acknowledges the many gods of this world but has praise for only one. Yahweh reminded Moshe: "This is my name for ever, and this is my memorial unto all generations" (Exodus 3:15). Why does the psalmist say, "According to thy name…so is thy praise?" Let's find out.

The original Hebrew alphabet was pictorial and often added some depth to the meaning of a word. Yahweh's sacred name begins with a *yod*, which depicts a hand and means either work or worship. The letter *hey* is next which depicts a man with his arms raised meaning look or reveal. The *vav* comes next and depicts a tent peg meaning hook or secure. Yahweh's name ends with another *hey*, thus two persons are depicted in it. However, the ancient Hebrews interpreted the meaning of Yahweh's name; it was nonetheless infused with awe and wonder of how He would one day *secure* His people by *revealing* His *raised hands*.

In the ancient Near East culture, a person's name held the same value as the person himself. In the Torah, Yahweh clearly reveals one Person Who bears His sacred name, thus His nature and character: "Beware of him, and obey his voice, provoke him not; for he will not pardon your transgressions: for my name is in him" (Exodus 23:21). A second witness later testified to this same truth: "Blessed be he that cometh in the name of the LORD" (Psalm 118:26). Exactly Who this divine Person was remained a mystery for a thousand years until multitudes of saints suddenly began ringing out this holy hymn towards Messiah Yeshua (Mark 11:9). Four days later His *raised hands* were driven through with iron *pegs* and His sacrificial body was lifted up on a tree and revealed for all Israel to *look* upon. The two *heys* in Yahweh agree to Yeshua's words, "he that hath seen me hath seen the Father" (John 14:9). Yeshua was both *Man* and *God* and secured salvation for both Jew and Gentile, male and female, rich and poor, free and bond. Today, praise Him for His amazing gift of divine atonement.

Foreshadows in the Exodus

Throughout the entirety of the Old Testament Yahweh sketches portraits of the two advents of Israel's glorious Messiah. His first coming is brilliantly portrayed within the events of the Exodus event and wilderness journey. The following are midrashic pictures of Messiah's substitutionary death, and the last one is of His springing to life again. Each epic event separately foreshadows *who* Messiah was; *what* requirements and blessings would result from His death; and *where, when, why* and *how* He would die. Enjoy discovering the monumental event that ended Israel's wilderness murmurings.

Death of the First Born
Part 1

"For I will pass through the land of Egypt this night, and will smite all the firstborn in the land of Egypt," (Exodus 12:12)

This dark, judgmental event foreshadowed exactly *Who* would one day die for all Israel's sins—*God's unique Son.* In John 3:16 Yeshua describes Himself as God's only begotten Son. Although Yeshua had an incarnate beginning on earth, He had no beginning whatsoever being eternally existent with the Father (Proverbs 8:22-30). At the set time a judgment of biblical proportion fell substitutionally upon God's firstborn Son that all nations might be spared the judgment they duly deserve for their own sins (John 3:16).

It is fitting that we identify with the trial and judgment that God's firstborn Son went through, for it was really our sins on trial and not His. Follow Him from Gethsemane where He was arrested, down the Kidron valley and up to Caiaphas' house. From there follow Him through the dimly lit streets of Jerusalem to Herod's palace, the next day to Pilate's judgment hall, and then to Golgotha's horrible hill. Stand beneath His towering cross. Hear him gasp for air, beg for water, lament His isolation and cry to heaven! This is your Elder Brother [the Firstborn] taking on your rightful pain and punishment. Take ample time today to thank Him for fully taking on your judgment.

Applying the Blood
Part 2

"Your lamb shall be without blemish, a male. And they shall take of the blood, and strike it on the two side posts and on the upper door post of the houses. and when I see the blood, I will pass over you, and the plague shall not be upon you to destroy you, when I smite the land of Egypt." (Exodus 12:5, 7, 13)

This necessary event foreshadowed *what* would be required after Messiah's death—*a claim upon His blood*. Had not a lamb's spotless blood been applied over the entrance of every Hebrew home and safety taken behind the door, they would have incurred the same loss as the Egyptians.

The placement of the blood was to be in an obvious place, the *doorposts*. The Hebrew word is *mezuzah*. The root of this word is *zeez,* meaning *conspicuous.* Yahweh instructed Israel that once they got into the Promised Land they should write Scripture directly upon their doorposts. This covenant token was not so much for the safety of their homes as it was for the sanctification of their daily lives. Scriptural references to Yahweh on their doorways reminded them Whom they served. Later the psalmist could say, "The LORD shall preserve thy going out and thy coming in from this time forth, and even for evermore" (Psalm 121:8). Today Jewish people still affix mezuzahs [decorative cases containing scripture] on the right side of their front door.

As the ancient lamb's blood was to be conspicuous upon the doorways of the believers' homes in Goshen, so today the blood of God's perfect Lamb must be prominent upon the entrance of the repentant soul's heart. This is what is required with Messiah's shed blood, and it is the Spirit Who supernaturally applies it. The blood makes you safe and the Book makes you *sure.* Before leaving your house this morning, thank the Spirit for His unseen work in your life. Ask Him also to lead you to someone that might need a little more understanding of why the Lamb's blood is so necessary for eternal life. As you come across such a person be ready to explain the gospel with simplicity (2 Corinthians 3:11).

The Great Exodus

Part 3

"And Moses said unto the people, Remember this day, in which ye came out from Egypt, out of the house of bondage." (Exodus 13:3)

Israel's flight from Egypt and baptism in the Red Sea severed all ties to their former physical bondage. Yahweh didn't want them ever to forget their day of salvation. He proudly declared, "the Egyptians whom ye have seen to day, ye shall see them again no more for ever" (14:13). This exodus from Pharaoh's house foreshadowed *what* effect Messiah's atoning death would one day bring—*freedom from spiritual bondage.*

A future Messianic liberation from sin's bondage was clearly prophesied by Isaiah, and Yeshua brought it to fulfillment in His very first sermon saying, "The Spirit of the Lord is upon me, because he hath…sent me to…preach deliverance to the captives, and…to set at liberty them that are bruised" (Luke 4:18). It is one thing to proclaim freedom to bound-up prisoners, yet another thing entirely to make it happen. Messiah "put forth His hand" often and literally set His people free from their many *physical* oppressions (Luke 5:13). This was a token to them of His ability to deliver from *spiritual* oppression.

When the Egyptian army and the Red Sea hemmed in Moses, he saved his people by his outstretched hand. Greater still, Israel's salvation from *spiritual* captivity came at a time when Messiah was hemmed-in between the Romans and the cross. It was there at that critical juncture that He turned, faced the cross and with His outstretched hands saved His people. Yeshua also wanted His followers to remember their New Covenant day of deliverance. This day was to be commemorated on future Passovers. As He said, "Do this in remembrance of me" (Luke 22:19). Paul also confirmed this sacred command (1 Corinthians 5:7-8).

If you want to experience freedom from spiritual bondage, you must do two things. When you feel trapped by sin, don't look at the *escarpment*; look for a way of *escape* that God has promised to provide (1 Corinthians 10:13). Second, deny your own *desires* and begin following your *Deliverer*. Today's freedom is enjoyed by being bound to His Words and His ways.

ᵥyater from the Rock
Part 4

"Behold, I will stand before thee there upon the rock in Horeb; and thou shalt smite the rock, and there shall come water out of it, that the people may drink." (Exodus 17:6)

This event foreshadowed *what* benefits would come from Messiah's death at Golgotha—*the outpouring of His Spirit.* The rock is a metaphorical type of God (Deuteronomy 32:4), and Yahweh's direct command to smite the rock runs in tandem with His command to "smite the shepherd" (Zechariah 13:7). Both of these pictures foreshadow Messiah being smitten for Israel's breach of the Law (Isaiah 53:4). In at least seven places, the Tanakh prophesies of Yahweh pouring out His Spirit upon His people (Isaiah 32:15).

Yeshua's Spirit rushed upon His followers ten days after His ascension. The Son of God spoke of this event saying, "If any man thirst, let him come unto me, and drink. He that believeth on me, as the scripture hath said, out of his belly shall flow rivers of living water" (John 7:37-38). Yeshua was not drawing from any single prophetic verse but was using a *summary fulfillment* from a variety of scriptures: "out of his belly" (Job 20:15); "rivers...shall flow" (Joel 3:18); and "living waters" (Jeremiah 17:13). Like the satisfying waters that flowed from Moses' smitten rock, Messiah's abiding Spirit satisfies the believer's thirst for the continual presence of God. "And because ye are sons, God hath sent forth the Spirit of his Son into your hearts, crying Abba, Father" (Galatians 4:6).

Does the deathly dryness of this drought-stricken world leave you parched and empty? Does the preaching of the modernists, liberals and counterfeits make you languish and feel like you have only experienced a mirage, something without substance or reality? Then come to the true Source and drink from that spiritual Rock—Lord Yeshua (1 Corinthians 10:4). His Spirit creates the supernatural oasis your soul daily needs. This morning ask the Saviour to make you more receptive to His Word and more yielding to His Spirit.

The Red Heifer

Part 5

"And ye shall give her unto Eleazar the priest, that he may bring her forth without the camp, and one shall slay her before his face." (Numbers 19:3)

No other sacrificial animal was ever ordained to be offered outside the Temple grounds. In the days of Solomon's Temple, the red cow [*parah adumah*] was led across a wooden bridge over to the Mount of Olives. There the high priest took some of her shed blood and sprinkled it in the direction of the Sanctuary seven times (v.3-4). The sacrifice was then burned till nothing remained but ashes. The ashes were then collected into three bronze containers and, over time, sprinkled sparingly in Temple waters to make them ceremonially clean. These purified waters made ritual purification possible for anyone who had come in contact with the dead. What a strange thing this was—making water pure with ashes from a dead sacrifice! Vestiges of this biblical injunction exist today when Jewish people withdraw from a graveside and wash their hands under a nearby water tap.

This event accurately foreshadowed *where* Messiah would die—*outside the walled city*. Yeshua was led outside one of Jerusalem's northern gates to "the place of a skull, which is called in Hebrew Golgotha" (John 19:17). Just as the red heifer's ceremonial blood was sprinkled seven times before the presence of God, so Messiah's blood ceremoniously sprinkled from seven places on His body: His hands, feet, head, back and pierced side. Peter highlights the sprinkling of the blood of Jesus Christ at the very beginning of his letter (1 Peter 1:2). Paul specifically alludes to the red heifer sacrifice saying, "Wherefore Jesus also, that he might sanctify the people with his own blood, suffered without the gate" (Hebrews 13:12). The apostle uses this as a banner for the Faith. The other side of the banner reads like this, "Let us go forth therefore unto him without the camp, bearing his reproach" (v.13).

Today as you go out of your house, follow Him unashamedly and with a whole heart. Ask for the Spirit's help.

$\mathcal{A}$aron $\mathcal{S}$tops the $\mathcal{P}$lague

Part 6

"And Aaron...ran into the midst of the congregation; and, behold, the plague was begun among the people: and he put on incense, and made an atonement for the people. And he stood between the dead and the living; and the plague was stayed." (Numbers 16:47-48)

This decisive event foreshadowed *why* Messiah would die—*to stop the nation's tendency to backslide*. Had not Israel's high priest made an atonement, Yahweh was going to "consume them all as in a moment" (v.45). God ended the Aaronic order 1500 years later and instituted a new one—the order of Melchizedek (Psalm 110:4). Messiah became Israel's eternal High Priest and stopped their spiritual plague through the offering up of Himself.

Aaron did three things in accomplishing Israel's healing. First, he ran and stood in the center of the plague-consumed crowd. Yeshua possessed this same fearless attitude: "when the time was come that he should be received up, he steadfastly set his face to go to Jerusalem" (Luke 9:51). Secondly, Aaron also put on incense that accompanied his prayer to Yahweh on behalf of the people. Yeshua did the same for Jew and Gentile when He cried out from the cross, "Father forgive them, for they know not what they do." The third thing Aaron did was to make a blood atonement for the people. Yahweh always required sacrificial blood in order to procure His forgiveness. This is why Yeshua shed His own holy blood on behalf of the nation. His voluntary sacrifice was the grandest atonement of all time (Isaiah 53:10).

Today, may your spirit rejoice and your soul confidently stand before the Father because of the intercessory work of His Son. All your sins are now behind you, even the worst of them, so leave your fear and dread behind, too. You can go out with full assurance because your loving, caring High Priest stands between you and your tendency to sin. But don't sin needlessly or carelessly. Do your utmost for Yeshua and the Spirit of Yeshua will do His utmost for you (1 Thessalonians 5:24).

Aaron's Rod that Budded

Part 7

"And it shall come to pass, that the man's rod, whom I shall choose, shall blossom: and I will make to cease from me the murmurings of the children of Israel." (Numbers 17:5)

The test of tribal princes was on. "And it came to pass, that on the morrow Moses went into the tabernacle of witness; and, behold, the rod of Aaron for the house of Levi was budded, and brought forth buds, and bloomed blossoms, and yielded almonds" (v.8). Moses got quite a surprise, didn't he? If you check the biblical record, you will find that Israel's prolific list of *murmurings* abruptly ended after this miracle and a measurable contentedness ensued for the remainder of the wilderness journey. Of all the miracles Yahweh performed for His people during their transition from slavery to freedom, this miracle was the most intriguing.

This spectacular event foreshadowed *that Messiah would sprout back to life!* Like Aaron's staff, which was once cut off from its life-giving source, so Messiah was "cut off out of the land of the living" (Isaiah 53:8). But after lying deathly still for three days before Roman witnesses, He miraculously sprang forth to effervescent life! Recall how Aaron's rod yielded buds, blossoms and fruit. Well, Yeshua's rising from the dead took place on *Yom HaBikkurim*, the springtime festival of *First Fruits*. This is the time of year when Israel's almond trees cover the landscape with plentiful white or pink flowers giving it a mystical freshness. In Israel, the almond tree is the first among fruit trees to wake from winter sleep. They burst into bloom while other trees are still dormant and bare. What a vibrant and colorful token Aaron's rod is to Yeshua's resurrection!

Like Israel's wilderness murmurings against God, which came to a complete end after the token, the miracle of Messiah's resurrection ends all discontent for His followers satisfying both Jew and gentile believers forever. Are you satisfied just knowing that Yeshua is risen from the dead? Is this not enough for you? Today, ask the risen Saviour to end your restlessness with a small application of His holy freshness.

The Serpent on a Pole
Part 8

"And the LORD said unto Moses, Make thee a fiery serpent, and set it upon a pole: and it shall come to pass, that every one that is bitten, when he looketh upon it, shall live." (Numbers 21:8)

Yahweh sent fiery serpents among the people, and they died in great numbers (v.6). Realizing their sinfulness the nation quickly repented and started begging Moses to intercede that Yahweh would take away the serpents—*seraphim,* meaning, *"burning* ones." The LORD did not end this reptile invasion as He did back in Egypt with the amphibious invasion of frogs, but He did provide a perfect remedy to combat sin's deadly sting. He told Moses to fashion a fiery serpent [*seraph*] and raise it up on a pole. Moses used brass—representing judgment. The word for pole is *nes, a standard bearer.* Nes comes from *nahsas* meaning to *gleam* from afar. The serpent and the pole together became the token of Israel's life. "And it came to pass, that if a serpent had bitten any man, when he beheld the serpent of brass, he lived" (v.9).

This strange event foreshadowed *how* Messiah would die—*lifted up on a stake for all to see!* The brass serpent was emblematic of the Adamic curse and mankind's judgment being averted; similarly, Messiah Yeshua was taken to a hill and fastened on a high cross for all Israel to behold. When Messiah was crucified they didn't recognize the symbolism at the time, yet this Messianic Deliverer had forewarned of the time when He would fall under sin's judgment saying, "as Moses lifted up the serpent in the wilderness, even so must the Son of man be lifted up: That whosoever believeth in him should not perish, but have eternal life...And I, if I be lifted up from the earth, will draw all men unto me" (John 3:14-15; 12:32).

Messiah's cross still gleams brightly today as a beacon of hope in a dark world. As a believer, your job is to point dying sinners to this source of eternal life. This morning ask God to help you get this vital message to someone who is experiencing the conviction of sin's eternal sting.

Father's Day Riddles

"Why do the heathen rage, and the people imagine a vain thing?"
(Psalm 2:1)

In the three following passages concerning God's Son, a riddle comes first. Here in Psalm 2 the riddle comes out front and center: *"Why do the heathen rage, and the people imagine a vain thing?"* They killed Yahweh's anointed [Heb. *mashiakh*], yet the Father took such great pride in His Son's atoning death that He raised Him from the grave. After doing so, His very first words to Him were, "Thou art my Son; this day have I begotten thee" (v.7). In Acts 13:33 Paul confirms that this verse refers to Yeshua's resurrection, not His incarnation. The Father was so delighted in His Son's redemptive work that He also set Him on the very throne of heaven (v.6). God the Father makes a third and final decree: "Kiss the Son lest...ye perish...Blessed are all they that put their trust in him" (v.12).

Later in the Psalms, another passage speaks of God's Son: "He shall cry unto me, Thou art my father, my God, and the rock of my salvation" (Psalm 89:26). No ordinary being could claim to have God as his Father. Only to one Who bears a unique relationship to Him could He say, "I will make him my firstborn" (v.27). The psalmist puts forth his riddle: *"Who in the heaven can be compared unto the LORD? Who among the sons of the mighty can be likened unto the LORD?"* (v.6). A helpful clue is then immediately given. Whoever is like Yahweh must also be able to rule the elements of earth: "Thou rulest the raging of the sea: when the waves thereof arise, thou stillest them" (v.9). When Yeshua twice calmed Galilee's raging sea before His disciples' eyes, He revealed His true identity as being like Yahweh (Matthew 14:32; Mark 4:39).

Wise Solomon set forth his grand riddle: *"Who hath established all the ends of the earth?"* (Proverbs 30:4). The same verse goes on to point the enquirer to God's unique Son saying, *"What is his name, and what is his son's name, if thou canst tell?"* A very revealing clue is given in the next verse. "Every word of God is pure: he is a shield unto them that put their trust in him" (v.5). Here Solomon cleverly reveals one of the Son's more exalted names—the Word of God (John 1:1; Hebrews 1:1-2). Thank the heavenly Father today for revealing His Son to you and in you.

The Trees of Paradise

"And God said, Let the earth bring forth grass, the herb yielding seed, and the fruit tree yielding fruit after his kind, whose seed is in itself, upon the earth: and it was so." (Genesis 1:11)

The Hebrew word for fruit is *priy*, which comes from the root *parah* meaning to bear fruit. It is no coincidence that the names of many fruits begin with the letter *p* and include an *r*: pacura, para guava, persimmon, pear, pommerac, pomegranate, prune and purple grapes. Among all the tender green trees Yahweh has planted in His garden, Yeshua remains at the very center as the Tree of Life. When we partake of this life-giving source, we abide forever. In picturesque tones of Yeshua, the Shulamite says, "As the apple tree among the trees of the wood, so is my beloved among the sons. I sat down under his shadow with...delight, and his fruit was sweet to my taste" (Song of Solomon 2:3).

God forbade Israel to cut down their enemies' fruit-yielding trees warning them, "the tree of the field is man's life" (Deuteronomy 20:19). When you repentantly call on the Lord for salvation and become born again, you re-sprout as a tree of the Lord and are "full of sap" (Psalm 104:16). You are also full of fruit. The psalmist says, "he shall be like a tree planted by the rivers of water, that bringeth forth his fruit in his season; his leaf also shall not wither" (Psalm 1:3). Wayfaring strangers in this world also need to be able to eat from your gospel tree and live. The spiritual fruit you bear—love, joy, peace, longsuffering, gentleness, goodness, faith, meekness, temperance—is produced when you yield to the Spirit (Galatians 5:22-23). If you are as fruit bearing as you ought to be, the homeless, hungry, hurting pilgrims of the world will be drawn to you. You can then point them to the foremost Tree of Life—Yeshua.

Consider Isaac's prayer of blessing, "God Almighty bless thee, and make thee fruitful" (Genesis 28:3). After finding your place of prayer this morning, ask the Holy Spirit to help you be more fruit bearing in all that you do today.

Why Would You Look Elsewhere?

"And John calling unto him two of his disciples sent them to Jesus, saying, Art thou he that should come? Or look we for another?" (Luke 7:19)

Often we find ourselves in the same spiritual shape as that greatest of all prophets—John. He maintained perfect *belief,* yet his extended stay in Herod's prison caused *disbelief* to rise. John was *faithful* unto the day of his showing (Luke 1:80), but lack of intervention from Yeshua caused him to become temporarily *doubtful.* We stand firm in the Saviour's light, yet we quickly fall faint when dark shadows creep in and pervade our life. The narrative doesn't tell us what became of John's lapse of faith. We don't know if he recovered or not; we can only assume that he did. But rather than focus on the shadows of doubt, Luke draws our attention to Messiah's marvelous faith-building invitation.

While sitting in Herod's dungeon news came to John that Israel's Deliverer had just halted a funeral and raised another person from the dead. John's reasoning was, "Well, if Messiah can raise the dead, then why can't He raise me out of prison?" If Yeshua had rescued John from Herod's prison, he would have been in a worse mental state three years later when he would have seen Yeshua's violent death. Every cloud, no matter how dark, has a silver lining in God's kingdom. John's silver lining in death was being spared the pain of a gut-wrenching heartache while watching the King and His kingdom fade into obscurity.

Small faith *sinks* when it focuses on *poor* circumstances, but great faith *soars* when it looks beyond to the perfect future. God holds tomorrow in His hand, and what He does with it is His business. Our business is to hold firmly onto His other hand in faith.

Whatever shadows of doubt this year may bring you, when the cloud thickens and grows dark, just lean heavily upon the King's firm words: "blessed is he, whosoever shall not be offended in me" (v.23). As you go to Him in prayer today, leave tomorrow's fear out of your thoughts.

June 21

The Capstone Commandment

"Now the end of the commandment is charity out of a pure heart, and of a good conscience, and of faith unfeigned." (1 Timothy 1:5)

The "end" [*telos,* goal] of God's commandments is to polish them with our obedience. The word capstone can mean "a crowning achievement." This usually comes towards the *end* of one's learning, practice or career in a given field of study. The capstone in which the apostle boasts in is not his own great grasp of Law, but in God's deep desire that His covenant people simply love Him and live for Him. Knowing God's Word is one thing, but living it out is another thing altogether. The righteous Judge will offer little reward for our academic achievements in the Law. Our acceptable actions will count the most.

Paul says that the capstone of the commandment is charity or love. The Greek word is *agape,* but in Hebrew, it is *chesed.* Love is an action verb; that is why *chesed* is translated loving kindness. Whoever loved someone without taking ample time to show it? You are to operate out of godly love in all that you do. When you are in love with someone, you conduct yourself with a *pure heart;* your love is not divided. You also conduct yourself with a *good conscience* meaning you don't focus on yourself, but upon another. In all good conscience, your mind works no ill because you only want the best for that person at all costs. Finally, you conduct yourself with *faith unfeigned.* Who could ever accuse you of pretending to love someone for whom you were pouring yourself out?

A revealing test that determines whether you're a keeper of God's commandments or not is the test of *charity,* the test of love. True love *shows.* True love also *shines* through all the abuse that is sometimes thrown right back at you. True love also *shelters.* Charity that comes from a pure heart, a good conscience and real faith, can never be stopped. That is why charity is the capstone of the commandments. Is your capstone of charity set properly in place? Ask the Lord to put a little extra 'glue' on your capstone today.

Coming Up Empty?

"Three times in a year shall all thy males appear before the LORD thy God...and they shall not appear before the LORD empty." (Deuteronomy 16:16)

The expression "coming up empty" refers to someone who has nothing to show for all of his or her labor. Yahweh didn't want Israel coming up to the three annual feasts empty handed. Although He desired Israel to come up with hands full of the physical fruits of their labors, He also expected them *not* to come up spiritually empty. If they brought Him no gift—that served as food for the priests—then their empty hands would be a token of the emptiness of their hearts.

In this fast paced world of ours, believers can also come up to the house of the LORD empty-handed and leave empty-hearted. God has more than proved His love for us, now we must prove ours. The word *tithing* is not found in the New Covenant, yet if a worshiper doesn't give regularly and generously then he has a heart problem. Consider three possible reasons for coming up with a spiritual deficit.

First, maybe you don't know how to *rejoice* in the things of God (v.14). God not only wants your heart to be healthy but to be happy. Second, maybe you are not in the place that the LORD has *chosen* for you (v.15). You might be in a good church, one that is bustling, but that's not where God wants you and your family to be at this present time. Maybe He wants you in that little church around the corner that is struggling. You would be a blessing to them and that would lift your own spirit, wouldn't it? Third, maybe you have failed to recognize *all thine increase* (v.15). God has overly blessed you so that you can pour out that overflow upon others. If your present material bounty is still not enough to your liking, then you probably have a spiritual deficit.

Seek the Father's help so that the next time you go *up* to His house, you go *in* with all of His fullness and go *out* with all of His joy!

The Common Community

"And the multitude of them that believed were of one heart and of one soul: neither said any of them that ought of the things which he possessed was his own; but they had all things common" (Acts 4:32)

The newly infused believers had such an uncanny zeal to meet the needs of fellow saints. Their hearts were overflowing like a river after a flash flood so that it could be said of them, "Neither was there any among them that lacked" (Acts 4:34). The reason for their communal love was that a communal love had been shown them through the Saviour's recent example—both in His life and in His death. With gratefulness, they reciprocated and held nothing back. They were fulfilling Scripture by dwelling together in unity (Psalm 133:1). They understood that in Yeshua they were truly one.

The Greek word for common is *koinos*, which literally means, "shared by all or several." What the first-century believers were doing went far beyond ordinary cultural practices of sharing food. That born-again community shared absolutely everything in their storehouses, including money, so that they could continue the unique oneness they had found. They didn't want to lose it.

Titus was a Gentile who, after responding positively to the gospel, found favor in the eyes of the chief apostle. Paul addressed him as "mine own son after the common faith" (Titus 1:4). From the beginning of Paul's new faith, he fully grasped that Yahweh was not the God of the Jews only. The Messianic community's understanding enlarged in a short time. They deemed every repentant creature under heaven as worthy to share in the common salvation that was once theirs alone (Jude v.3). Believing gentiles also thrived upon the aspect of community that the Messianic believers demonstrated so regularly and so wonderfully. They became one in Yeshua's love and were fully adopted into the commonwealth of Israel (Ephesians 2:12).

Today, share Yeshua's redeeming love with someone who might least be expecting it.

Having Withdrawal Symptoms?

"Then he openeth the ears of men, and sealeth their instruction, That he may withdraw man from his purpose, and hide pride from man." (Job 33:16-17)

We awaken each day with many purposes. Some plans are well-engrained habits like eating, conversing with friends, sports and career pursuits. Other plans hold such high priority that we write them down on the calendar months in advance. But how often do we set aside a portion of our time to the King's service? Moreover, how often do we hear of someone who withdraws from his or her own purposes to become entirely immersed in the purposes of God? The truth of the matter is this: The moment we became reborn we also became repurposed! God did not *save us* and then *set us aside* simply to continue being occupied with our former agendas.

Peter had to learn this lesson on withdrawal repeatedly until it sunk in. Messiah's death didn't fit into Peter's plans, so he returned to his favorite occupation—fishing. The lights came on for Peter when the risen Saviour unexpectedly appeared at the seaside. Lord Yeshua's presence drew Peter away from his boat and away from his purpose. At the shore, the Master pointed to the net full of fishes. And with a great tone of disappointment in His voice, asked His top student, "lovest thou me more than these?" (John 21:15). Peter answered affirmatively, but the Master had to ask Peter this same loaded question two more times before He could finally draw the lead disciple away from his own agenda. Peter's old purpose was to *fish,* but his new purpose was to *shepherd* Yeshua's sheep.

Imagine trading any love you have for the One Who loved you enough to die for you. Has your occupation become a preoccupation? Do you love *me* more than *Messiah*? Place yourself under the pierced feet of the Holy One today and call out to Him saying, "Draw me away. Draw me away. I am all yours."

The Highest Thing in the Universe

"I will praise thee with my whole heart...for thou hast magnified thy word above all thy name." (Psalm 138:1-2)

An old expression says, "A person's name is only as good as his word." In the Near East, to go back on your word is to reduce your name to nothing. Even the evil king Herod refused to reverse a pledge that had gone out of his mouth. On my first trip to Israel, my wife and I walked out of a souvenir store in Bethlehem with an 18-carat gold onyx ring—unpaid for. My wife had showed some hesitation about whether her mother would like it or not, so the owner said, "Take it with you, and if she likes it you can phone us back with your credit card details; if not simply mail the ring back." They trusted us based on our word and the good word of our Palestinian Christian tour guide.

The Orient has a long history of upholding truth and honor. In that culture, a person's name was equivalent to their very character. David knew that if he couldn't count on the surety of God's Word then His holy nature was also at risk. Unfortunately, rabbis of today do not hold the same reverence for God's Word as David did. Instead, they exalt man-made Talmudic opinions above the written words of Yahweh—as if He cannot say what He means with clarity. This makes a mockery of the God of Abraham.

In the above text, the Hebrew root for *word* is *ay-mer'* meaning, "something *said.*" David uses it again in verse 4, and is referring to the whole counsel of God—the Torah, Tehellim and Ketuvim. David makes it so clear when he says, "O let me not wander from thy commandments. Thy word [*ay-mer'*] have I hid in mine heart, that I might not sin against thee" (Psalm 119:10-11). Amazing as it may seem, the highest thing in the universe is not God or His throne, but His holy Word. No wonder Job said, "I have esteemed the words of his mouth more than my necessary food" (Job 23:12).

You can rest assured today that Lord Yeshua's words are "faithful and true" (Revelation 21:5, 22:6). His double promise to you hangs upon His most glorious and gracious of names. He is the "True and Faithful" witness (3:14, 19:11). This morning, read Yeshua's *true* and *faithful* words; hear them, receive them, keep them, meditate on them, and cherish them for they are eternal and eternally wonderful.

Ezekiel's Last Words

"It was round about eighteen thousand measures: and the name of the city from that day shall be, The LORD is there." (Ezekiel 48:35)

Ezekiel lived to witness a deeply traumatic experience—the destruction of Israel's beloved capital, Jerusalem. He also suffered the tragedy of being carried away to the Chaldean's capital, Babylon. It was there that he received both glorious visions and prophetic words from Yahweh. In Babylon Ezekiel reminded Israel of God's judgment, but he also gave them hope of a future national restoration. Eventually, the prophet died and was buried there. His venerable shrine can be found today in a village called Kifl. Inside the tomb, high up on the walls, are beautifully decorated Hebrew letters. Over the entrance is a prayer written to Ezekiel.

In the last four chapters of Ezekiel's writings he gives highly detailed measurements of a future Jerusalem—the one to come in the millennium. After going through all the measurements of the courts, walls and gates, he ends abruptly by giving us the city's new name. In that day it will no longer only be called by its familiar name—Yerushalyim; rather, it will be called *Yahweh Shamah*, "The LORD is there." The city's new name fits the Near East custom of renaming someone when he or she moves into an exalted position. Abram, Jacob, Joseph and Daniel were all renamed. The reason Jerusalem will undergo an incredible name change is obvious. Its nature will be changed by virtue of its then ruling, reigning and resting King—Yeshua, the incarnation of Yahweh. The people will no longer glory in the city's walls; instead, they will glory in the city's eternal King.

Today, glory in Lord Yeshua's presence for He dwells within the sacred walls of your heart by faith. Yes, "the LORD is there" and you're aware of it because He changed your nature the day He took His place upon your heart's throne. Don't go around today feeling lonely like some abandoned city or ghost town. You have Jesus dwelling in your innermost being, so "be glad [and]…exceedingly rejoice" (Psalm 68:3).

Praising God in Song or Silence

"But thou art holy, O thou that inhabitest the praises of Israel."
(Psalm 22:3)

After their victory at the Red Sea, the people couldn't help but recognize that Yahweh was dwelling among them. With timbrels held high in their hands, Miriam led the women into a time of praise shouting, "Sing ye to the LORD, for he hath triumphed gloriously" (Exodus 15:21). Prison walls once hemmed in Paul and Silas, yet they turned their shackles into musical instruments and sang praises unto God (Acts 16:25). As God drew near, the prison doors swung open. What an amazing token of how God inhabits the praise of His people! The psalmist stated this fact, but the actual words prophetically apply to the Saviour as He hung upon the cross. Now discover the wonder of how Yeshua praised God that day in silence.

The word for praise is *tehillah*, spelled *tav, hey, lamed, hey*. In this combination, the Paleo-Hebraic meanings of these letters are quite significant. The letter *tav* looks like a pair of crossed sticks and symbolizes a sign or <u>monument</u>. The letter *hey* pictures a man with his <u>hands held up</u>, and there are two of these letters in *tehillah*, thus depicting people with uplifted hands. The *lamed* represents a shepherd's staff. One of its meanings is to <u>bind</u>. When people bind their own hands together intermittently, it is called clapping and is a biblical form of praise (Psalm 47:1). Judah, *Yehudah*, was the tribe of people among whom Yahweh chose to place His Tabernacle. It's not a coincidence that Yehudah means praise or celebrated. God planned it that way.

As to Messiah's praise upon the tree, He couldn't sing because He could barely breathe. His praise was instead offered in silence. Theologically, there were two people represented on that *monumental* cross—the Son of Man and you. Yes, you! Paul agrees to this in Romans 6:6 and Galatians 2:20. From the cross, Yeshua praised the everlasting Father with His *hands held up*, each one being *bound* in place with ropes and nails. Your heart may be heavy today, but you can still praise God in song or in silence.

Messiah's Spirit Baptism

"I indeed baptize you with water unto repentance: but he that cometh after me is mightier than I, whose shoes I am not worthy to bear: he shall baptize you with the Holy Ghost, and with fire." (Matthew 3:11)

John's strange news pointed Israelites to a totally new form of baptism. What John did not know was that Messiah's baptism would also later become available to Gentiles as well. A proselyte of the Old Covenant had to undergo two Judaic rituals—circumcision and baptism, accompanied with a profession of the One True God. Entering into the New Covenant, however, requires a circumcision of the heart, which can in turn be evidenced by a changed life (Luke 3:8). The baptism of repentance is still required, but must be accompanied by a profession in Messiah as the Son of God. These two things are to be strictly enforced but can only come about "through the faith of the operation of God" (Colossians 2:11-12).

John's inter-testament baptism had to fade away, which John himself confessed (John 3:30). After Messiah's requisite blood was poured out, He could then—as High Priest in heaven—officiate over this new baptism in the Spirit (John 7:39). The *baptism with fire,* which John feverishly announced, was directed entirely at the Pharisees and Sadducees, those disbelieving souls who came out merely to spectate (Matthew 3:7). John prefaced and concluded his *burning* announcement with clear references to *hell fire,* a baptism to be avoided at all costs. He also clearly referred to whom Messiah would baptize in the unquenchable fire—unfruitful trees and undesirable chaff (v.10, 12). The choice of which baptism they would receive depended on whether or not they repented of self-righteousness and called on Yeshua's redeeming name.

The only second baptism that is actually required for a believer is water baptism. This should immediately follow Messiah's invisible Spirit baptism. Romans 8:9 states that a person doesn't even belong to Messiah if he doesn't have the Spirit of God, so salvation and the baptism with the Holy Ghost are synonymous acts, not separate. Today, take time to praise the Saviour for sparing you from baptism in the Lake of Fire.

Having Troubles?

"I marvel that ye are so soon removed from him that called you into the grace of Messiah unto another gospel: Which is not another; but there be some that trouble you, and would pervert the gospel of Messiah." (Galatians 1:6-7)

Within the Messianic fold, there are quite a variety of philosophies concerning worship and the Word. Paul was well aware of this reemerging problem and advised believers saying, "there are differences of administrations, but the same Lord. And there are diversities of operations, but it is the same God which worketh all in all" (1 Corinthians 12:5-6). The most critical issue is the matter of Yeshua's full deity. If He is not LORD, then we are still lost (John 8:24). These are His own words.

Most all Messianic believers agree that Yeshua is the *Son of God* (Messiah born of a virgin), but some do not behold Him as *God the Son*, the eternal Creator. This is not semantics; this is a sickness within the Messianic body! If any person attempts to rob Yeshua of His deity inside an assembly, they bring trouble. The apostle said that these kinds of troublers are accursed (v.9). Messianic leaders are to make Yeshua's Lordship crystal clear and to strengthen this theological position on a regular basis. In Isaiah 48:12 Yahweh speaks as the majestic Creator; however, in verse 16 He suddenly becomes heaven's sent One—the Messiah. This clearly teaches us that Yeshua is Yahweh and no less. The complementary passage to this is Zechariah 2:8-11 where Yahweh declares three times, in a triune way, that He is the sent One.

The aged apostle John helps believers who are faced with this ilk saying, "receive him not into your house, neither bid him God speed" (2 John 1:10). If you bless such a gospel heretic in any way, you are a partaker of his or her evil deeds (v.11). If someone like this is troubling you, go to your gospel shepherd and discuss the issue with him. It is his job to see to it that this person troubles you and your congregation no more. You can also equip yourself to counter this kind of heresy by studying Yeshua's deity throughout the Tanakh. Today, ask LORD Yeshua to help you become well versed on this subject.

ℒord of the ℬabbath

"And he said unto them, The sabbath was made for man, and not man for the sabbath: Therefore the Son of man is Lord also of the Sabbath." (Mark 2:27-28)

If Yeshua was under the spotlight on any given day of the week it was on the Sabbath of the LORD (Deuteronomy 5:14). He often chose to heal on this day to demonstrate His liberating power. This Sabbath the scribes and Pharisees watched Him closely as He walked along the edge of a cornfield. Messiah knew that Torah forbade harvesting on the Sabbath, but it didn't forbid eating straight from the earth's gloriously prepared table. Laws must also be interpreted, and there was no violation of holiness here. Yeshua was always ignoring or trampling on the rabbis' man-made oral traditions [*takhanot*] because they often superseded God's written Word.

Yeshua wanted to give His disciples rest from their hunger, so He lifted the intricate burdens of the Law. Knowing that the Sabbath police were watching, He may have whispered, "On the count of three, everyone grab a handful of grain." The moment they did, Pharisaical fingers came flying at them like poison darts. After asking Yeshua to explain the reason for His apparent breech of Law, He laid out a case precedent: "Have ye never read what David did, when he had need, and was hungry, he, and they that were with him?" (v.25). The protectors of the Sabbath thought it more holy for Yeshua and His students to just faint by the way, but Messiah thought it more holy to *show* them exactly Who He was—the Lord of the Sabbath. He did this in His closing summary.

Physical rest is found in ceasing from labor, but spiritual rest can only be obtained by ceasing from good works and trusting in Lord Yeshua's pierced, yet strong, arms. He won't let you go away hungry. Feeding you holy bread is His concern. Your concern is to simply draw near to Him and stay close. This morning after drawing near Him in prayer, thank Him for granting you rest from all your burdens, large and small.

God's Triple Pledge

"Thou art my servant...Fear thou not; for I am with thee: be not dismayed; for I am thy God: I will strengthen thee; yea, I will help thee; yea, I will uphold thee with the right hand of my righteousness." (Isaiah 41:9-10)

There are two focal points in this passage—fear and strength. One belongs to man and is natural; the other belongs to God and is supernatural. One has to do with what is in man's head, and the other has to do with what is in Messiah's hand. Fear and anxiety makes a person weak and powerless. Sometimes these negative emotions make a person cover his head with his hand(s). God tells His servant not to be dismayed; that is, not to *stare* at the problem or be *bewildered*. A fearful person is prone to focus only on the problem. Instead, the servant of God should focus on His two "I am's" and His three "I will's."

First, God says, "I will strengthen [*aw-mats'*] you." The three Paleo-Hebrew letters of *awmats* reveal just how strong your God will make you—like a *strong, mighty hunter*. Now, that's strong! Then God says, "I will help [*aw-zar'*] you." This word means to surround, protect or aid, but there's more. Its three Paleo-Hebraic letters depict the act of one who *shades* and *nourishes* another person's *head*. Fear can make a person faint. If you faint in the sun, you need someone to shade your head and give you water. Well, God the Son is indeed a Shelter in the time of storm and the Water of Life when you are spiritually dehydrated! Third, God says, "I will uphold [*taw-mahk'*] you." This word means to sustain, stay up, keep fast and follow close. Sounds good, doesn't it? It gets better! The three pictorial letters of *tawmakh* identify a person whom God has *marked* with inward *might* and a *tame* spirit. Wow! How blessed is that for being upheld when you were so weak a moment ago that you could hardly stand!

Yes, Elohim will do all three of these things for you today no matter what comes your way! He will make you strong. He will also surround you, shade you, protect you, nourish you and make you tame or calm. Begin this day by thanking Elohim for giving you such strength and assurance.

Your Elohim

"Thou art my servant...Fear thou not; for I am with thee: be not dismayed; for I am thy God: I will strengthen thee; yea, I will help thee; yea, I will uphold thee with the right hand of my righteousness." (Isaiah 41:9-10)

In yesterday's devotion, we examined all the wonderful things God [*Elohim*] does for His servant when he is overcome with fear or gets dismayed. Now let's look at the Paleo-Hebraic background of God's Hebrew title Elohim to discover the precious, priceless picture He draws of Himself that we might be filled with courage and calm. It is the overall picture of a shepherd who lives for the purpose of his sheep.

The first letter in Elohim is the *alef*, which depicts an ox head. An ox head pictures three ideas: *"strong, power, leader."* All these speak of your Great Shepherd. Next is the *lamed*, which depicts a shepherd's staff. This symbol means to *"bind, yoke."* Your loving Shepherd yokes Himself to you out of absolute duty and pure devotion. He will never leave you nor forsake you. Ever! Then the letter *hey* depicts a person with upheld hands and means to *"look,"* actually—"behold, look at me!" The Shepherd looks after you with His omniscient eyes, yet He also wants you to look at Him and know that He is always near. The letter *yod* depicts an arm with an open hand and means to *"work,* also to *throw."* A shepherd works diligently to keep his sheep fed, sheltered, rested, sheared and healthy. A protective shepherd will also throw things at approaching predators to ward them off. So if God be for you, then who can be against you (Romans 8:31)? Finally, the *mem* depicts three things: *"rough water, chaos, blood."* A faithful shepherd is willing to enter the wilderness arena and fight for his sheep and get bloody in the process if necessary (1 Samuel 17:34-36).

In Hebrews 13:20 Paul described the Son of God's role as "that great Shepherd of the sheep" and was careful to also note the chaos He endured and the means whereby He saved us—"through the blood of the everlasting covenant." Today, don't go out facing your problem; instead, go out facing your Great Shepherd, Yeshua. Look to Him! He's *your* Elohim.

About Face!

"Jude, the servant of Jesus Christ, and brother of James, to them that are sanctified by God the Father, and preserved in Jesus Christ, and called." (Jude 1:1)

Jude presents some of the most severe warnings in all of the New Testament. As one reads this letter, nothing less than a deep and profound respect can be held for the man who penned it. And who was this man? He was Yehudah, the half-brother of Yeshua.

At first, Jude was not an avid subscriber of Yeshua's groundbreaking theology. Neither was James [Yacob], another of Yeshua's half-brothers, a believer at first. In fact, Yeshua had four half-brothers (Matthew 13:55). Not even one of them adhered to His teachings until after His resurrection (John 7:5). And then only two of His half-brothers made an about-face that we know of. Jude and James turned 180 degrees from their former course of unbelief and suddenly became followers of the Way, the Truth and the Life. Afterwards James became president of the Jerusalem Council and like Jude, a contributor to the New Testament. What a big turn around these two men made! Yeshua's resurrection from the dead was what made the difference.

Maybe you have not fully made up your mind as to Yeshua's deity and you continue walking in unbelief. If so, then it is time for an about-face. If you are already a believer but have erringly grown cold on the Lord, then it is also time for an about-face! Maybe you have a relationship with God but you no longer have that full trust and confidence in His ability to guide you and provide for you. If so, you need to do an about-face. The Lord is understanding, patient and ready to do His part to bolster your faith once you turn fully towards Him.

This morning, ask the Lord to help you come face to face with Him in full agreement.

Three Levels of Sin

"But every man is tempted, when he is drawn away of his own lust, and enticed. Then when lust hath conceived, it bringeth forth sin: and sin, when it is finished, bringeth forth death." (James 1:14-15)

The Hebrew apostle speaks of man's battle with sin and its dreadful effects. A helpful acronym is LSD—lust, sin, and death. Let's examine the three levels sin. Even though a person may have been raised in a godly environment, that soul still possesses evil inclinations along with the rest of humanity. This is your inherent weakness that comes from Adam and the first level of sin. It is called iniquity, but in Hebrew, *ahvone*. Avon means perversity, moral evil, mischief. This has to do with our ungodly thoughts and emotions that often seem to come out of nowhere. These can become uncontrollable if not kept in check by confession and prayer. These sinful thoughts grieve God's Spirit, so we must turn from further enticement.

Sin is the next level and is noted by the Hebrew word *khet*, which implies an offence, a violation of one of God's holy laws. Solomon declares that "there is not a just man upon earth, that doeth good, and sinneth not" (Ecclesiastes 7:20). *Khet's* root word, *kha-tah*, means to *miss* the mark as if shooting an arrow. Paul says that we have all sinned and come short of God's perfection (Romans 3:23). This level of sin is like stumbling and can be done in ignorance or *shegagah* (Leviticus 4:2). *Shegagah* means a mistake, an inadvertent transgression, an error; and its root, *shegag*, means to *stray*. 1 John 1:9 tells us what to do when we stumble or stray.

Transgression or *peh-sha* implies deliberate sin. *Pesha* is an intentional action committed in defiance to God. Its root, *pasha*, literally means to *break* away; that is, rebel, revolt, apostatize, trespass—to cross over to the other side! At this point one is no longer "striving against sin," but is sinning willfully (Hebrews 12:4).

If you think a sinful thought today, don't say it. If you say it, don't do it. And if you do it, repent and don't do it again!

July 5

ℐℓ 𝒟ynamite 𝒟elivery

"And Stephen, full of faith and power, did great...miracles among the people...And they were not able to resist the wisdom and the spirit by which he spake." (Acts 6:8, 10)

Stephen is mentioned first in the listing of "men of honest report, full of the Holy Ghost and wisdom" (v.3). This is likely due to his ranking as first martyr of the New Covenant era. Even though Stephen was a Greek-speaking Jew, his speech was more like an angel's—not in eloquence, but authority. When the corporate body chose Stephen, they chose wisely. He was chosen along with six others mainly for ministering daily to the needs of Greek-speaking Jewish widows in Jerusalem; but he loved to proclaim the gospel as well. On this day, his salvation message was so riveting that the Hellenistic synagogue leaders stirred up the people and brought him to the council where false witnesses were waiting against him (v.12-13). Stephen so wonderfully fulfilled the requirement of being full of the Holy Spirit that "all that sat in the council, looking steadfastly on him, saw his face as it had been the face of an angel" (v.15). At his tribunal, he delivered the Word with great wisdom. His obedience to the faith earned him not only a title, *First Church Martyr*, but also a crown, which Lord Yeshua calls, "a crown of life" (Revelation 2:10). Stephen's name in Greek means crown or a wreath, so his name was highly prophetic.

Spirit-fullness, godly wisdom and honesty are all that any believer needs to accomplish the many daily tasks effectively. These three necessities, however, do come without some effort on the believer's part. Spirit-fullness comes through yielding to the Spirit moment by moment. Godly wisdom comes through study and prayer. And honesty comes through a steadfast determination to remain blameless. God wants every saint to be filled with the power of His Spirit, the depth of His wisdom, and the integrity of "just men made perfect" (Hebrews 12:23). This is His recipe for equipping the saints and winning the lost. Every believer operates on a different personality level, but we should all operate on the same level of commitment.

Get fully equipped this morning in the prayer closet, and then get busy ministering the Bread of Life to those in need!

£ord of the Rainbow!

"I do set my bow in the cloud, and it shall be for a token of a covenant between me and the earth." (Genesis 9:13)

The earth experienced an epic flood that seemed to come out of nowhere. From that time forward, God wanted every creature on earth to know that He would never repeat this same act again, lest panic set in every time it began to rain (v.11-12). He gave the inhabitants of earth a token of His forbearance—a rainbow. But there's more in a rainbow than meets the eye. A rainbow is a beautiful display of seven visible light waves emanating from heaven's electromagnetic spectrum. Seven is the number of perfection and completion, which accurately describes all of God's covenants with man. Now, here is the amazing part. Two more colors that are not visible to the human eye flank each end of the visible light spectrum. Beyond red is *infrared* light, and beyond violet is *ultraviolet* light. These remain out of our view for a very specific reason. It has to do with God's triune arrangement.

The Bible describes God metaphorically as light (1 John 1:5). Light is one continual spectrum, but only part of it is made available for viewing with the human eye. By this analogy we easily understand how a rainbow's visible light represents God's *Son*, for He is "the image of the invisible God" (Colossians 1:15). Paul says it another way. Yeshua is "the fulness of the Godhead bodily" (Colossians 2:9). Just as infrared and ultraviolet flank the visible light spectrum, so God *the Father* and God *the Spirit* flank God the *Son* on each side yet choose to remain completely out of view.

The top color on a rainbow is bright red. This speaks of the predominant way in which the Son of God protects His covenant people: "we have redemption through his blood, even the forgiveness of sins" (Colossians 1:14). Green, the middle color of the rainbow, speaks of the Son's eternal existence (Micah 5:2). John saw Yeshua seated in heaven with "a rainbow round about the throne, in sight like unto an emerald" (Revelation 4:3). Today, be reminded "God was manifest in the flesh" for your sake (1 Timothy 3:16), and take comfort in this.

Inspiration & Perspiration

"Then Solomon began to build the house of the LORD at Jerusalem in mount Moriah, where the Lord appeared unto David his father." (2 Chronicles 3:1)

Isn't it a bit funny how Yahweh's Temple has carried the additional name Solomon's Temple? Solomon was the chief architect and carried the most inspiration to see it through to completion. As you know, he originally obtained the inspiration to build God's house from his father. David understood why he could not initiate the actual building process, yet he chose to do what he could do. He laid up stockpiles of his own personal silver and gold to adorn the future Temple.

To use an adaptation from Edison's proverb: "Work is one percent inspiration and ninety-nine percent perspiration." Inspiration must have lots of follow-through. After the Temple's destruction by Babylon, its restoration came about because the people still had a willingness to work (Nehemiah 4:6). In building any large structure, one needs lots of workers.

Unfortunately, in establishing a New Testament assembly for Messiah, self-motivated and self-sacrificing volunteers are greatly needed. There were a great many of these individuals in the days of the first-century church, but in these last days just before the Master Builder returns some workers seem to be more than a little preoccupied. The divine Architect announced His plan: "I will build my church" (Matthew 16:18). But some saints have neglectfully forgotten that Messiah is still planting churches and still needs faithful volunteers. He is calling them. The question is—are they listening?

A pastor only has two hands, so he can't build an assembly of people all by himself. He's not short of inspiration; he's just short of help. Today, pray that the Master Builder will show you an area where you would be of valuable service in His kingdom-building program, then make your availability known to your pastor. He will be so glad.

Kiss & Tell

"And now they sin more and more, and have made them molten images of their silver, and idols according to their own understanding...Let the men that sacrifice kiss the calves." (Hosea 13:2)

God spoke this word of rebuke to "Ephraim," that is, the northern tribes (v.1). Jeroboam became the first king over Israel after Solomon's departure, but Jeroboam feared losing the people's allegiance if they continued travelling to Jerusalem to worship. His remedy was to raise up the old-time shrines, one in Dan and the other in Bethel. Two calves were fashioned of gold and placed in each city for Israelites to worship. Just as people kiss someone they have given their heart to, so the people of Israel adored one of the two golden calves with a ceremonial kiss as they offered up sacrifices to Baal, the bull god. Idol-worshipping Catholics touch or kiss the foot of St. Peter's bronze statue so much that it has been worn smooth.

Who or what one kisses tells the real story. Judas kissed Yeshua, but it was for the gain of money. Today the western world is regrettably smitten with the love of things. The list is exhaustive. To careless believers some of these things can easily become idols. Love is blind, and so there's a real possibility that a person can't see that they have fallen into the trap of "the love of the world and the things in the world" (1 John 2:15). Oddly, idols aren't just made of silver and gold anymore but also *plastic*! A television can possibly become a plastic idol. The worst plastic of them all is the plastic credit card that can easily lead to debt that leads to slavery. In contrast, an action-oriented love towards God will never take a person into debt. The believer can only store up real, lasting treasures through a consistent lifestyle of selflessness and adoration towards the *things of God*.

There is a healing remedy for the overt love of things—"turn thou to thy God: keep mercy and judgment, and wait on thy God continually" (Hosea 12:6). Today, ask the Saviour to help you love Him more and to love the world a whole lot less.

Days of Restoration

"And I will restore to you the years that the locust hath eaten, the cankerworm, and the caterpillar, and the palmerworm, my great army which I sent among you." (Joel 2:25)

The purpose behind the invading human armies God sent upon His people was pure and exacting. He was devoted to His covenant children, and therefore had to discipline them. But as a father who punishes his wayward child in measure and can then hardly wait to shower him once again with blessings, so Yahweh feels the same about Israel, His beloved son. The Hebrew play on words is absolutely beautiful in this text. The gracious Father says, "I will restore [*shilahmti*] the barren years I sent [*shilakhti*] upon you." The days of restoration now coming to Israel can be seen by way of the numerous and abundant fruitful orchards, vast vineyards, sweeping cornfields and hills lined with olive trees throughout their land. During peak season, a plane is daily loaded with watermelons, called the Queen's melon, and sent to England for their markets. And Jaffa oranges can be found in Australian vegetable markets. Joel would love to witness these wonderful days of his ancient homeland's dramatic restoration.

Maybe you've had an army of "locusts" invade your bank account, your health, your friends, your family, your career or maybe even your warmly lit library of dreams—your plans for the future. However, you can't point the finger at your heavenly Father and say, "Why did you do this to me?" David didn't lay blame to his faithful Shepherd. His attitude was, "It is good for me that I have been afflicted; that I might learn thy statutes" (Psalm 119:71). Difficult moments drive us to Messiah whether He is the designer of them or not. Grief, hunger, poverty, sickness, sorrow, shame or pain—all these "things work together for good to them that love God" (Romans 8:28).

Whatever is going on in your life today, fear not! Restoration is on the way! Joel assures you in 2:26 saying, "And ye shall eat in plenty, and be satisfied, and praise the name of the LORD...and...never be ashamed."

The Knowing

"Surely the Lord GOD will do nothing, but he revealeth his secret unto his servants the prophets" (Amos 3:7).

God never brought correction or judgment without first giving His anointed messengers a heads-up. The covenant people of God are never kept in the dark if they walk in the light of His currently revealed Word. For example, God didn't keep His servant Abraham in the dark about His prearranged plans to destroy two cities associated with Lot. When God reveals a thing, His messengers are certain of it as in the case of the "Revelation of Jesus Christ, which God gave unto [John], to show unto his servants things which must shortly come to pass" (Revelation 1:1).

The greatest time of destruction in man's history will be in the last days. Ever since Israel proclaimed statehood on May 14th, 1948, the countdown to Armageddon has accelerated. It is not God's desire that these last days overtake the planet by surprise. That is why the Son of God forewarned that earthquakes and storm surges would escalate at an ever-increasing rate before His return. He called these natural signs "the beginning of sorrows" which in Greek, means *birth pains* (Matthew 24:8). The earth has always had hurricanes, pestilences, earthquakes, famines and wars, but not at the pace that we see them happening today! They are coming closer together and in increasing intensity just as there is "travail upon a woman" (1 Thessalonians 5:3). Recently, destructive tsunamis have swept Indonesia and Japan "as a man wipeth a dish, wiping it, and turning it upside down" (2 Kings 21:13). Localized flooding has now escalated into regional flooding, and more and more countries are experiencing it.

As believers who regularly read God's Word, we have no excuse for not *"knowing* the time" (Romans 13:11). Tragically, the world has no way of knowing about the Lord's return unless we speak up. So let's tell them *"knowing* that the goodness of God leadeth [souls] to repentance" (Romans 2:4). One of Paul's life verses was this: *"Knowing* therefore the terror of the Lord, we persuade men" (2 Corinthians 5:11). Today, with the Lord's help, seek to get the message of Yeshua's certain deliverance to those who are not in the know.

$\mathcal{D}$ouble $\mathcal{V}$ision

"The vision of Obadiah. Thus saith the Lord GOD concerning Edom;
We have heard a rumour from the LORD, and an ambassador is sent among
the heathen." (Obadiah 1:1)

The first part of Obadiah's name is drawn from the root word *awbad,* which means to work or serve. An *obed* is a servant (Ruth 4:17). This word is the origin of the words *obedient* and *obey.* Even though Obadiah was a servant in the house of evil king Ahab, he proclaimed before Elijah to be a high servant of Yahweh saying, "I thy servant fear the LORD from my youth" (1 Kings 18:12). Then Elijah asked him to do something that he was fearful to do, but he did it obediently! Obadiah not only means to "work for Yah," but also to "worship Yah."

An *obed* will also, from his heart, do *obeisance.* Obadiah bowed and paid homage to the Most High God. He was still *serving* and *worshipping* Yahweh through his humble service to Ahab because God had him in that place for a specific purpose. Ahab's evil wife Jezebel attempted to purge the northern kingdom of Yahweh's true prophets, but Obadiah worked diligently to safeguard them. He hid one hundred of them in a cave and kept them supplied with bread and water (1 Kings 18:13). Obadiah had a wonderful case of double vision having a mind to *worship* Yahweh with empty, raised hands and to *work* for Him with full, busy hands.

Saint of the Most High God, do you have this same ready mindset to both work for God and worship Him as you humbly go about your daily routine? This kind of double vision will allow you to accomplish His will at every turn. He can use you wherever you are to carry out His sovereign will, and at the same time allow you to worship Him from the quietness of your heart. God needs faithful, work-minded, worship-minded servants all over the globe. Will you be this kind of double-visioned servant for the King of Kings?

Today, ask Abba to help you be a good *obed,* to be consistently *obedient* to His high commands and do *obeisance* to Him.

Losing the Plot

"Now the word of the LORD came unto Jonah the son of Amittai, saying, Arise, go to Nineveh, that great city, and cry against it; for their wickedness is come up before me." (Jonah 1:1-2)

Jonah's Hebrew name is profound, yet simple. At birth, his father called him *Yonah*, a dove. Jonah's father, Amittai (whose name means truthful, honest and dependable) wanted his son to be a symbol of *peace*. Yahweh sought to fulfill Jonah's prophetic name. He would send Jonah, the man of peace, to make peace between the people of Nineveh and the God of heaven. Jonah's job was to bring Nineveh to their knees in reconciliation to God through preaching one profound truth—that God would destroy the city-state in 40 days if they didn't quickly submit to Him. Jonah, however, wanted to escape his God-given responsibility by sailing away to Tarshish. Perhaps he preferred the atmosphere of revival that he was commanding back in parts of Israel (2 Kings 14:25). Jonah had a heart for his own people but very little for foreigners.

Even when Jonah changed his mind and went preaching to the people of Nineveh, he did so grudgingly. Afterwards he sat down peevishly to sulk. He had totally lost the plot; but God sought to bring Jonah back into line by comparing his pity for the wilted gourd to his lack of pity for a nation of lost gentiles. When Jonah lost the plot he went down (1:3), down (1:3), down (1:15), down (1:17) and down (2:6) until he had nowhere left to go but back up into God's will.

Have you lost the plot for evangelism? If you have, then the lost may lose their lot in the eternal kingdom. Has your pity for the lost been "swallowed up" by the affairs of this life? Winning the lost is the highest calling a believer possesses, but to turn from this calling is to descend into self-will. The key to *keeping the plot* is to recognize where you are supposed to be, observe where you presently are, and then see if the two line up. Occasionally we might temporarily lay aside the heavenly plot, but we should seek to stay in perfect synch with the Lord of the Harvest at all times (Luke 10:2). Spend some time today seeking the Lord's counsel and His estimation of your adherence to His divine call.

193

Who is Like Yah?

"The word of the LORD that came to Micah the Morasthite in the days of Jotham, Ahaz, and Hezekiah, kings of Judah." (Micah 1:1)

Micah warned Israel and Judah of future judgment, but he also extended hope beyond the years of their punishment to the golden Messianic age.

Micah (*mee-kah'*) is an abbreviation of Mikahyah, which means, "Who is like Yah?" The answer to this reasonable question is *no one*. Well, there is one exception and one alone. Micah calls Him the Judge of Israel (5:1), and he adds that, like Yah, this Judge is eternal in nature and walks before Him (5:2). Moreover, He judges in the majestic "name of the LORD" (5:4). Why? Because He is Yahweh's equal, His colleague, His "fellow" (Zechariah 13:7). Yeshua's equality with the Father is also confirmed in Philippians 2:6. Micah describes Yah's right-hand Man as coming forth out of his place to "tread upon the high places of the earth," and that when He does, the mountains will become molten under His feet (1:3-4). Micah boasts next in Yah's power to gather the remnant of Israel and put them together as sheep in a single fold (2:12). Micah also prophesies that Yahweh will build His earthly house upon an exalted mountain that will make all other mountains look like little hills (4:1). Who else but Yah or His companion Son can perform such things as these?

Are you lacking confidence in your beloved Redeemer, Yeshua? Do you sit solemnly somewhere in a corner waiting for a brighter day and better circumstances? If so, begin today contemplating the greatness of your God to the smallness of your problem. When you see that there is no real comparison, you will begin to see only Yeshua! Whether you have work difficulties, financial woes, family concerns, physical/mental sickness or heavy decisions to make, Yeshua stands ready to help you. He can do above and beyond what you would ever ask or dream (Ephesians 3:20). Today, just ask for LORD Yeshua's guidance and assistance. Praise Him while you wait patiently for His reply.

Perfect Confidence

"The LORD is good, a strong hold in the day of trouble; and he knoweth them that trust in him." (Nahum 1:7)

After Nahum pronounces a future worldwide destruction upon all the adversaries of God—namely Assyria—he pauses to give some comfort to those who are Yahweh's worshipers. He does this in fulfillment of his Hebrew name *nakh-oom*, which means comfortable. During Messiah's ministry, He took comfort in *kefar nakhum*, the town of comfort, Capernaum. This city overlooked the beautiful Sea of Galilee.

The prophet speaks of *trust*. In Hebrew, the primitive root of trust is *khasah* meaning "to flee for protection; figuratively to *confide* in: have hope, make refuge, put trust." The Modern Hebrew word for chair is *khiseh*—something you place all your confidence in to hold you up! Similarly, in the Bible, a king's chair is called a throne, *kisseh,* and the people take confidence in it. When a throne is vacant, the people worry. The writer of Hebrews wonderfully proclaims that in God "we might have a strong consolation, who have fled for refuge to lay hold upon the hope set before us: Which hope we have as an anchor of the soul" (Hebrews 6:18-19). Additionally, he speaks of "the forerunner," Messiah Yeshua, Who alone permits entrance into His Father's throne room. Nahum bids you not to worry about whether you will be allowed safe entrance. Paul quoted Nahum saying, "the Lord knoweth them that are his" (2 Timothy 2:19).

If you're feeling insecure this morning, shed all confidence in the many refuges this fallen world may afford. They are only false securities at best. In the last days God's adversaries who choose to hide themselves in mountains shall cast away all confidence in those geographical shelters and cry to the rocks that they might fall down upon them and hide them from the wrath of the Lamb Who sits upon the throne (Revelation 6:15-17). Nahum describes Yahweh as a stronghold, a *maoz*; that is to say, a fortress. Today, get *perfect confidence* in the prayer closet before venturing out.

The Great Selah

"I will stand upon my watch, and set me upon the tower, and will watch to see what he will say unto me, and what I shall answer when I am reproved." (Habakkuk 2:1)

Little is known about this pre-exile prophet apart from his brief writings at a time when the Chaldean armies were positioning themselves to overrun Jerusalem. Habakkuk carries on a dialogue with Yahweh asking Him many questions—primarily why a wicked nation is allowed to take over a righteous one. "And the LORD answered me, and said, Write the vision, and make it plain upon tables, that he may run that readeth it" (v.2). Judgment upon Judah was certain, and God's forewarning to flee the city while there was still time was one way of answering Habakkuk's plea: "in wrath remember mercy" (3:2).

Habakkuk ends his book with the words "on my stringed instruments," which may indicate that he was among the Levites who served musically in the Temple orchestra. In the midst of Habakkuk's description of how Yahweh's glory covers the heavens and His praise fills the earth, he inserts a musical notation into the text, a "selah," which is a *suspension* of music; that is, a pause (3:3). This word in its musical context appears nowhere else in Scripture outside of its prolific use in the Psalms. David prophesied upon the harp, and it appears that Habakkuk did also. Musically speaking, Habakkuk understood the power of silence at the appropriate moment. More importantly, he understood the spiritual necessity to talk to God, sing to God and praise Him audibly, but at times to be still and to wait and listen for His voice. Habakkuk whispers with his pen, "The LORD is in his holy temple: let all the earth keep silence before him" (2:20).

Habakkuk's name means *embrace* and appears to be a reduplication of a word that means to *clasp* hands. With this thought in mind, make your quiet time a little extra quiet today by sitting still and pausing in Adonai's presence with clasped or folded hands. Then just listen for His tender voice upon the strings of your heart.

Secreted in God

"The word of the LORD which came unto Zephaniah...in the days of Josiah...the king of Judah." (Zephaniah 1:1)

On the day this prophet was circumcised his parents gave him a deeply meaningful name. *Tsefanyah* means, "Yah has secreted." The first part of this name comes from *tsephan*, which means to *hide* by covering over. These godly parents placed their prized son in Yah's loving and protective hands, and they demonstrated this with a token. They gave their son a covenant name. In doing so, they were confessing their inability to keep their child perfectly safe. Only Yah could do that.

God's contracted name Yah appears about 50 times in Scripture. Where would Yah secret away the treasured souls that are most dear to Him? In His heart! If Yah measured the oceans in the palm of His hand and stretched out the heavens with the span of His hand, then the locket about His heart must be sufficiently spacious to enclose every soul seeking His refuge. If a mother fish hides her young in her mouth and a kangaroo hides her young in her pouch, should we think it strange that God hides His beloved ones next to His heart? Yahweh illustrated this spiritual truth with the following token. He had the names of Israel's tribes engraved upon a beautiful breastplate of 12 stones and instructed the high priest—a figure of Messiah—to bear it daily upon his chest next to his heart.

One thing Yah doesn't hide is judgment. He does not blindside His backslidden children but warns them to turn to Him while His mercy is still extended. Because of Zephaniah's prophetic warnings and Josiah's revival efforts, Judah had 20 years or more to obediently hide themselves in the Word of God.

The Holy One continues hiding away souls in His secret place in these modern times. If you've called upon Lord Yeshua for His eternal favor, then according to Colossians 3:3 "your life is hid with Christ in God." A safe within a safe! This morning call out to Yah and say, "Rock of Ages, cleft for me, let me hide myself in thee."

Your House vs. God's House

"Then spake Haggai the LORD'S messenger with the LORD'S message unto the people." (Haggai 1:13)

Haggai's name means *festive*. He was likely given this name because he was born upon one of the *haggim*, or feast days. When the remnant of Israel returned from Babylon, they settled in the heartland of Judea. They got busy rebuilding their houses and did not stop until they had put on the finishing touches—wood-paneling (v.4). At that time, their spirits became very festive. But they had forgotten to rebuild Yahweh's House first. It was still in ruins and stripped by Babylon of its entire glorious gilded wood paneling.

The LORD of the Festivals was so displeased by their gross oversight that He "called for a drought upon the land...and even upon all the labour of their hands" (v.11). A major part of Israel's last feast of the year, Tabernacles, includes prayers to the Almighty that He might grant sufficient rains over the winter months to ensure a sufficient crop come springtime. After the LORD took away the remnant's festive outlook, He sent along a messenger named *Festive* to turn things around. Haggai delivered the LORD's message, which was a simple one, "Consider your ways" (v.5, 7). The governor and the high priest fell into line with Haggai's message from the LORD and rallied the people to start rebuilding His House immediately. Only upon its completion could the Mosaic festivals have their most festive blessing from on high.

How are your festive plans going? Are you giving sufficient time and treasure toward the ongoing work of the LORD? If not, then maybe it is time to consider your ways, too! It is easy to get discouraged or even caught up in the everyday affairs of life. Sometimes church duties or even church attendance get set aside for a more convenient season until at last you finally remember that God's House has gone neglected. Today, take time to seek the LORD about something needful He may want you to do for Him.

God Remembers

"In the eighth month, in the second year of Darius, came the word of the LORD unto Zechariah, the son of Berechiah, the son of Iddo the prophet." (Zechariah 1:1)

Zechariah's name comes from two Hebrew words, *Zekar* and *Yah* meaning, "Yah remembers." In motivating the returning exiles to be loyal and rebuild the city, God brings to Judah's remembrance through Zechariah a very real fact saying, "The LORD hath been sore displeased with your fathers" (1:2). The returning exiles only had to look around at the surrounding ruins of Jerusalem to know firsthand just how displeased Yahweh was with their fathers' generation. Yahweh also remembers to show mercy and remembers His many promises, so He reminds the returning generation afresh saying, "My cities through prosperity shall yet be spread abroad; and the LORD shall yet comfort Zion, and shall yet choose Jerusalem" (1:17). Yahweh also reminds them of the forthcoming golden age when Messiah will sit and rule upon His priestly throne (6:13).

Some 500 years later another man who bore the name *Yah Remembers* declared the fulfillment of the Saviour's promised incarnation into the world. Filled with the Spirit of Yah, Zacharias spoke with overflowing joy saying, "the LORD God...hath visited...his people...to perform the mercy promised to our fathers, and to *remember* his holy covenant" (Luke 1:68, 72). On that atoning day when the Son of Yah was on the cross, the dying thief on His right side cast all his hope upon the Saviour with one simple request: "Lord, *remember* me when thou comest into thy kingdom" (Luke 23:42). One thing Yah will never forget is the soul who trusts in Him.

Beloved child of God, your heavenly Father is all knowing, all seeing and all present; nonetheless, He delights in being reminded of the promises He has made. After *reminding* Him today, it is then also up to you to *wait patiently* for Him to fulfill His good Word in His good way and in His good time.

God's Book of Remembrance

"Then they that feared the LORD spake often one to another: and the LORD...heard it, and a book of remembrance was written before him for them that feared the LORD, and that thought upon his name." (Malachi 3:16)

The fear of the LORD is addressed in nearly every book of the Tanach. It's central to upright and joy-filled living. The word for fear is *yareh* and means to *frighten*. Morally it means to *revere*. The dictionary defines revere this way: "to regard with respect tinged with awe." First-century messianic churches of Judea, Samaria and Galilee walked in godly reverence (Acts 9:31). Gentiles who were not full converts but highly regarded Yahweh and sympathized with Judaism in various degrees were called God-fearers. Cornelius was one example (Acts 10:2).

Malachi's name means "my messenger," and the people were to fear him as God's prophet. Malachi fulfilled his own name when he wrote of Yeshua, "the messenger of the covenant" Who was to come (3:1). Malachi greatly revered him calling Him "the Lord" and saying, "who may abide the day of his coming? and who shall stand when he appeareth? for he is like a refiner's fire" (3:1, 2).

At some point in our born-again life, we've all heard a nominal Christian say, "I don't fear the LORD." If you didn't take two steps back from such a person, you must have at least thought about doing so. And you probably didn't enjoy true fellowship with that person. When Malachi says, "they spoke often with one *another,"* he uses the word *rey-ah* which means "associate, brother, companion, fellow, friend, husband, neighbor." When the prophet says they *thought* upon Yahweh's name, he uses the word *khaw-shab,* which means "to *plait,* literally to *weave.*" Herein is a wonderful thing! God delights when any two saints come together that hold Him in high regard and make Him the tapestry of their discourse. He says, "They shall be mine, saith the LORD of hosts, in that day when I make up my jewels" (Malachi 3:17).

Today, ask the LORD to help you with your dialog. You will likely be talking with lots of unbelievers. Hopefully, they'll at least be God-fearers. Ask the LORD for you wisdom that you might successfully *weave* Yeshua into the fabric of your conversation and end up with something beautiful.

Weak but Waxing

"Gideon, and...Barak, and...Samson...Who through faith subdued kingdoms...out of weakness were made strong, waxed valiant in fight." (Hebrews 11:32-34)

Each of these men accomplished great things for God. Gideon defeated 30,000 Philistines in one battle. Barak defeated Jaban, the king of Canaan, and his mighty people who dwelt in Hazor; and Samson took down 3000 Philistines who were mocking him in their pagan temple. The amazing way each of these men went about gaining great victory was not in their own strength but in God's. The Almighty stripped them of their own ability so they would have to become reliant upon His ability.

At the beginning, Gideon didn't even have enough courage to thresh wheat in the open; he feared the Philistines would see him and come take his grain by force. But after God got through with him, he waxed strong. Barak was so weak in military genius that he insisted that a prophetess go into battle with him. Once Deborah went with him, Barak began to wax stronger. Samson had his eyesight taken from him, and that's about as physically challenged as a person can get. All Yahweh wanted in the first place was for Samson to have eyes only for Him. After Samson's weakness, he waxed strong in the end. The Hebrew word for wax is *halak*, which means to *walk*. They walked strong after fully embracing their weakness.

God has a purpose in bringing victories out of our weaknesses—mainly to get all the glory after the victory comes. Messiah set the example for us. "He was crucified through weakness, yet he liveth by the power of God" (2 Corinthians 13:4). This verse continues by saying, "For we also are weak in him, but we shall live with him by the power of God." And don't forget, God's grace and strength increases as your weakness increases (2 Corinthians 12:9). This is why Paul said, "Most gladly...will I rather glory in my infirmities, that the power of Christ may rest upon me" (v.9).

Today, your weakness is your advantage; so don't ask God to take it away. Instead, embrace it. After all, He gave it to you!

Going Out with Purpose

"Behold, there went out a sower to sow...So is the kingdom of God, as if a man should cast seed into the ground." (Mark 4:3)

The Son of God came from heaven with purpose—to sow the land of Israel with a fuller knowledge of God's Word. God revives His lifeless creation by quickening His Word within their hearts (Hebrews 4:12). Over time, much darkness covered the land of Israel resulting in a vacuum of the true light of God's Word primarily because the Torah was lorded over by evil shepherds (Ezekiel 34). God the Son became incarnate to dispel earth's spiritual darkness by being "the true Light, which lighteth every man that cometh into the world" (John 1:9).

Since Messiah didn't plan on staying long, part of His purpose was to train others to sow the good seed so that the next generation might also have the same opportunity to know and experience the Father's love. Messiah Yeshua found men casting nets for fish and taught them instead how to cast the gospel net for human souls. Before, these fishers had labored on water, but now they were to begin laboring on land. Because souls were to be found everywhere, Yeshua's instructions were simple: "Go ye into all the world, and preach the gospel to every creature" (Mark 16:15). The disciples in turn taught the next generation to do likewise. Peter informs us what lost souls truly need—to be "born again, not of corruptible seed, but of incorruptible, by the Word of God, which liveth and abideth for ever" (1 Peter 1:23). Peter's great desire was for the next generation to keep heaven's seed pure in both doctrine and delivery.

Today it is your turn to go out with purpose and make a difference to those who may not know the difference between truth and error. Cast the gospel net as you go out today and the seeds of the kingdom will sink into the hearts of men and women, boys and girls. The Holy Spirit will aid you in this wondrous work. After praying this morning, simply go out with purpose and a sack full of gospel seed.

The Character of God

"The LORD, The LORD God, merciful and gracious, longsuffering, and abundant in goodness and truth, Keeping mercy for thousands, forgiving iniquity and transgression and sin..." (Exodus 34:6-7)

This all sounds good if you are the one who might be standing in trouble with God, but what if someone has done you horribly wrong? Would you want them to be recipients of these same wonderful promises or would you wish the other side of God's flawless nature upon them where He warns that He will "by no means clear the guilty" (v.7)? We never shun the undeserved goodness of God upon our own lives, so why do we not pray that our enemies will receive the same?

The LORD understands your emotional suffering while you await His advocacy, so He explains: "For my thoughts are not your thoughts, neither are your ways my ways, saith the LORD" (Isaiah 55:8). The righteous Judge expects you to be more trusting in such a given situation. Look at the context of His plea in the prior verse: "Let the wicked forsake his way, and the unrighteous man his thoughts: and let him return unto the LORD, and he will have mercy upon him; and to our God, for he will abundantly pardon" (v.7). Because the LORD is so longsuffering, He waits and waits for hardened hearts to turn toward Him in repentance. He also facilitates people's heart change. God doesn't handle things as we would because He is not impulsive. Praise Him for that. What if He was as impulsive with us when we broke one of His high and holy laws? He treats us as He treats the lost—with extreme patience! Yahweh is angry at the wicked, but He is also "slow to anger" (Jonah 4:2). Some holocaust survivors are bitter towards God because of His inaction during their former time of need. They harden their hearts, which prevents them from turning to Him for what they *also* need most—forgiveness of sin.

Today, pray that the LORD will help you take on His character and to be patient and forgiving with that person who has wronged you.

The Acts Formula

"My voice shalt thou hear in the morning, O LORD; in the morning will I direct my prayer unto thee, and will look up." (Psalm 5:3)

In Bible College, the dean shared a wonderful little outline with us that we might use it as a guide when going into prayer. It isn't a magic formula, but it is a majestic one. Prayer should begin with *Adoration*. God is to be praised because of who He is, not just because of what He does for us. God is worthy to be praised regardless of our circumstances. If He can only be praised when things are going well, how then is He truly glorified? Believers living in cold, dark prison cells in persecuted lands don't come up short on praise just because their situation is miserable or horrible. They have come to realize that God is good all the time.

Confession must come up early in prayer, for without it our fellowship is hindered. The psalm writer said, "If I regard iniquity in my heart, the Lord will not hear me" (Psalm 66:18). God will always hear your praise, but He may not hear your petitions until your heart is in synchronization with His. Moreover, what is your praise to God if your walk with Him is not what it should be? Confession of faults in Yeshua's name puts them behind you so that you can go forward in might and manifold grace.

Now the time comes for *thanksgiving;* that is, thanking God for what He does on your behalf. The list of things to thank Him for can be endless. You can thank God for practically anything, even bad things that have come about recently. Tragedy is God's favorite building block for your house of triumph so long as you don't let your heart become hardened like mortar.

Prayer should end with *supplications*, petitioning God for various needs, not necessarily your own. Never pray without remembering the persecuted saints—"them that are in bonds...them which suffer adversity" (Hebrews 13:3). Give this prayerful outline a try today.

Paradise, the King's Garden

"And Jesus said unto him, Verily I say unto thee, Today shalt thou be with me in paradise." (Luke 23:43)

The word paradise isn't found in the Old Testament, but the concept is. The Aramaic word is *pardaysa*. It describes a *walled enclosure*, but specifically refers to a *royal garden*. Ezekiel referred to "all the trees of Eden, that were in the garden of God" (Ezekiel 31:9). Adam and Eve were evicted from this blissful enclosure. The Hebrews borrowed the Aramaic word and adapted it to read *pardes*. The three times it's found in the original text it is translated as *orchard* and refers to a king's garden. King Solomon said, "I made me gardens and orchards, and I planted trees in them of all kind of fruits" (Ecclesiastes 2:5).

Yeshua was born King of the Jews, but Israel was not interested in His rule and reign. Whenever this lowly King visited Jerusalem, He sought overnight solitude in the olive orchard at Gethsemane. It was in this pleasant orchard that the King surrendered His life for His subjects' true liberation. The next day, "in the place where he was crucified there was a garden," an orchard (John 19:41). On the cross—the greatest fruit bearing tree of all—Yeshua promised to take the repentant thief with Him into paradise. A few hours later Messiah's soul descended into the heart of the earth to a lovely place known as Abraham's bosom (Luke 16:22). This was paradise of the underworld—the Old Testament saints' resting place. Meanwhile, two devout men buried King Messiah's body right there inside the orchard's enclosure. After three days, the King of Souls proceeded to relocate paradise, and at His ascension led forth those former captives of the underworld into heaven (Psalm 68:16). These Old Testament saints are likely the "cloud" referred to in Acts 1:9.

Paul confirms that paradise's location is now in "the third heaven" (2 Corinthians 12:4, 2). If you want to dwell eternally in paradise with the King of Kings and have access to the Tree of Life, you must have no less faith than that of the dying thief. Think about the thief's remarkable confidence in Yeshua as Saviour even though this Saviour was about to die. The thief's eyes were fastened upon King Yeshua, the *Gateway* to paradise. Today, fasten your eyes on the King in your prayer time.

The Steko Principle

"Therefore, brethren, stand fast, and hold the traditions which ye have been taught, whether by word, or our epistle." (2 Thessalonians 2:15)

When Paul said to stand fast, he used the word *steko* from where we get our word "stay." Steko means, "to be *stationary*, figuratively, to *persevere*." Paul is the only New Testament writer to use the phrase *stand fast*, and he applied it to five areas of the Christian life.

The first is found in our text verse where he challenges believers to *stand fast by the apostolic teachings* that were being circulated through their preaching and handwritten letters. The newly formed Jerusalem church is commended in Scripture for doing exactly this (Acts 2:42). Secondly, he said to *stand fast in the faith* (1 Corinthians 16:13). Corinthian believers were being faced with the trendy philosophy of Gnosticism, but Paul told them that Yeshua possessed all the treasures of wisdom and knowledge and therefore, to seek hidden things only from Him. Third, Paul advised the Galatians to *stand fast in the liberty* in which Christ had made them free (Galatians 5:1). Some Pharisaic teachers in Galatia were attempting to bring believers back into conformity with Mosaic Judaism, which had been replaced by Messiah's new and living way (Hebrews 10:20).

On the fourth occasion, Paul also counsels us to *stand fast in one spirit* (Philippians 1:27). He ended his letter to the saints at Philippi by telling them to salute every saint. Most importantly, you are to *stand fast in the Lord* (1 Thessalonians 3:8). The Lord Himself is your daily source of joy, and it's hard to mature in godly character if you're purposely avoiding the adversity that naturally accompanies your salvation (v.3).

Today, ask the Holy Spirit to help you stand fast in all five of these areas. Yeshua doesn't want you migratory. He wants you to be stationary, so apply the *steko* principle to your everyday walk. He has already promised in Psalm 89:28 saying, "my covenant [mercy] shall stand fast with [you]."

The Testimony of Three

"For there are three that bear record in heaven, the Father, the Word, and the Holy Ghost: and these three are one. And there are three that bear witness in earth, the Spirit, and the water, and the blood: and these three agree in one." (1 John 5:7-8)

Under Mosaic Law, the testimony of two witnesses established a fact, and three made it irrefutable (Deuteronomy 17:6). At the dawn of the New Testament era Messiah Yeshua performed many mighty miracles. So that these could not be refuted later, He always took along His three witnesses: Peter, James and John. Yeshua also conveyed a great promise to us when He said, "For where two or three are gathered together in my name, there am I in the midst of them" (Matthew 18:20). This promise is valid whether saints are gathered for the purposes of judgment or for joyful praise (Psalm 22:3). We can see, of course, the divine origin of this number three. It emanates from the Godhead—heaven's undeniable, Triune Witness. The most significant titles of God all have three syllables: Elohim, El Shaddai, El Elyon, El Gibor, Adonai and His covenant name Yehovah.

Three things are necessary within every divine covenant made between God and man: God's word, blood and a token. An example of this can be seen in God's covenant with Noah. After the flood subsided, Noah shed animals' blood upon an altar; then God gave His word not to destroy the earth again in the same way. He accompanied His promise with the token of a multi-colored bow in the sky.

Concerning the greatest covenant of all times, salvation, John says three entities bear witness to its reality. First, the *water of God's Word* proclaims the news of our salvation, which we are also daily cleansed by (Psalm 119:9; Ephesians 5:26). The second entity is the spotless *blood drawn from Yeshua's veins.* When sinners are plunged beneath it, they lose all their guilty stains! The third entity is the *token of God's Spirit* Who has come to fill our hearts and now "beareth witness with our spirit, that we are the children of God" (Romans 8:16). The Holy Spirit is the divine token of your blood-bought salvation and permanently seals God's covenant Word with you. Today, praise the triune Godhead for their three-fold working in your life.

𝒫urchased & 𝒮ealed

"That we should be to the praise of his glory, who first trusted in Christ...after that ye heard the word of truth, the gospel of your salvation: in whom also after that ye believed, ye were sealed with that holy Spirit of promise, Which is the earnest of our inheritance until the redemption of the purchased possession," (Ephesians 1:12-14)

A 2000-year-old clay seal was recently unearthed along the southwestern corner of the Temple Mount. This seal from the Second Temple era is the size of a modern new Israeli shekel and has never been seen before. It brings much excitement to the archaeological world because prior knowledge of the use of seals in Temple liturgy has only come from ancient rabbinical writings. The cartouche [seal] bears the Aramaic inscription, "It is pure." Just below this engraving is the well-known, two-letter abbreviation for the name of Yahweh. It reads, "to Yah." Offerings carried to the Temple had to be stamped pure, for which this seal was used.

God the Father *purchased* your entire person with His Son's lifeblood. He bought you at a great price (1 Peter 1:19). Yeshua had this to say of the purchased possession, "him hath God the Father sealed" (John 6:27). You see, the moment you trust in the blood's saving power, the Father stamps you with the *eternal seal* of His own purity, thus making you pure and acceptable before Him forever (Ephesians 1:13). Your new obligation is simple, "glorify God in your body, and in your spirit" (1 Corinthians 6:20). In other words, stay pure. Paul says it like this: "grieve not the holy Spirit of God, whereby ye are sealed unto the day of redemption" (Ephesians 4:30). You are *sealed with God's pureness* immediately after believing, not after behaving satisfactorily, so this seal remains irreversible. This is why the above passage finishes like it began—"to the praise of *his* glory," not yours.

Today, go out with great joy remembering the words of Paul in 2 Timothy 2:19: "the foundation of God standeth sure, having this seal, The Lord knoweth them that are his."

Presented & Offered

"Present your bodies, a living sacrifice, holy, acceptable unto God, which is your reasonable service." (Romans 12:1)

The first-century-BC clay seal found near Robinson's Arch bears two Aramaic words: *Daka LeYah* meaning "Pure for God." Seal impressions, *khotamot*, were used as tokens. A worshipper seeking to offer an offering of any kind first went to a man in charge of the seals. He gave the man his money and purchased an offering. The man would give him a *khotam*, a clay signet that was used like a coupon today. The offerer would then take the *khotam* to another place in the Temple where he would actually receive his offering. The offerer then took his offering to the priests at the Temple. He presented it before Yahweh at the altar of sacrifice and gave it to the priests. They in turn offered up the sacrifice.

In Acts 20:28 Paul illustrates how God purchases the believer with His own holy blood, and then seals him with His Spirit. The word for holy in our text is *hagios*, which implies something that has been ceremonially consecrated. God stamps the pure impression of His own likeness upon us to show we belong to Him. The Father also stamps you as pure for service in His kingdom. This is why your immediate responsibility is to *present* yourself to Him. Yeshua is your daily advocate "to present you holy and unblameable and unreproveable in his [Father's] sight" (Colossians 1:22).

Paul rendered exceptional service, and if necessary, was willing to become a burnt *offering* (1 Corinthians 13:3). His zealous testimony was this: "I am ready...to die at Jerusalem for the name of the Lord Jesus" (Acts 21:13). However, it wasn't his time. Later he confidently said, "I am now ready to be *offered*, my time is at hand" (2 Timothy 4:6). The Father chooses when and how to offer you up. Your obligation until then is to be willing, waiting and working.

Are you daily, prayerfully presenting your body for service to Yahweh? Don't worry. He will give you dying grace when He is ready to *offer* you up, whether it is by way of martyrdom, sickness or old age.

God's Camp Fire & You

"The fire shall ever be burning upon the altar; it shall never go out."
(Leviticus 6:13)

God has chosen to represent Himself in many ways, but one theme that recurs throughout Holy Scripture is fire. At Mt. Sinai God appeared in the form of fire. In Deuteronomy 4:24 it says, "the LORD thy God is a consuming fire." God's Spirit sometimes consumed His enemies with fire. With this same holy fire, He also consumed Israel's sins, which had been transferred upon the heads of sacrificial animals. At the inauguration of the Tabernacle in the wilderness "there came a fire out from before the LORD, and consumed upon the altar the burnt offering and the fat: which when all the people saw, they shouted, and fell on their faces" (Leviticus 9:24).

This is how the altar originally gained its fire in the midst of the camp, and God instructed Moses saying that it should never be put out (Leviticus 6:12). This was crystal clear. Because of this command, priests were given round-the-clock assignments to tend the fire overnight. If a priest failed in his holy duty by lying down and falling asleep, then as a token of his disobedience hot coals could be brought from the brazen altar and placed on the edges of the sleeping sentinel's cloak. When his clothes summarily caught fire, he would abruptly awake and begin frantically shedding them.

The altar of incense was inside the sanctuary near the veil, which is where the prayers of Israel went up every morning and evening. Coals for this altar were taken from the brazen altar outside, so a link of prayer and continual fire is presented. Paul commands New Covenant believers to pray without ceasing (1 Thessalonians 5:17), and indeed we should. But as tragic as it may be, we too easily let the campfire of praise and prayer burn out.

Seek the Spirit of God in prayer today. Ask Him to help you, as a faithful member among the priesthood of believers, to remain vigilant in your intercessory duties and to keep His holy campfire of praise and prayer burning brightly night and day.

Kohelet & the Kehillah

"The words of the Preacher, the son of David, king in Jerusalem. Vanity of vanities, saith the Preacher, vanity of vanities; all is vanity." (Ecclesiastes 1:1-2)

In Hebrew, the book of Ecclesiastes is known as *Kohelet*, which means, *"preacher* or *lecturer."* We don't often think of Solomon as a preacher, but he sure preached hard and strong in his collection of Proverbs. He also preached eloquently in his poetic sermon entitled "The Song of Songs." The preacher was "wise, he…taught the people knowledge…he gave good heed…he sought to find acceptable words…upright…words of truth" (12:9, 10). Concerning the twelve-chapter-long message entitled "Vanity of Vanities" which the *kohelet* preaches to his *kehillah* [assembly], there is no way to improve upon it. Sadly, this message came to the preacher by way of his own meaningless experience. He had it all and experienced it all but was never satisfied with it—at all! In the end, the *kohelet* had but one message, *kol hebel* meaning, "all is meaningless."

Two Psalms are attributed to Solomon. In one, he summarizes man's many *meaningless* endeavors: "Except the LORD build the house, they labour in vain that build it: except the LORD keep the city, the watchman waketh but in vain. It is vain for you to rise up early, to sit up late, to eat the bread of sorrows: for so he giveth his beloved sleep" (Psalm 127:1-2). What he is saying is this: "If God ain't in it, then get out of it." However, he continues to summarize one thing in life that is fulfilling or meaningful. The preacher proclaims, "children are an heritage of the LORD: and the fruit of the womb is his reward" (Psalm 127:3). Solomon's whirlwind life was over the top, but his wisdom was not. God and family are the only two real pursuits in life worth investing in and praying for.

The wise person works in order to have something sufficient to offer back to his Creator and his family. It is easy to get sidetracked in life, so if need be ask the Father to help you place your labors today where they will be most meaningful and blessed.

𝒯𝒶𝓀𝑒 𝒥𝓉 & 𝐸𝓂𝒷𝓇𝒶𝒸𝑒 𝒥𝓉!

"And whosoever will, let him take the water of life freely." (Revelation 22:17)

God asks us to take many things unto ourselves. Many of these things we readily take, but others we have to think about often before embracing fully. If we're so ready and willing to take the *hallowed blessings* from God, we should also be ready to take the *holy burdens* from Him as well. My father used to give me advice from time to time. He would preface his advice with the words, "Now, you can take this or leave it." When it comes to our heavenly Father's perfect counsel, He doesn't say, "Take it or leave it." He says, "Take it and embrace it." The Lord asks us to take upon ourselves ten things. The first three are connected to salvation and experiencing God's love and fellowship.

He begins with an invitation to take the Water of Life (Revelation 22:17). This is a reflection on the Saviour's words, "Come unto me, and drink" (John 7:37). You are then invited to "take the cup of salvation, and call upon the name of the Lord" (Psalm 116:13). This is the Lord's Supper, which symbolizes fellowship in His sufferings. That is why He says, "Take, eat; this is my body, which is broken for you" (1 Corinthians 11:24).

After this, His advice requires more commitment. He challenges you saying, "Take my yoke upon you, and learn of me" (Matthew 11:29). "Take no thought for your life... [or] for tomorrow" (Matthew 6:25, 34). Most difficult of all, Yeshua says to daily "Take up your cross, and follow me" (Mark 8:34). Paul continues this *doctrine of taking* by saying that you should regularly "take upon...the ministering to the saints" (2 Corinthians 8:4), and daily "take...the whole armor of God," which includes "taking the shield of faith" (Ephesians 6:13, 16). When necessary, the apostle asks you to take wrong from others when you might otherwise be prone to take revenge (1 Corinthians 6:7).

Taking in these biblical injunctions and embracing them is a deliberate choice each of us should make in order to improve our usefulness to our King and His kingdom. Open your arms wide today in praise to the Most High and then enfold them around His holy Word.

Joseph's School of Obedience

"And a certain man found him, and, behold, he was wandering in the field." (Genesis 37:15)

Borrowing from R.T. Kendall's five-point outline on the life of Joseph, please allow this writer to make the following comments. Joseph had all the right ingredients for greatness; God just needed to cook him over the fire for a while. He first needed to learn *to trust God in the dark*. The LORD was with Joseph as he served in Potiphar's palace and labored in Potiphar's prison (39:7, 21, 23). This was a comforting lesson for Joseph, and you can take comfort as well. Joseph also needed to learn *that triumph comes after tragedy* in God's school of obedience. The psalmist records that "the word of the LORD tried him" (Psalm 105:19). Trying circumstances through life make you more spiritually fit in the end and more appreciative of the triumphant ending so that you can say like Eyobe, "when he hath tried me, I shall come forth as gold" (Job 23:10). Through his tragedies Joseph became more and more fit so that later under Pharaoh he could triumphantly order, "his princes at his pleasure; and teach his senators wisdom" (Psalm 105:22).

Joseph also needed to learn *that tears are part of the process*. There's no telling how many times Joseph wept during the course of his bitter experience. Paul also went through God's school of obedience and wrote that he served "the Lord with all humility of mind, and with many tears" (Acts 20:19). If you have no tears, then you are in the wrong school.

The golden boy needed to learn *that testimonies for God would come*. He had opportunities to testify before Potiphar's wife, before the chief baker and butler, and eventually before a great and mighty Pharaoh (Genesis 41:16). The Schoolmaster Yeshua taught that believers would be brought before kings and rulers for His name's sake and added, "it shall turn to you for a testimony" (Luke 21:13). Finally, Joseph needed to learn *that there are treasures greater than gold*. The long-awaited reunion between Joseph and his brothers was priceless.

Today, if you feel like you are wandering in life's field of dreams, pray that you will patiently pass all your lessons in God's daily school of obedience.

Satiated!

"With long life will I satisfy him, and show him my salvation."
(Psalm 91:16)

Psalm 91 is a favorite among Bible readers most likely because of the comfort it affords and protection it promises. Whenever God repeats a particular topic, He is inviting us to take a closer look. Such is the case with the phrase *ye-shu-ah-ti*, "my salvation," mentioned 32 times in the Tanakh.

Whenever people are in need of great help, great salvation, they are usually wide-eyed to see who it is that comes to their rescue. When God comes to our rescue, it is usually in the form of His Spirit. We know that the word salvation, *yeshuah*, is a noun, but when God pledges to show us His salvation, He is also promising to show us His Son Whose name is *Yeshua*. How exciting! The disciples and many others saw Him, and we, too, are promised that we shall one day see His face (Revelation 22:4).

Yeshua brings more than just deliverance from harm and help; He brings satisfaction. The Father proudly claims to the trusting one, "I will satisfy him." The Hebrew root for satisfy is *saw-bah* which also means to fill. Modern Israelis use a secular expression based on this word. It is "Sababa," which means, "No worries," "It's all good," or "I'm in a good mood." Most humans are never completely satisfied; they are only full of desire. But Yeshua's indwelling makes mankind's insatiableness cease! The Bible says, "in Him…all fullness [contentment] dwells" (Colossians 1:19). Yohanan made it clear that complete and lasting satisfaction came by Yeshua HaMashiakh, and that because of His outpoured life at Calvary and outpoured Spirit at Pentecost, "his fulness we have all received" (John 1:16). Yohanan highlighted the two main things Yeshua's fullness comprises—"grace and truth" (v.17).

No matter how urgent your need may be today, rather than focusing on *this* and *that*, try focusing on Yeshua's *grace* and *truth*. As you do, you will find your worries subsiding and the Saviour's presence ever abiding.

Mary & the Ark of God

"So David would not remove the ark of the LORD unto him into the city of David: but David carried it aside into the house of Obededom the Gittite." (2 Samuel 6:10)

The ark of God served as the resting place of God's glory and His first ten Torah commandments. This writer is not the first to point out what Scripture so clearly hints at, that Miriam [aka Mary] was an *ordained vessel*, like the ark, to contain what no man might otherwise look upon—the pre-born Son of God, the living Torah. Miriam's womb became the temporary, sanctified "resting place" for the incarnate Deity (2 Chronicles 6:41).

Like David who would not bring the ark into his own city, Mary left her own city, "and went into the hill country with haste, into a city of Judah" (Luke 1:39). As David carried the ark aside into the house of Obededom, so Mary "entered into the house of Zacharias, and saluted Elisabeth" (Luke 1:40). Just as the ark of God caused King David to start "leaping and dancing" (v.16), "when Elisabeth heard the salutation of Mary, the babe [John] leaped in her womb" (Luke 1:41). In the same manner in which "the LORD blessed Obededom" (v.11), Miriam was very "blessed...among women" (Luke 1:42). Just as David was earlier "afraid of the LORD...and said, How shall the ark of the LORD come to me?" (v.9), Elisabeth in the same way remarked about why she was so honored "that the mother of my Lord should come to me" (Luke 1:43). As "the ark of the LORD continued in the house of Obededom the Gittite three months" (v.11), so "Mary abode" in Zachariah's house "about three months" (Luke 1:56). Finally, just as "David went and brought up the ark of God into the city of David" (v.12), so Joseph took Mary and "went up...unto the city of David, which is called Bethlehem" (Luke 2:4).

These parallels are striking, and wonderfully illustrate Yeshua's holiness. The wooden ark housed the Law, and the human ark housed Yeshua, the Law-Giver. No glory should be given to the "ark" (Mary); rather, all glory and adoration goes to her beloved heaven-sent Son. Praise the Lord today for His condescension to you.

Stay by the Stuff

"So David went, he and the six hundred men that were with him, and came to the brook Besor...But David pursued, he and four hundred men: for two hundred abode behind, which were so faint that they could not go over the brook Besor." (1 Samuel 30:9-10)

David and his men had just returned home from a three-day journey. They arrived at Ziklag to find their village burned and looted of all possessions. David enquired of Yahweh and was informed that he would successfully recover all that pertained to them—wives, children and cattle (v.8). Weary and wasted they ran after the Amalekites. This running expended the last amount of energy in a third of David's men. There was no time to waste, so those that could still run took off again pursuing the enemy.

Not only had the 200 weary souls run out of strength, but apparently they had also run out of hope—*cheer*. There is a message tucked away in the brook's name. *Bes-or'* means cheerful, and its root, *baw-sar,* means "properly to be *fresh*; that is, *full,* figuratively *rosy*; to *announce* glad news." The flesh of the 200 weary soldiers was no longer fresh, their bellies were no longer full, and their faces were no longer rosy. David was running, however, with the good news that they would gain the full victory. His strength was supernatural because of the message of cheer God had given him. Upon their cheerful return to Besor David made a statute that lasted from that day forward: "The spoils of those that go into the battle will be shared equally with those that stay by the stuff" (v.24). After all, it was good that others had safeguarded their belongings!

In this day and time, it is not uncommon to be a weary warrior. This world tries to zap the very life out of you. Even friends and family can zap you. But be encouraged today and stay by the stuff! *Stay by the Bible* for it has the Words of life. *Stay by fellow believers* because the strong, cheerful ones at church will share their spoils of the victorious life with you and strengthen you. Most importantly, *stay by Yeshua* Who says, "be of good cheer" (John 16:33). Without fail, He has overcome the world and recovered all the power and dominion you will need for today.

Arabian Nights

"I certify you, brethren, that the gospel which was preached of me is not after man. For I neither received it of man, neither was I taught it, but by the revelation of Christ Jesus." (Galatians 1:11-12)

Yeshua personally apprehended Saul on the Damascus Road. It was there that he changed Saul's *nature* and his *name*. From that time on, he was known as Paul. He was a new man altogether! In some ways, the apostle's *nationalism* was also changed in that he had to adopt some new customs in order to win the gentiles. At the times when he ventured back to Jerusalem for the feasts, it became needful for Paul to put his former mantle back on. It was strange, yet straightforward for Paul to say, "unto the Jews I became as a Jew, that I might gain the Jews" (1 Corinthians 9:20). Most importantly, the Son of God changed the Pharisee of Pharisee's *narrative* giving him a brand new story to tell (1 Timothy 1:15)! Yeshua, however, had to quickly rein Paul in from his new evangelistic ministry and point him in the direction of Arabia where He could personally school the former disciple of Moses in the many fine points of the New Covenant.

Yeshua didn't save Rabbi Saul by grace just to release him to go and propagate Mosaic Law again. Paul was mightily saved, but he was still a novice concerning New Covenant theology. Later, Paul himself also forbade novices to teach (1 Timothy 3:6). Zeal without knowledge is a dangerous thing when it comes to teaching others. Leaving the good guidance of Moses the lawgiver, Paul had to submit himself to a new Teacher, Messiah the Grace-Giver. The gifted gospel herald tells us what made the real difference in his evangelistic efforts—three years alone in the wilderness getting New Covenant revelation directly from Lord Yeshua Himself (Galatians 1:12, 15-18).

There are no more revelations or prophecies to be received. This is why Lord Yeshua calls many to go aside into *fundamental* Bible colleges for a season to confer with teachers who have diligently studied the unchanging Word of God. The Holy Spirit gives some a special calling to preach, but we all need to study the word that we may receive His recommendation at the end of the day (2 Timothy 2:15).

ᴍasada & Strongholds

"And the hand of Midian prevailed against Israel...the children of Israel made them the dens which are in the mountains, and caves, and strong holds." (Judges 6:2)

The Hebrew word for stronghold is *metsadah*. Masada is the modern name given to the plateau fortress overlooking the Dead Sea, which was built by Herod the Great around 30BC. Though He built it as refuge for himself in the event of a revolt, one-century later 960 Jewish zealots hid within it until they were overcome by Roman legions in 73AD. The Hebrew resisters of Roman occupation committed suicide rather than surrender. At the end of the day, the earthen stronghold was just not strong enough to keep them secure. Today, soldiers entering the IDF are taken to Masada as part of their initiation. They are encouraged to be as vigilant as possible so that Israel will never again have to resort to living in dens, caves or strongholds. The book of Judges tells us why ancient Israel had to flee their homes and lands for other refuge. They "did evil in the sight of the LORD" (v.1). If they had stayed close to Elohim, they wouldn't have come near evil.

A stronghold is a place where you don't really wish to be. Kings make themselves strongholds for the day of trouble, but the trouble with strongholds is that they are neither comfortable nor completely safe. The truth is if you are in a stronghold, then the enemy has a very strong hold over you. He's got you in a tightly confined space where you have no freedom to move. Unless help arrives, you stand in jeopardy. The way to stay out of spiritual strongholds begins by daily surrendering to God's will in every area of your life and then staying clear of the enemy's many temptations. Forfeiting to surrender to God's perfect will, even for a moment, can possibly lead to a lifetime of being trapped by a formidable foe. If you want to be free from *metsada*, stay close to *Messiah*.

Today, guard your words and your thoughts by bringing every unchristlike thought into immediate captivity (2 Corinthians 10:5). This will allow you to experience freedom and keep you from being backed into a corner.

God's Helping Hand

"The hand of our God is upon all them for good that seek him;"
(Ezra 8:22)

If Ezra was impressed with the working hands of the returning remnant, he was even more impressed with the wonderful hand of Yahweh that so graciously rested upon them. Ezra was more than a construction foreman; he was a scribe in the Law of Moses and had much to do in restoring the people's hearts to it and its many rituals. He certainly couldn't have accomplished all that he did without God's helping hand, which he mentions six different times.

In time, the people of Israel began to intermarry with the heathen of the land. Eight different nationalities are mentioned. God's pure altar was meant for a pure people. Ezra sought God on this issue late one afternoon just after the evening sacrifice (9:5). He rent his garments, got on his knees, and spread out his hands to the Most High. He was fearful and ashamed to lift up his face to heaven because of the iniquities of his people, but he had to intercede for them. He began by rehearsing God's goodness in giving them "a little space of grace" and "a little reviving" (9:8). There was one other very incredible thing Ezra thanked Yahweh for—punishing them less than their iniquities deserved (9:13). Out of that little prayer meeting came a solution to Ezra's dilemma.

Maybe today you're looking for a solution to a problem that is way bigger than your little hands can manage. That's ok! God knows your hands are limited in power. All you need to do this morning is spread out your burden and your hands before Him and He will begin to show you just how big His hands are. Ezra had a wonderful motto: "The hand of our God is upon all them for good that seek him." By this Ezra is saying that the secret to acquiring Yeshua's helping hand is not just in seeking a solution; it's in seeking Him. He is the solution! This morning, enjoy seeking the Lord Yeshua's face and His hand will easily find its way into your demanding day.

219

Between a Rock and a Hard Place?

"And the angel of the LORD went...and stood in a narrow place, where was no way to turn either to the right hand or to the left." (Numbers 22:26)

The Hebrew word translated narrow is *tsar* meaning a *tight* place, which figuratively speaks of *trouble*. Balaam was determined to press on with his personal agenda, but things didn't go as he had planned. His donkey saw the heavenly Messenger and became fearful—understandably so. She attempted to turn away and crushed his foot, but Balaam adamantly forced her to go forward. The donkey was greatly troubled and in turn troubled Balaam by collapsing under him. He was in a real tight spot!

We can also find ourselves between a rock and a hard place when we determine to carry out our plans without first lining up with God. The narrow place we get in helps us to come to our senses so that we don't continue in the error of our self-absorbed way. It's good of God to intervene, for then we are saved from future heartache and headache. Sometimes we ask God to bless our plans, and then we're soon met with trouble in the way. This happened to Peter. An idea popped into his head, and he uttered his request. The LORD was standing right in front of him with the wind in His hair. Peter was given permission to proceed out of the ship with his shortsighted human plan to walk on water, but no sooner had he set out on his proud journey than he found himself like Balaam, pressed by a wall of water on one side and the boat on the other. And like Balaam's donkey that collapsed under him, the surface of the sea gave way underneath Peter.

Before setting out with your seemingly good plans, stop and ask the LORD if your plans meet His specifications. Ask the Holy Spirit to close the door that you have created if He has other plans more fitting. What may seem like a good idea to you may be in reality something interruptive to God's grand scheme of things. Today, don't pray that God will bless your plans; rather, pray He will show you *His* plan and help you to fulfill it.

The Great Shabbat

"And in this mountain shall the LORD of hosts make unto all people a feast of fat things, a feast of wines on the lees, of fat things full of marrow, of wines on the lees well refined." (Isaiah 25:6)

The *Siddur*, a Jewish prayer book, describes Shabbat as having three purposes. One of them is that the weekly Sabbath is "a taste of the world to come"—the Messianic Age.

God crowned His creative week with the Sabbath day. His ceasing from labor on the seventh day draws a marvelous picture of the ages of man on earth. Both rabbinical commentators and fundamental New Covenant scholars believe that man's labor and toil is to exist for six millennia, after which God ushers in a seventh millennium—one of perfect rest (Revelation 20:3). These 1000 years of peace and harmony are known as the Davidic kingdom. The current reckoning of 6000 years since Adam comes not only through the calculations of Gentile Bible scholars in the past, but also by modern Jewish scholars in Israel. They have now come out with the *Astronomically and Agriculturally Corrected Biblical Hebrew Calendar* showing that we have just crossed the threshold into the seventh millennium. We certainly live in momentous days according to God's faultless calendar.

Our text verse from Isaiah gives us a very brief summary of the great Sabbath rest. He describes Messiah's inaugural feast that will be held in the exalted mountain and eternal capital of the world—Jerusalem. Until the Son returns, we are not promised much rest from everyday conflicts. We are, however, to labor, strive and toil against our evil inclinations (Hebrews 12:4). This is man's greatest war, and it never seems to end. The day will come when Messiah gives all of His covenant ones a new body and a sinless nature like His (Psalm 17:15).

Take a spiritual rest today from your many daily cares and be reminded that a brighter day is coming soon. If you think that nobody loves you or cares about you, then rest in Yeshua's loving, caring and everlasting arms.

It's All or Nothing

"And he took the cup, and gave thanks, and gave it to them, saying, Drink ye all of it." (Matthew 26:27)

Following Lord Yeshua is not always an easy thing to do. It certainly wasn't an average task for the first-century disciples. They were constantly being faced with all-or-nothing decisions. When Peter felt confident that nothing stood in the way of his full commitment to Messiah, he proclaimed, "We have forsaken all and followed thee." But the lead disciple also attached a question: "What shall we have therefore?" (Matthew 19:27). The Master gave Peter the answer he was looking for at the time, but on another occasion He told Peter what else he would get for whole-heartedly following the Messiah—persecution.

When Lord Yeshua told the disciples to drink His entire cup, it was a foreshadowing of their own coming persecution. Drinking *all the cup* was a token of taking on persecution without shrinking back. In the Garden when Messiah had a choice whether or not to shrink back from suffering, His response was, "The cup which my Father hath given me, shall I not drink it?" (John 18:11). Messiah drank His entire cup of suffering, and He expects all who follow Him to do the same. It is not just a matter of volunteering for such adversity because *"all* that will live godly in Christ Jesus shall suffer persecution" (2 Timothy 3:12).

The average believer struggles with faithfulness or full commitment; however, the Lord's commands are never to be lived out in part. It is an *all* or nothing Faith. The pivotal point is whether you love Adonai Yeshua with *all* your heart, soul and strength or not (Deuteronomy 6:5). Did you know this command comes immediately after the Shema? The Lord says, "do *all* that I speak" (Exodus 23:22); "Bring ye *all* the tithes into the storehouse" (Malachi 3:10); "Shout for joy, *all* ye that are upright in heart" (Psalm 32:11); "In *all* thy ways acknowledge [me]" (Proverbs 3:6). Paul speaks for the Master and says, "live peaceably with *all* men" (Romans 12:18); "Whatsoever ye do, do *all* to the glory of God" (1 Corinthians 10:31). "Let *all* things be done decently and in order" (1 Corinthians 14:40). Today, hold nothing back from Yeshua. He deserves your very best, your all.

The Mighty Transformer

"...Christ Jesus: Who, being in the form of God, thought it not robbery to be equal with God: But made himself of no reputation, and took upon him the form of a servant, and was made in the likeness of men." (Philippians 2:5-7)

Having received abundant revelation, Paul clues us in on Yeshua's pre-incarnate existence saying that He was "in the form of God." The Greek word is *morphe* meaning *"shape*; figuratively, *nature."* In 1 Thessalonians 5:23, Paul calls Yeshua, "the very God;" however, Yeshua somehow maintained a distinct form separate from God. Another apostle verifies this concept saying, "the Word was with God, and the Word was God" (John 1:1). During Old Testament times the second Person of the Godhead appeared in different forms: creation Light, a smoking furnace, the angel of the LORD, a man speaking with his friend, a glory cloud, a pillar of fire, a shekinah glow, sometimes just audibly, and so on.

In the fullness of time, the infinite God transformed Himself into flesh and blood! Perhaps it is arguable which form He took on over the millennia was the most glorious. Perhaps it is His incarnate form. The wonder of it all is this: At the moment of the Son's resurrection it was forever determined what form He would remain in for the rest of eternity—a glorious mixture of both God and Man. Paul states, "For there is one God, and one mediator between God and men, the man Christ Jesus" (1 Timothy 2:5-6). After His resurrection, Yeshua appeared to Mary Magdalene, but she saw Him as a gardener. Shortly after that he appeared "in another form," to a pair of disciples walking to Emmaus (Mark 16:12). They perceived Him as some Torah scholar. Later along the Galilean seaside, it seems He appeared as an older man to youthful fisherman asking for a free fish (John 21:5). Many decades later John saw Yeshua's appearance much differently than he was accustomed—having snow-white hair and flaming eyes (Revelation 1:14). The day is coming when the mighty Transformer will fully transform us and "we shall see him as he is" (1 John 3:2).

Today, prayerfully seek to be transformed into a humble servant.

Touching the Ark

"And thou shalt put the staves into the rings by the sides of the ark, that the ark may be borne with them...they shall not be taken from it." (Exodus 25:14-15)

The ark, as you know, was a wooden cabinet overlaid with gold. It was the token of Yahweh's abiding presence (Exodus 25:22). The holy tablets within represented His pure nature, and the mercy seat above symbolized His readiness to dwell among men. Understandably, Yahweh's visible throne came with restrictions—No Touching Allowed! A reigning monarch's person was not to be touched; that is why he held out his golden scepter. In a similar way, God's servants were allowed to touch the rods that extended from the ark. Scripture records that tens of thousands died at once from touching the ark (1 Samuel 6:19). God even smote a righteous man for trying to save the ark from falling (2 Samuel 6:7).

Yeshua becomes the fulfillment of the ark's typology in several ways. The ark's wood and gold represents His humanity and His deity. The ark travelled with an outer garment; so did Yeshua. The ark was atoned with sprinkled blood, and so was Yeshua at Calvary. On one occasion, God's radiance and glory cloud emanated from the ark; so too with Yeshua at His transfiguration. Just as the law abided within the ark, Yeshua had God's law residing in His heart. The pot of manna and Aaron's budded-rod, which were placed in the ark, represent Yeshua, our daily Bread and eternal Life. There is one other notable aspect to consider.

During His public ministry many were quite fearful of touching His person; therefore, the sick attempted to touch only "the border of his garment" (Mark 6:56). They respected the holiness of His person, but the truth is He delighted in touching His kinsmen. He was constantly reaching out and touching others to bless or heal them (Luke 5:13). His favorite touch was for the mending of broken hearts. John rejoiced over his privileged opportunity when he said, "our hands have handled, of the Word of life" (1 John 1:1).

Hebrews 4:15 says you can touch Lord Yeshua today with your heart-felt prayers. Give this a try. What harm can it bring?

When "Nothing" Means Everything

"And it shall be unto them for an inheritance: I am their inheritance: and ye shall give them no possession in Israel: I am their possession." (Ezekiel 44:28)

It was not God's desire that the Tribe of Levi be caught up in the affairs of life. All their toils and labors were to be focused on Him and His kingdom. He in turn would provide their necessities through the continual offerings of all Israel. Since this priestly tribe could not possess land, they could live anywhere they wanted to among the other tribes. Only two weeks a year was a priest required to go live and labor at the Temple compound. Just as Israel was Yahweh's peculiar treasure among the nations, Levi was the peculiar tribe among the twelve. The Levites were to serve as spiritual guides in the cities where they dwelled, and the people would assist them in their daily living—even giving them tithes in the form of spices. The one thing the Levites were to lay daily claim to was God Himself, and He owns the cattle upon a thousand hills (Psalm 50:10).

Having received his New Covenant inheritance, the indwelling Spirit of Messiah, Paul became one who could no longer lay claim to earthly possessions (Philippians 3:12). This was also true because he suddenly received a gospel commission. His frequently unwelcomed gospel message left him homeless, hungry and destitute at times (2 Corinthians 11:27). Nonetheless, the apostle describes his attitude toward his new inheritance in this positive way: "As unknown, and yet well known; as dying, and, behold, we live; as chastened, and not killed; As sorrowful, yet always rejoicing; as poor, yet making many rich; as having nothing, and yet possessing all things" (2 Corinthians 6:9-10).

Maybe you have lost a child, a husband, wife or a friend due to a tragedy. Perhaps you have recently lost a good paying job, a house or even your life savings. You might have *nothing* left of value, yet you have inherited earth's greatest treasure—the Spirit of God's Son. You possess *everything*!

How Joshua Saved Israel

"And Moses called Hoshea the son of Nun Jehoshua." (Numbers 13:16)

It was Joshua, not Moses, who victoriously led Israel into their inheritance. He was a great type of the Messiah Whose name Yeshua is a shortened form of Yehoshua. This name originated in the mind of Moses and was bestowed upon Hoshea, which means salvation, thus *"saviour."* But Moses knew that Joshua could no more save Israel than he could, so he sought to enlarge Hoshea's name by adding one very important letter to it—a *yod*. Hoshea's new name, Yehoshua, not only signified his new position, but also suggests by its meaning "Yehovah is Saviour."

Joshua continued to bear the name of his earthly father "Nun" (pronounced *noon*) which means *perpetuity*. Joshua's surname, Nun, is phonetic, and its three Paleo-Hebrew letters [*nun, vav, nun*] are quite significant. The letter *nun* pictures a sprouting seed and means, "continue, heir, son." The letter *vav* pictures a tent peg and means, "add." The root word of Nun's name is also *Nun*, which means, "to *re-sprout*," thus; Joshua's surname was very prophetic. Hebrew babies who sprouted up in the wilderness under Moses would later re-sprout the next generation in the Promised Land under Joshua. As for Yeshua, He could not have completed Israel's salvation unless His dead body *re-sprouted* in newness of life (Romans 5:10). Messiah's body first sprouted from "the stem of Jesse" (Isaiah 11:1). Then, like a seed that dies when planted, Messiah's body *re-sprouted* from His lifeless body (John 12:24).

Most picturesque, Joshua saved Israel with *a spear* held in his outstretched arm, and he, like Yeshua Who awaited the nails, "drew not his hand back" (Jos. 8:26). Although Yeshua was already dead, His arms were still outstretched on the cross. At that time a Roman soldier stretched out *a spear* and "pierced his side, and forthwith there came out blood and water" whereby you are saved today (John 19:34)! Praise Yeshua today for His arm of salvation that was stretched out for you.

ᎧᏆow Ᏸeshua Ᏸaved Ᏸsrael

"God also hath highly exalted him, and given him a name which is above every name: That at the name of Jesus [Yeshua] *every knee should bow...And that every tongue should confess that Jesus Christ is Lord* [Yehovah]*."* (Philippians 2:9-10)

Yehovah, the self-existent One declared, "I have sworn by myself, the word is gone out of my mouth in righteousness, and shall not return, That unto me every knee shall bow, every tongue shall swear" (Isaiah 45:23). By rehearsing this mighty decree in Philippians 2:9-11 we come to know that the apostle is revealing Yeshua's truest identity. Yeshua is LORD; that is, Yehovah. The Greek word Paul uses, *kurios*, means supreme. This word can also be translated Lord, Master or God.

Around the time of Messiah's conception a token of God's salvation was given to Israel—Messiah's covenant name. The messenger decreed, "Thou shalt call his name [Yeshua]: for he shall save his people from their sins" (Matthew 1:21). Yeshua is an abbreviation of the formal name *Yehoshua,* which is comprised of two words, *Yeho* and *shua.* Bound together they mean, "Yehovah is a saving-cry." We find this particular cry for help very often in the Psalms. Notice the psalmist's great expectation when he cries out, "Save, LORD [Yehovah]: let the king hear us when we call" (20:9). Notice how the psalmist calls on Yehovah to save him from Hell: "Let...them go down quick into hell: for wickedness is in their dwellings...As for me, I will call upon God; and the LORD [Yehovah] shall save me" (55:15-16). One prophet promises Israel "whosoever shall call on the name of the LORD [Yehovah] shall be delivered" (Joel 2:32). Paul restates this in Romans 10:13, but makes it emphatic in verse 9 that your calling out to God must also include a confession that Yeshua is Yehovah—the self-existent One.

Your day ahead is likely to be as most others have been; that is, filled with great challenges. If today's challenges begin to swallow you up, just call out to *Yeshua* and He will save you from emotional distress and bring calm amidst your storm of life.

227

𝒟rawn to the 𝒮aviour

"Draw me, we will run after thee:" (Song of Solomon 1:4)

The Saviour first drew His covenant people out of Egypt—a type of the world—with His mighty and stretched out arm. The ten plagues made Israel marvel. Then with His glory cloud, the LORD drew Israel into the wilderness where they could have eyes only for Him. He also gave them one day a week in which to draw closer to Him. He facilitated this by removing the manna on the Sabbath day. Drawing Israel closer proved to be quite a challenge for the Saviour. Just before entering the Promised Land, He warned Israel not to "be drawn away, and worship other gods, and serve them" (Deuteronomy 30:17). His warning was met with obstinacy. He would have to draw them closer another way—"with cords of a man, with bands of love" (Hosea 11:4).

Israel's covenant-keeping God later allowed cruel armies to lay iron *bands* upon them, link them together with *man-made cords* [rope], and lead them into captivity. Simply put, God loved Israel too much to let them carry on in sin without regard for Him. In their captivity, they would regain earnest thoughts of the Holy One and learn to stop taking advantage of His infinite love. In the land of their captivity they could begin anew by responding to His call: "Yea, I have loved thee with an everlasting love: therefore with lovingkindness have I drawn thee" (Jeremiah 31:3).

King Solomon, a type of the Messiah, had betrothed a Shulamite. Her divided heart caused him continual trouble. She drew back into her comfortable lifestyle and lost her affectionate thoughts of him.

We, too, can behave like this with the Saviour, the One Whose mighty arm was outstretched upon the cross. Have you been recently "drawn away of your own lust, and enticed" (James 1:14)? If so, don't despise the firm manner in which the loving Saviour chooses to draw you back to Himself because His *bands of love* are tethered to the cross.

Grieving God

"I opened to my beloved; but my beloved had withdrawn himself, and was gone: my soul failed...I sought him, but I could not find him; I called him, but he gave me no answer." (Song of Solomon 5:6)

Solomon's betrothed bride represents the half-hearted nation of Israel. Yahweh says of them, "Forty years long was I grieved with this generation, and said, It is a people that do err in their heart" (Psalm 95:10). For their own spiritual wellbeing, the LORD smote that generation with divers plagues. Concerning the backslidden generation of his day, Jeremiah said to God, "thou hast stricken them, but they have not grieved" (Jeremiah 5:3). God's love is sometimes a very stern love, but He can never be blamed for loving us too little.

Solomon's bride explains what befell her after refusing to get up from her comfort and promptly open the door for her beloved. The king had waited there until his hair became drenched with the damp night air. She confesses, "The watchmen that went about the city found me, they smote me, they wounded me; the keepers of the walls took away my veil from me" (5:7). The bride is admitting her lack of spiritual vigilance. It was a custom for a betrothed virgin to go out in public with a veil on so others would know she was spoken for. When the watchmen snatched away her veil, it was a token against her signifying that she was really behaving like a woman without regard for her commitment.

We are sternly told, "grieve not the holy Spirit of God" (Ephesians 4:30). There are more ways to grieve God's Spirit than there are days in the year, so let us be prayerful and careful not to grieve Him in any way. This calls for extreme sensitivity. If the King of Saints has smitten your heart recently, He has only done so to shock it back into perfect rhythm with His. That is His only objective. If a New Covenant watchman, a brother or sister, exhorts you when you are careless, then remember Solomon's helpful reminder in Proverbs 27:6: "Faithful are the wounds of a friend."

Yeshua—the Great I Am

Part 1

"And he said unto them, Ye are from beneath; I am from above: ye are of this world; I am not of this world...for if ye believe not that I am he, ye shall die in your sins." (John 8:23-24)

Seven times in the Old Covenant Yahweh says, "I am he" using the words *ani hu*. They are as follows: "See now that I, even I, am he, and there is no god with me..." (Deuteronomy 32:39); "I the LORD, the first, and with the last; I am he" (Isaiah 41:4); "that ye may know and believe me, and understand that I am he" (43:10); "I am he; and there is none that can deliver out of my hand" (43:13); "I am he; and even to hoar hairs will I carry you" (46:4); "I am he...Mine hand also hath laid the foundation of the earth, and my right hand hath spanned the heavens" (48:12-13); "therefore they shall know in that day that I am he that doth speak" (52:6). Two times Yahweh uses the emphatic form, *anoki hu*: "I, even I, am he that blotteth out thy transgressions" (43:25); and "I, even I, am he that comforteth you" (51:12). This brings the total count to nine.

Some people say Messiah never claimed to be God, but this is so far from reality. Yeshua expressed Himself in a way that He could not be misunderstood. Yeshua clearly proclaimed He was the Great I Am. The New Covenant carefully records each instance. His use of the phrase, *ego eimi* meaning, "I am (he)" is found exactly nine times. They all appear in John's gospel: Read them in awe and wonder: "I that speak unto thee am he" (4:26); "It is I; be not afraid" (6:20); "if ye believe not that I am he, ye shall die in your sins" (8:24); "When ye have lifted up the Son of man, then shall ye know that I am he" (8:28); "Verily, verily, I say unto you, Before Abraham was, I am" (8:58); "when it is come to pass, ye may believe that I am he" (13:19); "Jesus saith unto them, I am he" (18:5); "As soon then as he had said...I am he, they went backward, and fell to the ground" (18:6); "I have told you that I am he: if...ye seek me, let these go their way" (18:8).

All nine *I am he* declarations from the Deutero-Isaiah text seem to align with the nine New Testament *I am he* proclamations in special ways. Yeshua didn't ever have to say, "I am God." All He had to do was say, "I am he," and when He did, the Pharisees began to pick up stones. Today, worship Yeshua for Whom He really is.

The Great I Am in Gethsemane
Part 2

"See now that I, even I, am he, and there is no god with me: I kill, and I make alive; I wound, and I heal: neither is there any that can deliver out of my hand." (Deuteronomy 32:39)

When observing this very first *I am he* declaration and comparing it to the four parabolic acts that transpired in Gethsemane, we find that this passage is extremely prophetic. John's gospel alone records the following event. The armed multitude entered Gethsemane by torchlight to arrest the lowly Son of God. When they drew near, "Jesus...went forth, and said unto them, Whom seek ye? They answered him, Jesus of Nazareth. Jesus saith unto them, I am he...As soon then as he had said unto them, I am he, they went backward, and fell to the ground" (John 18:4-6). What actually happened? He *killed* them; or to phrase it properly, they were slain of His Spirit. But He instantaneously *made* them *alive* again. When they got up, "he asked them again, Whom seek ye? And they said, Jesus of Nazareth. Jesus answered, I have told you that I am he" (v.7-8). In the midst of Messiah's two *I am he* declarations He presents striking tokens of His full Deity—He *kills* and *makes alive*.

Observe the next pair of chronological tokens: He *wounds* and *heals*. "Then Simon Peter having a sword drew it, and smote the high priest's servant, and cut off his right ear" (v.10). Just hours earlier in the Upper Room Messiah gave a command: "But now, he...that hath no sword, let him sell his garment, and buy one...And they said, Lord, behold, here are two swords. And he said unto them, It is enough" (Luke 22:36, 38). Hours later when the armed band stepped forward to bind Yeshua, Peter said, "Lord, shall we smite with the sword?" (v.49). Yeshua gave no stand-down order; thus the Master, via His student, *wounded* a man. Immediately Yeshua reached out and "he touched his ear, and *healed* him" (v.51). Yeshua fulfilled the fifth Deuteronomy 32:39 token when He successfully *delivered* His disciples by commanding the soldiers to "let these go their way" (John 18:8). When Yeshua rose up from the dead three days later, He most certainly fulfilled the sixth and seventh tokens of Deuteronomy 32:40, which read, "For I *lift* up my hand to heaven, and *say*, I live for ever." This seven-fold exhibition of Deuteronomy 32:39, 40 makes Yeshua to be the very God of Israel, Yahweh. Take perfect confidence in Yeshua today—as Lord of Lords.

Lord of the Sword
Part 3

"If I whet my glittering sword, and mine hand take hold on judgment; I will render vengeance to mine enemies, and will reward them that hate me...my sword shall devour flesh." (Deuteronomy 32:41)

The first "I am he" passage found in verse 39 continues to prove definitively that Yeshua was Governor of the sword in Gethsemane. When Lord Yeshua wounded the high priest's servant, He was sending a direct message to the high priest. Caiaphas was the one who had hatched the plot to destroy Him (John 11:51). Lord Yeshua's use of the glittering sword in the Garden was also a sign of what was to come.

His Word declares, "I will render vengeance to mine enemies, and will reward them that hate me." Indeed, Caiaphas hated Yeshua with a passion. This can be seen in the way he violently ripped his own robe at Yeshua's trial. Genesis 29:30, 33 defines one idea of hate as "to love someone less than another." Sadly, Israel was always doting on her other lovers. Yahweh once said of the nation, "I have delivered her into the hand of her lovers, into the hand of the Assyrians, upon whom she doted" (Ezekiel 23:9). The very same 24-hour day in which Lord Yeshua warned Israel with His glittering sword her leaders cried out, "We have no king but Caesar" (John 19:15). One generation later Yahweh was forced to deliver the unrepentant nation into the hands of the Romans upon whom she had boastfully doted.

Before entering the Promised Land, Moses urgently warned Israel of their reward for disobedience: "The LORD shall smite thee...with the sword" (Deuteronomy 28:22). Moses also lamented, "For they are a nation void of counsel, neither is there any understanding in them. O that they were wise, that they understood this, that they would consider their latter end! ...For the LORD shall judge his people" (Deuteronomy 32:28, 29, 36). All nations are to demonstrate their supreme love for the Saviour, because when He returns in power and glory, "out of his mouth goeth a sharp sword, that with it he should smite the nations" (Revelation 19:15).

Today, pray that Israel and the nations would find a burning passion their Kinsmen Redeemer.

Messiah's Token Hand

"My beloved put in his hand by the hole of the door, and my bowels were moved for him." (Song of Solomon 5:4)

Solomon's Shulamite bride was not enthusiastic about getting out of bed upon hearing his voice, but things changed when she saw his hand. In those days, opening the door to the wrong person could be dangerous. One solution was to place a very small square hole in the door. A very familiar person's hand could be easily identified when placed inside. This is where Solomon's anointed hand appeared. Though only traces of his perfumed oil were left behind, she magnifies the token of his memory saying, "I rose up to open to my beloved; and my hands dropped [oozed] with myrrh, and my fingers with sweet smelling myrrh, upon the handles of the lock" (v.5).

At the door of heaven (the cross), King Yeshua's hands dropped with pure crimson. He was also raised from the grave like no other resurrected man shall ever be—His hands still bearing the covenant tokens of Golgotha. Thus, He is set apart from all others for this reason alone.

When Habakkuk wrote of King Messiah's omnipotent return, he emphasized the covenant wounds in His hands. "God came from Teman, and the Holy One from mount Paran. Selah. His glory covered the heavens, and the earth was full of his praise. And his brightness was as the light; he had horns [rays] coming out of his hand: and there was the hiding of his power" (Habakkuk 3:3-4). We will never need to see a signet ring on our royal Sovereign's hand to identify Him sufficiently. Pure light will emanate from His nail prints for all to see, and "in his times he shall show, who is the blessed and only Potentate, the King of kings, and Lord of lords" (1 Timothy 6:15).

If you are discouraged today, don't let some difficult circumstance paralyze you and keep you from getting up to start your daily walk with the Holy One. Focus instead on the might and power of Messiah's Almighty hand. With it, He once bore your eternal pain, and yet now with both hands will bear you and your present burden all day long.

The Sons of Zadok

"But the priests the Levites, the sons of Zadok, that kept the charge of my sanctuary when the children of Israel went astray from me, they shall come near to me to minister unto me...saith the Lord GOD" (Ezekiel 44:15)

The sons of Zadok were a priestly family descending from the line of Zadok, the first high priest to officiate over Solomon's Temple. Zadok was a descendant of Eleazar, one of Aaron's four sons. Nadab and Abihu burned an unsanctioned mixture of incense before Yahweh and thus, "there went out fire from the LORD, and devoured them and they died before the LORD" (Leviticus 10:1-2). This left Aaron with two sons, Eleazar, the elder and Ithamar, the younger. According to the custom, the oldest son succeeded his father as high priest.

Sometime later in the wilderness, Phinehas, Eleazar's son, appeased God's wrath and won himself favored status. Yahweh announced to Moses, "Behold, I give unto him my covenant of peace: And he shall have it, and his seed after him, even the covenant of an everlasting priesthood; because he was zealous for his God, and made an atonement for the children of Israel" (Numbers 25:12-13). In Canaan Phinehas must have somehow failed in his duties. Perhaps he should have nullified Jepthah's pagan vow; we don't know. In any case, the priesthood was given over to the descendants of Ithamar; that is, Eli and his sons. After Eli let the Lamp of God go out in the Tabernacle, and after he allowed his two sons to carry on like men of Belial, the Aaronic priesthood reverted to the line of Eleazar. Yahweh prophesied to Eli through a man of God saying, "And I will raise me up a faithful priest, that shall do according to that which is in mine heart and in my mind: and I will build him a sure house" (1 Samuel 2:35). This came to pass in the days of David when he appointed Zadok to the priesthood.

Zadok means *just* and comes from a root word meaning to be *right, righteous*. Today, pray that the Spirit of God will help you to be more zealous of His commandments and to remain upright before the Father at all times. Remember, you have a godly heritage to pass on.

Rules of Engagement

"He that leadeth into captivity shall go into captivity: he that killeth with the sword must be killed with the sword. Here is the patience and the faith of the saints." (Revelation 13:10)

Messiah warned His followers that when they saw their beloved city surrounded by Roman armies to flee Jerusalem, not defend it. Pilate was puzzled on the issue of Yeshua's Judean Kingship because He never commanded His faithful followers to take up swords. He puzzled the Roman governor further when He said, "If my kingdom were of this world, then would my servants fight" (John 18:36). Earlier Yeshua remarked on John the Baptist's cruel death saying, "the kingdom of heaven suffereth violence, and the violent take it by force" (Matthew 11:12). Force was certainly not Messiah's method of bringing in His kingdom; the people had to receive it.

The sons of thunder, James and John, were thrown back by Messiah's stern rebuff when they wanted to call down fire from heaven that it might fall upon their unbelieving half-brothers of Samaria. Yeshua scolded them saying, "Ye know not what manner of spirit ye are of" (Luke 9:55). Peter, the chief of the three pillars, struck the high priest's servant once to defend his Master. But Messiah stopped him from proceeding any further. That night Peter learned a valuable kingdom principle. Much earlier Messiah commanded him to forgive others as many times as necessary. To Yeshua's many mountain-top listeners He proclaimed, "Love your enemies, bless them that curse you, do good to them that hate you, and pray for them which despitefully use you, and persecute you" (Matthew 5:44). The kingdom is installed on earth in this manner.

During those first three fiery centuries after Messiah's death, the persecuted saints refused to defend themselves in honor of the Lord's command. They still do even now. John received the rules of engagement for saints who seek to honor their Lord—exercise faith and patience (Revelation 13:10). Today, ask the Lord to help you use your faith and to have patience when, where and with whomever necessary.

𝒯ive 𝒮hekels for 𝒨ashiakh

Part 1

"The parents brought in the child Jesus, to do for him after the custom of the law." (Luke 2:27)

The Israelite nation had many customs. Let's not confuse one for another. Miriam and Yosef saw to it that their firstborn Son was ritually circumcised on the eighth day. This could be done anywhere (v.21). Mosaic Law also placed two additional requirements upon Miriam making it necessary to go up to the Temple. One requisite was to complete "the days of her purification" after childbearing (v.22). According to Leviticus 12:2-4 this was a total of 40 days. Until then she was not permitted inside the Sanctuary courts. Afterwards the mother was required to bring a pair of *young* doves as a sin offering, and if financially able, a *young* lamb as a burnt offering. We know that Miriam and Yosef were relatively poor because Luke only mentions the doves (Luke 2:24).

Luke records Miriam's last obligation: "As it is written in the law of the Lord, Every male that openeth the womb shall be called holy to the Lord" (v.23). He cites a portion of Exodus 13, which also explains how Yahweh's sparing of Israel's firstborn sons in Egypt entitled Him to set apart all future ones for Himself. Fortunately for the parents' sake—except for Levites—they were permitted to redeem or buy back their firstborn sons from the LORD (Exodus 13:13). The word here for redeem is *padah* which means to *sever*; that is, to *release, ransom*. This ceremony, *Pidyon HaBen*, Redemption of the Firstborn, could take place anytime after the child reached a month old and included a monetary exchange of five shekels (Numbers 18:15). This is why Miriam and Yosef also brought along baby Yeshua, to present Him to the Lord and buy Him back (Luke 2:22). Five is the number of grace, and through this five-fold token of grace, both parties achieved an enduring satisfaction.

Thirty-three years later, Mashiakh ransomed His parents and the world with five metallic tokens of grace, albeit, of a different kind! Today, praise the Father for His redeeming grace and love.

Five Shouts from Mashiakh
Part 2

"Be not far from me; for trouble is near; for there is none to help...Be not thou far from me, O LORD: O my strength, haste thee to help me...Deliver my soul from the sword; my darling from the power of the dog...Save me from the lion's mouth." (Psalm 22:11, 19-21)

Readers of the New Testament are familiar with Mashiakh's seven sayings from the cross, among which there was not a single plea for *heavenly* help. This psalm is prophetic in nature, but aren't we still meant to believe these words were indeed spoken from the cross sometime during the hours He hung upon it? Perhaps the reason why these five commands in Psalm 22 were not recorded in the New Testament is because they were not to be answered. In any event, these words are the most powerful and yet the most pitiful in all of Scripture. These are commands from the Son of God for divine intervention in His moment of crisis, but no help came. Why?

As if it were of great necessity, Mashiakh reminds His Father, "But thou art he that took me out of the womb...I was cast upon thee from the womb; thou art my God from my mother's belly" (v.9-10). The heavenly Father's firstborn Son hoped to find favor through this holy reminder, but there was a co-existing reality. Mashiakh's *earthly adoptive* father (Joseph) had legally purchased Him back from Yahweh for five shekels. When He sent out calls for grace, no grace was sent in reply. It was withheld from Him that it might instead be poured out on the rest of mankind. If the LORD had answered any one of Mashiakh's five distress calls, there would be no grace left available for us.

There is a third grouping of five to consider—*Five Sharp Implements for Mashiakh*. His body was pierced through with five metal objects. Triple fives equals grace personified: five coins, five distress calls and five piercings. From birth to death, grace's special number five marked Yeshua. Thus, He was the Personification of Grace.

Today, thank the heavenly Father for personifying and personalizing His grace toward you.

𝒟esperate for ℋim

"And he spake to his disciples, that a small ship should wait on him because of the multitude, lest they should throng him. For he had healed many; insomuch that they pressed upon him for to touch him, as many as had plagues." (Mark 3:9-10)

The rich seldom sought after Messiah for they already had what they wanted, and the religious tended to their religion. Those nationalistic zealots, who waged guerrilla warfare against Rome, were not interested in a passive King like Yeshua. However, one group sought Him desperately—the sick and needy.

Their numbers were large, their urgency was great, and their time was running out. Those who were diseased had *eyes* only for Him. The downside of their situation was that afterwards they chose not to give Him their *ears*. The infirm thronged Yeshua because of His power to grant physical deliverance, but they did not crowd around Him to receive spiritual enlightenment. They were desperate for healing, but after being healed not so desperate for Him. The lame, the blind, the maimed, the deaf and others like them were too self-absorbed to grasp what Messiah was really all about. He had come to set the captives free, not only from disease, but from spiritual darkness as well.

Sometimes we can be similar in our attitude towards Him. When we have a need our motto is, "He's all I need." By way of contrast, when all is well we tend to keep Yeshua in the background. The Lord places a priority in our everyday lives. He says, "I love them that love me; and those that seek me early shall find me" (Proverbs 8:17). People are desperate for love, and the Saviour is desperate for ours. That is why He compels us to direct our love towards Him. His word says, "Thou shalt love the LORD thy God with all thine heart, and with all thy soul, and with all thy might" (Deuteronomy 6:5). He wants His covenant people to draw near, not only to receive His love, but also to give Him *ours*.

Today, seek Yeshua's heart, not just His hand. Attempt to describe and express your love for Him.

If It's of God

"Unto the church of God which is at Corinth, to them that are sanctified in Christ Jesus, called to be saints," (1 Corinthians 1:2)

Paul was focused on Yahweh from an early age. Parents who wanted their sons to become rabbis started them out the moment they were weaned at age three. When Saul met the Son of God on the Damascus Road, the Pharisee of Pharisees forsook his self-righteousness for the true righteousness of God. After Yeshua commissioned him, Paul found a great challenge with the believers at Corinth. They were not behaving in accordance to God's character, but the world's.

As Paul wrote his first letter of correction to them, he began by making them aware that they were the church of God, and as a heavenly assembly they should act accordingly; that is, be saintly. He went on to tell them to focus on the preaching of the cross, which was the *power* of God, and Yeshua Himself Who is the *wisdom* of God (v.24). Paul came to Corinth, not with enticing words of men, but rather with the *testimony* of God (2:1). He encouraged them to seek out the *deep things* of God (2:10) and to be dependent on the *Spirit* of God (2:11) Who indwelled them as the *temple* of God (3:16). They were advised to respect people like himself who were the *stewards of the mysteries* of God (4:1) and not to judge people so quickly. He also encouraged them to work on proper *praise* of God (4:5) and to live out the *kingdom* of God daily (4:20).

Paul was trying to get the Corinthian believers to give attention to those things that were good; therefore, things had to be tested to see if they were purely from God or partly from this polluted world system. If it was of God, it had to be good. This was also James' testimony who said, "Every good gift and every perfect gift is from above, and cometh down from the Father of lights" (James 1:17).

If you have plans today that make you feel unsure about whether or not it is of God, ask Him if it is within His perfect will for *your* life.

Forms of God's Presence

"Repent ye therefore, and be converted, that your sins may be blotted out, when the times of refreshing shall come from the presence of the Lord." (Acts 3:19)

There are four forms of Yahweh's presence and each one speaks of the Son of God. Yeshua's most well known form is His *omnipresence*. David described this attribute in Psalm 139:7-10. Paul preached that the heathen "should seek the Lord...though he be not far from every one of us" (Acts 17:27). Yeshua's omnipresence was not entirely limited just because He dwelt in human form, for when He was on a mountain at night and His disciples were in the midst of the sea, "he saw them toiling in rowing" (Mark 6:48). Jesus also saw Nathanial under the fig tree (John 1:48).

The Son of God longs to visit with His own, so He takes on a *dwelling presence* whenever they praise Him (Psalm 22:3). He specifically said to Moses, "Let them make me a sanctuary; that I may dwell among them" (Exodus 25:8). He later came to dwell in Solomon's Temple where His presence gloriously filled the house (2 Chronicles 5:14). He also promised to dwell wherever two or three gathered in His name (Matthew 18:20).

Yeshua displayed His *manifest presence* at various times throughout the Old Testament period. He appeared many times to Abraham, Isaac and Jacob (Genesis 12:7, 26:2, 35:1). Yeshua also appeared to Moshe at the burning bush (Exodus 3:2-4). To Ezekiel He appeared as the Son of Man robed with fire and sitting upon a sapphire throne (Ezekiel 1:26). The time came when "God was manifest in the flesh" for a season (1 Timothy 3:16). And after His resurrection, He appeared to various believers. In the future He will manifest Himself yet again at His return (Acts 3:21).

A current form, and most sacred to us, is His *indwelling presence,* which was brought about ten days after His ascension to the Father's throne. He promises to make His abode with all who repent of their sins, place their trust in His atoning blood, and call upon His name (John 14:23). Today, take quality time to enjoy the Saviour's gracious, inwardly abiding presence.

Jotham's Parable

"And when they had platted a crown of thorns, they put it upon his head, and a reed in his right hand: and they bowed the knee before him, and mocked him, saying, Hail, King of the Jews!" (Matthew 27:29)

The prophets depicted many grotesque details of Messiah's suffering. Concerning His blessed face, they foretold that it would be spat upon (Isaiah 50:6), struck with a rod (Micah 5:1), and have the beard plucked out (Isaiah 50:6). All these dreadful things came to pass that Scripture might be fulfilled. One thing, however, that was not clearly foretold was the *wreath of thorns* pressed deep upon His head. The Saviour-King went beyond His call of duty in allowing this.

Thorns speak of the Adamic curse, and various species of them were used to chastise rebels during biblical times (Judges 8:7). Thorns can grow upon trees such as the *bramble*, a thorn tree mentioned in Jotham's parable—the story of the trees that went forth to anoint a king over them (Judges 9:7-15). Jotham was the lone survivor among Gideon's 70 sons, except for Abimelech who slaughtered them. Jotham, acting as the bramble, said unto the trees, "If in truth ye anoint me king over you, then come and put your trust in my shadow." Jotham's Hebrew name, *Yo-tawm,* means, *"Yehovah is perfect."* When used to describe a person, *tawm* means someone who is *perfect*; lacking nothing in physical strength, *wholesome*; a quiet sort of person; *complete*; morally innocent. These definitions describe Yeshua the Nazarene, "the root of David" which grew into a sheltering tree of life (Revelation 5:5; Jeremiah 33:15).

Jotham's parable, when viewed in the greater prophetic light of Messiah, envisions the following. Upon the tree perfect Jehovah hung, and with thorns about His head and sharp spikes in His hands and feet a picture is drawn of a cursed bramble tree, which challenges man to freely trust in its revitalizing shade. Messiah's destiny is for "the fig tree" [Israel] and "all the trees" [Gentiles] to receive Him as "Prince of the kings of the earth" and to "anoint [Him] as the Most Holy" (Luke 21:29; Revelation 1:5; Daniel 9:24). Anoint Yeshua afresh in your heart today.

Torah vs. Gospel

"Forasmuch as we have heard, that certain which went out from us have troubled you with words, subverting your souls, saying, Ye must be circumcised, and keep the law: to whom we gave no such commandment:" (Acts 15:24)

The apostles wanted gentile converts moving forward in Messiah's doctrine, not backwards to Moses' doctrine. James gave his ruling, which specified four Mosaic do-nots (v.20). These were a compliment to Yeshua's two affirmative Torah principles—to love God with all your heart and to love your neighbor as yourself. This total comes to six, but God's number of completion and perfection is seven. So what is the seventh general rule of practice for Jew and Gentile alike? To keep Yeshua's sayings. If He said it, you can do it. He has even given you His Spirit to aid you in the process.

According to Matthew 7:24, Yeshua's sayings are the believer's new foundation or "rock" upon which to build. Moses' teachings were good, but now fall way short of Messiah's. Moses said, "Do not commit adultery," but Messiah's higher law says even not to look at a woman with lust. Moses said not to murder, but Messiah's higher law says that if you hate someone then you have a murderer's heart. The vast majority of the Gentile Christian world is greatly hesitant about studying the New Covenant in light of its Hebraic foundation. While it's true they are missing out on many wonderful truths, they're afraid of where it might lead, and rightly so. Additionally, when lost Jews go into a Messianic congregation and see Moses' name exalted and Yeshua's name hardly mentioned—or not at all as the case sometimes is—they, too, become confused. A group of blood-washed saints parading around a Torah scroll in a New Covenant assembly is comparable to a group of university graduates in full regalia celebrating by holding up their old high school diplomas. Yes, that foundational grade schooling was once necessary, but it is now insufficient to enter the career world.

Today, marvel over the beauty of the five gospel books of Messiah—Matthew, Mark, Luke, John and Acts.

Temporal vs. Eternal

"For which cause we faint not...for the things which are seen are temporal; but the things which are not seen are eternal." (2 Corinthians 4:16, 18)

Paul understood the end game with great clarity and was always making comparisons like the Old Covenant vs. the New Covenant, law vs. grace, old man vs. new man, corruptible vs. incorruptible, mortal vs. immortal, Moses vs. Messiah, and so on. He understood the vast difference one makes over the other, and so He makes three comparisons in this passage.

He compares the outward man with the inward man and says that one will perish but the other one is renewed day-by-day (v.16). No matter the amount of proper diet, exercise and rest you give your outward man, it is still going to maintain its predetermined course of decline. Yet when you have a daily intake of Bible time and prayer, accompanied with constant yielding to God's Spirit, your inward man grows stronger and more mature in stature.

Next, the apostle contrasts "our light affliction which is but for a moment" with our future "exceeding and eternal weight of glory" (v.17). For this reason, you need not worry about all the shame, ridicule and possible hardships that may come from making your Saviour known to a lost and dying world. If it comes, endure hardness as a good soldier and labor on for the LORD.

Lastly, Paul compares the temporary, fleeting nature of the things that are seen—that shall vanish one day and be replaced—with eternal things that are not seen (v.18).

With this last point in mind, don't be overly attracted to the glittering trinkets this world has to offer you today. Rather, invest your heart, life and treasures in the coming kingdom. You'll have no regrets when the kingdom's fullness comes.

Messiah's Door of Mercy

"Behold now, thy servant hath found grace in thy sight, and thou hast magnified thy mercy, which thou hast showed unto me in saving my life." (Genesis 19:19)

Here in the words of Lot we have the first occurrence of mercy in the Bible. It is the word *khesed* and is often translated as kindness. Mercy is defined as "compassionate or kindly forbearance shown toward an offender." Mercy is a well-known attribute of Yahweh and, therefore, Lot thanked the angels of God for showing mercy to him. Mercy can also be translated as pity, and it was Job who looked for just a little of this from his friends but found none (Job 6:14).

Mercy is a trait that is to be equally found in God's people. Ruth showed kindness to Naomi, Rahab showed kindness to the two Hebrew spies, the Kenites showed kindness to Israel, and David showed kindness to the house of Saul after his death, namely to Mephibosheth. When we study the word *khesed* in its ancient pictorial form, a beautiful illustration of mercy and kindness comes forth. Khesed has three letters: *khet*, which pictures a wall, *samekh*, which pictures a thorn, and *dalet*, which pictures a door. Together these letters depict the work of a loving shepherd who builds a secure, four-sided *wall* [with a *doorway*] made from *thorny* brush material to enclose and protect his helpless sheep. The shepherd makes a doorway; an entrance through which the sheep may come in, but then guards that doorway to make sure no predators can enter. The shepherd himself becomes the *door* and puts himself in harm's way, especially at night when he sleeps there. He does this only because he loves his sheep.

This is the very illustration Messiah chose to describe His loving kindness and mercy for you. He says, "I am the door of the sheep...by me if any man enter in, he shall be saved [safe], and shall go in and out, and find pasture. The thief cometh not, but for to steal, and to kill, and to destroy: I am come that they might have life...I am the good shepherd: the good shepherd giveth his life for the sheep" (John 10:7, 9-11). Today, thank the Good Shepherd for His mercy and kindness.

When Dead Men Listen

"Marvel not at this: for the hour is coming, in the which all that are in the graves shall hear his voice," (John 5:28)

Knowing that His listeners were very much dull of hearing, Yeshua encouraged them to pay close attention to the spiritual concepts He was teaching. His advice: "He that hath ears to hear, let him hear" (Matthew 11:15). The emphasis was on hearing, not just listening. There's a vast difference between the two. He that has ears to hear refers to one who has a *teachable spirit* and wants to benefit from what he hears. This person is also going to be a doer of Messiah's Word because he loves his Teacher devotedly.

There are some interesting, visible features about the word hear. Visually speaking, the word "hear" is an *ear* with an *h* placed in front of it. What could the hidden meaning be behind this little letter? The *h* is a soft sound and is produced by simply using one's breath; therefore, to *hear from God* is to catch His breath upon your ear. The word "hear" is just one letter short of "heart." Herein lies the key to godly hearing. One must catch God's *breath* and take it to *heart*. It is one thing to listen with your ears, but another matter altogether to listen with your heart. When God speaks to you, either from His written Word or from His indwelling Spirit, "Deep calleth unto deep" (Psalm 42:7). God longs to reach our innermost being.

It is far better to listen *willingly* to the Son's call in this present life, than to listen *woefully* in the afterlife, "for the hour is coming, in the which all that are in the graves shall hear his voice. And shall come forth; they that have done good, unto the resurrection of life and they that have done evil, unto the resurrection of damnation" (John 5:29). How well a believer listens now determines whether the Son will say to him or not, "Well done thou good and faithful servant," at the Judgment Seat (Matthew 25:21). This is what Paul may have been talking about in Philippians 3:11. He was more concerned with how he lived for God than how he would die.

Today, ask the Lord to help you to be sensitive to His still, small voice and to His indescribably deep and holy Word.

Spirit Taught

"*But this spake he of the Spirit, which they that believe on him should receive: for the Holy Ghost was not yet given; because that Jesus was not yet glorified.*" (John 7:39)

The Spirit was sent to us by Yeshua's command (John 15:26), made available to us by Yeshua's blood, and given to us that we may become more like Him. Concerning the Holy Spirit, Yeshua said, "He shall not speak of himself" (John 16:13). We know that the Holy Spirit's role is to teach us about the Father and the Son, but what else does He teach us?

The Spirit teaches you how to *sit still*. "The same day went Jesus out of the house, and sat by the sea side" (Matthew 13:1). Though you are a servant, you're not always to be busy or moving. The Master Himself knew how to sit. Notice His determination: "And great multitudes were gathered together unto him, so that he went into a ship, and sat" (v.2).

The Spirit teaches you when to *stay quiet*. False accusers told lies about Messiah before His very face. He could have defended Himself, but Jesus held His peace (Matthew 26:63). The Father can do a much better job of defending us than we can do all by ourselves. So the time may be when you should let Him because He knows how to silence the crowds.

The Spirit teaches you to *wait patiently*. Messiah will come to your rescue if you have the patience to wait for His delivering power. "He giveth power to the faint; and to them that have no might he increaseth strength. Even the youths shall faint and be weary...But they that wait upon the LORD shall renew their strength" (Isaiah 40:29-31).

The Spirit teaches you to *speak discerningly*. Yeshua always had the right words at the right time. Jeremiah was but a youth and needed much discernment in speaking with the hardened hearts of his day. His testimony was this, "The Spirit of the LORD spake by me, and his word was in my tongue" (2 Samuel 23:2). Ask the Holy Spirit to be your Teacher and Tutor today.

The Daughter of Zion
Part 1

"Sing, O daughter of Zion; shout...be glad and rejoice with all the heart, O daughter of Jerusalem...the king of Israel, even the LORD, is in the midst of thee: thou shalt not see evil any more." (Zephaniah 3:14-15)

Zion is a specific hill within Jerusalem, but is also another name for the City of God. The term "daughter of Zion" also refers to Jerusalem. In our text, Zephaniah emphasizes that Yahweh is the King of Israel. A later prophet, Zechariah, presents Yeshua as both of these rolled into One. He writes, "Sing and rejoice, O daughter of Zion: for, lo, I come, and I will dwell in the midst of thee, saith the LORD [*Yahweh*]" (Zechariah 2:10). As Zechariah continues writing he gives one additional bit of information about this coming One: "Rejoice greatly, O daughter of Zion; shout, O daughter of Jerusalem: behold, thy King cometh unto thee: he is just, and having salvation; lowly, and riding upon an ass" (Zechariah 9:9). Using the *remez* [hinting] principle, Zechariah makes it irrefutably clear—Israel's God, Yahweh, will come in lowly, fleshly form!

In the ancient Near East, cities other than Jerusalem were tagged with the name "daughter of" like Tyre and Tarshish. The term daughter points to her parent-city, which looks down favorably upon her from the heights above. This is entirely true of Jerusalem. *Yerushalayim* is plural revealing that there are indeed two Jerusalems—one terrestrial and one celestial. Paul referred to Zion's parent-city calling it, "Mt. Sion...the city of the living God, the heavenly Jerusalem" where innumerable angels dwell (Hebrews 12:22). He confirms this saying, "Jerusalem which is above is free, which is the mother of us all" (Galatians 4:26). A resident of this celestial city can only procure his or her permanent citizenship through being born *again* [Gr. *anothen*: from above] (John 3:7). This very same spiritual rebirth concept is presented in Psalm 87:3-6: "Glorious things are spoken of thee, O city of God...And of Zion it shall be said, This and that man was born in her...The LORD shall count, when he writeth up the people."

Today, thank Yeshua for coming down to earth, sending His Spirit back to breathe new life into you, and for making you a permanent citizen of heaven.

The Daughters of Zion

Part 2

"Go forth, O ye daughters of Zion, and behold king Solomon with the crown wherewith his mother crowned him in the day of his espousals, and in the day of the gladness of his heart." (Song of Solomon 3:11)

The daughter of Zion is the *city* and the daughters of Zion are its *citizens*. However, some citizens have yet to receive their Messianic King. When this remainder whole-heartedly embraces Yeshua at His return, the earthly Zion shall glow as no city ever has or ever shall. "And it shall come to pass...he that remaineth in Jerusalem, shall be called holy, even every one that is written among the living in Jerusalem: When the Lord shall have washed away the filth of the daughters of Zion, and shall have purged the blood of Jerusalem...by the spirit of judgment, and by the spirit of burning" (Isaiah 4:3-4). Afterwards King Messiah will create a wedding canopy over earthly Zion for His newly reborn Israelite bride (v.5).

At the end of King Yeshua's lowly first advent, a clarion call went out to the daughters of Zion from the mouth of Pontius Pilate—"Behold your King!" (John 19:14). When they looked, they only saw that He was *crowned* with thorns. Nevertheless, it is written: "for the joy that was set before him [He] endured the cross" (Hebrews 12:2). On His way to the cross that day Yeshua said, "Daughters of Jerusalem, weep not for me, but weep for yourselves, and for your children" (Luke 23:28). He said this due to His knowledge of the long, dark days that lay ahead for Israel. All Israel's lamenting will be overshadowed when the Son of God returns "in the day of his espousals, and in the day of the gladness of his heart." The *sod*, or deep, hidden level of Song of Solomon 3:11 foretells of the Messianic King being *crowned* by His mother; that is to say, heavenly Zion. He will return already "having on his head a golden crown" (Revelation 14:14).

Today, pray that the current faithless daughters of Zion would have a change of heart and receive by faith their soon-returning King, and be spiritually joined to Him.

ᾼalk About Zion

Part 3

"Let mount Zion rejoice, let the daughters of Judah be glad, because of thy judgments. Walk about Zion, and go round about her:" (Psalm 48:11-12)

The psalmist boasts in the defensible, earthly city of Jerusalem saying, "Beautiful for situation, the joy of the whole earth, is mount Zion, on the sides of the north, the city of the great King" (v.2). Let's proceed with an application, a *midrash* on Zion, based on King Messiah's death just outside Zion's walls. Is not this the most pivotal event in Zion's long history?

Mt. Zion is a specific mountain adjacent to Mt. Moriah, the Temple Mount, but its exact location is uncertain. The psalmist says that Mt. Zion is situated on the sides of the north. This is entirely true of the heavenly city (Isaiah 14:13). But if the psalmist is referring to the north part of the earthly city, then this is exactly where a hill named Golgotha and Calvary is situated. This is precisely where Israel's King took upon Himself our *judgment for sin*. Could this horror be what some saw when they walked about Zion one day? "For, lo, the kings were assembled, they passed by together. They saw it, and so they marveled [*tamahh*–to be astonished]; they were troubled, and hasted away. Fear took hold upon them there, and pain, as of a woman in travail" (Psalm 48:4-6). A few centuries later another prophet foretold this event in much the same way saying, "Behold, my servant...As many were *astonished* at thee; his visage was so marred more than any man, and his form more than the sons of men: So shall he sprinkle many nations; the kings shall shut their mouths at him: for that which had not been told them shall they see; and that which they had not heard shall they consider" (Isaiah 52:13-15). The psalmist is also careful to say, "that ye may tell it to the generation following" (48:13).

No wonder the psalmist says at the end of his song, "For this God is our God for ever and ever: he will be our guide even unto death" (v.14). Let Yeshua be your guide as you go out today, wherever that may be.

cHannah's Prophecy

"And Hannah prayed, and said, My heart rejoiceth in the LORD, mine horn is exalted in the LORD: my mouth is enlarged over mine enemies; because I rejoice in thy salvation." (1 Samuel 2:1)

Hannah's prayer is not only a song born out of triumph, it is a prophecy which shall be completely revealed in due time. Hannah's prophetic utterance begins due to the reversal of her barrenness and having a son. Her prophecy concludes in verse 10 with a full expectation that Yahweh will send His anointed King at an appointed time and render judgment upon all that strive against Him. In other words, Hannah prophesies about the installation of Earth's final Governor, Messianic Yeshua. Interestingly, He would be born from a virgin's womb.

This 12th-century BC handmaid of the LORD has her prophetic song rehearsed in another age altogether, this time from the lips of Yahweh's handmaid *Miriam* who actually brings forth the Saviour King. Miriam's exaltation of the LORD in Luke 1:46-55, known as the *Magnificat,* closely follows the themes of Hannah's canticle and in the same order. Miriam's paraphrase of the ancient prophecy is succinct but sublime. It rises within her heart upon receiving knowledge that she is carrying inside her belly the incarnate Lord (v.43). Hannah's prophecy, perhaps recited by countless expectant Hebrew mothers through the centuries, suddenly becomes realized through the virgin Mary. Let her words encourage your downcast spirit today.

"My soul doth magnify the Lord, And my spirit hath rejoiced in God my Saviour. For he hath regarded the low estate of his handmaiden: for behold, from henceforth all generations shall call me blessed. For he that is mighty hath done to me great things; and holy is his name. And his mercy is on them that fear him from generation to generation. He hath showed strength with his arm; he hath scattered the proud in the imagination of their hearts. He hath put down the mighty from their seats, and exalted them of low degree. He hath filled the hungry with good things; and the rich he hath sent empty away. He hath helped...Israel, in remembrance of his mercy; As he spake to our fathers, to Abraham, and to his seed for ever."

Hannah's Song

"They that were full have hired out themselves for bread; and they that were hungry ceased: so that the barren hath born seven; and she that hath many children is waxed feeble." (1 Samuel 2:1)

Hannah's name, *khanah*, means *favored,* yet for many years, her life seemed anything but blessed because the LORD had shut up her womb (v.5). Hannah's life was wrapped up in misery, especially at the annual pilgrimage to Shiloh when her husband's other wife, Peninnah, became her adversary and provoked her the whole time (v.6). Peninnah is the feminine form of *paniyn,* which means, a *pearl.* As you know, a pearl forms by encasing an irritant. Peninnah was a pearl to her husband but only an irritating factor in Hannah's life. It got to the point that Hannah could never enjoy the feast; all she could do was weep excessively year after year (v.7).

Hannah's barrenness was eventually reversed. She named her son Shemuel, weaned him and gave him up to serve the LORD at Shiloh. Hannah's reversal turned her trial into triumph and her weeping into worship. She mentions more than ten reversals in her song. The one in our text is that *the barren hath born seven.* A wonderful reversal not mentioned in her song is the manner in which she was now able to go up to the Tabernacle yearly without weeping. Each year she went up with joy as she took little Samuel a proper-fitting, handmade coat (v.19).

Maybe Hannah's song has not yet become your song, but keep in mind that once you have given your petitions to God they belong to Him. There is great depth of meaning in Samuel's Hebrew name, you see. *Shemuel* means, *heard of God.* God hears a saint, but then carefully chooses when to answer. All four matriarchs of Israel had to wait on God to heal them of their barrenness. Epic events in God's divine plan can only unfold through the process of time.

Today, trust that the Father has heard your request and then trust equally in the perfect timing of His response.

251

The Shout of the King

"...Israel: the LORD his God is with him, and the shout of a king is among them." (Numbers 23:21)

Many could have misunderstood Balaam's prophecy about Israel, because a nation's strength was found in the *physical* presence of their king. Nations believed that the gods set up mortal kings to carry out their eternal will. Thus, nations viewed kings as an earthly extension of heavenly rule. For this very reason, they seldom went into battle without them. But Israel's King was not like other kings; Yahweh was completely unseen. A physical token of His presence preceded Israel as they journeyed—His golden mercy seat carried on staves by priests. Through experience, Israel learned to find sufficient confidence in their King's empty chair as they went into battle after battle so victoriously.

Even though Yahweh remained out of view, He commanded His people to shout in faith just the same (Joshua 6:5). Their first major test was a success. When the people shouted the walls of Jericho fell flat. In a later, decisive moment the Ark of the Covenant came into the camp and "all Israel shouted with a great shout, so that the earth rang again" (1 Samuel 4:5). This greatly unsettled the Philistine camp, and even they acknowledged that the ark was synonymous with the God of Israel's abiding presence (v.6-7). Isaiah reminded his people to be confident, saying, "cry out and shout...for great is the Holy One of Israel in the midst of thee." (Isaiah 12:6).

On the day Yeshua presented Himself as their long-awaited Messianic King, they "took branches of palm trees, and went forth to meet him, and cried [shouted], Hosanna: Blessed is the King of Israel that cometh in the name of the Lord" (John 12:13).

That period of the King's physical presence was short lived, but you can take courage that the King of Kings is ever present with you as you journey from home today. If you get discouraged, depressed or upset today, don't ask God where He is or to show Himself; instead, show yourself to Him by shouting the victory in Yeshua's high and holy name!

Showing Up for Rehearsals

"These are the feasts of the LORD, even holy convocations, which ye shall proclaim in their seasons." (Leviticus 23:4)

Gentile believers often refer to these seven recurring observances as Jewish festivals, but in verse 2 Yahweh says, "these are my feasts." Most Christians believe that these Old Testament feasts are of no real importance in this current New Testament dispensation, and so sadly, they remain unaware that this Age of Grace was inaugurated on a Jewish feast day, the fourth one—Shavuot. God has a holy timeline and Israel's entire history is laid out according to these seven feasts.

Yahweh calls each of His feasts a holy "convocation." This word in Hebrew is *miqrah* meaning "something *called* out, a public *meeting*." God is calling a meeting basically, and His people are commanded and expected to respond by showing up and participating. This lends to the alternate meaning of miqrah, a *rehearsal*. A rehearsal is a private practice for a future live performance. This is amazing! You see, every time Israel came together they were not so much observing the feast as they were rehearsing the feast and getting ready for the big day when Messiah would come in as the Feast's main Character. After nearly 1500 Passover rehearsals, Messiah appeared center stage as the *Passover Lamb* and offered His protective blood right on cue. He also came in sinlessly as *Unleavened Bread* being buried with our sins. On *First Fruits*, He rose from the dead and raised others with Him to present them before the Father as a wave offering. Fifty days later, He sent forth His Spirit on the day of *Shavuot*, the Feast of Ingathering! Woefully, most Israelites today think they are still in rehearsal for the Spring Feasts, but Act One has already been fully played out causing Messiah to exit the stage and the intermission to commence until Act Two begins—the Fall Feasts.

The Lord is publicly calling you to come meet at His house this week. It is a weekly rehearsal time of praise and worship preparing you for that eternal day when you will suddenly become ushered into His glorious presence where you praise Him as never before!

Rehearsals—Shouting Your Lines!

"These are the feasts of the LORD, even holy convocations, which ye shall proclaim in their seasons." (Leviticus 23:4)

Each feast was a convocation or calling, a *miqrah* wherein the people were supposed to *qarah*—call out. *Qarah* is the Hebrew word meaning, "to proclaim, publish, pronounce, read, say." These things can all be done aloud. There was much to proclaim at the festivals. There were also many readings from the Torah and Haftorah, pronunciations of prayers and songs of all Yahweh's greatness. And like any drama, there were props [ex. *succah's*] to be set up and actions to be performed.

On that grand performance day when Messiah came to play out His sacred part in the Spring Feasts, many of the designated performers temporarily forgot their lines [ex. Peter didn't speak up when he should have]. However, after the final scene of Act One, *Shavuot* [Pentecost], things quickly changed. At that time, "the number of the disciples multiplied in Jerusalem greatly; and a great company of the priests were obedient to the faith" (Acts 6:7). This number also included many recently obedient Pharisees (15:5). During the strategically planned intermission, thousands of Judean citizens suddenly began calling out their newly scripted lines, preaching the good news of Messiah's love in Jerusalem, Judea, Samaria and soon after, to the nations. Messiah's star performance was so amazing that other actors were compelled to go out into the highways and hedges to publicly call those who were totally unaware of what was going on at center stage—Jerusalem.

If you're born again, then you also have a calling to go out and proclaim Messiah's spectacular Act One performance and His upcoming Act Two return where He will finish what He started. Act Two is certainly not to be missed! *Proclaim* it to your friends. *Pronounce* it to your neighbors. *Publish* it in a tract and distribute it widely. *Read* it in nursing homes. *Say* it as you go about your day today. Be sure to ask God for the Spirit's help as you seek to tell someone of Messiah's incredible selfless performance and saving name.

Trumpet Rehearsals!

"In the seventh month, in the first day of the month, shall ye have a sabbath, a memorial of blowing of trumpets, an holy convocation." (Leviticus 23:24)

The first four rehearsals are over having been successfully played out live in Jerusalem, but there are three more to go—in the Fall Feasts. The first of these is *Yom Teruah*, the Day of Trumpets. Teruah means "clamor or alarm" and refers to battle sounds. Messiah will return to earth at the end of the Great Tribulation and as King of Kings will likely appear on the very day of Trumpets, and announced by an epic earthquake (Zechariah 14:4). After Israel's ten-days of mourning and repentance—having seen the nail prints in His hands (Zechariah 13:6)—He will, as Great High Priest, wash their sins clean away on *Yom Kippur*, the Day of Atonement (Zechariah 6:13; Isaiah 4:4). This event will quickly usher in *Sukkot*, the Feast of Tabernacles, at which time He will, as Lord of Lords, create one glorious wedding canopy over Jerusalem for the born-again nation. This will be the return of the glory cloud, "a flaming fire by night...And a shadow in the daytime from the heat, and...a covert from storm and rain" (Isaiah 4:5-6).

Seven years prior to this end-time fulfillment, King Yeshua's blood-bought followers, Jew and gentile, dead or alive, will be caught up in the air with a prophetic noise which Paul calls "the last trump" (1 Corinthians 15:52). Could this event also take place on a future Feast of Trumpets? The Church Age *began* on a Feast day. Could it not also *end* on a Feast day? When Yeshua said, "ye know neither the day nor the hour wherein the Son of man cometh," was He also at the same time giving us a big hint (Matthew 25:13)? Could He have been referring to a well-known fact of that day? The day of Trumpets was the only Levitical Feast day that commenced on the first day of a month, and a new month could only be determined after visually sighting the first sliver of the new moon over Jerusalem's horizon.

As Messiah's disciple, you must be rapture-ready at all times, every day, every hour and every moment. You don't have to have your eyes glued to the calendar, but you should have your eyes on the skies because the trumpet rehearsals are about to go live!

255

Yahweh & Yahweh

"Then the LORD rained upon Sodom and upon Gomorrah brimstone and fire from the LORD out of heaven." (Genesis 19:24)

A Ph.D. in Semitic studies writes, "The ancient Israelite believed in two Yahwehs—one invisible, a spirit, the other visible, often in human form. The two Yahwehs at times appear together in the text, at times being distinguished, at other times not. There was no sense of a violation of monotheism since either figure was indeed Yahweh."

Referring to Yahweh in heaven, Yeshua said, "Ye have neither heard his voice at any time, nor seen his shape" (John 5:37). This emphatic declaration, by the visible, incarnate Yahweh, leads us to conclude that all Old Testament visible appearances of Yahweh were Yeshua. Notice how another Scripture presents Yahweh as being two distinct Persons. "Trust ye in the LORD [*Yahweh*] for ever: for in the LORD [*Yah Yahweh*] is everlasting strength" (Isaiah 26:4). Look back at our text verse. During that single moment in time, one Yahweh stood upon the earth while the other Yahweh resided above in the heavens. The Yahweh on earth is the same One Who appeared unto Abraham in the plains of Mamre on the eve of Sodom's destruction (Genesis 18:1). And He remained on earth until its judgment was accomplished.

If Yahweh does not exist in two forms then the following three verses remains irreconcilable. "And the LORD [*Yahweh*] spake unto Moses face to face, as a man speaketh unto his friend" (Exodus 33:11). A few verses later Moses is told by Yahweh: "Thou canst not see my face: for there shall no man see me, and live" (33:20). Another passage exalts Yeshua, the visible Yahweh, in a wonderful way: "And the LORD descended in the cloud, and stood with him [*Moshe*] there, and proclaimed the name of the LORD" (Exodus 34:5). Yeshua's role has always been to exalt the Father, yet the Father only seeks to glorify the Son. Herein is a marvelous thing! When you glorify One, you are actually glorifying them both. Today, exalt Yahweh the *invisible* Father and Yahweh the *incarnate* Son.

Oneg Shabbat

"If thou turn away...from doing thy pleasure on my holy day; and call the sabbath a delight [oneg], the holy of the LORD...and shalt honour him, not doing thine own ways, nor finding thine own pleasure, nor speaking thine own words..." (Isaiah 58:13)

Yahweh presented His people with a great challenge. Regrettably, they needed lots of coaxing to turn them from their self-focused ways. Even today, it is sad to hear some of the ordinary, mundane conversations that take place in God's house on the day believers should be delighting in Him. God instructed Israel to cease from their everyday behavior on the seventh day and to engage in loftier pursuits with a delightful attitude, not grudgingly. If the people turned willingly He promised them the sky: "Then shalt thou delight [*anag*] thyself in the LORD; and I will cause thee to ride upon the high places of the earth, and feed thee with the heritage of Jacob thy father: for the mouth of the LORD hath spoken it" (v.14).

Oneg Shabbat means *enjoying* the *rest day;* thus, the people are to engage in simple activities such as eating, singing and spending time with family. Most modern families live such busy lives that they barely take time to eat one meal together on a given weekday. Your *day of rest* should be different. It's a time to slow down and sit down in the Almighty's presence. In Ezekiel 44:3, the prophet gives a beautiful picture of the seventh millennium, that great Sabbath when Messiah shall sit in the Eastern Gate and eat bread before the LORD. Yeshua will indeed delight His way through the entire 1000-year sabbatical. There will be lots of gathering and singing praises to His high and holy name.

Do you delight in the Lord's Day? Do you seek to spend more time in His Word, more time around those who also love Him, or do you try to take up one of your ordinary, daily pursuits? Today, perhaps you could go visit a lonely shut-in or pick up the phone and encourage someone who has been sick for an extended period. Seek to lift Yeshua's name joyfully on high today. It is He Who has given you eternal rest from your sins.

September 15

Apples & Honey

"*Stay me with flagons, comfort me with apples: for I am sick of love.*" (Song of Solomon 2:5)

The Jewish New Year is accompanied by a double token—sliced apples dipped in honey. Both are sweet to the taste and quite healthy. Eating apples dipped in honey is a parabolic act symbolizing one's desire for health and happiness throughout the coming year. This is why it is customary at the New Year season to give friends and loved ones these two symbolic tokens of prosperity. Apples and honey are clear biblical metaphors. Solomon says, "A word fitly spoken is like apples of gold" and "Pleasant words are as an honeycomb, sweet to the soul, and health to the bones" (Proverbs 25:11; 16:24).

The Shulamite bride mournfully requests Jerusalem's king to *prop* her up and *refresh* her by giving her *pressed* fruits (juice) and apples, her favorite fruit to eat. Why is it that the bride is so weak and bedridden? Because she languishes for spiritual renewal and longs to be close to her Soul Mate, Jesus.

The world is also spiritually lovesick in the sense that there is so little godly love available in these last days (Matthew 24:12). Believers should be ready year-round to share a kind word because it's like a balm that has the power to heal emotional and spiritual hurts. People are in constant need of restoration whether they are lost or saved. The soul is a fragile thing indeed, and so a kind word given at the right time and in the right way can be like "honey out of the rock"—it helps another become instantly satisfied (Psalm 81:16).

As you set out into the Jewish New Year, determine in your heart to be a rich source of blessing to others who are spiritually down. Don't be the bearer of rumors, bad news or complaints. Go out bearing "all the words of this life" in Yeshua (Acts 5:20). Today, ask the Holy Spirit to help you accomplish this worthy goal.

Why the Third Day?

"Thus it is written, and thus it behoved Christ to suffer, and to rise from the dead the third day." (Luke 24:46)

Behoove means *necessary* or *needful*. Even though many Scriptures speak of the manner in which Messiah would suffer, die and be buried, no particular Old Testament verse or passage can be found which specifies that Messiah would rise again on the third day. However, Yeshua's statement to the men on the road to Emmaus has to do with summary fulfillment. He is taking from the whole of Scripture to make his analogy of His dramatic third-day resurrection.

It all begins in the Torah. On the third day, the chief butler was lifted out of prison and had his life restored (Genesis 40:20). Later, Joseph put his brothers into prison for three days and on the third day said to them, "This do, and live" (Genesis 42:18). This third-day typology appears twice in Genesis, like two witnesses, that it might be established as a truth. Next, Moses declared, "We will go three days' journey into the wilderness, and sacrifice unto the LORD" (Exodus 8:27). Levitical Law required that the remainder of a sacrifice be burned with fire on the third day (Leviticus 7:17). It wasn't considered corrupt until it went beyond the third day. A prophecy was given that Messiah's soul would not stay in the grave long enough to see corruption (Psalm 16:10); thus, as the perfect Sacrifice for sin, He would have to rise before the end of the third day—and He did! The fourth book of Torah requires a defiled person to go through a separation process on the third day (Numbers 19:12). In the underworld, Messiah was separated from the living, but resurfaced alive on day three to rejoin the living.

In the historical books David, a clear type of the Messiah, said unto Jonathan, "let me go, that I may hide myself...unto the third day" (1 Samuel 20:5). Yahweh spoke to Hezekiah saying, "behold, I will heal thee: on the third day thou shalt go up" (2 Kings 20:5). The prophetic books speak next: "And Jonah was in the belly of the fish three days and three nights" (Jon. 1:17). This was the only sign Messiah gave to authenticate His Lordship. Hosea says of Israel, "in the third day he will raise us up, and we shall live in his sight" (Hosea 6:2). Today, may the surety of Yeshua's life-restoring Word and sin-healing blood enliven you.

God's Spiritual House

Part 1

"That Christ may dwell in your hearts by faith; that ye, being rooted and grounded in love, May be able to comprehend with all saints what is the breadth, and length, and depth, and height;" (Ephesians 3:17-18)

The Hebrew Bible begins with the letter *bet* as in *B'risheet*—"in the beginning." The Paleo-Hebraic letter *bet* depicts a *tent* floor plan, which represents a house or family, and we would do well to follow this trail to see what God is up to. The first occurrence of the word *house* is where God tells Noah to bring his whole house into the ark (Genesis 7:1). What is most important about a house is not its structure, but its contents—the people. This point becomes amplified when one considers Noah's prophecy: "God shall...dwell in the tents of Shem" (Genesis 9:27). The Shemite line gave rise to the Hebrews. Yahweh said to this tent-dwelling clan, "let them make me a sanctuary; that I may dwell among them" (Exodus 25:8).

Paul attempts to describe the immense spiritual capacity of God's house to the believing community of Ephesus. He mentions the divine aspects of its breadth, length, depth and height. The first thing Paul teaches about God's spiritual house is that it is a house of faith. The letter *bet*, when placed in front of a word, means *in*. All who enter God's house must enter *in* by faith, and that's why Paul calls it the household of faith (Galatians 6:10). God fills His house only with those souls who have placed their full faith *in* His Son. Around 175 times Scripture identifies God's family as those who alone are *"in Christ, in Christ Jesus*, or *in him."*

The Son has charge over the Father's house; therefore, it can bear the name *Beit HaMashiakh*—"House of the Messiah." All nations are invited to enter this most sacred house. Those that come by faith "are no more strangers and foreigners, but fellow citizens with the saints, and of the household of God" (Ephesians 2:19). Today, ask God to direct you to that special soul whom He has prepared so that you can speak to them of Messiah's spacious and gracious house.

God's Spiritual House

Part 2

"And the LORD said unto Noah, Come thou and all thy house into the ark;" (Genesis 7:1)

God told Noah to build an ark against the coming cataclysmic flood. Though Noah built the floating house, it could equally be considered God's house because He was the Architect and the Provider of all the know-how, wood and other materials including the tar so that it wouldn't sink. Knowing that He was about to flood the world in a week's time, God prompted Noah to bring his family into the safe confines of the boathouse. They entered by faith; that is, believing and trusting.

The Hebrew word for house is *bah-yit*. In its pictogram form, *bahyit*'s three letters reveal the following: *bet* pictures a tent and represents a house; *yod* pictures a hand and represents work and worship; and *tav* pictures two crossed sticks and represents a sign. Thus, *bahyit* implies *a house with a hand-sign*. In ancient times, an upright hand stamped in red upon one's doorway was viewed as a mark of favor with the god with whom he kept covenant. One hundred years ago, red or blue handprints could still be seen upon the houses of Jews, Christians and Muslims throughout the Holy Land. [See *The Threshold Covenant* by Trumbull]. After Noah and his family entered the ark, "the LORD shut him in" (Genesis 7:16). Yahweh sealed His safe house by the sign of His own hand.

For God so loved the world that He made a flood-proof house for the world's safety. Sadly, only those who loved Him went in. This tells us that God's house is not only a house of faith, but also a house of love. That is why Paul challenges believers "to know the love of Christ, which surpasseth knowledge" (Ephesians 3:19). By exercising faith in God, you show that you *trust* Him, and by loving Him, you show that you *treasure* Him. "For we know that if our earthly house of this tabernacle were dissolved, we have a building of God, an house not made with hands, eternal in the heavens" (2 Corinthians 5:1). Today, ask the Holy Spirit to help you understand, experience and appreciate the love of God in a much deeper way.

God's Spiritual House

Part 3

"And the flood was forty days upon the earth; and the waters increased, and bare up the ark, and it was lift up above the earth." (Genesis 7:17)

We want to venture on to discover the highly symbolic meaning of the word ark—God's spiritual house of faith and love. The Hebrew word is *teh-baw'*, and its three Paleo-Hebrew letters *tav-bet-hey* paint a vivid picture. *Tav* represents a sign or mark, and this symbol became the sign of the <u>covenant</u> for the people of God. What is more, *tav* also represents a <u>monument,</u> and Noah's ark certainly qualified as one! The letter *bet*, as you know, means <u>house</u>; and the third letter, *hey*, has an added meaning that is carried over from the Phoenician alphabet—a <u>window</u>. God designed the ark to have one long window in it (6:16). The Hebrew word window means light. Putting these three letter-meanings together they show us a *monumental covenant house* with a *light*—a perfect picture of the ark.

The ark, with its long window to receive heavenly light, reminds us of Yahweh's future covenant house in Jerusalem. God gave the Temple plans to Solomon, and "for the house he made windows of narrow lights" (1 Kings 6:4). When the inaugural day came, God filled His covenant house with His Shekinah glory. Almost one thousand years later Yahweh sought to create and inhabit a very different kind of house, the household of Messiah. On the feast day of Shavuot, 120 of Messiah's devotees banded together in the Temple courts, perhaps under one of the many porticos. There, God suddenly "filled all the house where they were sitting" (Acts 2:2). This moment marked the completion of Moses' Old Testament house and the start of Messiah's New Covenant house. The four gospels remain under the dispensation of the Law.

The Father's spiritual house is entered by faith, is furnished with love, and never lacks light. Paul said, "the house of God...is the church [ekklesia, *called-out assembly*] of the living God" (1 Timothy 3:15). Today, God's house is a people not a place. This morning, ask the Father to show you what is the "breadth, and length, and depth, and height" of His Son's love; then go tell it to languishing souls!

God's Holy Offspring

"And I will bring forth a seed out of Jacob, and out of Judah an inheritor of my mountains: and mine elect shall inherit it, and my servants shall dwell there." (Isaiah 65:9)

When God brought forth His Genesis creation, each life form possessed seeds of their own likeness. Some two thousand years later God saw Abraham and—as if he were a tender sapling—plucked him up from Ur and replanted him among the wellsprings of Canaan. God promised Abraham, the father of the Hebrews, "in thy seed shall all the nations of the earth be blessed" (Genesis 22:18). Abraham's promised seed, Isaac, was eventually born. He then begat Jacob who begat twelve sons who became the nation of Israel. In Isaiah 41:8 Israel is called the seed of Abraham. By this phrase, the prophet is referring to righteous souls, not merely raw offspring.

John the Baptist told the Pharisees not to think they were righteous simply because Abraham was their forbearer. He declared, "God is able of these stones to raise up children unto Abraham" (Luke 3:8). Yeshua made it clear what the seed is that gives spiritual life to God's offspring. He said, "The seed is the word of God" (Luke 8:11). Peter reconfirmed this saying that we are not "born again...of corruptible seed, but of incorruptible, by the word of God, which liveth and abideth for ever" (1 Peter 1:23). When you give God's Word a lodging place in your heart, new life manifests within. John the beloved emphasized that Messiah Himself is the Word of God, so this seed within redeemed humanity is most holy (John 1:1). For this specific reason he also said, "Whosoever is born of God doth not commit sin; for his seed remaineth in him: and he cannot sin, because he is born of God" (1 John 3:9). God's offspring comes to life by "faith that...the promise might be sure to all the seed; not to that only which is of the law [*Jews*], but to that also which is of the faith of Abraham [*Gentiles*]; who is the father of us all" (Romans 4:16).

You were born-again by faith. So live today by faith, be holy by faith and in practice.

The Bread of God

"My Father giveth you the true bread from heaven. For the bread of God is he which cometh down from heaven, and giveth life unto the world." (John 6:32-33)

Recently in Horbat Uza, Israel a ceramic bread stamp bearing the image of the seven-branched Temple menorah was unearthed. This stamp from the 6th century confirms the presence of a Jewish community existing alongside the Byzantine Christian community of Akko. It would have been necessary to mark baked goods as kosher with a Jewish symbol if they were being supplied to Jews dwelling in neighboring Akko.

Messiah fed a multitude of starving souls with fresh-baked bread from His divinely stamped hands. The next day people tracked Him down wanting more loaves. What they actually needed was Him. Yeshua referred to Himself as the most cosmically kosher bread in the whole world declaring, "him hath God the Father sealed [Gr. *sphrag-id'-zo*: to stamp]" (v.27). He informed them that they should rather desire spiritual bread that their souls might live forever and presented them with a proverb: "I am the bread of life: he that cometh to me shall never hunger" (v.35). His miracle was still not enough to convince them. He said, "ye also have seen me, and believe not" (v.36). The people of little faith required an even greater stamp of authority that God had sent Him to earth. For the time being He continued, "This is the bread which cometh down from heaven, that a man may eat thereof, and not die" (v.50).

The people would receive God's most convincing stamp in due time. As all bread must *go into* and *out of* the furnace, Yeshua proclaimed, "I am the living bread...and the bread that I will give is my flesh, which I will give for the life of the world" (v.51). After dying, His unleavened (sinless) body was placed in the earth. It came forth three days later eternally fresh! From that day forward the timeless prayer, "Blessed are You O LORD our God, King of the universe, Who brings forth bread from the earth," had new emphasis for believers. Today, thank the Father for sending you His very best Bread!

A Yom Kippur Poem

"For the life of the flesh is in the blood: and I have given it to you upon the altar to make an atonement for your souls: for it is the blood that maketh an atonement for the soul." (Leviticus 17:11)

Though our Messiah came down as a man,
    His form was meek and gentle as a lamb.

Despised and rejected He bore our grief,
    yet Jacob's lil' flock stand in unbelief.

False stories of His claims He sadly heard,
    from His station answered He not a word.

Dark enemies He scattered, great and small
    while the guilt of our sins on Him did fall.

Our dreaded scourge and shame on Him was laid;
    for crimes we did commit He gladly paid.

Wrapped, buried—sealed out of sinners' sight,
    in his dark tomb He lay for Israel's plight.

From Pesach until Shabbat He did rest;
    but to His rising the prophets still attest.

One grand design seen on Golgotha's hill;
    in all of this, it was the Father's will.

On Pesach Yeshua made the atonement through His bloody death, at His rising from the grave He became the Great High Priest, and on a future Yom Kippur He will stand in this office and ceremonially apply His atoning blood over the remnant of Israel (Isaiah 66:8; Zechariah 6:13).

Today, pray that Jews worldwide will presently receive Messiah's atoning blood one by one.

September 23

Repairing the Altar

"And Elijah...repaired the altar of the LORD that was broken down." (1 Kings 18:30)

Scholars differ on exactly which tribe the mighty prophet was from, but they agree that he was from one of the northern tribes. Elijah's ministry to the backslidden Baal-leaning Israelites was not an easy one. Israel enjoyed their syncretism (the combining of different beliefs), but Yahweh was always given second place in their lives. This is the reason why Elijah challenged the people with the question, "How long halt [*limp*] ye between two opinions?" (v.21). Elijah's aim was to make Yahweh's rebuilt altar the token of Yahweh's supremacy.

The word for altar is *miz-bay-akh*. Its four Paleo-Hebrew letters perfectly depict an altar's purpose. The first letter, *mem,* means blood. *Zain* represents a mattock and means to cut. *Bet* means family, and the *khet* pictures a wall meaning to divide or halve. An altar was a specially designed place for a family to meet with God. They came with an animal, shed its blood, divided it in half and then prayed. It was the place where sin was done away with, but not without the cost of a life.

Since our beloved Messiah, the Son of God, has been once and for all sacrificed on our behalf, an altar no longer needs to be constructed. We can now pray anywhere and have our sins forgiven so long as we plead the blood of God's sinless Lamb. It's easy in these fast-paced days to let our quality prayer time fail. When this happens, we need to rebuild our altar of prayer. Reestablishing a *special place* to pray is something that is suitable, and a *special time* can be rewarding. The family altar is so precious and fruitful; it must be rebuilt if it has not been given adequate attention.

Today, get a vision of a blazing fire lit upon your personal or family altar and keep that *special fire* burning all day long and until Messiah returns.

266

God Will Make a Way

"Behold, I will do a new thing; now it shall spring forth; shall ye not know it? I will even make a way in the wilderness, and rivers in the desert." (Isaiah 43:19)

A wilderness is not known for being hospitable. Although it can be an inspiring place to visit, it's not the kind of place you want to call home. The desert is no friend to strangers. Only those who are experienced with its terrain can endure its harshness. All the Arabian Desert had to offer Israel other than the occasional cluster of Palm trees was bitter waters, scorching sands, searing heat, cold nights, scorpions, vipers and vultures. The desert in and around Mt. Sinai simply had no kindness to offer the wayfaring pilgrims. That is where Yahweh came in as both Guide and Guard.

In place of the bitter waters, He caused birthright water to pop up wherever He chose. Instead of palm trees, His Shekinah cloud shaded them from the searing heat. The pillar of fire gloriously provided warmth for them by night. He guided them through the unfamiliar territory, not only with Moses, but more importantly, with His special Angel. This same Angel also protected them from many unfriendly nations. At the end of the day, it was the harshness of the environment that allowed Israel opportunity to come to appreciate God's overall goodness and grace. Yahweh was reassuring Israel that He could do this same thing again if they would only *wait* upon Him and stop being *weary* with Him (v.22).

You may be weary today, but don't give up on God. He calls for your utmost trust before showing you His utmost tenderness. He is waiting for the right time to come through for you. You'll be glad when He does. In the meantime, just follow His simple directives. Make offerings to Him (v.23). He even likes sugar cane (v.24)! Don't weary Him with a careless attitude towards His commandments (v.24). Praise Him for blotting out your transgressions (v.25). Put Him in remembrance as much as you can (v.26). Today, even if things look out of season, begin looking for God's new thing because He has promised to bring it.

Double Assurance

"My sheep hear my voice, and I know them, and they follow me: And I give unto them eternal life; and they shall never perish, neither shall any man pluck them out of my hand." (John 10:27-28)

Far too many believers fall short of taking Yeshua's words at face value. A loving Shepherd would never cast one of His own sheep over a cliff or into a fire. Such a thing would be unthinkable, so take comfort. Yeshua defines His sheep as the ones who *hear* and *receive* His words. Because the divine Shepherd sees deep into the heart, He *knows* which ones are His. The Shepherd also says that His sheep will *follow* Him. Now, you may be one of those sheep in the back of the flock or wandering off constantly, but you still belong to Him. This wayward behavior doesn't disqualify you; rather, it brings the Shepherd's swift attention because He is responsible for your soul, your very life.

Your double assurance begins with the Shepherd's boast, "You shall *never* perish!" When the Son of God says never, that's exactly what He means—never! The Greek text describes never with much more emphasis. A double negative is given—*never at all* and *in no case.* By this definition, perishing becomes impossible. The reason you cannot perish is because you are in the Shepherd's hand, and He has declared that no one is able to pluck you out of it.

Secondly, Messiah says, "My Father, which gave them me, is greater than all; and no man is able to pluck them out of my Father's hand" (v.29). The translators supplied the word *man* in verses 28 and 29; therefore, Messiah's claim actually implies that *no one* exists, terrestrial or celestial, mortal or immortal, who is capable of removing you from God's strong grip.

Rejoice in your strong Shepherd today. Don't fear being left to the wolves; that would be a blemish on the Shepherd's reputation as Keeper of the Flock. So go about your day praising Him for His unconditional love and protective nature.

Grace in the Wilderness

"Thus saith the LORD, The people which were left of the sword found grace in the wilderness; even Israel, when I went to cause him to rest." (Jeremiah 31:2)

Yahweh could not pour out grace upon His people while they were immersed in idolatry throughout the land of Judah; that would be a perversion of His holiness. But after killing some, and wounding and chasing some out of their inheritance with His chastening sword, He could begin to show favor toward them once again.

Israel needed to *cease* from their worship of other gods. The pagan deities to whom Israel succumbed were numerous. In Babylon, they would hang their harps for a time and begin to reflect on who they were as a people. There, in the wilderness of their captivity, they found favor among their captors and built houses and prospered. They also for the first time built synagogues in an attempt to reestablish their faith and practice. Having no Temple and no altar, they couldn't sacrifice. This would allow Israel to simply rest and focus on obedience for a while. They had not been keeping the sabbatical years, so the land of their former inheritance could also rest for 70 years.

Maybe you've been going through a wilderness of your own—or of your own making—and it just seems to have no end in sight. Well, God knows when relief is coming, but for now, He wants you instead just to see Him and rest from your worries. Perhaps His grace has been active in your life recently, but you've been too focused upon your problems to notice His interaction with you. As strange as it may seem, Yeshua can't be your shelter unless you somehow see the need for His shade. The greater your wilderness, the greater His grace will shade and shelter you.

Look for His grace in your life today, and then thank Him for it. Look for places He is providing shelter for you through friends, Christian fellowships, Bible studies, church and prayer.

September 27

No Strings Attached!

"But God commendeth his love toward us, in that, while we were yet sinners, Christ died for us." (Romans 5:8)

Today is not a day for doubting; it is a day for diving into the Saviour's big, strong arms. The Son of God stretched out His arms for you 2000 years ago to take your punishment for sin. He did this because He loves you. His arms remain stretched out today for another reason; He longs to hold you and hug you. He likely hugged His disciples in a brotherly way every day, and in good time, He will get His arms around you, too.

Salvation is not so much about you as it is *about Him*. He did the suffering, the bleeding, the crying, the dying—not you. When He was on the cross all your sins were *before Him*, and praise God, they are all now *behind Him*. You can no more lay hold on your sins than you can lay hold on yesterday. Yeshua isn't going to bring up those horrible deeds again because they are in "the depths of the sea" (Micah 7:19). He put out His promise before the entire nation of Israel saying, "I will forgive their iniquity, and I will remember their sin no more" (Jeremiah 31:34). If He can do this for a whole nation, then certainly He can do it just for you. When He sees you for the first time and wraps His arms around you, what He will not want to bring up is *your past*, but *His*! He may even allow you to touch those covenant wounds He received in the past. That will definitely cure your doubts as to whether or not His love for you is irreversible.

Yeshua saved you and changed your nature so that you might bring Him glory on earth. Whether you choose to glorify Him with your life or not, His past death assures your future safety forever. Paul says, "Much more then, being now justified by his blood, we shall be saved from wrath through him" (v.9). That's about as plain as it gets. You may lose heart, but one thing is certain, Yeshua did not, cannot, and will not. He is "the same yesterday, and today, and for ever" (Hebrews 13:8). He loves you with no strings attached, so cling to this thought all through the day.

Absolutely Full

"Beware lest any man spoil you through philosophy and vain deceit, after the tradition of men, after the rudiments of the world, and not after Christ. For...ye are complete in him," (Colossians 2:8-10)

The world pushes its vain, empty promises upon us day after day, but we find them untrue year after year. They say, "Use this product and you'll look ten years younger," or "Wear our brand of clothing and you'll be content." Their favorite claim is, "Take this product and you'll instantly feel on top of the world!" The world can never satisfy a child of God's true longings. Sometimes we have to find this out the hard way.

A similar philosophy is prevalent in some Christian circles. False teachers will push you to receive a second filling, a second work of grace or a second baptism. Their aim is to help you get filled up with all of God's Spirit, and thereby have all joy and satisfaction. They are sincere, but sincerely wrong. The truth is you're already as full as you ever will be or can be. You may not feel like you are full of God's Spirit, but you are. He fills you full with the Spirit of His Son the moment of your new birth—just like a baby draws in two lungs-full of air upon entering the world. God never does anything half way. Giving the reigns of your life fully over to Him is the real daily struggle.

Scripture says that Yeshua Himself is the definition of divine fullness: "For in him dwelleth all the fullness [*play'-ro-mah*] of the Godhead bodily" (v.9). The next verse says, "Ye are complete [*play-ro'-o*] in him" (v.10) which means, "made *replete, full*, literally *level* to the brim." You cannot fill something that is already full. When Paul says to "be filled with the Spirit," he means be *controlled* by it (Ephesians 5:18). Believers are not to chase after more fillings from God. Instead, they are to make the most of what they already have—the fullness of God's Son.

Today, enjoy the fullness of Yeshua's Spirit and be more respectful of His leading in your life. Become more of a true servant and make Him your true Master.

It's No Secret!

"Jesus answered him, I spake openly to the world; I ever taught in the synagogue, and in the temple, whither the Jews always resort; and in secret have I said nothing." (John 18:20)

Yeshua has just been brought to the high priest after being apprehended at Gethsemane. The very last phrase of His statement was a quotation of Yahweh's words from Isaiah 45:19—"I have not spoken in secret." The lowly Nazarene was drawing their attention to something needful; He was more than meets the eye. By quoting that short but key phrase, He invited Israel's counselors to consider that the whole passage was shedding divine light upon Him.

What else then does Isaiah chapter 45 speak of concerning Yeshua? *"I am the LORD...though thou hast not known me"* (v.5). How true this statement was at that time! *"Woe unto him that striveth with his Maker!"* (v.9) The chief priests and elders had been striving with Messiah from the beginning of His ministry, which was now reaching its peak. *"I have made the earth...stretched out the heavens"* (v.12). Yeshua twice created loaves and calmed the winds to prove this point. *"Assemble yourselves and come; draw near together"* (v.20). The priests had assembled themselves and drawn near to Yeshua but in the wrong spirit. *"Look unto me, and be ye saved, all the ends of the earth"* (v.22). At that moment, they were looking upon Messiah, and His atoning blood was already flowing from Gethsemane's agony. *"I have sworn...unto me every knee shall bow, every tongue shall swear"* (v.23). Every one of those chief leaders was refusing to bow to their heaven-sent King.

Yeshua's key phrase also pointed to Isaiah 48:16 which says, "Come ye near unto me, hear ye this; I have not spoken in secret from the beginning; from the time that it was, there am I: and now the Lord GOD, and his Spirit, hath sent me." Yeshua is the *Sent One* and, at the same time, the *Sovereign One* (48:12). Just verses later Yahweh says this: "O that thou had hearkened to my commandments! then had thy peace been as a river, and thy righteousness as the waves of the sea" (48:18). Yeshua tearfully alluded to this very verse just days earlier while overlooking Jerusalem (Luke 19:42). Today, *bow* before Yeshua and praise His name.

On Loan from God

"God said unto him...this night thy soul shall be required of thee."
(Luke 12:20)

These words were spoken to the self-centered man in Yeshua's parable of the rich fool. After building a barn to store his bounty, the rich man prepares to celebrate his success but is interrupted with thundering words from above. He is told that it is his time to die, and then he is challenged with the rhetorical question: "Whose shall those things be?" (v.20). Even though there is no mention of family or friends in the parable, certainly he has a community he can share them with; but miserably and miserly he thinks only of self. The rich man felt sure that "my goods" and "my soul" were his very own to keep (v.18, 19). He got a shocking surprise when he discovered that they were actually only *on loan* to him.

In the Hebrew language the words *my* and *mine* do not exist. Instead, something that belongs to me is *to me*. With this Hebrew lesson in mind, Yeshua says that we are to be "rich toward God," not towards ourselves (v.21). We should share our abundance with those around us rather than just keeping it all to ourselves. God gives *to us* that He might spread it abroad *through us*. He loans things to us to see if we will loan them to others expecting nothing in return.

Yeshua put forth another helpful life principle: "beware of covetousness: for a man's life consisteth not in the abundance of the things which he possesseth" (v.15). When we keep things to ourselves, we only show our inward poverty, but when we give, we show that we are rich and have more than we really need. Paul quotes Yeshua as having said, "It is more blessed to give than receive" (Acts 20:35). Remarkably, there is a certain unexplainable contentment in giving. God had one Son and He gave Him freely for the benefit of the world.

Be reminded today that your life and life possessions are on loan to you. What you do with them can further your wishes or they can further God's will. Ask the Holy Spirit to direct you in your choices today.

273

Your Glorious Sin-Bearer

"Who his own self bare our sins in his own body on the tree, that we, being dead to sins, should live unto righteousness: by whose stripes ye were healed." (1 Peter 2:24)

Ellen G. White, the founder of the Seventh Day Adventist Reform Movement, made the following heretical quote: "It was seen, also, that while the sin offering pointed to Christ as a sacrifice, and the high priest represented Christ as a mediator, the scapegoat typified Satan, the author of sin, upon whom the sins of the truly penitent will finally be placed" [*The Great Controversy*, pg. 422]. This false prophetess spoke blasphemously by robbing Yeshua of His chief glory as our rightful Sin-bearer.

In reality, White's theology is not much different from someone who claims that a New Covenant believer can lose their salvation, and be brought back into jeopardy to *bear the burden* of their own sins for eternity. This equally makes mockery of Yeshua's role as Sin-Bearer. His pain was your gain. When a person comes to Messiah by faith and asks for forgiveness of sins, he proceeds on the truthful assumption that Yeshua bore those sins to Golgotha's tree, and he would be right for it is written, "the LORD hath laid on him the iniquity of us all" (Isaiah 53:6). Not only did Messiah bear our sins to Calvary, He bore them to *Sheol*, the grave. And He left them there, too.

Messiah represents both Atonement Day goats—the one that was sacrificed and the one made into a *scapegoat*. This word for scapegoat is *azazel* and is comprised of two words meaning "a she-goat" and "to *go away*;" hence, to disappear. Did not the Saviour disappear into the heavens soon after making complete atonement and annulment for our sins? Yes, and He *went away* with all the glory of the Father.

Today, if you doubt your eternal security, turn from such thinking and praise Yeshua for what He has already done. Your loving Sin-Bearer has cast all your sins into the depths of the sea (Micah 7:19)! This is the very reason why Paul could write Romans 8:30. Now, go out today rejoicing in your High Priest's completed work of salvation.

The Way of the Ant

"Go to the ant, thou sluggard; consider her ways, and be wise:" (Proverbs 6:6)

Ants only sleep about seven hours a day because they have so much work to do. And ants can't live on their own; they need a colony. This reminds us of how busily the first-century church "continued daily with one accord in the temple and breaking bread from house to house" (Acts 2:46). We are warned not to forsake the assembling of ourselves together because we need each other (Hebrews 10:25). Did you know that ants have two stomachs, one to feed self and one to feed others? As believers, we take in the Word of God, the bread of life, for our own benefit as well as the benefit of others. When a worker ant has found a source of food, it leaves a scent trail to attract others in the colony to it. In the same vein, "we are...a sweet savour of Christ, in them that are saved" (2 Corinthians 2:15). The average ant can lift 20 times its own body weight. This reflects a similar truth that you "can do all things through Christ which strengtheneth" you (Philippians 4:13).

Did you know that ants build trap tunnels to keep out the rain? This is a great idea and reminds us that we need to work diligently to keep various destructive forces out of our assemblies like envying, strife and divisions (1 Corinthians 3:3). Each colony of ants has its own distinctive smell and can detect an intruder easily. We should be on alert when visitors come in with destructive doctrines "lest Satan should get an advantage of us: for we are not ignorant of his devices" (2 Corinthians 2:11). Some ants follow light patterns from the sun. This is a good thing also for "if we walk in the light, as he is in the light, we have fellowship one with another, and the blood of Jesus Christ his Son cleanseth us from all sin" (1 John 1:7).

Today, ask the Lord to help you be awake, productive, sharing, helpful, sweet, strong, constructive, watchful and steadfastly walking in His holy light. Don't let the ants outwork you today!

The Pouring-Out Ceremony
Part 1

"And they gathered together to Mizpeh, and drew water, and poured it out before the LORD, and fasted on that day," (1 Samuel 7:6)

Israel performed this *pouring-out* ritual in a final act of consecration to Yahweh after they willingly obeyed Samuel in putting away their strange gods—Baal and Ashtaroth (v.4). But what did the ritual represent? Jacob poured *a drink offering* onto a pillar he had set up for El Shaddai after his personal encounter with Him (Genesis 35:14). Also, when David was in battle against the Philistines and in dire thirst, three of his mighty men succeeded in bringing water back from a well outside Bethlehem; however, "he would not drink thereof, but poured it out unto the LORD" (2 Samuel 23:16). It was a *libation,* an act of high worship in honor of a deity (v.17). If the Hebrews knew anything about their God, Yahweh, it was this: He was in the pouring-out business if they met His requirements (Malachi 3:10). In David's case, he was mirroring what he wanted Yahweh to do for him—to pour out a blessing on the battlefield.

Elijah also performed the ancient pouring-out ceremony. It had not rained for the past three years. Before the prophet expected Yahweh to restore the parched land with rain, he ordered water to be poured out on his biblically built altar (1 Kings 18:33). Elijah was testing the backslidden tribes to see if they had any thirst left for the One True God's blessing. Yahweh received Elijah's drink offering and sacrifice. He sent down fire and it "consumed the burnt sacrifice...and licked up the water that was in the trench" (v.38). Not long after, Yahweh reciprocated. A cloud arose out of the sea and grew until it sent down a great rain for the people (v.45).

The LORD has promised you blessing for both body and soul, for both you and your children. He says, "For I will pour water upon him that is thirsty, and floods upon the dry ground: I will pour my spirit upon thy seed, and my blessing upon thine offspring" (Isaiah 44:3). This morning pour out your heart to the God of Abraham. If you are real thirsty, then pour out your heart till it is empty of *self,* and then wait to see what He will do!

The Pouring-Out Ceremony
Part 2

"Therefore will I divide him a portion with the great...because he hath poured out his soul unto death:" (Isaiah 53:12)

Yahweh ordained that His people present Him a *token*, to pour Him out a drink offering of water at the Temple, but only during the seven-day feast of Tabernacles. Each morning at dawn, the Levites would ceremonially descend to the spring of Siloam with one golden pitcher. There one of the priests would draw up a pitcher full of fresh spring water. They would all then proceed back up to the Temple where it was poured out at the brazen altar. Accompanying this annual water libation was the daily wine libation, which, at Tabernacles, created a dual pouring-out ceremony. In return for their obedience and prayers, they expected Yahweh to send ample rain throughout the coming agricultural year. This would be *the token* of His commitment to them.

The first miracle Messiah ever performed was highly symbolic; it involved the pouring out of both water and wine (John 2:1-11). This parabolic act mirrored the water and wine libations of Sukkot, and therefore painted Him in the light of a priest who labors ceremonially to secure Israel a heavenly blessing. One Sukkot, on the last day of the Feast, Yeshua confirmed that He was the source of Israel's finest blessing. He shouted, "If any man thirst, let him come unto me, and drink. He that believeth on me...out of his belly shall flow rivers of living water" (John 7:37-38). The miracle at Cana, an honorable gesture of pouring out water and wine, prefigured the greatest out-pouring that would ever be seen.

On the day Yeshua was being offered up for our sins, His body was extremely dehydrated. He cried out for water, but none was given Him. Through the psalmist, His testimony was this: "I am poured out like water, and...all my bones: they look and stare upon me" (Psalm 22:14, 17). The most incredible, dual pouring-out ritual of all time came very soon after this. A "soldier with a spear pierced his side, and...there came out blood and water" (John 19:34). This made it all possible for the Father, in return, to "pour upon...the inhabitants of Jerusalem, the spirit of grace and of supplications" (Zechariah 12:10). Today, be sure to thank the Son of God for His incredible pouring-out ceremony on your behalf.

The Truth of the Matter

"To this end was I born...that I should bear witness unto the truth. Every one that is of the truth heareth my voice. Pilate saith unto him, What is truth?" (John 18:37-38)

John the Beloved was fascinated with Yeshua's heavenly wisdom. While the youthful disciple walked with Messiah, he clung to Him, and after He was gone, he clung to His many truths. If John was at Yeshua's initial trial and at the cross, it is likely that the "clingy" disciple was with Yeshua also at many other places in between. The early church record states that John's father, Zebedee, was a Levite and closely related to the high priest's family. This afforded John opportunities not available to the other disciples during Yeshua's trials.

The beloved disciple is the only gospel writer to include Yeshua's brief exchange on Truth as He stood before Pilate. If John were close by when the Master spoke these words, he would have greatly desired to shout the answer back to Pilate: "Yeshua, *He* is the truth!" While Matthew and Mark mention *truth* three times each and Luke just five times, John mentions truth 22 times in his gospel account. Later in his three short epistles, the *disciple of truth* spoke about *truth* 18 times. It was such an important doctrine that the apostle sought to pass its worth along to his own disciples. Let's have a quick look at just his third epistle.

He begins by cordially addressing his close friend, Gaius, to whom he says, "I love in the truth" (v.1). Here, and in the remainder of the letter, John uses the word *truth* interchangeably for the *gospel.* Gaius was John's convert through the preaching of the gospel. John then exclaims, "I have no greater joy than to hear that my children walk in truth" (1:4). The gospel is the pilgrim's handbook, and because it takes so many hands to pass it along to the next generation, John encourages others to be "fellow helpers to the truth" (v.8). The aged apostle complimented one saint in particular, but we should each be in "good report of all men, and of the truth itself" (v.12).

Today, seek to bless others with the precious truths of the gospel of Yeshua.

$\mathcal{K}$nown of $\mathcal{G}$od

"But now, after that ye have known God, or rather are known of God, how turn ye again to the weak and beggarly elements, whereunto ye desire again to be in bondage?" (Galatians 4:9)

Paul faced a sad problem with the gentile believers of Galatia. The legalistic Torah teachers from Israel had come and tripped them up during his long absence. He had this to say to the Galatian converts, "Ye observe days, and months, and times, and years. I am afraid of you, lest I have bestowed upon you labour in vain" (v.10-11).

One remedy was to explain how following Abraham's faith superseded the following of Moses' law (3:18). Paul set forth his best argument knowing that they understood the class distinction between a servant and a son. He said, "God sent forth his Son, made of a woman, made under the law, To redeem them that were under the law, that we might receive the adoption of sons. And because ye are sons, God hath sent forth the Spirit of his Son into your hearts, crying, Abba, Father. Wherefore thou art no more a servant, but a son and if a son, then an heir of God through Christ" (v.4-7). A servant only knows his master in formal, outward ways, but a son knows his father in personal, intimate ways. Paul challenged these new converts to be aware of adopting old rituals.

Why approach your heavenly Father with a *siddur* [prayer book] when you have His face before you? Why swing a *lulav* [a ceremonial palm branch] when you can swing from Abba's arms? Why cover your head with a *kippah* [a cap] when Messiah covers your head with His majestic wings (1 Corinthians 4:7. 11)? If you're a new believer, begin building upon the new foundation that has been laid. Stand firm in the New Covenant; that is why Yeshua made it for you.

Today, celebrate that you're now *known of God* through the simple forms of repentance, forgiveness, prayer, praise and thanksgiving. Take extra time today getting to *know* God better through fellowship, not formality.

A Feast Worth Keeping

"Therefore let us keep the feast, not with old leaven, neither with the leaven of malice and wickedness; but with the unleavened bread of sincerity and truth." (1 Corinthians 5:8)

Paul emphasized keeping the Feast of Passover even though the Corinthians were gentile, but did he imply the Mosaic Passover? He certainly sets a strong case for a modified, Messianic Passover when he says, "For even Christ our Passover is sacrificed for us" (v.7). The New Covenant Passover is an illustrated gospel message and has taken on the popular name *The Lord's Table*. Concerning future Passovers, Yeshua instructed to do it "in remembrance of me" (Luke 22:19). Yeshua's Last Seder was actually the whole nation's last Mosaic Seder because Messiah, as the firstborn, birthright Son died within the House of Israel. While Messiah was dying, God reinstated the ninth plague, darkness, as a token that the Light of Israel was being rejected.

God has blocked the way back to a complete observance of the Mosaic Passover. He removed the earthly Temple and thus the sanctioned Mosaic lamb, which was to be slaughtered before its very doors. The new Messianic Passover Lamb is to be eaten in the form of unleavened bread and to be accompanied with fruit of the vine. Yeshua said to observe this as often as desired. Annually observed Messianic Passovers are even more beautiful and educational to participate in. Can a Jewish believer partake in the annual Mosaic Passover with his unsaved relatives? Sure. This is only natural, but he doesn't find spiritual fulfillment in it.

Paul gave no commands to keep any other Feast during this dispensation, but this doesn't mean we can't observe them in ways that show how Messiah rests at the heart of each one. When Messiah Yeshua returns to permanently tabernacle with Israel He will reinstate the yearly observance of Tabernacles (Zechariah 14:16). For the past 2000 years, the focus has been on the spring feasts; the Millennium will focus on fall festivals.

Begin preparing your heart today for your next scheduled communion service. Ask the Lord to make it a special one.

The Omega & the Omnigatherum

"And he gathered them together into a place called in the Hebrew tongue Armageddon." (Revelation 16:16)

From the courts of Heaven Messiah declared Himself to be "the Alpha and the **Omega**, the beginning and the end." Our times are in His hands. Despite such majesty, some regard Him little more than an **omelet**. Warning! Clear **omens** of His Second Advent abound. Upon His arrival an **omer** of perfect justice will He grant to everyone. In the presence of the Omega, the mighty men will seem no bigger than an **omicron**. The awful tribulation that precedes His appearing is looking more and more **ominous** for the countless Christless masses.

The nations' careless attention to His supreme laws is in no way **omissible**. Each and every **omission** of His supernal statutes will not be lightly judged as if those willful souls had merely been ignorantly **omissive**; rather, they will have forced the Judge of all the Earth to **omit** the dispensing of His infinite mercy. Their failure individually to adhere to His eternal and holy **omnibus** will be found completely inexcusable. Their excuses of inability to keep His commandments properly shall be met with the fact that His righteous laws were made **omnidirectional**. As the guilty stand before the Holy One, their pleas for leniency will become **omnifarious**.

At the outset of Armageddon day, His global opposers—dead or alive—shall fall prostrate at the sight of His **omnipotent** sword. Omega's sudden and visible **omnipresence** at the end of days shall polarize the nations causing them to turn from fighting antichrist and instead join him to resist the Almighty Christ. Even though the amalgamated forces attempt such a proud thing, the **omniscient** One calculates their move and commences His pre-determined annihilation of that unholy **omnigatherum**. With just one word from the Alpha and Omega, the antichrist, who devoured the helpless sea of nations like an insidious **omnivore**, shall be cast into the **omnivorous** pit.

Today, share the message of Messiah's might and mercy with someone who has yet to accept it.

October 9

Did Yeshua Ever Receive Worship?

"And when they were come into the house, they saw the young child with Mary his mother, and fell down, and worshipped him: and...they presented unto him gifts; gold, and frankincense, and myrrh." (Matthew 2:11)

Yeshua was no less Lord before His resurrection than afterwards (Philippians 2:6); however, some say that Yeshua never accepted worship from His countrymen until after His resurrection. Well, then, try explaining what the Magi were doing before Yeshua's crib. Some messianic believers like to quote Messiah saying to Satan, "Thou shalt worship the Lord thy God, and him only shalt thou serve" (Matthew 4:10). When Yeshua said, "Get thee hence Satan," the dark prince went away, which demonstrated who was servant and Who was Lord!

The word worship in Greek means, "to *prostrate* oneself in homage; crouch, kiss, adore, reverence." A woman of Canaan had a daughter possessed of the devil, and she came "and worshipped him, saying, Lord, help me" (Matthew 15:25). Did He tell her to get off the ground and to stop her *prostration* and pleading? No. There "came a leper and worshipped him." Did Messiah tell him to stop *crouching*? No. A woman began to weep and to *kiss* the Master's feet while He sat at meat. Did He tell her to cease? No, He gladly received her form of worship in exchange for the great forgiveness He had granted her. When Yeshua and Peter stepped into the boat after walking on water the wind ceased. "Then they that were in the ship came and worshipped him saying, "Of a truth thou art the Son of God" (Matthew 14:33). Did He command His students to stop *adoring* Him? No. A blind man impressed with Messiah's gracious words said, "Lord, I believe. And he worshipped him" (John 9:38). Did Lord Yeshua tell him to dispose of his *reverence*? No. Yeshua never refused worship because He was worthy of worship. Though His divinity was veiled, His blameless, flawless, sinless humanity was not. They frequently called Him *Lord* or *Master,* which is to say, "Adonai"—a title belonging to Yahweh.

Today put your knees and face to the floor and give the Son of God all due adoration, reverence and worship.

The Visible God

"And the Father himself, which hath sent me, hath borne witness of me. Ye have neither heard his voice at any time, nor seen his shape" (John 5:37)

Messiah's clear statement forces us to re-examine just Whose form was manifested to men in those assorted Old Testament appearances. The Scriptures specifically record that the LORD [Yahweh] appeared unto Abraham, Isaac, Jacob, Moses and Solomon. He appeared to others as well. We normally assume this Person was God the Father, but that is impossible based on Messiah's personal and definitive testimony. To cite just one example: when the biblical narrative of Exodus 33:11 states that "the LORD spake unto Moses face to face, as a man speaketh unto his friend," only one conclusion can be drawn—this was God the Son in a pre-incarnate form.

Paul's special revelation adds to our understanding. He declares that the Son was "in the form of God" and "equal with God" before His incarnation (Philippians 2:6). He also says, "in him dwelleth all the fullness of the Godhead bodily" (Colossians 2:9). Elsewhere he describes the Son in relation to the Father: "being the brightness of his glory, and the express image of his person" (Hebrews 1:3). No wonder Lord Yeshua spoke in such a disapproving tone saying, "Have I been so long time with you, and yet hast thou not known me, Philip? he that hath seen me hath seen the Father; and how sayest thou then, Show us the Father?" (John 14:9). Paul knew all too well that the Son alone dwells "in the light [*the Father*] which no man can approach unto; whom no man hath seen, nor can see" (1 Timothy 6:16). John also tells us that God is light (1 John 1:5). So when Yeshua tells us that He is the light of the world, we are to understand that He is the visible substance of the Father (John 9:5). Paul describes Yeshua as being "the brightness of His [*the Father's*] glory, and the express image [*exact copy*] of his person" (Hebrews 1:3).

In your quiet time today, lift up the Son as the great and exalted Most High God. Praise Him as all-God with all your heart and be blessed all day long.

283

Finders Keepers!

"For the Son of man is come to seek and to save that which was lost." (Luke 19:10)

Zacchaeus was "chief among the publicans [tax collectors]," but nothing was going to stop him from seeing the Saviour that day. He ran and climbed up in a tree and waited for Yeshua to walk by. However, the Messiah didn't just walk by; He stopped by. "And when Jesus came to the place, he looked up, and saw him, and said unto him, Zacchaeus, make haste, and come down; for today I must abide at thy house. And he made haste, and came down, and received him joyfully. And when they saw it, they all murmured, saying, That he was gone to be guest with a man that is a sinner" (v.5-7). Zacchaeus was not a bigger sinner than most, just richer; and like Solomon, Zacchaeus had long since discovered that riches don't really satisfy. He had observed other people's satisfaction in just being around the Messiah, so he gave that a try and fell in love with the Master at first sight.

There's something interesting and prophetic about Zacchaeus' Hebrew name Zaccai, pronounced *zak-kah'ee*. His parents named him this after a good, chief ruler (Ezra 2:9). Zaccai means *pure* and comes from the root *zaw-kak'* meaning, "to *be transparent* or *clean,* physically or morally." During the festive time in Messiah's presence Zacchaeus quietly received Yeshua into his heart and life, and as a result, he suddenly became very *transparent.* He also decided to come *clean.* "Zacchaeus stood, and said…Behold, Lord, the half of my goods I give to the poor; and if I have taken any thing from any man by false accusation, I restore him fourfold" (v.8). Yeshua found Zacchaeus, not the other way around. Yeshua could have passed right by Zac and his gold-filled sack, but He didn't. He sought him, saved him, and gave him a *purity* that he did not possess earlier that day.

Yeshua is the Seeker-Saviour. If He found you and saved you by His grace, He's going to keep you by His grace. He's not going to lose you. That's a guarantee! Today, praise the Son of God for seeking you out and not passing you by.

The Stone Ezel

"Then Jonathan said to David...when thou hast stayed three days, then thou shalt go down quickly, and come to the place where thou didst hide thyself...and shalt remain by the stone Ezel." (1 Samuel 20:18-19)

Jonathan and David had a covenant between them, and part of covenanting included holding no secrets. This is why Jonathan reminded David saying, "if I knew certainly that evil were determined by my father to come upon thee, then would not I tell it thee?" (v.9). Jonathan took David for a short walk in the field to explain his covert plan for David's safety. Referring to the upcoming day, Jonathan said, "I will shoot three arrows on the side thereof, as though I shot at a mark. And, behold, I will send a lad, saying, Go, find out the arrows. If I expressly say unto the lad, Behold, the arrows are on this side of thee, take them; then come thou: for there is peace to thee, and no hurt; as the LORD liveth. But if I say thus unto the young man, Behold, the arrows are beyond thee; go thy way: for the LORD hath sent thee away" (20-22). As the story unfolds, David did have to run away after all.

The irony of this story is that the very place in which David was hiding bore the name "Departure." Ezel (pronounced *Eh'-zel*) means departure, and comes from the root *aw-zal'* meaning, "to *go away*; hence, to *disappear*." It's almost as if the memorial stone had already foretold the future. The story has a progression: Jonathan departs from his father's feast table; the arrows depart from Jonathan's bow; the lad departs from Jonathan to bear his armor back home; and finally, after tearful farewells, David departs from Jonathan.

Life often brings in unexpected and unwelcome circumstances. Suddenly we are called upon to depart from our pre-planned schedules and are forced to rush away to a hospital or some other emergency. When these times come, fear not and remember that God is still in control. Don't ever depart from your steadfast faith. Moreover, always be ready to depart this world unexpectedly by sudden death or sudden rapture!

Glory Seekers

"He that speaketh of himself seeketh his own glory: but he that seeketh his glory that sent him, the same is true, and no unrighteousness is in him." (John 7:18)

This saying was prompted by a mistaken philosophy among the crowd. "Now about the midst of the feast Jesus went up into the temple, and taught. And the Jews marveled, saying, How knoweth this man letters, having never learned?" (v.14-15). Not only were they marveling over Messiah's unique wisdom, but also it was the Sabbath day and He had just healed someone. He made this point clear saying, "I have done one work, and ye all marvel [admire]" (v.21).

Yeshua was certainly worthy of admiration and glory, but He came to bring glory to His Father, not Himself. This is why He said so transparently, "My doctrine is not mine, but his that sent me" (v.16). He could have easily taken credit for His high wisdom, but instead sought to give the Father glory.

Now that the Son has gone back to His throne in heaven, the Holy Spirit has come. But do you think He has come to bring glory to Himself? No, not at all! The Holy Spirit has come to bring the Son of God glory. As Yeshua said, "for he shall not speak of himself" (John 16:13). Our text verse lays out the concept that we are to seek the glory of the Sender. That is precisely what the Spirit of God is busy doing now; He is glorifying God the Son. But guess what? We are also now sent ones. Yeshua said, "as my Father hath sent me, even so send I you" (John 20:21). The moment the Son of God saved us, He began equipping us to be sent into the world that we might bring Him glory. We'll never accomplish this job if we spend too much time drawing attention to ourselves.

Today, no matter where you seek to go or what you seek to do, seek to do it to the glory of God (1 Corinthians 10:31). Seek also to bring the message of Yeshua's glorious salvation to as many as you can.

Messiah's Inaugural Baptism

"And it came to pass...that Jesus came from Nazareth of Galilee, and was baptized of John in Jordan. And straightway coming up out of the water, he saw the heavens opened, and the Spirit like a dove descending upon him:" (Mark 1:9-10)

There were many reasons for ritual immersions in Mosaic times, and they all required the same thing—"plenty of water" (Leviticus 11:36). This is why John was found "baptizing in Aenon near to Salim, because there was much water there" (John 3:23). The water had to be high enough so a person could go straight down and come back up again. "And Jesus, when he was baptized, went up straightway [straight, level, true] out of the water" (Matthew 3:16). Messiah was completely flawless in Torah observance and entirely incapable of sinning in His deified, human form. As King of the kingdom, He was unequalled, eternal, immortal and impeccable. Thus, there was no cause for Him to be baptized for *repentance;* however, one reason He submitted Himself to it was to endorse John's ministry.

Baptisms [ritual washings] were also required for *consecration* into priestly service at age 30, *cleansing* from any form of defilement or ritual impurity, *converting* to Judaism, being *crowned* king, becoming a *son of the commandment* [bar mitzvah] or becoming a *rabbi.* Yeshua also went under those ritual waters for a reason that is not widely known. When a rabbi *acquired his own yoke* and became the authoritative figure over his own rabbinical school he was ceremonially immersed. Yeshua invited the masses to take upon themselves His yoke and authority, which was lighter and less burdensome than other rabbinical masters were (Matthew 11:28-30). Many who were not His personal followers still respectfully called Him Master because of His yoke. Two irrefutable tokens were presented that day to validate Israel's new Master—the visible, dove-like form of the Spirit and the audible voice of the Father Who said, "Thou art my beloved Son, in whom I am well pleased" (v.11).

Today, renew your respect for the Master, renew your zeal to His school of obedience, and yoke up to Him wherever He goes.

A Changed Life!

"Come and hear, all ye that fear God, and I will declare what he hath done for my soul." (Psalm 66:16)

Yeshua ben Elohim, Jesus the Son of God, has always been in the business of changing people's hearts and lives. Here is what He has done for my soul.

I grew up in a Baptist home and from the age of two went to Sunday school and worship service every week. By age 15, I knew Who Jesus was, and knew that I needed to be reconciled to the Father. Before this could happen, I had to repent of my sins and ask for forgiveness directly from Him. One day during the invitation time of a worship service, I felt the Holy Spirit's strong call and managed to loosen my grip from the pew in the back row of the balcony. I went forward in front of 300 people and made my stand with the Saviour. Beyond a shadow of a doubt, I knew from that very moment that my soul had been born anew.

The pastor baptized me two months later with some other young people, but I was never discipled in my new faith. What I needed was for someone to show me how to get involved right away with the Son of God in a daily walk. Nearly ten long years went by in servitude to self until I was handed my very first book having anything to do with Jesus. One summer day—25 years old and newly married—I walked in the back door of my childhood home and my mother had her hand held out with a book in it on the signs of the Lord's soon return. I gladly took that book and quickly found out what to do—*live for Him as if He could come back any day*! My life now had purpose, joy, direction, fulfillment and a very certain hope.

Five years later the LORD called me to preach, so I enrolled in Bible College and stayed until receiving a graduate degree. I was changed forever, and wanted to see others change also. "Blessed be God, which hath not turned away my prayer, nor his mercy from me" (v.20). Today, thank the triune God for redirecting your life for His glory.

The Breath of God

"And the LORD God formed man of the dust of the ground, and breathed into his nostrils the breath of life; and man became a living soul." (Genesis 2:7)

The Hebrew word for soul is *nefesh,* which means *breathing,* and refers to any breathing creature. In the Jewish world, they regard this as a person's soul. All life comes from God; that is why the psalmist commands, "Let every thing that hath breath praise the LORD," and then fulfills the command by saying, "Praise ye the LORD" (Psalm 150:6).

The root of nefesh is *nafash* meaning "to *breathe*; passively, to *be breathed* upon, figuratively, *refreshed* as if by a current of air." On the first day Messiah rose from the grave He came to the disciples in the Upper Room; there "he breathed on them, and saith unto them, Receive ye the Holy Ghost" (John 20:22). This is often an overlooked event, but it is vitally linked to the Genesis account of man's creation.

Adam was fully formed with flesh and blood, but he couldn't breathe, talk or enjoy fellowship with the Creator without first being infused with life, so Yahweh breathed upon him. When Yeshua walked into the Upper Room, the disciples were spiritually lifeless. Even though Messiah had previously spent considerable effort *fashioning* them for ministry, they were still passive and motionless with the gospel at that point. That's when He *breathed* on them and gave them the Spirit, or *breath of life*. No doubt, they were *refreshed* until a lasting measure could be given them at Pentecost. When one puts these two accounts together it places Yeshua in the exalted position of Creator God and Giver of eternal life. John made this point clear in the first verses of his gospel narrative.

Yeshua breathed His very last breath for you. He loved you that much. He has also given you of His everlasting breath that you might praise Him with it wherever you go. Today, take in a deep breath and then fellowship with Him, talk with Him and enjoy His holy presence all day long.

The Kingdom—Now & Not Yet

"He said therefore, A certain nobleman went into a far country to receive for himself a kingdom, and to return." (Luke 19:12)

Matthew's gospel mentions the kingdom 55 times. His gospel was primarily to the Jews and originally written in Hebrew. He wanted to document King Messiah's arrival and as much of His teaching on the kingdom as possible. By way of contrast, John's gospel, which was written to the world at large, only refers to the kingdom a few times. Matthew emphasizes the literal, tangible nature of the kingdom. He does this by recording the King's declaration: "But if I cast out devils by the Spirit of God, then the kingdom of God is come unto you" (Matthew 12:28). On the other hand, John stresses the spiritual, invisible aspects of the kingdom by exclusively recording Messiah's two statements: "Except a man be born again, he cannot see the kingdom of God" and "My kingdom is not of this world" (John 3:3; 18:36).

Both aspects of the kingdom exist side by side. A literal kingdom requires three things: a *land*, a *lord* and *subjects*. These three things were tangibly in place during King Messiah's earthly ministry. His subjects were few in number, however, so He left a door of opportunity open over the past two millennia for more subjects to bow. At the King's glorious return all Israel will become subservient to Him, for it is written, "Thy people shall be willing in the day of thy power" (Psalm 110:3).

Now consider the spiritual kingdom. A real *land* exists in the unseen realm of heaven. In that highest domain, a resurrected *Lord* sits upon His throne. The angels who dwell there are His willing *subjects,* and number in the thousands of millions. We subservient humans here below are part of that spiritual kingdom as well. We sing praises and pray to our majestic, seated King, and He hears us when we do. By His Spirit He directs our daily movements and carries out His will on earth.

Today, bend your knee and confess Yeshua as LORD; then, with your surrendered heart, reconfirm your allegiance to Him.

Be Faithful to Your Word

"Wherefore he called that place Beersheba; because there they sware both of them." (Genesis 21:31)

Abimelech's servants had taken over Abraham's well. To settle the matter permanently, Abraham "took sheep and oxen, and gave them unto Abimelech; and both of them made a covenant" (v.27). The Hebrew language sheds some additional light as to what actually happened to the animals. The word "made" is *ka-rawt'* and it means to *cut*. This means that the animals had to die. Covenant making took place all the time in biblical days. This was a way of strengthening a pact between two people whether they were friends or adversaries. Not only did the patriarch make a league with the king of Gerar that day, he also purchased back his old well. "And Abraham set seven ewe lambs of the flock by themselves. And Abimelech said unto Abraham, What mean these seven ewe lambs which thou hast set by themselves? And he said, For these seven ewe lambs shalt thou take of my hand, that they may be a witness [token] unto me, that I have digged this well" (v.28-30).

Throughout the covenant making process, Abraham vowed a total of seven times that he would not deal falsely with Abimelech or his descendants (v.23). Moreover, he "called that place Beersheba; because there they sware both of them" (v.31). The word for swear is *shaba*, which means, "to *seven* oneself," that is, to swear seven times. Thus, he named the site Beersheba meaning the "well of the seven-fold oath."

Concerning matters of the heart, Messiah said to "Swear not at all...But let your communication be, Yea, yea; Nay, nay" (Matthew 5:34, 37). He wants His followers to be known as trustworthy people whose words match their new natures. The expression, "Say what you mean, and mean what you say" has great worth. If you make a promise, no matter how insignificant or ridiculous it may later seem, stay true to it. Don't make any promises you can't or won't keep (Ecclesiastes 5:4).

Today, ask God to help you be as true to your word as He is to His.

Resting from the Sabbath?

"Let no man therefore judge you in meat, or in drink, or in respect of an holyday, or of the new moon, or of the sabbath [days]:" (Colossians 2:16)

The gentile believers at Colossi had been drawn into various legalistic trappings like *asceticism* that was characterized by certain forms of abstinence—"touch not, taste not, handle not" (v.21)—and *Judaism* that was characterized by 39 Sabbath do-nots. Paul didn't want these new converts adopting Mosaic rituals. He wanted them simply to walk in Messiah and be established in the faith, growing in His love, and abounding with thanksgiving (v.6-7).

In our text verse the translators have added the word *days*; thus, the chief apostle clearly refers to the Sabbath day. This is also understood by its placement in descending order—year, month and day. Paul warned the believers at Colossi to "Beware lest any man spoil you through philosophy and…tradition of men…and not after Christ" (v.8). He made it clear: "ye are complete in him" (v.10). Paul wanted gentile converts to be *resting* in the Redeemer, not *wrapped* in rituals. Outward form had been replaced with inward faith and "shadows" replaced with substance (v.17). If the Judaizers succeeded in getting Colossians to cling to the Sabbath, then they would never truly know what it meant to cling to the Saviour.

Word for word, each of the Ten Commandments are repeated in the New Testament *except* for one: "Remember the Sabbath day to keep it holy." In 2 Corinthians 3:7 Paul tells you why this token of the Law is not repeated in the New Testament; namely, it is ceremonial in nature and was to be done away with. For this same reason, tithing is also not carried over into the New Testament. The Sabbath was what set the Jews apart from the gentiles. Thus, the two cannot be joined if Sabbath injunctions remain. Paul does not say that it's wrong for a Jew to worship on the seventh day, or a Gentile to worship on the first day. He simply says, "Let every man be fully persuaded in his own mind" (Romans 14:5). Messiah has removed the law's heavy, demanding yoke from you and replaced it with His own, lighter yoke. Take some time to rest in Him today—free from any entanglements.

Yoked Together—Yeshua & Yishrael

"In all their affliction he was afflicted...in his love and in his pity he redeemed them; and he bare them, and carried them all the days of old." (Isaiah 63:9)

Messiah chose to identify Himself closely with Israel in almost every way. As a result, He suffered many of the same things they did. Let's examine some similarities. Both spent a portion of their life *exiled in Egypt* (Hosea 11:1; Matthew 2:14). Both were *afflicted from their youth*. Israel was afflicted with whips just prior to their exodus as a young nation (Psalm 129:1-2). In Messiah's case, He likely suffered taunts from other youths, and as an adult the Pharisees rudely remarked that He was conceived out of wedlock (John 8:41). But Psalm 129:3 turns to record dramatically Messiah's ultimate affliction by whipping at the tender age of thirty-three. Both also experienced *rejection among their brethren*. The northern tribes constantly scrapped with the two southern tribes and Messiah was always at odds with the Pharisees. Both *found themselves cornered* at one time by staunch enemies—Israel at the Red Sea and Messiah at the brow of a hill in Nazareth (Luke 4:29).

Israel had a *wilderness experience* lasting 40 years and Messiah had one lasting 40 days. During these times they both encountered *great thirst*. Both faced *a giant* at the end of a 40-day testing period. Israel faced Goliath and Yeshua faced Satan. Both lived under *a glory cloud* for a brief period—Israel in the wilderness and Messiah when He was on the Mt. of Transfiguration (Mark 9:7). Both had *sin laid* to their charge (Isaiah 1:6; 53:6). Both suffered a *serpent's bite* upon the heels. When Messiah's heel was pierced at the cross, it fulfilled Genesis 3:15. Both lived under a supernaturally *blacked-out sun* for a duration (Exodus 10:22; Luke 23:44). Both endured *Roman crosses*. Josephus estimated 1.1 million Jews died in this manner. Both shall have their *enemies subdued* under them (Psalm 110:1). Both have prophesies written of their suffering followed by *exaltation* among the nations (Zechariah 8:23; Philippians 2:11). Both shall experience a *resurrection* from the dead—Messiah has already received His.

Today, thank Yeshua for His steadfast identification and faithfulness to His covenant people, and pray that they would presently recognize this truth and repent one by one.

Supplication & Symbolism

"Hear the voice of my supplications, when I cry unto thee, when I lift up my hands toward thy holy oracle." (Psalm 28:2)

In Hebrew, the word supplication is *takh-a-noon*. Its root is *khana,* which means, "to *bend* or stoop in kindness to an inferior." Let's look at the Paleo-Hebrew picture language of *takhanun* to find out what this word implies.

Tav is the first letter and is depicted by a pair of crossed sticks meaning a *mark, sign* or *signal.* Supplication and prayer are marked by humility. God says, "to this man will I look, even to him that is poor and of a contrite spirit, and trembleth at my word" (Isaiah 66:2). As a sign that you've humbled yourself, you kneel *stooping low* upon your knees and bending your neck. This lowering process is a parabolic act, which signals to God what you want Him to do in return—stoop down from heaven with kindness. *Kaph* is depicted by an open palm and means, to *allow.* So when the psalmist says, "Hear the voice of my supplications," he means, "God please *allow* my prayer to reach your ears." The physical token of the open palm towards heaven is also incorporated. "I lift up my hands toward thy holy oracle." The psalmist also expects God to reciprocate by opening His own hand because he says, "Arise, O LORD…lift up thine hand: forget not the humble" (Psalm 10:12).

Nun is depicted by a sprouting seed and means to *continue.* Prayer is to be a continual part of our lives, and we should continue in prayer and never give up (Colossians 4:2). Paul says, "Now she that is a widow indeed, and desolate, trusteth in God, and continueth in supplications and prayers night and day" (1 Timothy 5:5). *Vav* is depicted by a tent peg and means *add*; also *secure.* The petitioner is asking God to continue making him feel secure and to add blessings in his day-to-day life. *Nun* shows up again at the end. The sprouting seed also means *heir* or *son,* so the one supplicating is asking God to allow him to continue living securely as if he were His own heir or son.

Today, present your needs to God with bended knees, a bowed head and uplifted palms. He is bound to hear you.

Lord of *Breakthroughs*

"The Philistines also came and spread themselves in the valley of Rephaim. And David inquired of the LORD, saying, Shall I go up to the Philistines?...And the LORD said unto David, Go up: for I will doubtless deliver the Philistines into thine hand." (2 Samuel 5:18-19)

The word *Rephaim* means giants. This day the giants were Philistine, and they were attempting to prevent David from extending his kingdom any further. However, Yahweh routed the heathen armies that day, and David acknowledged this by renaming the valley *"Baalperazim"* meaning "Lord of Breakthroughs" (v.20)! This new name became the memorial token of Israel's victory that day. So great was the victory, that the Israelites piled up the useless idols the Philistines left behind and burned them (v.21).

Even though David's army sent the Philistines running with fear, they came back some time later to the same valley ready to do battle again (v.22). When David inquired of the LORD, he was told to attack their flanks, which were over against the mulberry trees (v.23). The Lord of Breakthroughs also gave David a divine token of assurance for this battle. He said, "when thou hearest the sound of a going [*tseh-aw-dah*, a march] in the tops of the mulberry trees...then shall the LORD go out before thee, to smite the host of the Philistines" (v.24). The Spirit's timing was strategic. Not only did David hear the supernatural sound of a marching army, the Philistines did, too. This gave David great confidence and the Philistines great consternation!

No matter what kind of valley experience you are facing today, the victory is yours in Yeshua's name. The Spirit of Messiah will break through the enemy's strongest line of defense, but only when the time is right. Today's valley may seem wide and daunting to you, but don't have a *breakdown;* instead, have a *breakthrough*! Half the battle is in your mind. So begin to break through by focusing your mind on the Lord of Breakthroughs.

Samson's Prophetic Riddle

"And Samson said unto them, I will now put forth a riddle unto you…Out of the eater came forth meat, and out of the strong came forth sweetness." (Judges 14:12, 14)

As you know, Samson killed a lion on the way to Timnath where he and his parents were going to participate in his engagement ceremony. After the ceremony they went back home, and after a season came back with him to the wedding. On the way to Timnath, Samson "turned aside to see the carcase of the lion: and, behold, there was a swarm of bees and honey in the carcase of the lion. And he took thereof in his hands, and went on eating, and came to his father and mother, and he gave them, and they did eat" (v.8-9). Later that day as the celebration got underway, Samson placed his riddle [*khee-dah*; dark saying] before 30 Philistine companions who were brought in to make the wedding cheery. At the end of the weeklong celebration, the answer came forth: "What is sweeter than honey? and what is stronger than a lion?" (v.18).

We understand the plain meaning of Samson's answer, but there is a hidden [*sod* level] meaning here which speaks of Messiah, Judah's Lion (Revelation 5:5). Messiah's death was a great tragedy, but out of His death came forth great spiritual sustenance for the family of God. The first half of Samson's riddle was, "Out of the eater came forth meat [food]." Messiah is the fearless *Eater* Who *ate up* our adversary the devil and made all our sins disappear at the cross. Praise His holy name! Referring to the remarkable quality of *sustenance* that would *come forth* from His death, Yeshua said, "Whoso eateth my flesh, and drinketh my blood, hath eternal life…For my flesh is meat indeed, and my blood is drink indeed" (John 6:54-55). The second half of Samson's riddle, "out of the strong came forth sweetness," is equally true of Messiah Yeshua. One of His titles is *El Gibbor* meaning "the Mighty God" (Isaiah 9:6). Out of His mighty love came our redemption. Now "we are unto God a sweet savour of Christ" (2 Corinthians 2:15).

Ask the Spirit to help you carry the sweetness of the Saviour's sustaining life and strong love into the workplace today.

Samson's Greatest Foe

"Then went Samson down...and came to the vineyards of Timnath: and, behold, a young lion roared against him. And the spirit of the LORD came mightily upon him, and he rent him as he would have rent a kid, and he had nothing in his hand:" (Judges 14:5-6)

Archaeologists have recently unearthed a tiny, gray stone seal that depicts a man facing a lion. It was discovered in Beit Shemesh, a city that was close to the Philistine cities of Gath and Ekron. Samson's Hebrew name, *Shimshon*, means sunlight and comes from the word *shemesh* meaning "to be *brilliant*, the *sun*." Thus, Samson is linked to the city where the stone was found. Moreover, the layer of dirt the seal was dug from dates to the time of the judges—circa 11th Century BC. The seal's existence at least proves there was a story in circulation about a legendary figure that conquered a lion.

Samson conquered the lion but found it incredibly difficult to conquer his own inborn weakness. Satan first tested Samson's physical strength, but was forced to find another way to bring him low. Samson had a weakness for pleasure, and this became his downfall. He shone brightly for a season, but then his brilliance waxed dim, and the prince of darkness put out his candle. Samson had opportunity to turn around and get back on track but got lost in his lust.

A good opponent studies his enemy, and Satan studies you closely. He wants to bring you down so you can't be a champion for God. This is why Peter tells you, "Be sober, be vigilant; because your adversary the devil, as a roaring lion, walketh about, seeking whom he may devour" (1 Peter 5:8). The Saviour has warned you to stick to the divine plan and not to lose your brilliance. He says, "Remember therefore from whence thou art fallen, and repent, and do the first works; or else I will come unto thee quickly, and will remove thy candlestick out of his place, except thou repent" (Revelation 2:5).

Ask the LORD to help you gain strength today in areas where you are currently weak and vulnerable to the enemy's attack.

Following the Lamb!

"These are they which follow the Lamb whithersoever he goeth."
(Revelation 14:4)

When the Lamb of God walked the earth He asked many to follow Him, but few took up His challenge. For many the cost was just too great. Various ones made their excuses to the Lamb's face. Some reasons seemed to be reasonable enough to us, but they were all insults to the Holy One Who had forsaken all for them. Besides the twelve, there was one man in Jericho, a blind man, who didn't make excuse. After receiving His sight from the Lamb, he "followed him, glorifying God" (Luke 18:43).

Following the Lamb requires a *willingness* to forsake all. There were those who followed the Lamb as circumstances allowed. One gospel records that "a great multitude from Galilee and Judaea followed him," and some of these were able to follow Him triumphantly into Jerusalem singing, "Blessed is he that cometh in the name of the Lord" (Mark 11:9). On His way to Golgotha there "followed him a great company of people, and of women, which also bewailed and lamented him" (Luke 23:27). A handful soon followed the Lamb to His tomb, and 40 days later hundreds followed Him as far as Bethany to behold His heavenly departure. When the Lamb sent down His Spirit to indwell repentant hearts permanently, they were so filled with His infinite love that they began to follow Him by faith to their own appointed deaths. James was the first of these. Over the centuries, millions have followed the Lamb to their own place of martyrdom.

For those of us who follow the Lamb today, we are told to *"follow* after charity" (1 Corinthians 14:1). We should also *"follow* that which is good" (1 Thessalonians 5:15), and steadfastly *"follow* after righteousness, godliness, faith, love, patience, meekness" (1 Timothy 6:11). As well, we are to *"follow* peace with all men, and holiness, without which no man shall see the Lord" (Hebrews 12:14). Peter wonderfully summarized, "For even hereunto were ye called…that ye should *follow* his steps" (1 Peter 2:22).

Today, prayerfully look for the Lamb's pathway.

Prophesies Shall Fail

"Charity never faileth: but whether there be prophecies, they shall fail; whether there be tongues, they shall cease; whether there be knowledge, it shall vanish away." (1 Corinthians 13:8)

A coworker once showed me a mural he had just painted on his church's sanctuary wall. While there, he said that a woman had recently given a prophecy that "there will be 318 people in this sanctuary before Jesus returns." Seeing that only about 175 people could have been squeezed into the sanctuary, reconstruction was necessary even to fulfill the woman's prophecy. The failure of that prophecy was that it did away with the imminence of the Lord's return. Something else had to happen before He could come back—a building project.

A Christian weatherman in Israel recently prophesied on a *messianic* TV show that the Shekinah cloud would return and rest over Jerusalem before Messiah returned. He further stated that the cloud might not stay, but rather come and go. This prophecy shall certainly fail because God's true prophet already stated emphatically that the glory cloud will not rest over the Holy City until the "Branch of the LORD," the Messiah, takes up residence there and until "the Lord shall have washed away the filth of the daughters of Zion" (Isaiah 4:2, 4).

Paul clearly taught that the sign gifts would stop, and he told us why. "But when that which is perfect [*telios*, complete] is come, then that which is in part shall be done away" (v.10). That which is now *complete* is the collection of the New Testament Scriptures. That which was *in part* refers to the *miraculous* sign gifts. These powers were only given to Messiah's handpicked apostles (Acts 2:43; 5:12) and temporarily at that (2 Timothy 4:20). Apostles could in turn appoint others, but this was not to extend to future generations. Signs and wonders were always temporary and were only meant to lead to a prearranged destination. Signs are no longer needed once you arrive; you just begin enjoying where you are.

Peter wrote, "We have...a more sure word of prophecy; whereunto ye do well that ye take heed" (2 Peter 1:19). Today, lean on the clarity of God's completed Word. It will never, ever fail you or make a fool of you.

How Do They Read You?

"Ye are our epistle written in our hearts, known and read of all men." (1 Corinthians 3:2)

Paul's colorful expression has not been lost over the centuries. It is still widely used today when said this way, "I can read him like a book!" A book doesn't talk to you, but as you read each word within, it delivers its message. In the same way, the believer is to be a living message, sort of like an open book—one that is *observed,* not just listened to. Paul not only suggests this to the believers at Corinth, but to you also. He says, "ye are manifestly declared to be the epistle of Christ" (v.3).

People should be able to read your Christian or Messianic life with just a glance. In fact, sometimes a glance is all they may ever get. If someone sees you in a market square and observes you helping an elderly person, they immediately know you are caring; thus, you will be the one they may decide to share their burden with some day. The old saying, "I would rather see a sermon than hear one" accurately describes the manner in which the lost often discover the gospel. You may not always sense it, but the certain reality is that your co-workers and neighbors have their magnifying glass on you. Maybe you don't feel comfortable with others peering into your life at random, but they want to see if Jesus is as real as you make Him out to be.

If you have announced that you are a Bible believer, are you then *known* and *read* of all men or do they have to ask around to make certain? Can they read you as *content* if you're always *complaining*? Can they read you as *faithful* if you're always *falling*? Instead, let them read you loud and clear by your dynamic daily walk.

Seek the joy of the Lord in your prayer time today. And take that joy wherever you are going so that others will have someone joyful and faithful to read. Amen?

Rise & Shine!

"For a just man falleth seven times, and riseth up again" (Proverbs 24:16)

Self-improvement is not a bad thing. Other people benefit from it, too. There seems to be nothing worse than watching someone who is able to improve his or her situation but refuses to budge. That's when they need a nudge! James laid out the nudge principle. He said that believers could and should help other believers when they stray from the truth (James 5:20). Even so, the one who has fallen must have some desire not to remain down for the count. The longer he stays down the harder it is to get back up.

If you are powerless to rise from your fall, there is One standing ready to assist you. He will do for you as He did for a poor soul whom the devil had constantly picked on. "Jesus took him by the hand, and lifted him up; and he arose" (Mark 9:27). The Saviour was also known to walk up to fallen ones and say, "Thy sins be forgiven thee...Arise, and walk" (Matthew 9:5). Lord Yeshua wants you to get back up when you fall. He wants you on your feet moving forward by faith. If you're lying in the way, then others may accidentally trip over you as they do their best to walk the straight and narrow path. Don't be a discouragement to others. Be an encourager by showing others how to move on after failing spiritually. If you fall down, don't stay down. Get up, and be quick about it. The Lord wants to keep fellowship as unbroken as possible.

Maybe your fall has been great and you're afraid of what others might think or say about you when you get back up and into service for the King. If so, then listen to the words of your Master: "Arise, and be not afraid" (Matthew 17:7). Maybe your fall has given you the feeling that you're *spiritually* dead. Pay no attention to that lie. The Son of God will do for you as He did for Jarius' *lifeless* daughter. He "took her by the hand, and called, saying, Maid, arise" (Luke 8:54). Whatever state you're in today, rise up and walk with the Lord; and if you're able, seek to help a brother or sister who has stumbled.

ᴀAre You Well Suited?

"And there were certain Greeks among them that came up to worship at the feast: The same came therefore to Philip, which was of Bethsaida of Galilee, and desired him, saying, Sir, we would see Jesus." (John 12:20-21)

Philip was from Bethsaida, a peaceful city near the shores of the Kinneret. John presents this disciple as the first person Messiah called to follow Him (John 1:43). Philip quickly became fond of Israel's Redeemer and wasted no time finding someone else who he thought might be interested—Nathanael. When this fellow Galilean initially responded with a measure of skepticism, Philip simply replied, "Come and see" (John 1:46).

Philip was very missions hearted and apparently well suited to handle spontaneous enquiries. When some Greek-speaking people came from abroad and were seeking to know more of the Saviour, the tame-natured disciple later felt well suited enough to cross cultural barriers and go to Samaria. There both he and his message of the resurrected Messiah were gladly received (Acts 8:5). Dispatched by the Holy Spirit from Samaria, Philip was particularly suited to answer the eager questions of an Ethiopian man who was lacking one necessary detail for his salvation (8:27). He needed to know whose atoning blood to which the prophet Isaiah was referring. Philip courteously placed one question to the Ethiopian man: "Do you understand what you are reading?" That one question so well suited the man's overflowing curiosity that he urged Philip to come up into his chariot and sit with him (8:31).

How well suited are you for satisfying other people's longings to know the Redeemer? Are you "peaceable, gentle, and easy to be entreated, full of mercy and good fruits, without partiality, and without hypocrisy?" (James 3:17) If so, your friends, neighbors and workmates will readily and confidently come to you in their time of need. This is the type of godly man or woman seekers will need in order to see the Saviour clearly. Today, ask the Spirit to continue suiting you for your gospel calling.

How's Your World Vision?

"That was the true Light, which lighteth every man that cometh into the world. He was in the world, and the world was made by him, and the world knew him not." (John 1:9-10)

A believer doesn't have to look around very long to realize that the world is a very dark place. This is especially true when the darkened hearts of mankind are revealed in the various daily news sectors. Yeshua, "the *Light of the World*," came to change the darkness by shedding His holy light upon it. John spread Yeshua's true light, and you can continue spreading the light of His Word wherever you go in this dark world.

Another title belonging to Him is "the *Lamb of God*," because He took away the sin of the world (1:29). He took the immeasurable weight of the world's sin and carried it to His cross dying there with it. Today, anyone who sees his or her sin upon that Lamb and mournfully identifies with Him, and asks Him for forgiveness receives a full pardon. This is the message that you can now carry to anyone in the world.

John recounts Messiah's words: "For God so loved the world, that he gave his only begotten Son" (3:16). Yeshua reflects the Father's love overwhelmingly and can easily be called "the *Lover of Souls*." You can now go in His love and melt the hearts of those who think no one really loves them. The Son of God proved His love, and all that is left to do is for you to preach it! So many are waiting for this good news, and they live all around you.

The good news doesn't include good works (Ephesians 2:8, 9). Only Yeshua's atoning blood can claim and cleanse a person. Tell others simply to surrender at Calvary where their Saviour stands ready to meet them. Yeshua is the *Light* of the world, the *Lamb* of God, and the *Lover* of souls. He is the One Who died for sin, forgives sin, washes away sin's guilt, and replaces it all with the fullness of His Spirit. Catch this world vision today and take it prayerfully with you as you go.

The Supply Line

"But my God shall supply all your need according to his riches in glory by Christ Jesus." (Philippians 4:19)

Paul was able to blaze one foreign trail after another and was willing to go anywhere with the gospel torch because he knew he had a steadfast supply line. There was hardly a day when the apostle to the gentiles was not in some needy situation. Paul knew *Who* would always come through for him—Yeshua. If Paul knew how to count on anyone, it was Yeshua, and the apostle wanted all of his disciples to look to Him in their time of need.

The great pioneer missionary not only knew *where* the supply line originated, but also *what* the supply actually was—the wonderful "supply of the Spirit of Jesus Christ" (1:19). The human body can go days without water and weeks without food, but the inner man cannot so much as move unless the Spirit's breath continually fills his spiritual house. Knowing precisely *why* the spiritual supply comes, Paul informs us of his subsequent supernatural motivation saying, "I can do all things through Christ which strengtheneth me" (4:13). This same divine supply that enabled Paul to go the distance will also assist you in your life's journey.

This first herald of God's grace among the nations did not know exactly *when* much needed physical supplies would reach him, but he labored on without fainting knowing that those things would reach him at the right time and in the right way. And he knew *how* it would arrive to him—through the prayers of the saints (1:19). God will not ignore the faithful, fervent prayers of a righteous saint. How much more, then, will He hear and answer hundreds and thousands of saintly prayers? Despite his great physical lack at various times, Paul could always say, "I have all, and abound" (4:18).

Don't give up the spiritual fight today or even entertain the thought. Instead, claim Yeshua and His Spirit as your all in all and stay on the firing line until He comes.

Seeing Him

"Then said Jesus unto them, Be not afraid: go tell my brethren that they go into Galilee, and there shall they see me." (Matthew 28:10)

Having majestically ascended from the depths of His dark grave, the risen Messiah could hardly wait for His kinsmen to see Him; but they would not see Him for very long in the religiously congested city of Jerusalem where it all ended. Rather, they would see Him at length where it all first began—on the gently sloping hills of Galilee. Unbelief is an obstacle which prevents the lost from seeing the Son of God; however, believers can also have obstructions which cloud their vision.

Fear is one obstruction that hinders believers from fully serving the Saviour where they would otherwise experience Him in blessed ways. *Doubt* also creates obstructions to seeing Him. The women who went to the empty tomb doubted seeing a living Lord. No wonder Mary supposed the risen One was just the gardener! We often don't proceed with our holy assignments because of crippling doubts concerning His protection and provision. *Slothfulness* doesn't help either. On the very day the Master predicted His resurrection, the men were still staring at the dull-gray Upper Room walls. At the very same time, the ardent women were staring at the Saviour's radiant face! Slothfulness kept the men from seeing Him first, and lack of diligence will keep you from having close encounters with the beloved Son.

Disappointment is an obstruction that is all too real. The disciples were tremendously disappointed in themselves having abandoned their Master in His hour of need. Like them, we also can become disillusioned and reclusive when we look too long at our many shortcomings. *Failures* need to be confessed and forgotten because Yeshua is the only truly perfect Man. In order to see Him as He is, we should stop looking at ourselves and simply ask for restoration and get back to our appointed places. Today, may God's Spirit help you see the Saviour more clearly.

One Sacred Kiddush Fountain

"In that day there shall be a fountain opened to the house of David and to the inhabitants of Jerusalem for sin and for uncleanness." (Zechariah 13:1)

The word *Kiddush* means sanctification. It is a Jewish prayer recited to sanctify or set apart the Sabbath day or other Jewish holidays from the ordinary days of the year. Kiddush comes from the word *kadash,* which means, "to *be clean,* hence *holy;* causatively to *consecrate, hallow."* On Friday evenings just before sunset Hebrew families throughout the world gather around their family tables and begin various prayers by saying, "Blessed are you O LORD, our God, King of the Universe, Creator of the fruit of the vine." The father or leader pours wine or grape juice into a Kiddush cup, takes a sip, and then passes it along to each person standing. At one of Messiah's sanctified gatherings, Passover, He "took the [Kiddush] cup, and gave thanks, and said, Take this, and divide it among yourselves" (Luke 22:17).

A Kiddush fountain is also sometimes used on Shabbat. This is an apparatus that holds anywhere from four to twelve tiny cups. The host takes his full Kiddush cup and pours the sacramental drink into the top of the fountain; tubes then distribute the liquid evenly into each little cup. As the red juice is poured out and shed abroad into individual cups, it wonderfully illustrates a *fountain of salvation* that would only be recognized by followers of the New Covenant. This Kiddush fountain becomes a beautiful, visual token of how Yeshua's holy, cleansing blood was shed for us. We hold communion at our church this way. Before pouring the sacramental red grape juice into the top of the fountain we recite the text verse above plus Yeshua's sacred words, "For this is my blood of the new testament, which is *shed* for many for the remission of sins" (Matthew 26:28).

Thank Yeshua today for breaking open His soul-cleansing fountain and making it available on your behalf. Also, thank Him for His fountain's restorative value—how it revived your parched soul while wandering through death's valley.

Gloriously Transformed

"My little children, of whom I travail in birth again until Christ be formed in you," (Galatians 4:19)

Paul was as interested in salvation's ongoing work as he was its finished work. Many of the Galatian believers (Gentiles) seemed helpless in their turning back to a works-based faith, which was due to the invading influence of Judaizers from Jerusalem. The Galatians' spiritual growth had now come to a halt, and Paul was desperately grieved. Yes, doctrine does affect development. What one feeds on determines his final stature. It wasn't enough for Paul just to bring Messiah to the Galatians; he wouldn't stop helping them until they became *like* Messiah.

Paul, the most likely author of Hebrews, was also greatly concerned with saved Jews in Jerusalem who were compromising some of their beliefs and practices to relieve part of their persecution. He reminded them repeatedly of the *better* way. He wanted to see them fully transformed into their Saviour's marvelous character regardless of the price paid. Paul warned that it's not enough just to have "a form of godliness" (2 Timothy 3:5). This will never do! David didn't have a mere form of godliness; he had a heart for God, and that makes all the difference. David also grieved over the fact that he was trapped in his earthly human form. His heart's cry was, "I shall be satisfied, when I awake, with thy likeness" (Psalm 17:15). The aged apostle John also longed for that glorious, transforming day. He wrote, "Beloved, now are we the sons of God, and it doth not yet appear what we shall be: but we know that, when he shall appear, we shall be like him" (1 John 3:2).

What hinders you from becoming fully formed into His image: a friend, a workmate, a family member, a career or a sport? *Lack of love* for the One Who died for you is usually the underlying reason. Rekindle your *first love* on a daily basis. This is easier than starting all over when your wood is all wet. Today, don't be satisfied that you are called a son of God. In fact, don't be satisfied until people begin "confusing" you with the Son of God. Oh, to be like Jesus—a life-long journey! Pray also for a brother or sister who has yet to let the Son be fully formed in them.

November 4

𝒯urning 𝒲ater into 𝒲ine

"And there were set there six waterpots of stone, after the manner of the purifying of the Jews, containing two or three firkins apiece. Jesus saith unto them, Fill the waterpots with water. And they filled them up to the brim. And he saith unto them, Draw out now, and bear unto the governor of the feast. And they bare it." (John 2:6-8)

This miracle draws out a beautiful contrast between the old order and the new. The old Mosaic rituals of purification have been surpassed by Messiah's new Spirit baptism (1:31-34), and His one sacrifice for sin replaces the old, repetitive offerings. John illustrates this truth by showing Yeshua driving out all the sheep and the oxen from the Temple (2:15). An amazing feature in this story is the huge quantity of wine created—about 120 gallons—and its exceeding quality. This symbolizes the abundant, rich supply of Yeshua's Spirit imparted to every believer at the moment of the new birth. John writes, "of his fullness we have all received" (1:16). In Ephesians 5:18 Paul contrasts the surpassing need of now being controlled by the Spirit rather than by old wine.

The Hebrew word for wine is *yayin* meaning effervescent. Its root, *ayin,* refers to a fountain of water that bubbles up from the ground. Miriam's stressful call, "they have no wine," signifies the believers' heart-felt cry for joy that never runs dry. John the Baptizer's joy was fulfilled after laying his eyes on the Source of it—Yeshua, the heavenly Bridegroom (3:29). How much more joy is yours having been given access to the very Source!

Today your heavenly wellspring of inner satisfaction is effervescent and steadfastly independent of any other events that might take place. The Son of God has solemnly pledged, "that my joy might remain in you, and that your joy might be full" (15:11). You see, *His* joy has become *your* joy! Even though He has given you His unique joy, you may still have to make the conscious choice to be joyful today in spite of your circumstances. Either way, it is a win-win situation for you.

Dealing with Discouragement

"And John calling unto him two of his disciples sent them to Jesus, saying, Art thou he that should come? or look we for another?" (Luke 7:19)

If anyone was convinced that Yeshua was the long-awaited Messiah, it was John the Immerser. He leaped in His mother's womb when he first came into the presence of the Saviour (v.41). Thirty years later he saw the Spirit in the form of a dove descend upon Messiah, and he heard the audible voice of God declaring that He was the sent One. Then he proclaimed to those standing by that Yeshua of Nazareth was the Lamb of God Who carries away the whole world's sin. Just months later John was in great *loneliness* and utter *despair* in Herod's prison. He was also in real *doubt*. John thought that Messiah's coming should have ended the martyrdom of God's prophets. He was wrong. There would be more—including Yeshua. Messiah sent a message back to John speaking of all the miracles He was doing in fulfillment of Scripture, plus one other very pertinent message: "And blessed is he, whosoever shall not be offended in [*because of*] me" (v.23).

It seems the more you want to do for God, the more discouragement you face. But what the Son of God allows or disallows in His servants' lives is really His business, not yours (Matthew 20:15). If you will focus on what the Master is doing around the world, you won't have much time left to focus on what He is not doing for you. Job was tested by God's silence, and in the same way, John was tested by Messiah's silence. If the LORD said that He "would dwell in the thick darkness," then sometimes He must also dwell in thick silence (1 Kings 8:12). When God is silent, we sometimes get nervous. Instead, we should just get busy. That's what John Bunyon decided to do. From his dark prison cell, he wrote *The Holy War*. From Paul's prison cells, he wrote several letters found in the New Testament. Maybe the Baptizer should have picked up a pen. Yeshua also endured silence from heaven at the cross, but He labored on and secured your salvation.

Today, prayerfully thank Him for doing just that, and then labor on in His will!

Packaging Grace

"And he said unto him, If now I have found grace in thy sight, then show me a sign that thou talkest with me." (Judges 6:17)

Gideon wanted a token of God's grace; but before he could receive it, he had to give his own token of graciousness. The mighty angel requested, "Bring forth *my* present" (v.18). After cooking up some tender goat, fresh pita, and a pot of gravy, Gideon brought it and presented it to him (v.19). The angel told Gideon to place his token gift on the nearby rock. "Then the angel of the LORD put forth the end of the staff that was in his hand, and touched the flesh and the unleavened cakes; and there rose up fire out of the rock, and consumed the flesh and the unleavened cakes. Then the angel of the LORD departed out of his sight" (v.21). Gideon now had his token. Yahweh's angel consumed the Midianites in the same manner He had consumed the meal—with a fiery zeal.

The LORD often packages grace in interesting ways. When my twin brother and I were born, my mother began encountering sciatic nerve problems. My father worked rotating shifts, so my mother was left to tend the twins on her own. One day she cried out to God for grace. Grace soon showed up! It was a small-statured woman bearing the visible marks of childhood polio. And what was her name? Grace! Yes, Grace Dixon, and she was the LORD's handmaiden and my mother's handmaid for that season. At some point her family had to move to another city, but from the few times I saw her in the later years of my childhood I could tell there was something truly special about her. Even though she had her own burden to bear, she was kind, gracious and very happy. Her husband was also extremely joyful and friendly. Thus, God had given Grace *much grace* by sending her a loving, caring, strong husband.

God is in the grace-packaging business. His greatest package came in the form of a Man on a cross, and "of his fullness have all we received, and grace for grace" (John 1:16). Today, ask the LORD to show you someone to whom you can take a portion of His grace and kindness.

Justice or Just Ice?

"To do justice and judgment is more acceptable to the LORD than sacrifice." (Proverbs 21:3)

The Hebrew word for justice is *tsedakah,* and it means rightness. God wants us to live uprightly all the time. This is not easy, but He expects this behavior to come from those who have His just nature residing within. He wants us to *be right* with Him and *do right* by His Word in our daily lives. He has given us the cloak of His own righteousness, and He intends for us to wear it well.

He also wants us to do right by others. When we don't, the Holy Spirit will certainly reveal in our hearts His displeasure. Children have an inborn sense of justice, and they are quick to let others know when an injustice has been done. But grown-ups won't usually tell you when you've offended them in some way; they just hold it in.

God wants believers to execute justice lest injustice prevail; however, when we attempt to sort out others who are doing wrong we can sometimes go about it in the wrong way or at the wrong time. The wrong way usually involves a wrong approach—one that is cold and lacking in compassion. There may also be times when we don't need to approach a person at all because what we really desire is judgment for the one who has troubled us. We come at them with our own brand of *justice,* which is *just ice.* What may equally be needed at these times is a measure of mercy. This is also worth dispensing. Justice must be mixed with mercy because this action reflects how God has dealt with you.

Today, ask God to warm your tepid heart so that you can go out with a warm, holy glow and do right by Him, by His Word and by others. There's a world full of fragile people out there, and God doesn't want you to be the straw that breaks the camel's back.

Is Your All on the Altar?

"And thou shalt burn the whole ram upon the altar: it is a burnt offering unto the LORD: it is a sweet savour, an offering made by fire unto the LORD." (Exodus 29:18)

Not every sacrifice was to be eaten by the offerer and the priest. Some sacrifices were to be consumed wholly by God. The sacrifice remained on the altar until all was gone which teaches us a great spiritual lesson.

We know that we are to give God our whole hearts and not be half-hearted towards Him. Once we've done this, He sometimes asks us to make good on our promise. The LORD can be pleased that we give Him one out of seven days for worship and one out of ten dollars for stewardship, but He is none too pleased when we give Him one-tenth of our heart and soul. He wants our all on the altar.

Some saints are fearful of total surrender. They're fearful of the unknown, and that makes them uncomfortable. After all, who wants to be sacrificed? Who wants to be burned? John the Baptizer was entirely sold-out to Yahweh, but did he die at age 30 because Herod took him or because God took him? David Brainerd put his all on the altar of prayer and died at age 29. But did he die because his poor health consumed him, or did he die because the love of God had consumed him?

We need to live full lives for God because we never know when our time here below will expire. Do you have ten years to serve God? Do you even have ten days? Only the LORD knows this, and, therefore, you should put your all on the altar today. Wouldn't you rather go out burning than to go out "bemoaning" (Jeremiah 31:18)? Wouldn't you rather die in the "midst of the battle" like Jonathan than die in the midst of your basement making little toy sailboats (2 Samuel 1:25)? How will your heart and service be remembered?

Today, offer yourself afresh and anew, pledging your all to the One Who put His all on the altar of sacrifice for you.

Parable on the Harp

"I will incline mine ear to a parable: I will open my dark saying upon the harp." (Psalm 49:4)

The parable was a metaphorical tool used by wise teachers of the Near East. Solomon spoke in proverbs and parables—3000 of them (1 Kings 4:32). Although the use of parables preceded Messiah, no one ever used them with His level of authority and expertise. He spoke them as He heard them from His Father (John 5:30). This fact coincides with our text verse. With great power and effect, Yeshua uttered His parables mainly upon the hills of Galilee and its nearby sea, which resembles the shape of a harp. Modern Israelis call this sea the *Kinneret* taking the word from *kinor,* the Hebrew word for *harp.*

The prophets of old called for stringed instruments in order to bring the Spirit of the LORD upon them (2 Kings 3:15). The chief reason the Psalms are so prophetic in nature and speak so often of Messiah is that they were written under inspiration of Davidic-style harps. One gospel writer defines Yeshua's wide use of parables as fulfilled prophecy that belongs directly to God (Matthew 13:35). "Give ear, O my people, to my law: incline your ears to the words of my mouth. I will open my mouth in a parable: I will utter dark sayings of old" (Psalm 78:1-2). When Messiah spoke, it was God speaking. Messiah's habit was to incline His *ear* to the Father and then open His *mouth* in superior parabolic form.

Messiah continues speaking in the Psalm from which our text is drawn. Regarding His coming crucifixion, He says so beautifully: "Wherefore should I fear in the days of evil, when the iniquity [*perversity: punishment*] of my heels shall compass me about?...But God will redeem my soul from the power of the grave: for he shall receive me" (v.5, 15). And oh, how the Father received Him! As Yeshua ascended into heaven after His resurrection, the Father said to Him, "Sit thou at my right hand, until I make thine enemies thy footstool" (Psalm 110:1).

This morning get quiet and incline your ear to LORD Yeshua to see what He will say to your *harp-shaped* heart.

Purity in the Tongue

"For then will I turn to the people a pure language, that they may all call upon the name of the LORD, to serve him with one consent." (Zephaniah 3:9)

Zephaniah spoke this prophecy around 630BC. Three decades later his Hebrew-speaking countrymen were carried off into Babylon, the land of the Chaldeans. There they conveniently adopted an Aramaic tongue and even returned home with it 70 years later. Aramaic remained a dominant language in Israel even to the time of Yeshua. Hebrews also frequently spoke Koine Greek in Yeshua's day. One generation after Messiah, Israelites were scattered throughout the earth and were forced to take on a host of languages.

Hebrew was known in Yeshua's day, but in the Diaspora, it became such a forgotten language that it had to be reinvented. God had promised that this would occur just after the judgment of nations—Israel included (v.8). Yahweh says to His own people after judging them: "The remnant of Israel shall not do iniquity, nor speak lies; neither shall a deceitful tongue be found in their mouth" (v.13). God's intention is to change Israel's tongue as well as their heart because the two are *spiritually* attached. In the near future, this will be true of all nations. They, too, will learn Hebrew, at least as their second language, having their hearts inclined to the Hope of Israel—Lord Yeshua.

When God transforms your heart, He transforms the language of your heart. He *tames* your tongue because "the tongue can no man tame; it is an unruly evil, full of deadly poison" (James 3:8). God also *tones* your tongue to speak soft words, not harsh ones. After salvation, the Spirit-filled tongue learns to speak with holiness instead of hatefulness, "For in many things we offend all. If any man offend not in word, the same is a perfect man" (James 3:2). Because "the tongue is a little member, and boasteth great things," God *tunes* your tongue to speak the wonderful Words of Life (James 3:5).

This morning ask the LORD to help your tongue become as a fountain sending forth only the purest, sweetest gospel water.

ᐧ𝒲𝑎𝑙𝑘𝑖𝑛𝑔 𝑖𝑛 𝒞𝑜𝑣𝑒𝑛𝑎𝑛𝑡

"I beseech thee, O LORD, remember now how I have walked before thee in truth and with a perfect heart, and have done that which is good in thy sight. And Hezekiah wept sore." (2 Kings 20:3)

In the Near East, establishing a covenant walk with another person involved nine steps, but all nine were not required to make the covenant binding. In their rush, Jonathan and David performed at least three significant steps. They *exchanged robes* (1 Samuel 18:3-4). This pictures the "garment of salvation" the Lord has given us (Isaiah 61:10). They *exchanged weapons* that represent protection. God has given us His spiritual "armor" (Ephesians 6:13). The two also *swore allegiance* to each other while reciting covenant obligations (1 Samuel 20:17). Paul speaks of our unwavering allegiance before Yeshua and of His allegiance to us (Hebrews 10:23).

Central to making or *cutting a covenant* was dividing an animal in half, laying it in two piles, and walking a figure-eight in the midst (Jeremiah 34:18-19). Abraham and Yahweh performed this ritual except Abraham was put into a deep sleep to show that salvation is unconditional (Genesis 15:8-12). Messiah also cut the New Covenant with His own blood and stood alone in the thick darkness. The two covenanters also made incisions in their right arms, raised them, and joined them together to *mix their blood*. Yeshua's sinless blood became supernaturally mixed with our sinful blood while He hung upon the cross. The covenanters turned their incisions into *permanent scars* by rubbing ashes into them. Yeshua was raised from the grave with His covenant marks remaining (John 20:27).

The next step involved *exchanging names*. Believers are called Christians (Acts 11:26), and in Israel they are referred to as Messianics. Thus, we bear the Saviour's title in one way or the other. And when you get to heaven He will write His name directly upon you (Revelation 3:12). The two men would also *eat a covenant meal*. At the very least they ate bread and wine (Joshua 9:12-15). We see this several times in the Old Testament and most vividly at the Last Supper. Finally, the two would *plant a memorial tree* and sprinkle it with the blood of the slain animal. Peter mentions the sacred New Covenant "tree" Yeshua planted for you, which He sprinkled with His own blood (1 Peter 2:24). Today, take heed to the way in which you walk with your Covenant Partner, Yeshua.

Jaffa Oranges & Jesus' Coming

"He shall cause them that come of Jacob to take root: Israel shall blossom and bud, and fill the face of the world with fruit." (Isaiah 27:6)

This verse makes a great piece of *poetry*, but it makes even greater *prophecy*. I first became aware of this prophecy while riding through one of Israel's huge orange orchards on a tour bus. In former days, Israel's fruit did not likely get exported further than the Middle East, but today her fruit can be found as far away as Australia. I'll never forget the day I was walking through a vegetable market of Sydney, Australia—the end of the world—when suddenly a mound of oranges got my attention. The oranges were labeled *Jaffa* and in much smaller print, *Suntina #3030*. I bought an orange and stuck the fruit label in my Bible right beside Isaiah 27:6.

Yes, exported Jaffa oranges do point to Messiah's second coming. Israel is also one of the world's leading citrus producers and exporters of grapefruits, tangerines and the pomelit. Isaiah prophesied that Jews would return from their long exile, settle back down in the land, and begin farming and exporting fruit all over the world. There's hardly a fruit that doesn't grow in their heaven-blessed land.

Isaiah predicted a stream of returning exiles, and so it is that every day an airplane lands in *Eretz Yishrael* with at least a handful of *olim* [pilgrims]—sometimes a whole plane full—who desire to make *aliyah* [become citizens]. Isaiah declares, "ye shall be gathered one by one, O ye children of Israel" (v.12). He also speaks of exiles returning out of dire necessity, "And it shall come to pass in that day, that the great trumpet shall be blown, and they shall come which were ready to perish in the land of Assyria" (v.13). Assyria is modern-day Iran where nearly 25,000 Jews currently live. Why are they still dwelling there today? They are awaiting the great trumpet blast.

Are you rapture-ready if the great trumpet were to sound today? Let today's prayer be a preparation for His imminent return.

The Trust Factor

"The LORD is good, a strong hold in the day of trouble; and he knoweth them that trust in him." (Nahum 1:7)

Repeatedly throughout Scripture, the faithful and obedient ones were asked to have implicit trust in Yahweh. When the enemy came in like a flood, sadly Israel was too often found trusting in nearby nations to protect them. The LORD pledged that He would allow Israel to experience the sad consequences of trusting in their "fenced walls" instead of trusting in Him (Deuteronomy 32:52). Whenever Israel trusted in the One True God for supernatural fortification, He made good on His holy promise.

When we examine the Paleo-Hebrew letters for the word *trust*, we get an amazing picture. The word is *khasah*. It is a primitive root meaning "to *flee* for protection; figuratively, to *confide* in." The first letter in khasah is *khet*, which is depicted by a *wall* and gives forth the idea of dividing. The next letter is *samekh*, which is depicted by a *thorn*, means protect. The final letter is a *hey*, which is depicted by a *man* with his *hands raised*, and it means look. When all three letters are interpreted together, they give the following concept of trust: "to get behind the *walls* belonging to the *man* who has sworn to *protect* you with the oath of his *raised hands*." In the Near East, if a person was seeking refuge from harm he could run into a man's tent or house and request protection. If the man swore his protection, the fleer was safe!

This exact same picture of trust is drawn in the New Covenant where you are implicitly told to look to "the man Christ Jesus" (1 Timothy 2:5). Those who sense eternal danger are to *flee* immediately to the fortified *walls* of this covenant *Man's* house for everlasting refuge. He stands at the door with both *hands raised* [and pierced] as an oath of allegiance to *protect* you (Luke 24:50). No wonder the psalmist exclaims, "For our heart shall rejoice in him, because we have trusted in his holy name" (Psalm 33:21). Today, meditate on Yeshua's raised hands on your behalf and go out into your busy day with joy and calm assurance.

317

Four Levels of Interpretation
Part 1

"I am the good shepherd: the good shepherd giveth his life for the sheep." (John 10:11)

Since God's Word is likened unto a "seed" in Luke 8:11, we should go on to discover the wonders of the four rich layers of soil it takes life in.

The surface level is *Pashat* meaning "plain, simple." This is the passage's *literal* interpretation and is derived through examining its literary, historical, and cultural contexts. A simple reading of the text usually sheds sufficient light and truth. Keeping a word or phrase within the context of the passage prevents it from becoming distorted.

The next level is *Remez*, which means, "hinting." A Scripture may hold *implications* of a deeper truth than what is found on the surface. The reader is called to look back within the text for a word or phrase's pre-established meaning. Zechariah 9:9 presents Messiah coming on a donkey, but his key words "rejoice O daughter of Zion" hint back to 2:10 where Zion's daughter rejoices because the coming One is the LORD.

Going further down, we come to the *D'rash* level meaning, "search." This involves reading into the text and searching the Bible—true *commentary*—for further comparison and application. Typology (Matthew 2:15) or allegory (Galatians 4:24) may be found, but not to the point where the literal, plain meaning is done away with.

The final level is *sod* meaning "deep, hidden." God's Word does hold secrets. This is why Solomon said, "It is the glory of God to conceal a thing: but the honor of kings is to search out a matter" (Proverbs 25:2). The word *mystery* appears 18 times in Scripture and each one is in the New Testament. Here all the mysteries of the Old Testament begin to unfold.

Today, ask God to help you study and experience fuller and deeper expressions of His infinite Word.

Four Levels of Interpretation
Part 2

"I am the good shepherd: the good shepherd giveth his life for the sheep." (John 10:11)

Let us take the four Hebraic hermeneutical principles discussed yesterday and apply them to the following verse to see what we might find. The *Pashat* level furnishes Messiah's *simple* claim to be a new shepherding figure over the spiritually impoverished nation. His pledge of unfailing commitment is an invitation for them to trust Him implicitly.

The *Remez* level *hints* that Yeshua is no ordinary Shepherd. He calls Himself good. Since previous texts within the Word of God already declare that "there is none that doeth good, no, not one," Yeshua must be strongly *hinting* of His sinless nature and divine origin (Psalm 14:3). Hints of the Shepherd of Israel's goodness and glory were laid out by the prophet long before: "Behold, the Lord GOD will come...and...He shall feed his flock like a shepherd" (Isaiah 40:10, 11).

The *D'rash* level sends out a *search* for a possible typology and discovers one—Messiah's most noble ancestor, David who voluntarily put himself in harm's way for one of his sheep (1 Samuel 17:34-35). David's further testimony presents a spectacular allegory. The commentator quotes David saying, "moreover, the LORD that delivered me out of the paw of the lion, and out of the paw of the bear, he will deliver me out of the hand of this Philistine" (v.37). After Messiah fought the "wolf" (John 10:12) and gave His life for the sheep, He was delivered from the clutches of the giant whose name is death. The Father raised Him back to life as if He never died!

The *Sod* level now unearths this verse's grandest *hidden* treasure. Yeshua is the very Shepherd spoken of in the 23rd Psalm—"the LORD." In our text, Messiah did not say He was "a" shepherd, but rather "the" Shepherd. For this cause, the valley of death is but a shadow to Him. He passes clear through it into the light of endless day, and His sheep gladly follow such a powerful and loving Protector.

Four Levels of Interpretation
Part 3

"The secret things belong unto the LORD our God: but those things which are revealed belong unto us and to our children for ever, that we may do all the words of this law." (Deuteronomy 29:29)

The four gospels occur under the dispensation of the Law, and Yeshua dies under its curse for mankind. It may be plausible that God has written the four gospels individually along the four levels of Hebrew Hermeneutics. Let's see.

Matthew appears to use the *D'rash* method more than the others do. He speaks of "fulfilled" Scripture more than John does, twice as much as Luke, and four times that of Mark. Matthew *searched* the Tanakh repeatedly to see how events of Messiah's ministry compared to what was previously foretold. His search of Old Testament *commentary* usually led him to say, "that it might be fulfilled which was spoken of the Lord by the prophet." He makes midrashic applications in 2:15, 16-18 and 19-23.

Mark clearly writes on the *Pashat* level. H wrote in a vernacular style with an abundant use of sentences beginning with "and." The brevity of his gospel points to the fact that he wanted to make his narrative *simple* and *direct* to his non-Jewish readers.

Luke seems to favor the *Remez* approach. He *hints* back to history and eyewitness accounts that you might "know the certainty of" what happened (1:4). Concerning Messiah's inception, Luke 1:48 records Mary's Magnificat which *hints* at Hannah's prophecy of an anointed King (1 Samuel 2:10). Luke hints at Isaiah's description of the seven-fold Spirit resting upon young Yeshua (2:40, 52). Before Luke presents the parable of the vigilant widow, he gives us a *hint* to what it's about (18:1). Luke's use of the word parable(s) exceeds that of the other gospel writers. He must appreciate the way in which Yeshua *hints* through His proverbial speech.

John begins his gospel in typical *Sod* fashion speaking of Yeshua in *hidden* ways such as the Word of God, the Light of the World and the Bread of Life. Today, may the Spirit speak to your heart through the wonders of His Word.

The Great Rolling Away

"And they said among themselves, Who shall roll us away the stone from the door of the sepulchre? And when they looked, they saw that the stone was rolled away: for it was very great." (Mark 16:3-4)

Everything about Yeshua is great in Mark's gospel! It was customary for the Son of God to rise up a great *while* before day (1:35), to pray and then to have a great *multitude* (3:7) following Him throughout the day to hear His gracious words. He alone was able to speak to a great *storm* of wind (4:37) and bring about a great *calm* (4:39). Yeshua was constantly doing great *things* (5:19) that brought about great *astonishment* (5:42). The great *Physician* (2:17) often told His healed patients to tell no man, but instead, "a great *deal* they published it" (7:36). On behalf of the poor, Yeshua tried to level the playing field with those who had great *possessions* (10:22). The Son of Man also inspired His followers by speaking of His majestic return in the clouds with great *power* and *glory* (13:26).

After such a great ministry and dying in such great agony—where the sun was greatly darkened and the earth greatly shaken—would we expect to find anything less than a great stone sealing the Messiah's tomb? When the women found the stone rolled away, that was a great burden removed (Mark 16:3). At that moment, what they didn't realize was that an even greater burden had been rolled away—the debt-load of their sins! The Son of God "was delivered for our offences, and was raised again for our justification" (Romans 4:25).

The rolled-away stone at Golgotha is a beautiful token revealing how God has greatly *rolled away* our sins. At Gilgal, Yahweh said to Israel, "This day have I rolled away the reproach of Egypt from off you" (Joshua 5:9). Well, here is the spiritual connection between these two holy places. In Hebrew Gilgal means "a *wheel;* by analogy, a *rolling* thing," and Golgoltha means "a skull." Just below this rocky, round and rolling hilltop, your sins were rolled away forever. Take time today to praise your great Saviour thoroughly for this great thing He has done!

Got Heart Burn?

"And they said one to another, Did not our heart burn within us, while he talked with us by the way, and while he opened to us the scriptures?" (Luke 24:32)

When the risen Messiah first came alongside these two downcast men headed to Emmaus He inquired of their sad countenance (v.17). They had yearning hearts, but the three full days Messiah predicted He would be in the grave had elapsed. A golden day had since dawned, and most of His followers were missing out on the excitement. Their hearts should have no longer been yearning but burning.

The promises of God are sometimes so amazing that we just stand back somewhat in disbelief. If He said to them, "I will arise in three days," then why weren't they back in Jerusalem? And what's the matter with *us*? When He says, "I will uphold thee," why do we instead hold back confidence in Him? When He says, "forgive," why do we forget to do it? When He says, "I will come again," why do we count the years instead of the days? In the Saviour's absence, prayer *to Him* and reading Scripture *about Him* will keep our hearts burning brightly *for Him*.

The only other verse in the New Testament where *heart* and *burn* appear together is when a scribe quoted to Yeshua the Torah's command on the degree to which our hearts should burn for God. The scribe said, "And to love him with all the *heart*, and with all the understanding, and with all the soul, and with all the strength, and to love his neighbor as himself, is more than all whole *burnt* offerings and sacrifices" (Mark 12:33). Here we find that if our hearts are burning properly for our Father they will also burn brightly for our fellow man. We will seek the good of the gospel for each and every one.

Today, draw close to God's unchanging Word and gain heart and strength from it. After drawing close to God and His Word, draw close to your neighbor or even a stranger. Take your burning heart to that person and with the Spirit's help show them the Saviour's burning love for them.

Faith, Courage & Loyalty

"There was...a...priest named Zacharias...and his wife was of the daughters of Aaron, and her name was Elisabeth. And they were both righteous before God, walking in all the commandments and ordinances of the Lord blameless. And they had no child, because that Elisabeth was barren, and they both were now well stricken in years." (Luke 1:5-7)

In his book entitled *52 Bible Lessons*, William Rodgers makes this note: "Luke begins the Messiah story with familiar Hebrew themes of *faith, courage,* and *loyalty* to God; all to be woven later throughout the narrative fabric." Let's examine these three Hebrew themes using Luke's opening story.

There was no lapse of *faith* in Zachariah and Elizabeth for their testimony was that they were both righteous before God. Their *loyalty* to God also couldn't be put into question because it says they were blameless in carrying out His commandments. However, when a call to take *courage* suddenly arose, Zachariah staggered. It was his lot to burn incense inside the Temple, and of all the places an angel could have possibly been standing when Zachariah went in, he was at the altar of incense where Israel's prayers went up daily. God was ready to reward the couple's long-running faith and loyalty. That's why the angel said, "Thy prayer is heard; and thy wife Elisabeth shall bear thee a son" (v.13). Even though Zachariah was expressly told that his son would possess the *courageous* spirit of Elijah, he himself lacked personal courage to act upon the good news. His reasoning: "I am an old man, and my wife well stricken in years" (v.18). He asked the angel for a token, but he got one he wasn't expecting—his speech was taken away. Perhaps his hearing was taken also because "they made signs to" him what the child's name should be (v.62).

God calls for strong attributes of *faith, courage* and *loyalty* to be active in your daily life. When one or more of these attributes aren't as active in your life as God desires, He may give you a nudge. Today, pray for the Spirit's help in any one of these areas where you may be lacking.

Yeshua—the Alpha & Omega

"Thus saith the LORD the King of Israel, and his redeemer the LORD of hosts; I am the first, and I am the last; and beside me there is no God." (Isaiah 44:6)

Like two pillars of truth, Yahweh repeats this creed in Isaiah 48:12. The Almighty seems to glory in this very descriptive, self-appointed title, yet in the Book of Revelation, Yeshua HaMashiakh bears this same title repeatedly. When He returns no one will be confused as to His infinite power and illustrious position within the Godhead. His unveiling will prove Him to be our perfect, undiminished Deity.

Yeshua says to John for the first time, "I am Alpha and Omega, the beginning and the ending" plainly declaring that He is "the Almighty," that is to say, *El Shaddai* (Revelation 1:8). When He says, "I am Alpha and Omega...What thou seest, write in a book, and send it unto the seven churches," He is revealing Himself as Author of Holy Scripture (1:11). When He proclaims, "I am the first and the last: I am he that liveth, and was dead; and, behold, I am alive for evermore," He discloses the fact that He alone possesses the keys of hell and of death (1:17, 18). The next time He claims to be "the first and the last," He reveals that He is the omniscient One saying, "I know thy works" (2:8, 9). Near the end of John's vision Yeshua says, "I am Alpha and Omega, the beginning and the end" (21:6). In this one verse He reveals that He is the One Who quenches men's thirst as the Fountain of Life and proudly proclaims, "I will be his God, and he shall be my son." At the end of Yeshua's unveiling, He combines all the titles together saying, "I am Alpha and Omega, the beginning and the end, the first and the last" (22:13). Here He discloses that He is Judge of all the Earth for He says, "I come quickly; and my reward is with me, to give every man according as his work shall be" (22:12).

May you be refreshed in your mind and spirit today knowing that Yeshua is the infinite, infallible, illustrious *God of the Universe* forever and forevermore! Take confidence in Yeshua's all-sufficiency today.

Bearing Hebrew Fruit

Part 1

"But the fruit of the Spirit is love, joy, peace, longsuffering, gentleness, goodness, faith, meekness, temperance: against such there is no law." (Galatians 5:22)

There are nine different aspects of the Spirit's fruit bearing in our lives. They seem to stem outward in three triune clusters, but we want to examine each individual manner of fruit from its Hebrew word and from its first usage.

Love comes from the word *aw-hab* and means "affection." The very first time it appears it has to do with Abraham's love for his only son Isaac (Genesis 22:2). This greatly typifies God's love for His only begotten Son. The first time love is used in relation to man and God is in Exodus 20:6 where love for Him is accompanied by keeping His commandments. May you show your love for Him today by doing exactly that!

Joy comes from *sim-khah* and means "glee." Its root, *saw-makh*, means to *brighten* up. The first time joy is used has to do with the manner in which we are to serve the LORD God (Deuteronomy 28:47). Times of sadness will undoubtedly come, but the steadfast sign of any true believer is a bright face. If a child of God doesn't possess authentic joy, then what does a lost person have to gain? Joy should not diminish because of suffering. Messiah had joy set before Him in the form of a cross (Hebrews 12:2). May Yeshua's joy shine through your darkness today.

Peace is translated from *shalom* and is first presented to us in Genesis 15:15 where God tells Abraham that he will be *safe* and *well* when he departs this life. Having perfect *peace* begins at salvation, not in the cemetery! If you're afraid to live the Christian life, you will not have very much confidence when it comes time to die a Christian death. After the Spirit applies the blood to your soul, He accompanies this with divine assurance: "The Spirit itself beareth witness with our spirit, that we are the children of God" (Romans 8:16). The Bible also gives you peace and assurance. May you enjoy much peace as you read God's Word today.

Bearing Hebrew Fruit

Part 2

Longsuffering is comprised of two words—*aw-rek* and *ah-feem*. Together they literally mean "slow nostrils." When a person gets very upset, their nostrils flare as they begin to breathe irregularly. This person is not really in control of their emotions; rather, his emotions are controlling him. Since the heat of anger and fire of retaliation burn so readily, the believer should breathe slowly, stay calm and delay his anger. The opposite of longsuffering is being short-tempered. Solomon said, "He that is soon angry dealeth foolishly" (Proverbs 14:17). The first time *longsuffering* appears in the Bible, Yahweh proclaims it is one of His main attributes before Moses; therefore, to be longsuffering is to be like God (Exodus 34:6). This day will likely provide you with an opportunity to become soon angry, so pray early on that the Spirit might bear the attribute of longsuffering through you if the need arises.

Gentleness comes from the word *an-aw-vah*, and it means "condescension." The first appearance of gentleness is where David says of the LORD, "thy gentleness hath made me great" (2 Samuel 22:36). He is so impressed with Yahweh's condescension that he repeats the compliment in Psalm 18:35 and prefaces it by saying, "thy right hand hath holden me up." The Son of God came down on our level and greatly lowered Himself for our benefit. Let us do the same for others and esteem them better than ourselves (Philippians 2:3). By lowering yourself beneath another like a servant, you will lift them up emotionally and hold them up spiritually. By becoming small in your own eyes, you will become great in God's eyes. Today, condescend to someone who least expects it.

Goodness in Hebrew is the word *tobe*. Its identical root word means "good." All believers testify that God is a good God. By this, we mean that He is not a vindictive God. "And Jethro rejoiced for all the goodness which the LORD had done to Israel" (Exodus 18:9). Live out the goodness of God today by being good and doing good whenever and to whomever possible.

Bearing Hebrew Fruit

Part 3

Faith in Hebrew is the word *eh-moon* and it means "established or trustworthy." God views Faith's first mention in the Bible as a sorely lacking quality among His covenant ones (Deuteronomy 32:20). Faith's twin is *faithful*. The Hebrew word is *aw-man* and it means, "to build up or support." Faithfulness was a treasured quality found in God's leading servant, Moses. He attempted to build up national support for God's holy laws. Yahweh placed Moses as overseer of His earthly affairs and said that he was "faithful in all mine house" (Numbers 12:7). We are to be trustworthy pillars in Messiah's house, helpful in building up the faith of weaker saints, as well as fostering faith among the lost who have no other spiritual support structure. Make this your holy aim today.

Meekness is derived from the word *an-vah* meaning "mildness." It is first used regarding Moses who was mightily infused with power and authority (Numbers 12:3). With Moses in mind, meekness cannot therefore imply weakness. To be mild is to be temperate and not extreme. Believers are to use the authority and power given them as children of the Most High God, but not parade it around with a "look-at-me" kind of attitude. Ask the Spirit to help you be mild mannered today.

Temperance means self-control. Solomon counsels young people to learn restraint and to be mindful of their conduct at all times. He says, "keep thy father's commandment, and forsake not the law of thy mother: Bind them continually upon thine heart, and tie them about thy neck" (Proverbs 6:21). When Solomon suggests fastening biblical principles to your heart, he speaks figuratively. But when he suggests tying it around your neck, he is speaking literally of an endearing Near East custom where a person would take a loved one's vows, write them down on parchment, fold it up into a small square, encase it in metal or leather and wear it proudly on a necklace. Tangible reminders (tokens) are good, but if the Spirit hasn't already written God's holy laws on your heart, His nine different spiritual fruits can never fully blossom in your life.

The House of Mercy

Part 1

"Now there is at Jerusalem...a pool, which is called in the Hebrew tongue Bethesda, having five porches. In these lay a great multitude of impotent folk, of blind, halt, withered, waiting for the moving of the water." (John 5:2-3)

This pool was located just outside Jerusalem's northern city walls. Its original construction in the 8th century BC was simplistic. It was a reservoir in the Beth Zeta Valley and was made to catch winter rains that could be conveyed into the city via a channel. Centuries later, it was enclosed with five porticos that provided adequate shelter for its many users and qualified it to be called a house. In time, invalids lingered the longest. Yahweh would seasonally dispatch a heavenly servant to step down into the waters and stir them, "whosoever then first after the troubling of the water stepped in was made whole of whatsoever disease he had" (v.4). Because of this reoccurring miracle, the edifice took on the name House of Mercy.

The Aramaic word for grace or mercy is *hesda*. Its Hebrew counterpart *khesed* means *kindness*. The House of Mercy stayed filled with kindred souls who found little pity or mercy elsewhere. At the Mercy House, hopes were higher for those closest to the edge of the water, except for a certain man who had an infirmity 38 years. He evidently lay there with his bed unable to move (v.5). In this man's condition, he needed extra grace and mercy. Yeshua, the embodiment of mercy, was soon to pass by, and He was the one Whom needy souls *always* called the "Son of David" if they needed His special brand of mercy (Mark 10:47).

Are you that committed to a soul in need or at least briefly available to stir such a soul to trust in God's saving grace and sin-healing mercy?

The House of Kindness
Part 2

"When Jesus saw him lie, and knew that he had been now a long time in that case, he saith unto him, Wilt thou be made whole?" (John 5:6)

Within the House of Mercy, this poor man sought to receive a little extra kindness or he would never see a normal life again. The Great Physician arrived on the scene with requisite and remedying compassion. The feeble man answered Yeshua's question not knowing who He was. He replied, "Sir, I have no man, when the water is troubled, to put me into the pool: but while I am coming, another steppeth down before me" (v.7). The paralytic's skepticism quickly vanished as the Physician's healing power coursed through his very being with the accompanying words, "Rise, take up thy bed, and walk" (v.9). Like Israel who wandered in the wilderness for 38 years, this man was finally brought into the place of blessing. His patient waiting was wonderfully rewarded.

Though Scripture does not reveal the man's name, he was certainly known by name among the many other infirm, if not most of them. After catching their breath, those nearest this miracle must have begun to cry out for the same level of kindness to be shown upon them; but according to the miracle, only one could be made whole. Even though a multitude was in that place, Yeshua "conveyed himself away" (v.13). In contrast, the Son of God later extended His unparalleled mercy and kindness to the whole house of Israel and a world that was stricken with sin. At Golgotha He "bowed His head and gave up the ghost" (John 19:30). In Hebrew, the word for "bow" is *khasad*. This is the root word of *khesed*, which means, "to be *kind*." No greater kindness can ever be shown than Yeshua's agonizing death on the cross.

Today, focus on being kind to others. This may come more naturally for friends or family, but be on the lookout for further opportunities to show pity and demonstrate kindness towards those whom you barely know.

Thanksgiving—a Jewish Holiday?

"When ye have gathered in the fruit of the land, ye shall keep a feast unto the LORD seven days." (Leviticus 23:39)

We know that the American concept of Thanksgiving came from the Pilgrims, but from where did they get it? From the Bible. The Puritan immigrants were very devout, and their completely fresh start allowed them to pattern some of their ways after biblical Israel. In their zeal they even considered at one point making Hebrew the national language of the new land. Look at some of the Ivy League university school seals. You'll find actual Hebrew lettering on them. Dartmouth's 1769 seal displays the Hebrew letters for EL SHADDAI. These shine down upon two feather-clad Indians walking and reading an open Bible in front of the stately institution. Yale boldly inscribed the Hebrew words for URIM V'TUMIM meaning "lights and perfections" within an open Bible. America's forbearers were indeed grateful to the God of Israel for their newly found freedom and manifold blessings. So they wanted to attribute a form of thanksgiving to Him that would honor Him as their covenant-keeping Provider.

The Pilgrims took note of Israel's autumn celebration of the Feast of Tabernacles, which was the ordained season to give thanks to God for all His bountiful blessings. Today, displays of Indian corn, squash and other late summer fruits and vegetables are a reflection of the ancient, required offerings the Israelite pilgrims once brought up to Jerusalem for their annual festival. The LORD reminded His people saying, "when ye have gathered in the fruit of the land, ye shall keep a feast unto the LORD seven days" (Leviticus 23:39).

Don't let the TV or the turkey steal the show this coming Thanksgiving Day! Rather, as the doxology says, "Let all creatures here below praise God, from whom all blessings flow." Thanksgiving is a holy day, but it is spelled *holiday*. Make this year's Thanksgiving Day a holy day and fill it with as much thanksgiving and gratefulness as possible.

What Has It Cost You?

"And Gad came that day to David, and said...Go up, rear an altar unto the LORD in the threshingfloor of Araunah the Jebusite." (2 Samuel 24:18)

David wasted no time in carrying out the plan. When Araunah saw the Judean king coming with his servants he knew something monumental was about to transpire. Araunah curiously enquired about David's coming. David's response was swift: "To buy the threshingfloor of thee, to build an altar unto the LORD, that the plague may be stayed from the people" (v.21). The Jebusite king not only generously offered his land as a gift, but also his oxen and their wooden implements for the sacrificial fire. Araunah went beyond the call of duty, but David couldn't accept the gracious gift. He said, "Nay; but I will surely buy it of thee at a price: neither will I offer burnt offerings unto the LORD my God of that which doth cost me nothing" (v.24).

David paid the Jebusite king six hundred shekels of gold by weight for the prime hilltop real estate (1 Chronicles 21:25). We often offer God things that have cost us something; however, very little discomfort was felt in the process. It's a human tendency to give in a way that doesn't rearrange your life. Sometimes it's good to give to the point where you know your lifestyle has been somewhat altered. You can't compare your gift with any other person's. The amount of money you made in one hour in an air-conditioned business transaction, may have in contrast, taken another saint all day to earn while he was standing on concrete in a hot warehouse wielding steel with arthritic pain.

The LORD loves sacrificial giving, whether it's your time, talents or your *treasures*. We don't always have to give to the point of robbing ourselves, yet it is well pleasing to God to offer Him our very best. Ask God to measure your heart today so that you can more perfectly measure your next gift.

The Ephod of God

"And David said to Abiathar the priest, Ahimelech's son, I pray thee, bring me...the ephod. And Abiathar brought...the ephod to David." (1 Samuel 30:7)

Upon returning to Ziklag David and his warriors discovered it burned and pillaged by the Amalekites. Even their families had been taken into captivity. Instinct should have immediately sent them running to recover their families, right? No. David had to run it past God first. John Wesley says, "David was sensible of his former error in neglecting to ask counsel of God by the ephod, when he came to Achish, and when he went out with Achish to the Battle; and his necessity now brings him to his duty, and his duty meets with success."

The ephod was the high priest's signature garment, an apron-like vest that displayed the securely sewn breastplate. Behind the breastplate was a pouch containing two stones that may have been used for yes or no answers. Whether David actually put it on cannot be known for certain, but he did ask Yahweh with heart and soul, "Shall I pursue after this troop? shall I overtake them? And he answered him, Pursue: for thou shalt surely overtake them, and without fail recover all" (v.8).

Even though this curious ephod *is not* presently available to you, the same God Who led and guided David *is* (Hosea 3:4). David himself gives you this assurance. He writes of Yahweh's watch-care: "For this shall every one that is godly pray unto thee in a time when thou mayest be found: I will instruct thee and teach thee in the way which thou shalt go: I will guide thee with mine eye" (Psalm 32:6, 8). David's son adds, "In all thy ways acknowledge him, and he shall direct thy paths" (Proverbs 3:6). You see, if you love God and seek to please Him daily—which includes confessing sin—then you can't go wrong. When you bring God into the picture at any given time, you are placing the outcome in His hands. That doesn't mean you ask God to bless your pre-chosen steps; rather, you should ask God to guide your steps along the path He has chosen. Let Him be your eyes today!

Mission Possible

"If ye have faith as a grain of mustard seed, ye shall say unto this mountain, Remove hence to yonder place; and it shall remove; and nothing shall be impossible unto you." (Matthew 17:20)

Lord Yeshua lays out the most impossible task one would ever dare attempt—to move a mountain with words. Even so, He says that it can be done, but not by human will and effort. Something way beyond our normal powers is required to accomplish such a feat. Messiah calls it faith, and we're told that God has "given to every man the measure of faith" (Romans 12:3).

Does it take great faith to move mountain-sized problems in your life? No, Yeshua says that you need only a little faith. A little child's faith believes that his parent can do anything, and sometimes a child actually asks for it to be done. You see, a child is incapable of adult reasoning; therefore, he acts on his rationale—believing only in the possible.

When God brings a slave-holding nation like Egypt to its knees, He does it with a little old man and a little stick (Exodus 4:2). When God defeats an innumerable army like the Midianites, He does it with a small band of men with little rams' horns (Judges 7:16). When God wants to take down a ten-foot giant, He sends a little lad with pebbles. Even still, in these three examples only the lad went out in faith. The other two adults went out because God gave them no choice in the matter.

What mountain is in your way today? Unemployment, a mean boss, a nasty co-worker, a besetting sin, worry or depression? Don't worry! Your mountain is not too big for God to move: "For with God nothing shall be impossible" (Luke 1:37). He just asks you to pray in faith believing. Be reminded that He will always act on your behalf but not always on your *behest*—your command, dictate or mandate.

Today, don't stare at your mountain. Stare at your mighty Messiah for He forms mountains and takes them down at will.

333

Success!

"Behold my servant, whom I uphold; mine elect, in whom my soul delighteth; I have put my spirit upon him...He shall not fail nor be discouraged, till he have set judgment in the earth." (Isaiah 42:1, 4)

The word *servant* appears 226 times in Scripture. That's a lot! Not all servants mentioned were successful, nor desired to be. Those that did succeed did so after much failure, but there was One Who never failed. His name is Yeshua. The Father chose Him, sustained Him, delighted in Him and empowered Him. The Father is so proud of His incredible Servant Son that He simply says, "Behold Him!"

What was this Servant sent to do? Convince Israel? No, not entirely. It was to convince the gentiles that they might make Him to be their Judge, their Governor, their Ruler and their Sovereign (v.1). How would He go about accomplishing this task? By shouting and demanding they make Him their King? No. The Bible says, "He shall not cry, nor lift up, nor cause his voice to be heard in the street" (v.2). Would He get discouraged when some did not understand His mandate? No. "A bruised reed shall he not break, and the smoking flax shall he not quench" (v.3). He holds out hope to all. In fact, hope is the banner around which He rallies the nations.

God proclaims with a smile on His face, "My Servant shall succeed!" —And He did! Do you want to succeed in your ministry wherever it may be and whatever it might involve? Do you want to be successful like Messiah? Well, start by deciding to steer away from discouragement. The enemy's attack begins in your mind. It all starts with some *disappointment* in your life that may lead to *discouragement*. Discouragement then leads to *despair,* which can also lead you to *doubt.* The next thing you know, your doubt has turned to total *disbelief* concerning God's ability to bring you to success. You come to an impasse, a road that has no outlet.

If you're faced with some disappointment today, get with God and He will turn it into an appointment with success.

𝓔litzur & the 𝓔lixir of 𝓛ife

"And whosoever will, let him take the water of life freely." (Revelation 22:17)

Since the dawn of civilization, alchemists have searched for a panacea, a cure-all for man's ills and woes. Such a mixture is called an *elixir*. This word is taken from the Arabic word *Al-Ikseer* meaning combination or mixture. Elixirs are to be taken orally, like cough syrups that guarantee to remedy one's persistent cough. Emperor Jiajing in the Ming Dynasty died from drinking a dosage of mercury, which was supposed to be an Elixir of Life. Throughout time, dissatisfied or skeptical customers have labeled elixirs to be nothing more than snake oil. The desire for eternal life has led to the legend of the Holy Grail or Cup of Christ. This legend purports that if one actually found it and drank from it, he would live forever. Although this is only a fanciful story, the reality is that an "elixir of life" does actually exist, but it's a spiritual formula.

God once caused life-giving water to flow out of a donkey's skeletal remains for Samson (Judges 15:19). He also caused water to flow from a prominent rock in the Arabian wilderness curing millions of thirsty Hebrews from their worries of death. After this miracle, God became familiarly known as Elitzur meaning "God of the Rock" (2 Samuel 22:47).

Paul wrote that the Israelites "did all drink the same spiritual drink: for they drank of that spiritual Rock that followed them: and that Rock was Christ" (1 Corinthians 10:4). This spiritual drink is still available to all, yet it can only produce the desired benefit when "mixed with faith" (Hebrews 4:2).

Yeshua is not only your Remedy for *eternal* anxieties but also *today's*. This morning, mix the water of God's Word with your faith and you'll be blessed for life.

ℐeshurun & ℐerusha

"The ways of Zion do mourn...all her gates are desolate...And from the daughter of Zion all her beauty is departed:" (Lamentations 1:4, 6)

Jeshurun is a beautiful, poetic name for all Israel meaning *upright* (Deuteronomy 33:5). Jeshurun was christened and crowned at birth. She was also calmly cradled within her Father's arms, and for her many fond memories made. But she "waxed fat and kicked...and forsook God" (32:15). As a result, the time came when Jeshurun began to be called by another name [in midrashic thinking], *Jerusha* meaning *possessed* or *occupied* (2 Kings 15:33). Judah, the heart of Israel, was shamefully sent away into captivity.

Her laughter quickly turned to lament as she tried to make her new home by the rivers of Babylon. There Jerusha found a bit of humble desert shade and began to pine: "there we sat down, yea, we wept, when we remembered Zion. We hanged our harps upon the willows in the midst thereof. For there they that carried us away captive required of us a song; and they...required of us mirth, saying, Sing us one of the songs of Zion" (Psalm 137:1-3). Since songs come deep from the heart, Jerusha found no ability to make a melody. She only managed to lament of her true love: "How shall we sing the LORD's song in a strange land? If I forget thee, O Jerusalem, let my right hand forget her cunning. If I do not remember thee, let my tongue cleave to the roof of my mouth; if I prefer not Jerusalem above my chief joy" (v.4-6).

The believer's life can slowly dwindle from a bright flame down to a flicker. The fire finally goes out, and the sad thing is that you didn't even notice it. This is when God steps in. But He does not bring you bitterness or barrenness; rather, He brings you opportunities for brokenness (Psalm 34:18). In due season, the King will fill your heart with a glad song as He heals it and restores it. Today, ask God to help you through your trials and trails and to store your repentant tears in His bottle (Psalm 56:8).

ꟿaking ꟾbba ꟼroud

"That we should be to the praise of his glory, who first trusted in Christ." (Ephesians 1:12)

Immediately after a faith-filled believer places all his trust in the Saviour, the heavenly Father places the Spirit of His Son within the newly adopted child. From that point onward the Father expects the child to abandon his basement full of bad habits and take up a new, lofty life—one that reflects the life of His flawless Son. It is for His pleasure, not ours, that we are created (Revelation 4:11).

The heavenly Father wants us to live daily for Him in such a way that as we interact with others He will be able to shout, "Hey, that's my boy!" or "That's my girl!" He wants us to make Him proud. Nothing makes a parent prouder than when his or her child does something good, noble, courteous, selfless or outstanding. The way a believer lives his life points to the One he is living for.

If we were honest, we would have to say that we don't always make Abba proud, do we? At times when we carelessly err, we do the opposite of bringing Him praise; instead, we bring Him sorrow. Instead of lifting His countenance, we lower it. Even so, the wonders of His love remain steadfast. He would never disown us because He has paid so dearly for us.

Paul says that when we heard the gospel of our salvation, believed it, and trusted completely in it, we were immediately sealed with the Holy Spirit (v.13). He goes on to inform us that the Holy Spirit's inwardly abiding presence is the guarantee or down payment that we hold as a promise until we inherit our new bodies. He also adds that this will be "to the praise of his glory" (v.14). The Father longs for us to have a redeemed body like the Saviour, but we must wait for that day.

The truth is we cannot live a perfect life here and now. It is impossible due to the fact that we live in unredeemed bodies. However, we should strive to make Papa as proud as possible because He picked us out of the crowd for His name's sake.

When Little is Much

"And Jesus sat over against the treasury, and beheld how the people cast money into the treasury: and many that were rich cast in much. And there came a certain poor widow, and she threw in two mites." (Mark 12:41, 42)

Little is much to God when *your heart is big.* Israel's humble King was always quick to point out the value of a pure gift. He explained to His talmidim saying, "this poor widow hath cast more in, than all they which have cast into the treasury: for all they did cast in of their abundance; but she of her penury did cast in all that she had" (v.43-44). The widow's greatest treasure was not what was in her hands, but what was in her heart. Tithing is part of the Mosaic system of gift measuring. Paul says of the giver, "as he purposes in his heart, so let him give" (2 Corinthians 9:7). God no longer measures the size of your gifts, but your heart.

Little is much to God when *that's all you have.* The widow woman of Zarephath only had a "handful of meal...and a little oil in a cruse" (1 Kings 17:12), but that's all God needed with which to work. The impoverished gentile willingly gave her last bit of meal to Elijah. Not only did the Hebrew prophet receive it, Yahweh also received it as if it were a holy, Levitical meal offering.

Little is much to God when *it is mixed with faith.* A little lad had only five bread rolls and two tiny fish. Andrew didn't think too much of it as he compared it to the massive crowd of 15,000 hungry souls clutching their growling stomachs. Andrew minimized the child's freewill offering saying, "what are they among so many?" (John 6:9). The Master answered His faithless disciple in a way that must have left him humbled. The little lad left with a big thank you and became a hero.

As humans, we have our limitations, but as believers, we are never to think that God has any whatsoever. Like you would let a doctor place a stethoscope to your heart to make sure all is well, allow the Holy Spirit to check your spirit today. He will make the necessary heart-rate adjustments and then bless not only your gift, but also you as the giver.

When Bitter is Better

"The full soul loatheth an honeycomb; but to the hungry soul every bitter thing is sweet." (Proverbs 27:7)

If any person knew what it was like to be full and satisfied, it was King Solomon, but his satisfaction never seemed to satisfy him. What he learned in the end was that having less is somehow much better than having everything. Having everything leaves nothing to be desired. It only leaves misery. Solomon grew up in the palace with a silver spoon in his mouth and a golden cup in his hand. Peering out his lattice window, Solomon probably found measurable contentment in viewing the lower class ranks of his day being satiated with just a simple meal, a bland soup or even the taste of well water. At the end of the day, Solomon loathed his vast prosperity. What should have made him full only increased his inner emptiness.

Those who have everything seldom smile, but those who have little usually resonate with hope and their faces show it. To the hungry, even bitter (*maw-rah*) things somehow taste sweet (*maw-took*). Those who have everything in life struggle not only with satisfaction, but also with being grateful.

Ungratefulness is a bad trait to be found among God's people. John the Baptist said, "be content with your wages" (3:14). In Hebrews 13:5 Paul said to "be content with such things as ye have" and "having food and raiment let us be therewith content" (1 Timothy 6:8). The apostle experienced the bitterness of rejection, hatred, hunger, homelessness and imprisonment, yet he testified, "But I have all, and abound: I am full" (Philippians 4:18). The simple necessities of life were to him a sweet smell. Out of his bitter-filled life came his sweet-filled testimony: "I have learned, in whatsoever state I am, therewith to be content" (Philippians 4:11).

Can you say this right now? If you have been out of a job for any great length of time, you know that any line of work will satisfy. Today, ask God to help you make the most of your bitter situation. Remember, the joy of the Lord, and His sweetness, is your strength.

Ask, Seek, Knock

"Ask, and it shall be given you; seek, and ye shall find; knock, and it shall be opened unto you: For every one that asketh receiveth; and he that seeketh findeth; and to him that knocketh it shall be opened." (Matthew 7:7-8)

When Eliezer went to find a bride for his master's son Isaac, he placed a simple request before his master's God. At the well Eliezer *asked* Yahweh to give him an unmistakable sign (Genesis 24:12). The humble servant of Abraham *received* the answer he was looking for and returned home the next day with a wonderful bride for Isaac and a big smile for himself.

When Joseph went *seeking* his half-brothers on behalf of his aged father, he was met with perplexity at Shechem when the brothers weren't there. Yet, with God's timely intervention a certain man found Joseph wandering in the field and enquired of him saying, "What seekest thou?" When he responded, "I seek my brethren," he was confidently told that he would *find* them in Dothan (Genesis 37:15-16).

John the beloved was the last apostle to die, yet his brother James was the very first to go. Herod sought to kill Peter next, so he put him in prison until after Passover. "But prayer was made without ceasing of the church unto God for him" (Acts 12:5). They were *knocking* on heaven's door at this stage. If they had prayed for James, they were now pleading for Peter. God heard their incessant knocking and *opened* every door in the prison house until Peter was safely out. Then God sent an amusing token to the house of prayer. Peter arrived at the prayer meeting *knocking*, and Rhoda came to the door. When she found out that it was Peter, she excitedly forgot to open the door and instead ran back to tell the others. "Peter continued knocking" until they *opened* the door (v.16).

Sometimes God quickly gives you the answer for which you are *asking*. At other times, He shows up at a reasonable hour to help you find what you are *seeking*. But then there are those times when He pauses for a season to listen quietly to the repeated *knocking* sound of your desperate supplications. Today let Adonai hear the longings of your heart.

The Lamp of God's Assembly

"And being turned, I saw seven golden candlesticks; And in the midst of the seven candlesticks one like unto the Son of man," (Revelation 1:13-14)

At the time of Yeshua's revelation to Yohanan, the Temple no longer stood and its glorious solid-gold menorah had vanished into complete obscurity. God, however, had fashioned a new flaming candelabra to burn brightly before Him. The Saviour bent down and laid His hand on John saying, "the seven candlesticks which thou sawest are the seven churches" (v.20).

May we be reminded of the Church's source of light and life. The aged prophet saw "in the midst of the seven candlesticks one like unto the Son of man...and his eyes were as a flame of fire...And his feet like unto fine brass, as if they burned in a furnace" (1:13-15). The very fire of the Son's holy presence gives life to the lamp of God's assembly. This lamp stays lit because the Son walks "in the midst of the seven golden candlesticks" as would be expected of any temple dwelling priest (2:1).

The Great High Priest of heaven sends His holy reminder to His oil-supplied saints: "Remember therefore from whence thou art fallen, and repent, and do the first works; or else I will come unto thee quickly, and will remove thy candlestick out of his place, except thou repent" (Revelation 2:5). If Messiah removed His perfect light from Jerusalem's stone Temple, then He could just as easily remove that same light from New Covenant assemblies. Messiah admonishes each of us to burn fervently before Him and before a darkened world that knows nothing of His salvation light.

Is your lamp trimmed today or are you a bit dull in the way you burn because yesterday's soot encrusts you? Do you have a fresh supply of the Spirit's oil for the day ahead? In prayer today, ask the Holy Spirit to help you do your part as one small-illumined lamp in a very dark world.

341

December 8

A Wall of Grace

"But Noah found grace in the eyes of the LORD." (Genesis 6:8)

The Hebrew word for grace is *khane*, and it means "kindness, favor." This word comes from *khanan* meaning "to bestow, to have pity upon, to show mercy." *Khane* is made up of two Hebrew letters, *hket* and *nun*. When we bring back their ancient Paleo-Hebraic meanings, the main idea behind grace becomes more concrete. The letter *hket* depicts a wall and means divide. The *nun* depicts a seed and means continue. Thus, the word for grace pictures someone who *divides* from or shields another so he can *continue* prospering.

Grace isn't given to a person because he deserves it; then it would no longer be grace (Romans 11:6). God graciously allowed Noah to build a structure that would *divide* him and his family from the floodwaters so they could *continue* living. God's grace appeared next to Lot, Abraham's undeserving nephew. The angels airlifted Lot and his family to safety just outside Sodom and stood like a *dividing* wall between them and the doomed city. The angel told Lot not to stay in the plains but to *continue* up to the mountains. At that moment Lot said, "thy servant hath found grace in thy sight" (Genesis 19:19).

David, a man who committed adultery and murder, provides for us yet another example of God's grace that comes in the form of a protective wall. He said, "For the LORD God is a sun and shield: the LORD will give grace and glory" (Psalm 84:11). David knew that when his army's shields faced into the sun it blinded the enemy and prevented their advance. The Judean warrior speaks of Yahweh as One Who protectively *divides* him from his enemies so he can *continue* among the living.

As you have seen in these three examples, God's grace comes to the undeserving. Who can truly say that they are worthy of God's favor? Grace always comes because of God's willingness to give it, not our deserving to have it. According to Romans 8:31, you can leave your house with confidence today knowing that God's grace allows Him to be *unconditionally* for you.

Messiah's Name Kept Secret

"Listen, O isles, unto me; and hearken, ye people, from far; The LORD hath called me from the womb; from the bowels of my mother hath he made mention of my name." (Isaiah 49:1)

Many Jewish people naturally inquire, "If Jesus was the Messiah, then why wasn't his name predicted in Scripture?" Well, Isaiah wrote seven centuries prior to Messiah's first advent and told us that Messiah's covenant name would be kept secret until the time concerning His birth. This was already a standard custom among the Hebrews. Typically, children were not given a name until after being born (Luke 1:62). In Messiah's case, He was named at the time of His glorious conception.

Names in biblical days were not just to identify one person from the next; rather, they were often prophetic in nature and revealing of that person's very character or destiny. In the dispensation of time, an archangel was dispatched to earth that he might announce Messiah's entrance into the world, yet in a clandestine way. The messenger, Gabriel, was given express permission to reveal Messiah's anointed name only to two people—His parents. He used a beautiful play on words to describe the anointed Child's coming mission. Gabriel declared to Yosef, "and thou shalt call his name Jesus [*Yeshua*]: for he shall save [*yoshia*] his people from their sins" (Matthew 1:21).

Yeshua's name is a shortened Aramaic version of the formal Hebrew name Yehoshuah meaning, "Yehovah is Saviour." Yeshua was Jehovah incarnate just as Isaiah had wonderfully foretold. The Holy Spirit moved him to give Messiah the title *Emmanuel* meaning "God with us" (Isaiah 7:14). This speaks not only of Yeshua's nature, but also His destiny. When the Baby Messiah was fully formed, the virgin "brought forth her firstborn son; and he [Joseph] called his name" Yeshua (Matthew 1:25).

Many gentiles have never heard the name Jesus, nor have countless Jews heard the wonderful saving name of Yeshua, so take time today to share this *name above all names* with someone who does not know Him in a saving way.

343

Got Joy?

"And the angel said unto them, Fear not: for, behold, I bring you good tidings of great joy, which shall be to all people." (Luke 2:10)

Doctor Luke opens his gospel story with the greatest headlines of all time: "A Saviour is born, which is Christ, the Lord" (v.11). The joyous message the angels brought to the outcast shepherds was so joyous in scope that they foretold the news wouldn't stop being spread until it had reached *all* people. Messiah's goal was that the good news "be preached in his name among all nations" (Luke 24:47). Even in the dark days of the Great Tribulation when radio and television signals will be restricted in their capabilities (because of an irradiated atmosphere), an angel will fly across the globe having the everlasting gospel upon his lips to proclaim it unto every nation, kindred, tongue and people (Revelation 14:6). God doesn't want anyone to miss out on this fantastic opportunity.

What is it that is so special about this joyous news? Well, it is not only the vital information on how to obtain eternal life instantly, but also on how to obtain eternal joy instantly. Peter discovered Messiah's indwelling joy to be so incredible he could only describe it as unspeakable joy (1 Peter 1:8). Let's backtrack for just a moment to Luke's very first usage of the word joy (Luke 1:44). The teenaged Miraim, pregnant with Yeshua, went to visit her aged cousin Elisheva who was also pregnant. As soon as Miriam entered with a customary greeting, baby John kicked with joy in Elisheva's belly. Did you know that Luke both begins and ends his gospel with *joy*? As Messiah ascended into the heavens His followers "worshipped him and returned to Jerusalem with great *joy*" (Luke 24:52).

No matter what you're going through today, the joy of the Lord is available to you, and it alone is your strength (Nehemiah 8:10). Be strengthened today with the joy that the Spirit placed in you the day you were born again.

Hanukkah—a Miracle Season

"And it was at Jerusalem the feast of the dedication, and it was winter. And Jesus walked in the temple in Solomon's porch." (John 10:22-23)

Hannukah, like Christmas, should be a season of celebrating miracles, not myths. Neither of these festivals is mandated in the Bible but both nonetheless came about through the course of time.

Hanukkah draws its name from the Hebrew word for *dedication*. In 165BC, after three years of resistance against Greco-Syrian occupiers, Jewish warriors reclaimed Jerusalem and quickly began cleansing the Temple courts of pagan sun-god influences. In the process of reinstituting proper worship, tradition [myth] says that one day's supply of oil for the Menorah was found which burned for eight days till more could be made. Neither the 1st or 2nd Book of Maccabees records this event, but they did state that an eight-day feast was held. This was obviously a late observance of Tabernacles, which was the most celebrated event among the seven Feasts. Better late than never! It is ok to light your *Hannukiah*, but speak of the true "oil of joy" that gives off Messiah's "true Light" (Isaiah 61:3; John 1:9). And hold to Titus's helpful words: "Not giving heed to Jewish fables, and commandments of men, that turn from the truth" (Titus 1:14).

Most Christians aren't fully aware that Christmas is really based on pagan sun-god worship. Ancient mythology taught that Tammuz, the sun god, died on the winter solstice and was reborn three days later on the 25th of December. The Hebrews were guilty of honoring this pagan deity (Ezekiel 8:14-16). The Roman Catholic Church made sure it continued by holding a mass on the venerable day of the sun, December 25th. This Christ [Tammuz] mass became known as Christmas. Catholics also usually include some imagery of the sun along with icons of the cross. Peter warned against following "cunningly devised fables" (2 Peter 1:16). Much earlier, Jeremiah advised not to learn "the way of the heathen…For the customs of the people are vain: for one cutteth a tree out of the forest…with the ax. They deck it with silver and…gold" (Jeremiah 10:2-4).

The *nativity scene* wonderfully depicts Messiah's birth. Keep this central to this season of miracles and thank the Father for sending the true light of His only begotten Son.

The Shield of Faith

"Above all, taking the shield of faith, wherewith ye shall be able to quench all the fiery darts of the wicked." (Exodus 25:14-15)

The great gospel warrior Paul speaks of the most needed piece of armor in the spiritual battle arena—faith. The Greek word for shield means, "*door* shaped." Shields could not only be small, but also body length and rectangular like a door. This offered full protection against an oncoming barrage of arrows. Faith is a door that *opens* opportunities for God to work in our lives, but faith is also a door that we *go behind* to shield us from the enemy's destructive work.

In the first mention of shield God said "Fear not, Abram: I am thy shield" (Genesis 15:1). Here we discover that our shield is the very presence of God. We can't see Him, but by faith we can experience His protective power. When Abraham neglected to use his divine shield of faith in Abimelech's country, his wife Sarah was taken from him. When Deborah affirmed that there was not "a shield or spear seen among forty thousand in Israel," Shamgar went out by faith and slew 600 men with an ox goad (Judges 5:8). When David went out to battle Goliath, he threw off Saul's manmade armor and proceeded with Yahweh's shield of faith. David later wrote a song about God's sheltering power saying, "in him will I trust: he is my shield" (2 Samuel 22:3).

In its ancient pictorial form, the three-letter Hebrew word for shield, *magen*, draws a powerful picture for us. *Mem* means chaos; *gimel* means walk, and *nun* means continue. They reveal a person in the midst of *chaos* who *walks* through it and *continues*! Paul tells us how to walk through Satan's battlefield and continue standing, "by faith, not by sight" (2 Corinthians 5:7). Satan wants to separate you from your faith in God. The reason is not so that you will lose your salvation—that is impossible—but so that you will lose your certain advantage over him.

The star on David's shield blazed with faith. How does your faith shine in times of chaos, trouble or uncertainty? Ask the Spirit to empower you with great faith today. You'll probably need it.

Who Are the Weak?

"We then that are strong ought to bear the infirmities of the weak, and not to please ourselves." (Romans 15:1)

Paul was witness to the material prosperity of some churches scattered about the Mediterranean world. When he preached the gospel and established them in the faith, one of the main purposes he gave the church was to help those in need, particularly believers who were suffering in poverty and persecution. Paul described them as being infirm and weak. Does this not accurately describe the Persecuted Church who lives mainly in Africa, Asia and the Middle East? Churches in the West are financially strong but often forgetful that the persecuted ones would be pleased with some financial help. Paul pointed out an inherent flaw that needs our attention.

The apostle goes on to say, "Let every one of us please his neighbor for his good to edification" (v.2). Does not the Persecuted Church qualify as the prospering church's neighbor? Paul has already affirmed so. He makes his case saying, "For even Christ pleased not himself; but, as it is written, The reproaches of them that reproached thee fell on me" (v.3). The reproaches coming from millions of Islamists, Communists and Hindus fall as a constant barrage upon the heads of faithful believers throughout the world. By way of contrast, the reproach that falls upon the financially strong western church is their lack of concern for the Lord's faithful martyrs worldwide.

Paul, a persecuted preacher himself, admonishes us: "For whatsoever things were written aforetime were written for our learning, that we through patience and comfort of the scriptures might have hope" (v.4). The Persecuted Church has plenty of patience, yet needs plenty of comfort and hope. This may come in the form of medicine, winter clothing, school supplies, food and Bibles. Bibles are unwelcome or even outlawed in many countries, thus Scriptures need to be printed abroad and brought in.

Today, ask the Father to receive your financial gift for the cast-down believers and multiply it exceedingly on their behalf. Voice of the Martyrs is prepared to run into the fire with your holy offering.

December 14

Glowing Faces

"But we all, with open [unveiled] *face beholding as in a glass the glory of the Lord, are changed into the same image from glory to glory, even as by the Spirit of the Lord."* (2 Corinthians 3:18)

This chapter is Paul's New Covenant midrash on Moses' veil (Exodus 34:29-35). Moshe spent forty days in God's presence; the Hebrew word means *face*. When Moshe came down his face was aglow. This not only resulted from staring at God's glorious face, but also from staring at the gloriously fashioned law which God engraved with His own hand (31:18). When he came down, the people were afraid to approach Moshe and strongly urged him to veil his face.

The apostle tells us in verse 7 what we might not otherwise have known: that the Ten Commandments' reflective *glory faded* from Moshe's face. In verse 13, Paul also tells us that after Moshe's face stopped glowing he continued to wear his veil so that the people would not think less of God's glorious Law. In verses 14 and 15, the apostle uses Moshe's veil as a token of Israel's current blindness. He states that to this very day it is as if they willingly wear a thick veil when reading the Torah and cannot plainly see that its glory has faded away in light of Messiah's coming. Paul once had this problem himself. In verse 16, he does say that if Israel will only look to their glorious Messiah, He will lift that veil and take it from them as He has done for many, Paul himself being one example.

Torah scrolls are still highly revered and even paraded around in some Messianic congregations, but Paul says that this very thing is mankind's death sentence, his condemnation (v.9). Adhering to Mosaic Law will not change you, but adhering to Lord Yeshua will. The Son of God now stands firmly by His blood-sprinkled New Covenant, and it has an amazing heavenly glow—particularly in the first five books (v.6). Why don't you try lifting up this life-changing book at your next meeting?

Today, if you will *lift* it up, *live* by it and rely on the Spirit of the Lord, you will be changed a bit more into the likeness of the Lord.

Your Divine Repairman

"I will put none of these diseases upon thee, which I have brought upon the Egyptians: for I am the LORD that healeth thee." (Exodus 15:26)

In the preceding verses, Yahweh speaks of Israel's responsibility strictly to adhere to His commandments—to hear them, learn them and then perform them. God inspires His people to walk uprightly before Him, and in return to receive from Him all of His goodness. He boasts in His divine ability to *heal*. The Hebrew word is *rapha*, which means to mend or cure. The concept behind the word *rapha* is "to repair or make whole" which can be applied to a variety of situations.

Yehovah-Rapha is able to repair the worst of man's conditions whether they are related to the physical, mental or spiritual realm. Israel's Great Physician came to them in the form of their promised Messiah. He restored eyes that had gone blind, hands that had withered, legs that had gone limp, skin that had grown leprous, minds that had gone mad, souls that had become possessed, and bodies that had grown cold with death.

When Yeshua repaired people's sick bodies, this helped to repair families and restore widows' impoverished homes. But Messiah's main objective was to restore the nation spiritually which involved mending bruised spirits, broken hearts and battered souls. For this, a very special remedy was needed. The Healer would have to place Himself in a situation where He Himself would need to be healed. What a paradox, but it is true! At the beginning of His ministry, He read to the Pharisees from the Scroll of Isaiah, "Ye will surely say unto me this proverb, Physician, heal thyself" (Luke 4:23). If He healed Himself too early then we would *not* benefit from it. If the divine Healer healed Himself while on the cross, then we would remain *unchanged* and still be in our sin-sickness. However, Yeshua did heal Himself three days after dying for our sins—then He began healing us from within!

Michael Card says it like this: "When we in our weakness believed we were strong, He became helpless to show we were wrong." Today, thank Yeshua for taking all those awful stripes by which your sins are healed (Isaiah 53:5). Ask your divine Repairman to heal other areas of your life—perhaps from your sordid past. He can heal any hurt.

Shining Lights

"Do all things without murmurings and disputings: That ye may be blameless and harmless, the sons of God, without rebuke, in the midst of a crooked and perverse nation, among whom ye shine as lights in the world." (Philippians 2:14-15)

Paul, the proponent of the "new and living way" and the "more excellent way," uses three couplets in the two verses above. First he mentions *murmuring and disputing*—something that we more than occasionally engage in. The writer then compares this sort of behavior with that which best describes the unbelieving world—*crooked and perverse*. Between these two couplets of bad and worse, Paul zeros in on the believer's expected model performance—*blameless* and *harmless*.

The children of this world reflect darkness; but when the children of light display the same attributes that they do, such as complaining and arguing, then unbelievers lose their last glimmer of hope. With the help of his scribe, Paul penned this letter from a moldy, dark prison cell in Philippi. He must have had a very fond appreciation for the warmth and light of day, and perhaps this is why he chose to use *light* as a metaphor for the world's *hope*. James also knew that a wonderful source of encouragement to lost souls is when the adopted children of "the Father of Lights" shine as they were supposed to (James 1:17). Paul says that when we conduct ourselves in a godly way we shine like lights in the darkness.

With this in mind, let us completely do away with unbecoming behavior between saints and display the best we have for the lost who so desperately need to see the way to heaven more clearly. Paul explains that when we do, it is as "holding forth the word of life" to the lifeless (v.16).

Today, seek to let your light shine as brightly as possible whether in your work place, or wherever you are headed. Ask the Father to illuminate your good testimony.

Are You Still Breathless?

"Of which salvation the prophets have inquired and searched diligently, who prophesied of the grace that should come unto you:" (1 Peter 1:10)

It seems from the teachings of this New Covenant prophet that the Old Covenant prophets were "breathless" in their anticipation of the coming One Who, all by Himself, would change things for the better. Peter says that the former prophets steadfastly searched to discern the timeframe when Messiah would arrive "and the glory that should follow" (v.11). Peter also explains that since this long-awaited time has clearly arrived, "the angels desire to look in" on this new thing (v.12). Yes, even the angels of heaven are breathless to get a closer look at people like you who have received Spirit-life and immortality through the gospel of grace. You were breathless when you first got saved, but the question is, "Are you still breathless?"

This incredible new thing that once made prophets muse and angels now marvel Peter simply calls "the grace that should come." The fact that you never deserved what you now so wonderfully possess—namely, forgiveness and infilling—ought to make you overjoyed, ecstatic, bright-eyed and *breathless*! This is normally the feeling at the time of the new birth; it is something indescribable. Beyond making you breathless, the grace that has come unto you ought to make you more *devout*. Peter goes on to say, "As obedient children, not fashioning yourselves according to the former lusts in your ignorance: But as he which hath called you is holy, so be ye holy in all manner of conversation [behavior]" (v.14-15).

Today, if needed, ask God to help you get your enthusiasm back—your fire, your zeal, your wow! The Spirit of Grace will help you with your waning excitement and lacking devotion because He has such great plans for you! His aim is not to *drag* you along, but to *draw* you along! It is now your turn to give the world a true desire to want to know what makes you satisfied! If need be, take time today to get your awe and wonder back.

351

When Faith Faces Shipwreck

"Holding faith, and a good conscience; which some having put away concerning faith have made shipwreck:" (1Timothy 1:19)

Paul knew firsthand what it meant to be shipwrecked. He uses this event as a metaphor for *spiritual catastrophe*. You may not have abandoned your ship of faith just yet, but the hull has a crack, is taking on water fast, and you're standing on the bow's edge waiting to jump into this world's frigid waters. If you don't do something quick, you're sure to be treading water soon. Faith may seem easy to rely on when all is going well, but when life's circumstances begin to overwhelm you; this is not the time *to let go*. This is the time for your faith *to let God* do the unusual! Here are some vital things to do when you feel a spiritual shipwreck coming on.

First, *throw out your anchor* before you hit any more rocks! Paul calls this an "anchor of the soul" and says that it is your best hope (Hebrews 6:18-19). Decide here and now that you're not going to be pushed any further into Satan's snares and spiritual decline. Next, *pray for favorable weather*. Paul says that prayers and intercessions should be made "that we may lead a quiet and peaceable life" (1Timothy 2:2). Prayer changes things, so ask the Spirit to improve things by sending some help your way—a friend, a neighbor, a verse of Scripture or a song in the night.

Next, *look for fair lands*. Paul speaks of saints that face some severe storms in life. Here is what he has to say about them: "But now they desire a better country, that is, an heavenly: wherefore God is not ashamed to be called their God: for he hath prepared for them a city" (Hebrews 11:16). The day you got saved is the day your gospel ship set sail; and until it arrives on heaven's bright shores there are more storms to come. This means you need to develop sailor's blood and toughen up.

Most importantly, *draw close to the Captain* of your salvation; He's standing behind the ship's helm (Hebrews 2:10). Your present faith may not be what it should, but the Captain's courage will strengthen your faith hour by hour.

The 10 Lost Tribes Myth

"For the Levites left their suburbs and their possession, and came to Judah and Jerusalem: for Jeroboam and his sons had cast them off from executing the priest's office unto the LORD:" (2 Chronicles 11:14)

A myth is "an unproved or false collective belief." Scripture proves that there is another side to the 10 Lost Tribes theory. Tracking down the *unrepentant* members of Israel is a lost cause, but tracking the remnant is a different story. The *unrepentant* Israelites did go into captivity, and their whereabouts were known up to the first century AD, but the fact of the matter is, Israel was never completely lost because a *remnant* of every northern tribe returned to the south, the land of Judah 250 years before the Assyrian captivity even took place. The Levites returned first. "And after them out of all the tribes of Israel such as set their hearts to seek the LORD God of Israel came to Jerusalem" (v.16). This included "Ephraim, Manasseh, and Simeon…in abundance" (2 Chronicles 15:9).

Additionally, at the time of the Assyrian invasion [722 BC] Hezekiah sent letters calling for those who had "escaped out of the hand of the kings of Assyria" to return to their spiritual home in Jerusalem (2 Chronicles 30:6). One hundred and twenty years when Judah went into Babylonian captivity [606 BC], remnants of the other ten tribes went with them. This is why Jeremiah speaks of Yahweh bringing the scattered sheep of Israel again to his habitation (Jeremiah 50:17-19). Why was Yahweh determined to bring all twelve tribes back home? Because He planned on establishing His New Covenant with them. (Jeremiah 31:31). A short time after Persia conquered Babylon [536 BC], Artaxerxes made a decree that "all they of the people of Israel" were free to join Ezra to go up to Jerusalem. (Ezra 7:12-13). From that very time forward, Judah became synonymous with Israel. This is why Peter addressed his Pentecost sermon to all the house of Israel (Acts 2:36).

Whenever God speaks to your heart and says, "You have gotten off the path of righteousness, get back in the way," you had better repent and do it quickly. Today, praise the LORD for refusing to lose you. Rehearse His faithfulness in tracking you and calling you back home unto Himself.

353

What's in the Name Saviour?

Part 1

"And Jehoahaz besought the LORD, and the LORD hearkened unto him: for he saw the oppression of Israel, because the king of Syria oppressed them. And the LORD gave Israel a saviour." (2 Kings 13:3-5)

The Bible's first usage of the word *saviour* pertains not to God, but to man. Nehemiah makes note of the many saviours that were sent to Israel saying, "in the time of their trouble, when they cried unto thee, thou heardest them from heaven; and according to thy manifold mercies thou gavest them saviours, who saved them out of the hand of their enemies" (Nehemiah 9:27).

The saviours acted as wartime generals, but afterwards were made peacetime judges called *shoftim*. "Nevertheless the LORD raised up judges, which delivered them out of the hand of those that spoiled them...And when the LORD raised them up judges, then the LORD was with the judge...all the days of the judge...And it came to pass, when the judge was dead, that they returned, and corrupted themselves" (Judges 2:16; 18-19). Here we see the key to Israel's salvation. It was found in the life of their anointed saviour/judge—whoever he happened to be. As long as the saviour/judge was alive, Israel was safe. Yeshua is Israel's everlasting **Saviour/Judge**. He expressed this saying, "the Father...hath committed all judgment unto the Son" (John 5:22). To demonstrate this truth, He graciously released some people of their legally binding sin-debt and signified it once with a token—making a lame man rise up and walk (Mark 2:9).

The word saviour in Hebrew is *moshiah*. It gave rise to the word *moshiakh* meaning "anointed one" which is translated Messiah. The root of *moshiah* is *yasha*, which means, "to be *open, wide, free*; by implication, to be *safe*." Did not our New Testament Saviour paint a lovely picture of the believer's safety when He said, "I am the door: by me if any man enter in, he shall be saved [*safe*], and shall go in and out, and find [*wide-open, free*] pasture" (John 10:9)? Today the Saviour/Judge has set you free! He lives forever and will keep you safe from harm and self-corruption. So go out in joy and be led forth with His peace tucked away in your bosom.

What's in the Name Saviour?

Part 2

"I bring you good tidings of great joy, which shall be to all people. For unto you is born this day in the city of David a Saviour, which is Christ the Lord." (Luke 2:11-12)

Yeshua of Nazareth was no ordinary man and certainly no ordinary saviour; therefore, this Saviour's birth came with an unusual token. He was wrapped in grave clothes and placed in a stone box, a manger. This greatly prefigured His atoning death and entombment—a strange way indeed to save a captive people! About one month after the Saviour's birth there was a second token given of His death, yet this time it was a token of His resurrection also. An aged priest named Simeon declared, "Behold, this child is set for the fall and rising again [Gr. *anastasis*; a *standing* up again; literally, a resurrection] of [among] many in Israel; and for a sign [token] which shall be spoken against" (Luke 2:34).

Israel needed a great saviour/priest, one who could offer an eternal sacrifice for their many sins. Yeshua became that **Saviour/Priest** and even *offered* Himself for all of our sins—past, present and future. He was *crucified* for them and *buried* with them, but He couldn't be an eternal Saviour if He remained dead. We would stand in eternal jeopardy. So the Father raised Him from the dead, paraded Him home and seated Him at His own right hand as Melchezidek Priest over His people (Psalm 110:1). How's that for a Saviour/Priest!

The truth is your eternal salvation does not at all depend on whether *you live* for the Saviour; rather, your salvation depends upon whether the Saviour *lives for you* (Philippians 1:6). We know that He does because God's word tells us so: "But this man, because he continueth ever…is able also to save them to the uttermost that come unto God by him, seeing he ever liveth to make intercession for them" (Hebrews 7:24-25).

This morning go to your Saviour/Priest and thank Him for His eternal offering and for His continual prayers on your behalf.

What's in the Name Saviour?
Part 3

"Thou shalt call his name Jesus [Yeshua]: *for he shall save* [yoshia] *his people from their sins."* (Matthew 1:21)

The angel gave this token to Miriam just before the Saviour's conception. She clung to it the rest of her life. Yeshua is an abbreviation for Yehoshua, which consists of two words, *Yeho* and *shua* meaning, "Yehovah is a saving-cry;" that is to say, God's name is a cry for help. We find this concept very often in the Psalms. It is connected to being saved from various types of trouble. Notice how the psalmist expects to be physically saved when he calls upon the One True God: "Save, LORD [Yehovah]: let the king hear us when we call" (20:9). The psalmist also spiritually calls on Yehovah to save his soul from hell (55:15-16).

The crucified sinner on the Saviour's right side was destined for hell but in faith called out to Yeshua for help: "Lord, remember me when thou comest into thy kingdom" (Luke 23:42). Messiah immediately saved his soul and assured him with these comforting words: "Today shalt thou be with me in paradise" (v.43). Only days earlier impoverished crowds of Israelites in Jerusalem cried out, "Hosanna to the son of David...Hosanna in the highest" (Matthew 21:9). The people's plea for urgent salvation from Roman oppression was drawn from Psalm 118:25 which says, "Save now, I beseech thee, O LORD: O LORD, I beseech thee, send now prosperity." This means that their cry to Yeshua was a cry to Yehovah! No wonder the Pharisees tried to stop them from their emotive chanting.

A blind man once loudly cried out, "Son of David!" expecting instant physical salvation. He immediately received it. Son of David was a lofty title for Messiah's role as a **Saviour/King** (Matthew 12:23). Israel never had a king like this before! Any king could *hear* the people's cries, but only this One could *eliminate* the people's cries.

What is it that you need saving from today? No problem is too big for the Saviour! Call on His matchless name now, and He will draw near. The King will also deliver you from sin's daily grip.

What's in the Name Saviour?

Part 4

"And Jesus stood still, and called them, and said, What will ye that I shall do unto you?" (Matthew 20:32)

Your Saviour wants you to gain more assurance of His salvation. We learned that saviour in Hebrew is *moshiah* and its root *yasha* means to be safe. *Yasha* also means *to free, help, defend, deliver, preserve, rescue, save and get victory*. Let's see how each of these definitions relates to Yeshua in His role as **Saviour/Shepherd** and to us as His helpless sheep.

To Free: Yeshua said, "If the Son therefore shall make you free, ye shall be free indeed" (John 8:36). Sheep often need to be freed from various entanglements. *To Help*: An undeserving Gentile woman came to the Saviour. Like a bleating sheep she cried out, "Lord, help me" (Matthew 15:25). Did He help her? Yes, and through no merit of her own. Paul encouraged all sheep to come to the Saviour to get help in time of need (Hebrews 4:16). *To Defend*: Did the Saviour defend a woman about to be stoned for adultery? Yes, He defended her like an ewe lamb from a pack of circling wolves. *To Deliver*: The Saviour's first sermon was a message of His delivering power. "The Spirit of the Lord is upon me...he hath anointed me to...preach deliverance to the captives" (Luke 4:18). By definition, the word deliver means, "to carry and turn over to the intended recipients." This is precisely what the Saviour did for a demon-possessed child. "Jesus rebuked the unclean spirit, and healed the child, and delivered him again to his father" (Luke 9:42).

To Preserve: It was a shepherd's job to keep the sheep alive and well. That's why Paul could say of Yeshua, "the Lord...will preserve me unto his heavenly kingdom" (2 Timothy 4:18). *To Rescue*: Paul was about to be "pulled in pieces" one day at the Temple until the Saviour/Shepherd stepped in and rescued him (Acts 23:10, 27). *To Get Victory*: Paul spoke of the sinner's absolute victory in glowing terms: "But thanks be to God, which giveth us the victory through our Lord Jesus Christ" (1 Corinthians 15:56).

Today, praise the Saviour/Shepherd and exalt His most wonderful name for His continual and unconditional salvation.

Messiah & the Manger

"And she brought forth her firstborn son, and wrapped him in swaddling clothes and laid him in a manger; because there was no room for them in the inn." (Luke 2:7)

A brief look around at Megiddo will reveal to the Bible student that a manger [Heb. *shoket*, a trough] is not generally made of wood as artists often portray. Such a manger would be routinely kicked over by animals and the precious feed lost. Further still, it could easily be crushed under hoof or chewed in pieces by restless animals. The feeding trough that the newborn Messiah was placed in was rectangular and cut out of rock. When you view one of these mangers, a better imagery of the Nativity scene begins to emerge.

Yeshua made the following comparison of Himself before a gathering of Pharisees: "Did ye never read in the scriptures, The stone which the builders rejected, the same is become head of the corner?" (Matthew 21:42). To commence building His spiritual house, God made His Son to be the architectural *pattern*—the first laid stone by which all other stones are aligned. He made His Son like a chief cornerstone: perfect, fundamental and indispensable. The Chief Cornerstone of God's spiritual Temple was rejected only a short time after His birth because Herod sought to kill Him. Then at the beginning of His brief public ministry, the chief rulers in Nazareth sought to push the Chief Cornerstone off a cliff.

Another aspect of a cornerstone is that such a stone is very often *ceremonially* laid. Historically, they have also been inscribed and hollowed out to contain historical documents or other objects. Thus, the imagery of the world's infant Redeemer being ceremonially laid in hollowed-out rock and ascribed with great glory is now etched upon our minds (Luke 2:11). The Babe lying in a stone box tightly wound in strips of cloth also dramatically foreshadows His death and temporary resting place—a hollowed-out limestone tomb.

Today, begin to make more room in the hollow of your heart for the Son that He might continue building upon your life's work.

$\mathcal{D}$elivering $\mathcal{M}$essiah to the $\mathcal{W}$orld

"Behold the handmaid of the Lord; be it unto me according to thy word. And the angel departed from her." (Luke 1:38)

In delivering Messiah to the world, Mary did her part as an awaiting virgin; she was an *alma for God*. Some nine months later, "she brought forth her firstborn son, and wrapped him in swaddling clothes, and laid him in a manger" (2:7). Immediately, heavenly messengers came to deliver the good news of Messiah's arrival. These were *angels of God,* and they told some nearby shepherds exactly where they could find Israel's long-awaited Messiah (2:8-14). They were so successful in delivering their news that the shepherds took off running to see this wonder of wonders for themselves (2:15-16).

Messiah's ministry was short-lived, and He left a great work for others to continue. The very first men to begin delivering His message of love and forgiveness were known as *apostles of God*. These devotees labored diligently thinking they had only one generation to do so before Messiah's return. We would do well to follow their pattern.

Messiah knew all along that this great work would have to be passed along to many succeeding generations before His return in power and glory; therefore, with great trust He has "committed unto us the word of reconciliation" (2 Corinthians 5:18-19). Paul lays a title upon all believers calling us *ambassadors of God;* that is to say, "ambassadors for Christ" (v.20). He does this so that we might feel the weight of this calling more strongly and thus carry out our duties more thoroughly. As His ambassadors to the nations, we should not be short on compassion, patience or prayer. That's how Yeshua went about His great commission. The incredible news of Messiah's soon return desperately needs to be delivered today. The hour is late! For this to be accomplished the high King of Heaven needs royal ambassadors in every city in the world.

Being the goodwill ambassador that you are, ask His Royal Majesty to help you accomplish His sovereign will today. The current city you dwell in is not by accident. It is by assignment!

359

ℋow to 𝒯ruly ℬless 𝒢od

"Now when Daniel knew that the writing was signed, he went into his house; and his windows being open in his chamber toward Jerusalem, he kneeled upon his knees three times a day, and prayed, and gave thanks before his God, as he did aforetime." (Daniel 6:10)

All the presidents, princes and rulers of Babylon consulted together to establish a royal statute that whosoever asked a petition of any deity except of king Darius during the next month should be cast into a pit of lions. The king established the decree by signing it into law. It then became unalterable. The new decree, however, didn't alter Daniel's prayer habit one bit. He continued to kneel and pray facing Jerusalem three times a day.

Daniel loved to pray and bless the name of Yahweh, and it seems that the only way the prophet knew how to do this was on his knees. This was not mandated in the Torah, but Daniel felt that the God Whom he served whole-heartedly night and day deserved the very best respect. You see, in the Hebrew there is a direct connection between the words *kneeling* and *blessing*. The word for knee is *beh'-rek* and the word for kneel is *baw-rak.'* Barak is also the formal word beginning a host of Jewish prayers; it means, "to *bless*." The Jewish world normally prays while standing, but this very word that begins most of their prayers calls for them to bend the knee. This was the truest Hebraic form of adoration and worship and survived through the Second Temple period.

When devotees of the Son of Man came before Him to make their request, they did so upon bended knee. They crouched low before their high King, and the Authorized Bible calls their bending and stooping "worship" (Matthew 15:25). How true!

Yeshua is King of Kings and Lord of Lords; so let your knees make contact with the floor today if you really want to bless His name.

God's Little Detours

"And I will bring the blind by a way that they knew not; I will lead them in paths that they have not known: I will make darkness light before them, and crooked things straight. These things will I do unto them, and not forsake them." (Isaiah 42:16)

Sometimes God allows us to go down a path we have not been down before. At first, it can be a bit alarming. What detour has the Lord taken you on recently? Maybe you are on one right now—a detour of financial reversal, of physical decline, of some broken relationship or a new responsibility. Maybe God is calling you to walk a new path of His choosing faithfully. Are you willing to walk it and to let Yeshua be your eyes, your Leader, your Shepherd and your Guide?

Detours call for new understanding. First, understand that you are not supposed to be in control—God is. He is the One Who has made you temporarily "blind." Detours may seem chaotic and uncomfortable, but God knows where He is taking you. Your detour can be used as an opportunity to say to God, "Not my will, but thine, be done."

Secondly, understand that you don't necessarily need to know the reason for the detour. It is okay to ask God why, but don't expect a quick answer or one at all. God's little detours aren't supposed to make sense to you; they're just supposed to make you more trusting. This just might be the very reason for the whole detour, to see if you will follow without fretting.

Thirdly, understand that you are not alone. The Shepherd is on the path with you and promises His oversight so that you don't stumble and fall. He says so calmly, "I will lead them…and not forsake them." No matter how strange the detour may seem, and no matter how alone you feel, you are not alone, nor are you forsaken (2 Corinthians 4:9). All that is important is that you stay close enough so that Yeshua can direct you with His shepherd's staff.

Expect a possible detour in the near future. When things don't go as you planned, just go on trusting the Author and Finisher of your faith.

December 28

Lost Your Identity?

"For whom he did foreknow, he also did predestinate to be conformed to the image of his Son." (Romans 8:29)

The moment a person receives the new birth he is faced with a new opportunity. The believer can become an entirely "new man" if he so desires (Ephesians 4:24). This will take the better part of a lifetime, but this is no reason to delay the process. John the Baptizer had a great motto from which we can benefit. Speaking of Messiah he said, "He must increase, but I must decrease" (John 3:30).

Paul was also determined to take on a new identity in Messiah. To the church at Corinth—that was suffering from an identity crisis—Paul proclaimed his personal method whereby he would achieve this. His motto was very simplistic: "I die daily" (1 Corinthians 15:31). This means that we should bury our self-centered desires before beginning each day. Just before the apostle said this, he put a riddle or proverb before the carnal Corinthian believers saying, "What shall they do which are baptized for the dead, if the dead rise not at all? Why are they then baptized for the dead?" (v.29). Paul was contrasting a heathen practice to the concept of true Christian baptism whereby the repentant believer comes up from the baptismal waters as a completely new man. Dead people have no aptitude for change, but if you are alive in Messiah, then there is plenty of potential (2 Corinthians 5:17).

Paul reminded Corinthian believers that a danger remains in hanging on to one's old identity. He warned of the carnal believer's possible premature death. To the church with the identity crisis he said, "For this cause many are weak and sickly among you, and many sleep [are dead]" (1 Corinthians 11:30).

Today, ask the Father to help you fully rid yourself of your old identity as well as old things so that in Messiah, you may become more and more the new person He purposed you to be.

362

𝒮tay 𝒯ocused

"Princes also did sit and speak against me: but thy servant did meditate in thy statutes." (Psalm 119:23)

When David returned to Ziklag and discovered it burned to the ground, he was greatly distressed, and so were his own mighty men. The people spoke of stoning him (1 Samuel 30:6). But what did David do? He encouraged himself in the LORD his God. When he was on the run for more than a decade dodging Saul's accusations and arrows, what did he do? He meditated on God's promises and even wrote down his feelings in poetic form. We call these prayerful writings the Psalms. When he was on the run from his own son, Absalom, his life was not sustained by thoughts of revenge or even self-pity; the *water* of God's Spirit, the *bread* of God's Word and the *salt* of God's friendship sustained it.

Anyone who serves God long enough will have no shortage of adversaries. The gospel enterprise stirs up plenty who will stop at nothing to get you to back up or quit. They will attempt to sideline you, sidetrack you, even attack you and turn you upside down if that helps them accomplish their goal. Even worse, friends may turn into *fiends*, family may turn into *foes*, and associates within your Christian circle may turn into *assassins* concerning your good name. Times like these will tempt you to consider whether it is worth continuing on or not, but it is!

When sinners attempt to halt your gospel progress, misrepresent your intentions or flat out lie about you, it is easy to be overtaken with a host of emotions. If you are, then they have succeeded. You then become sidetracked with the issue of clearing your name. But is this *your* job or God's? It is your duty as a believer to be so *occupied* with things pertaining to the King and His kingdom that you have no time to become *preoccupied*. The gospel must ever stay on the go. This is central to the kingdom.

May you do as David did with his distraction. While princes were sitting and *plotting* how to take him down, David just kept on *plodding* along with the work of the Lord and the statutes of the Lord.

Could Yeshua Sin?

"For such an high priest became us, who is holy, harmless, undefiled, separate from sinners, and made higher than the heavens;" (Hebrews 7:26)

The reoccurring question, "Could Yeshua sin?" is not a hypothetical one. It's a hyper-dimensional question that directly challenges the Son of Man's incarnate deity. When this question arises on earth, angels in heaven grasp their swords. A quote from Ralph H. Sexton, Sr. is helpful: "To say there is a possibility that Jesus could sin is to say there is a possibility that God could sin." When the Son came to earth, He did not empty Himself of Godhood; He only emptied Himself of the outward appearance of such. This is why Paul says, "Jesus Christ the same yesterday, and today, and forever" (Hebrews 13:8). Perhaps the apostle was paraphrasing Psalm 90:2 that says, "from everlasting to everlasting, thou art God."

Yeshua "was in all points tempted like as we are, yet without sin" (Hebrews 4:15). But those that take the "yes" position say that if Messiah was not actually able to sin, He really wasn't tempted. Wrong! If the Son of Man could have sinned, Satan would not have left Him alone until he had succeeded. One only has to look at the Greek word for *without* to see that it wasn't possible. In our text verse, the word without in Greek means "at *a space*; separately, apart from, beside, by itself." Additionally, the word "separate" in Greek means, "to *place room* between." There was a great gulf separating sinful mankind and the God-Man; there still is.

Just look at His miraculous inception. He had the *Holy Spirit* as His Father (Matthew 1:20). Thus, Yeshua could have sinned if and only if the Holy Spirit could have sinned, which is utterly impossible. John stated, "in him is no sin" (1 John 3:5). Peter declared that Yeshua "did no sin" (1 Peter 2:22). And Paul proclaimed plainly that the incarnate Son "knew no sin" (2 Corinthians 5:21). Here the Greek word "know" means to "*be aware*." Yeshua had no sin nature in Him to be aware of, but we do. Thus, let us walk fearfully, prayerfully and reverently today.

Unto the End

"And he that overcometh, and keepeth my works unto the end, to him will I give power over the nations." (Revelation 2:26)

Walking with God is the grandest of all privileges, something you hope will never end. *Working* for God is also the greatest of earthly privileges. However, it is not a part-time job that you tend to at your convenience or only when you feel spiritual. Lord Yeshua has commissioned us and crowned us with His loving statutes; therefore, we should never seek to lay aside such an ornament, even temporarily.

Sometimes difficult circumstances can bring you to your wit's end. You can be tempted to lose heart and give up. *Fox's Book of Martyrs* records the testimonies of many rock-solid believers who refused to quit on God, even when tied to the stake. Some were so anointed that they proclaimed the greatness and love of God while in the early stages of being burned alive. Yet many believers in the West want to quit on God at the drop of a hat. Keeping the faith and keeping Messiah's commands aren't just to be carried out when winds are favorable. The believer must prepare to set sail every single day, even when the dark clouds loom low and the winds blow at gale force. The believer should also set sail even if there is no wind at all, for God is able to breathe upon lifeless skies.

We need to overcome our desires for mediocrity. What we do daily for Yeshua should flow from an overwhelming love for Him. He overwhelmingly loved us all the way to the cross. "When Jesus knew that his hour was come that he should depart out of this world unto the Father, having loved his own which were in the world, he loved them unto the end" (John 13:1). How is that for overcoming unto the end! The Persecuted Church overcomes on a daily basis "by the blood of the Lamb, and by the word of their testimony; and [because] they [love] not their lives unto the death" (Revelation 12:11).

Today, determine to follow Yeshua all the way to the end no matter what and no matter where.

About the Author

Kyle Sutton was born and raised in Kinston, North Carolina. Growing up in a non-Jewish home—yet living one block from the only synagogue in town—he weekly attended a local Baptist church from age two. At age 15, he committed his life to the Lord Jesus Christ and was promptly baptized. The tragedy is, he wasn't properly discipled, and therefore, did not begin living fully for the Lord until age 25.

It was at this stage that he got married and began studying the Bible from cover to cover as it pertained to the nation of Israel—the people to whom it was written. Approximately five years later the Lord called him to preach. He enrolled at Trinity Baptist Bible College in Asheville, North Carolina and graduated in 1998 with a Bachelor of Theology degree. Upon graduation, the Lord quickly placed a strong calling upon him to go to the children of Abraham with the Good News.

This calling forced him to dig even deeper into the many intricate details of the Jewish culture, religion, and mindset of the Bible. As a wild branch grafted in to the rootstock of Israel, Sutton enjoys drawing comparisons between Old and New Covenant concepts. Over the past ten years his passion has been to share with others what he has found.

Other Books by this Author

Available on Kindle and in other eBook formats:

I Am Joseph (2009)
> Features more than 100 comparisons between the stories of Joseph and Jesus. Captivating! —253 pgs. Available at Amazon.com

A Prophet Like Moses (2003)
> Details 75 similarities between the mediators of the Old and New covenants—51 pgs.

Walking in Covenant (2007)
> Explains all nine steps in the blood covenant ceremony and exclusively chronicles how these steps were performed between God & Israel within the Exodus. Enlightening! —55 pgs.

The Need for the Second Birth (2010)
> A Hebraic approach: examining the cultural differences between a firstborn son and the second born. Judgment vs. Mercy—22 pgs.

The Day Yom Kippur Overshadowed Passover (2011)
> Compares the high priest's Day of Atonement duties and how Messiah performed these on Passover. Fascinating! —54 pgs.

Messianic Haggadah The Festival of Freedom (2011)
> A Siddur for Pesach—30 pgs.

Salt & Covenant (2012)
> Why God demanded it as the basis of relationship—36 pgs.

Ancient Betrothal Ceremony as seen in the Last Supper (2012)
> Understanding our role in the NT engagement period—38 pgs.

Wearing Messiah's Mantle (2012)
> Comparing Elijah's mantle and Yeshua's—33 pgs.

Other Bestselling Books from A FONTLIFE Publication, LLC

The *Winning With WordPress* series consists of Basics, Advanced and Security. Designed for all levels of user, they cover WordPress up to its latest release. *Winning With WordPress Basics* is for the beginner with little or no technical knowledge. You'll learn the fundamentals for setting up and using WordPress to its full advantage.

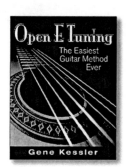

Open E Tuning by Gene Kessler is, without a doubt, the easiest guitar method ever to learn. This instructional book takes the beginner through all the basics of guitar playing and teaches basic music theory that will help the budding musician become proficient when playing at advanced levels.

The Ultimate Guide to the SDLC is the most comprehensive resource available to help you navigate the System Development Life Cycle. This book contains the most complete collection of 21st century IT best practices to help you increase your project success rate and save time and money while doing so.

CPSIA information can be obtained at www.ICGtesting.com
Printed in the USA
BVOW04s2106121113

336129BV00008B/176/P